FISH IN ART

MILLAIS SCHOOL
ART DEPARTMENT

FISH IN ART

Christine E. Jackson

REAKTION BOOKS

Published by
Reaktion Books Ltd
33 Great Sutton Street
London EC1V 0DX, UK

www.reaktionbooks.co.uk

First published 2012

Printed and bound in China by C&C Offset Printing Co., Ltd

British Library Cataloguing in Publication Data
Jackson, Christine E. (Christine Elisabeth), 1936–
Fish in art.
1. Fishes in art.
I. Title
758.3'7-dc23

ISBN 978 1 86189 899 9

Contents

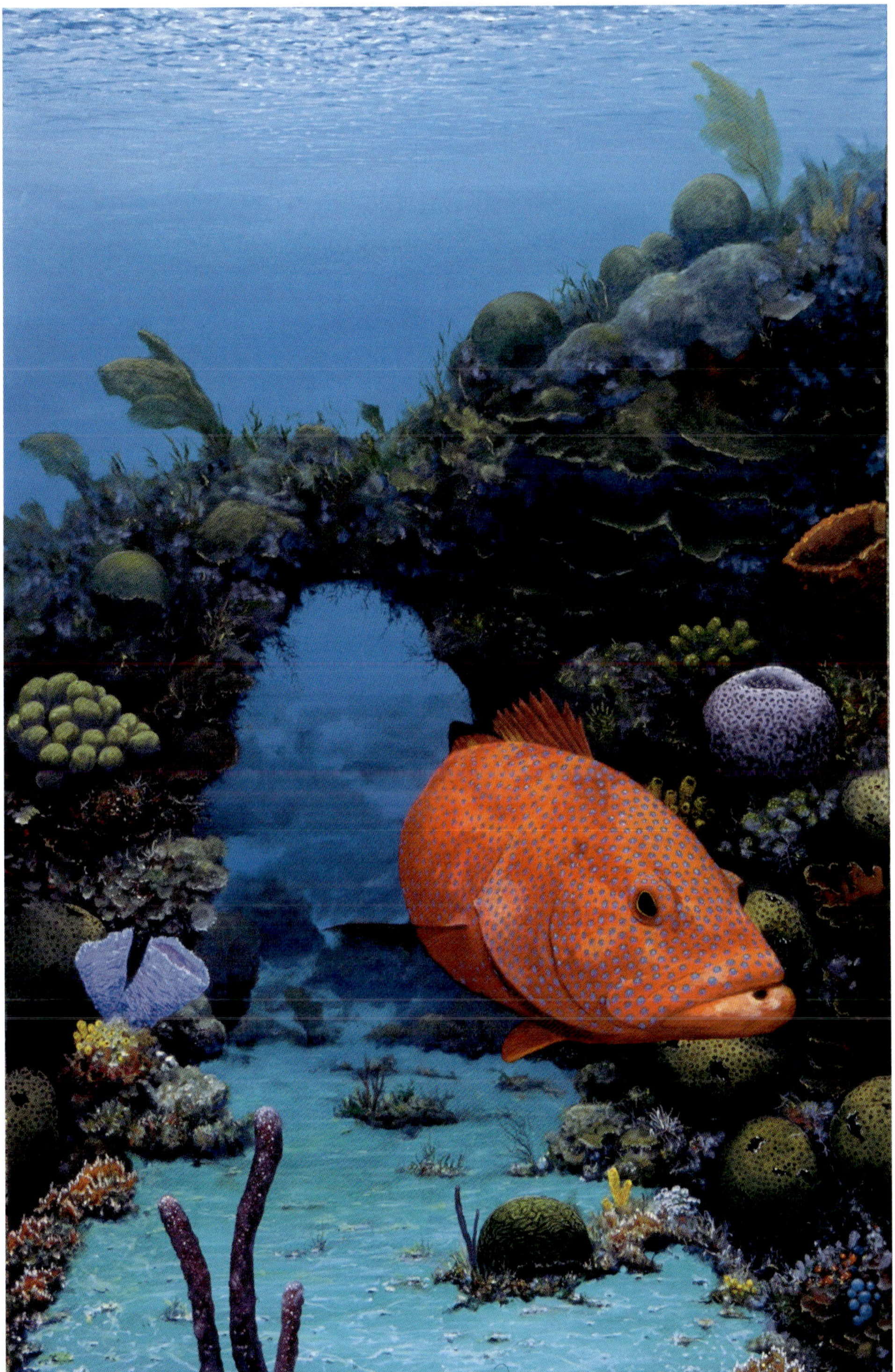

1 Patrick Chevailler, *Grouper*.

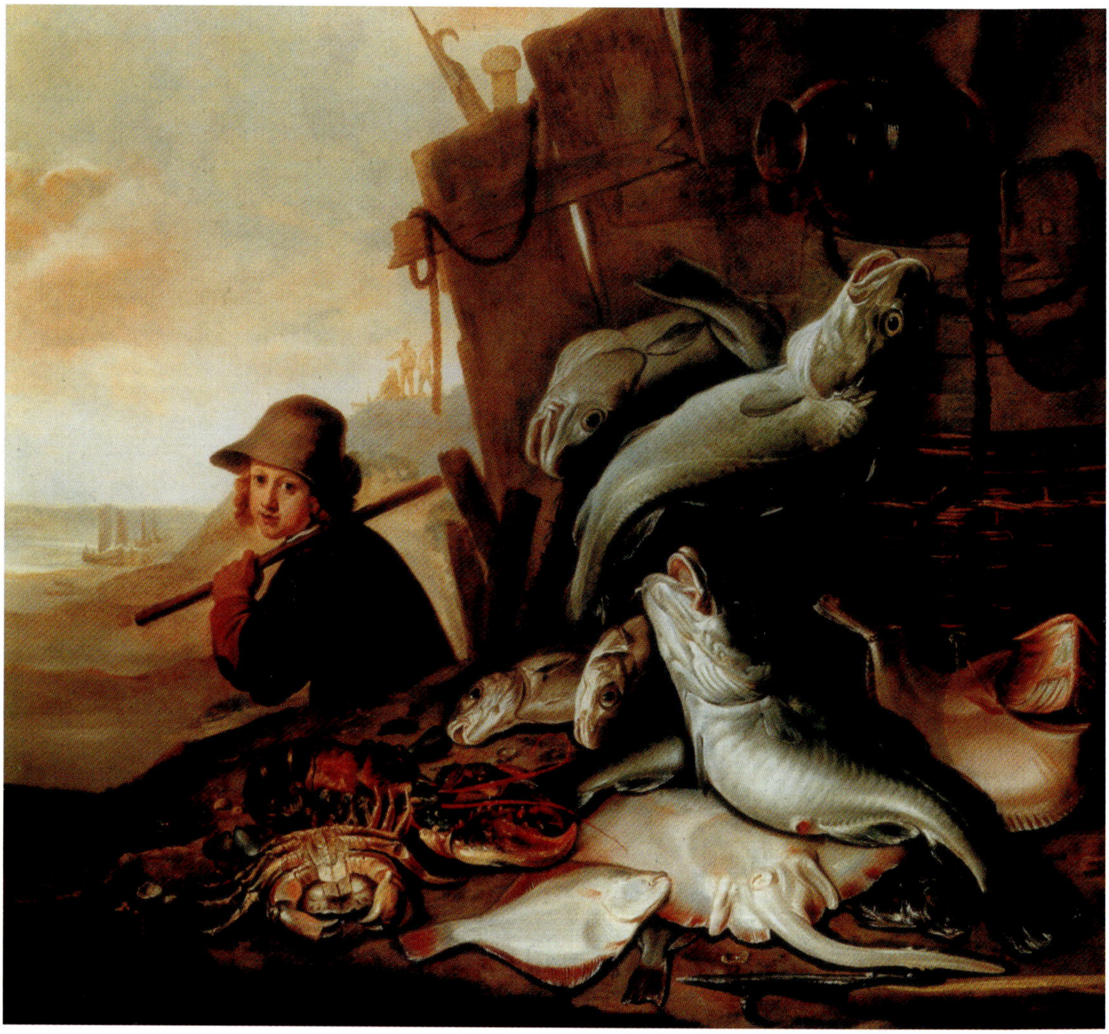

2 Jan de Bont, *Still-life of Landed Fishes*, 1653, oil on canvas.

INTRODUCTION

Fish is a basic food for people across the world, which has meant that artists have been sufficiently interested in them to paint their image from the earliest times to the present day. 4,000 years ago in Egyptian tombs images were painted on walls, later on papyrus and paper, depicting angling scenes and fishes in rivers and ponds or lifted from the water. In the seventeenth century the medium most often used was oil on panel or canvas. A variety of species occurs in pictures from different localities, though some fishes have such a wide distribution that artists of several nationalities have delighted in painting them. The Chinese were painting fishes in ink and colours on silk during the Song Dynasty (960–1279).

Since there has been no previous book on fish in two-dimensional art, the aim here is to chart the development of fish in art within a social and historical background. Fish have had a huge impact on European social history, politically (for example, the Hanseatic League disputes and the Cod War between Britain and Iceland), economically (forming the basis of the wealth of the Low Countries) and religiously (great quantities of fish being required following the edicts of the Roman Catholic Church on eating no meat in Lent and on Fridays). Commercially, there was the influence on fish markets of ice and salt and the technologies of drying, salting, smoking and pickling. The effects of steamships and railways, refrigeration and canning are also a part of the story of fish being brought to the table in a fresh condition.

When countries and empires are wealthy their art flourishes. Most fish paintings were commissioned within these prosperous periods. The

Low Countries' golden age of painting, with scores of wonderful sea fish paintings, occurred in the sixteenth and seventeenth centuries. Dutch and Flemish Old Masters loved to display their dexterity in painting iridescent scales or the colourful shells of lobsters and crabs. They showed fishes arranged decoratively for banquets or simply with just a lemon and loaf of bread for breakfast. They also painted fishes when unloaded from boats and laid on the beach. Market stalls with heaps of fishes were another favourite subject. Jan de Bont's *Still-life of Landed Fishes*, signed and dated 1653, is a typical example. The painting is crowded with cod, plaice, whiting, ray, crab and lobster, beautifully painted with clear delineations of the different species. Once purchased, the fishes were stored in larders and in the kitchen, providing further scenes and opportunities for artists.

The British were at their most powerful in the nineteenth century, when their newly rich aristocracy and gentry preferred to fish in home rivers, and the art of the period reflected this. Watercolours were added to the media in which the artists worked, producing angling paintings and carefully delineated portraits of fishes laid on riverbanks. American artists followed the British pattern of painting fishes but added a new dimension in the twentieth century by creating some memorable images of big game fishes and sea angling. In the second half of the twentieth century it became possible to dive into the depths of the oceans and new, vibrantly colourful tropical species never seen before became available to artists. Throughout the centuries artists have revelled in fishes' infinite variety of shape, colour and surface texture, producing pictures of them that delight the eye and whet the appetite.

About 60 per cent of the total number of roughly 25,000 fish species live in salt water, the other 40 per cent in fresh water. Marine species are regarded as tastier than the majority of freshwater fishes. Initially, edible marine species were chosen almost exclusively by artists and their patrons for fish paintings. Men braving the oceans in small boats and bringing home catches that they landed onto a beach and sold there, or moved to a market, were the subject of many Continental fish paintings. The history of painting freshwater species differs from that of marine fish art. The British painted freshwater species, again almost exclusively, in the nineteenth and twentieth centuries. The reason was that angling had become a sport in Britain as well as a means of catching food. Izaak Walton and Francis Barlow were responsible for the story of angling for freshwater species taking such a different course. The publication of Walton's *The Compleat Angler* (1653) and the sporting prints of *Angling*, *Fishing* and *Salmon Fishing* by Barlow in the mid-seventeenth century led to the sport becoming so important and popular as to eclipse demand for other kinds of fish pictures in Britain. In the late twentieth century British fish painters began to paint living fishes in small sections of rivers and streams, and the old formats of marine fishes laid on beaches and freshwater fishes laid on riverbanks were finally abandoned.

The aim of this book is to cover the stages of these two histories and the effects they have had on artists who responded by producing different kinds of paintings in response to changing fashions. We have excluded paintings of whales, dolphins and porpoises because they are mammals, not fishes. Although regarded as fishes until the mid-eighteenth century, including them would have widened the scope of the subject, fishes in art, and trespassed on the field of mammals in art. However, we have included paintings that feature crustaceans – lobsters, crabs and shrimps. The artists themselves regarded these as fishes and could never resist their wonderful colours to add a touch of glamour and red highlights to their compositions. Oysters and mussels supported large numbers of the poorer members of society for centuries since they were harvested in enormous quantities and so were cheap to buy. If we need another excuse for including them, it is that crustaceans and molluscs are known universally as shellfish. Otherwise, we have chosen paintings of true fishes, both freshwater and marine.

Book illustration of fishes is a wholly different topic with a separate development both of choice of species depicted for scientific description and the methods used to illustrate them. Only a few book illustrations, milestones in recording fishes, have been included.

To paint fishes on inn signs successfully, a simple design, clear outlines and bold images are needed to arrest the attention of passers-by. Special paints are used for the boards, which need repainting every seven years or so because of weathering. Three inn signs have been included, painted by artists specializing in this skill.

When examples of Chinese and Japanese art were first seen in the West, their strangeness was a barrier to their being understood and appreciated. The vertical perspective in Chinese paintings was, and is, astonishing to Western eyes accustomed to paintings arranged in planes above and below a horizon. The thoughtful use of space and universal spatial awareness in Chinese art make Western fish paintings look haphazard and crowded. The Korean, Japanese and Chinese emphasis on spirit, or life, in a painting as being the greatest inspirational element has led to less concern with correct anatomical or colour details. Western painting of fishes concentrated on physical form and markings for identification purposes. The oriental deep respect for life precluded the painting of dead animals. This reverence for all living things is at variance with Western man's idea of his own species' superiority, concomitant with his exultation in hunting trophies. Eastern equality in valuing all living species also meant that the painting of flowers and birds, fishes and insects, was regarded as only a little inferior an occupation to that of painting portraits, scenes of palace life or landscape. In the West painting live animals was regarded as a very inferior form of painting and of little esteem. Western landowners liked hunting trophies, so dead fishes were acceptable as subjects of serious paintings and accepted as 'fine art' (still-life) – but not live specimens (see Jan de Bont, illus 2). From the first, fishes painted in relation to their river or sea environment was a constant ideal in the East, but a much later way of representing fishes in Western art, only in the last two centuries becoming normal practice. Eastern fish art was not subservient to scientific demands for searching for and recording new species with little or no background. The beauty of the fishes seen in detail or in context with their water element provides a constant source of pleasure when looking at

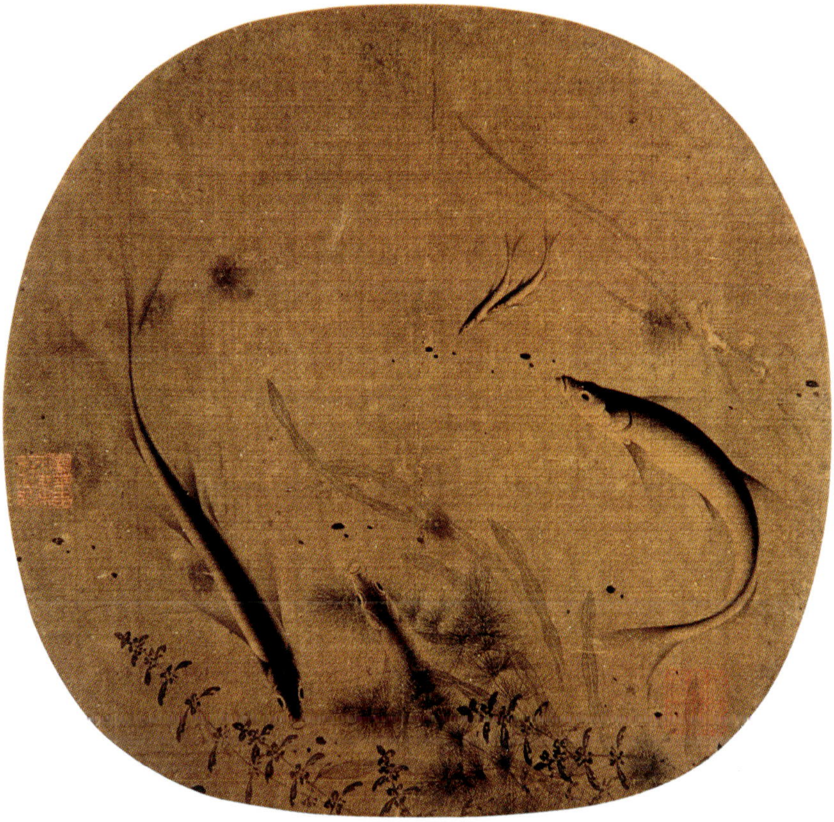

3 *Fish at Play among Grasses*, Song Dynasty, fan leaf on silk, ink and colours, artist unknown.

Chinese and Japanese fish art. The living fishes seen in flowing movement painted on a silk fan leaf in ink and colours in the Song Dynasty captures the spirit of the fishes in the Chinese manner.

Contemporary Western painting of fishes by specialist fish artists is closer to the Eastern ideal, with the fish in the water surrounded by pebbles and plants natural to its environment. Modern paintings that do not portray fish realistically but use their interesting shapes are represented here by some famous names and recent exponents of the use of fishes in art.

We have sought to include beautiful and surprisingly colourful paintings of various species by fish artists of many nationalities of a standard to satisfy art critics as well as to give pleasure to freshwater anglers and sea fishermen.

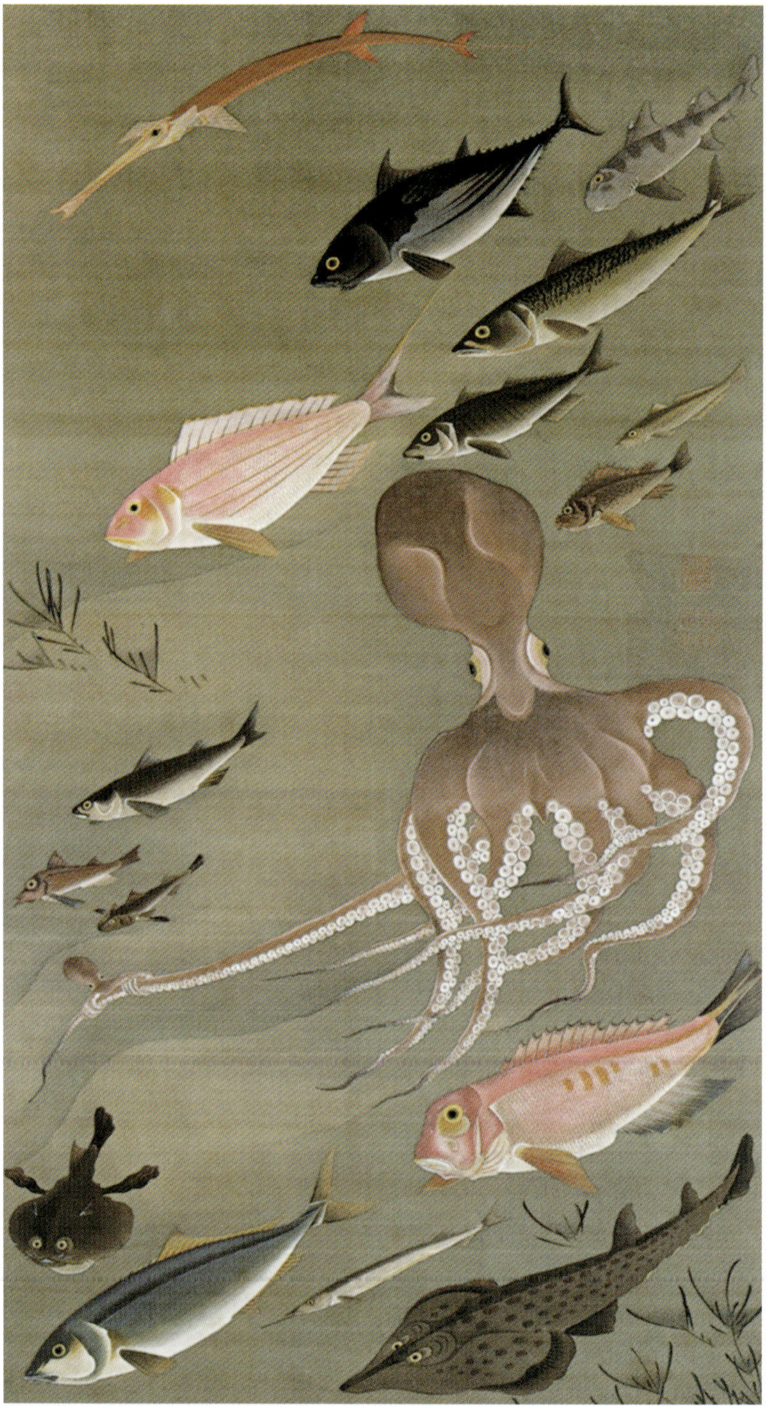

4 Ito Jakuchu (1716–1800), *Fish and Octopus*, ink and colour on silk. Jakuchu was born and lived in Kyoto near the markets. He specialized in painting the exotic birds he kept in his garden and Buddhist subjects. He was a solitary, eccentric figure in the history of Japanese painting because of his realist technique. The composition is on a strong diagonal and the fishes are seen from above – characteristic of Japanese paintings of natural history subjects. The sea has to be imagined, but carefully placed weed suggests plant growth in the sandy seabed.

one
Fish in the Sea

The sea covers more than 70 per cent of our planet's surface, yet this vast area is the environment about which we know the least. Not until the mid-twentieth century was it possible to explore its depths and the rich variety of life that inhabits the oceans, including thousands of fish species.

The first deep-sea sounding was taken by Sir James Clark Ross in the Southern Atlantic Ocean on 3 January 1840. Since that time various expeditions have studied not only the varying depths but the physical characteristics of the water masses and the biota (the plant and animal life) living there. Discoveries include major features such as oceanic ridges, basins and trenches, and smaller features like seamounts and isolated patches of very deep water. Just as exciting has been the recording of extremely colourful fishes in the warmer waters of the Caribbean, the Indian Ocean and South Pacific, living among beautiful plants, brightly coloured corals and hollow-bodied sponges, strange molluscs and other sea creatures. Artists attempting to paint these newly discovered species need a paint-box with the widest range of tints imaginable. Most of these species have lived for thousands of years unseen by, unknown to and unmolested by man. It is only comparatively recently that artists have had the opportunity to depict them.

Boats were so small and fragile that it was dangerous for men to venture far out to sea. Those that were brave enough to explore the world, from the fifteenth century onwards, were terrified of lurking sea monsters. Some pictures of these sea monsters appeared as drawings in the seas of sixteenth-century hand-coloured printed charts and maps of the world. These maps included whales, dolphins and porpoises spouting from blowholes, or the more frightening and spectacular slapping of the surface by whales' huge tails. They were thought to be fishes but were correctly classified for science as mammals by Carl Linnaeus in 1758. Before these voyages of exploration and discovery only those species that live close to shores and move in shallower waters were encountered. Even as late as the seventeenth century the doughty Dutch and Flemish seamen could land only some forty to fifty different local fish species for their countrymen to eat and their artists to paint.

Throughout history people who lived by the sea ate better quality food, and more of it, than those who lived inland. In the European winters it was preserved fish that helped to save Scandinavians, the British and people living on the northern sea coasts of continental Europe from starvation. Most people who were familiar with fishes – herring and cod if no other – never saw marine fishes alive in water. Consequently, nearly all artists painted fishes out of water, although there were a few who imagined how they would look underwater and attempted to portray fish in the sea. Fishermen saw fishes swimming in the sea briefly – before hauling them out in nets or when a shoal passed their ships. Some shore-dwellers saw a few species kept alive in rock pools by fishermen until the market required them. Fishes were also kept alive in large half-barrels or tubs, several of which feature in paintings of Dutch market scenes. For the most part marine fish paintings were of fishes being hauled out of the sea, or in boats where the catch was being sorted.

The map of Scandinavia published in 1539 to accompany Olaus Magnus's *A Description of the Northern Peoples* has enjoyable small scenes both on land and in the sea. Men are depicted fishing through holes in the ice for fishes lurking underneath, in rowing boats across fishing lakes and driving the fishes into a net. Mariners are suffering untold miseries from colossal sea serpents crushing their ships in their coils and whales swamping them. The imaginary nightmare sea creatures of these previously uncharted and unsurveyed oceans are larger than the ships. Their dragon-like bodies and forked tails make them look like watery devils. Clearly, the stories brought home and told to the map makers have had a great impact, and many of the fishes in this map are frightening. There are some more normal, because familiar, fishes tied up in bundles on the land in Norway (opposite the sea-serpent and island of Helgala).

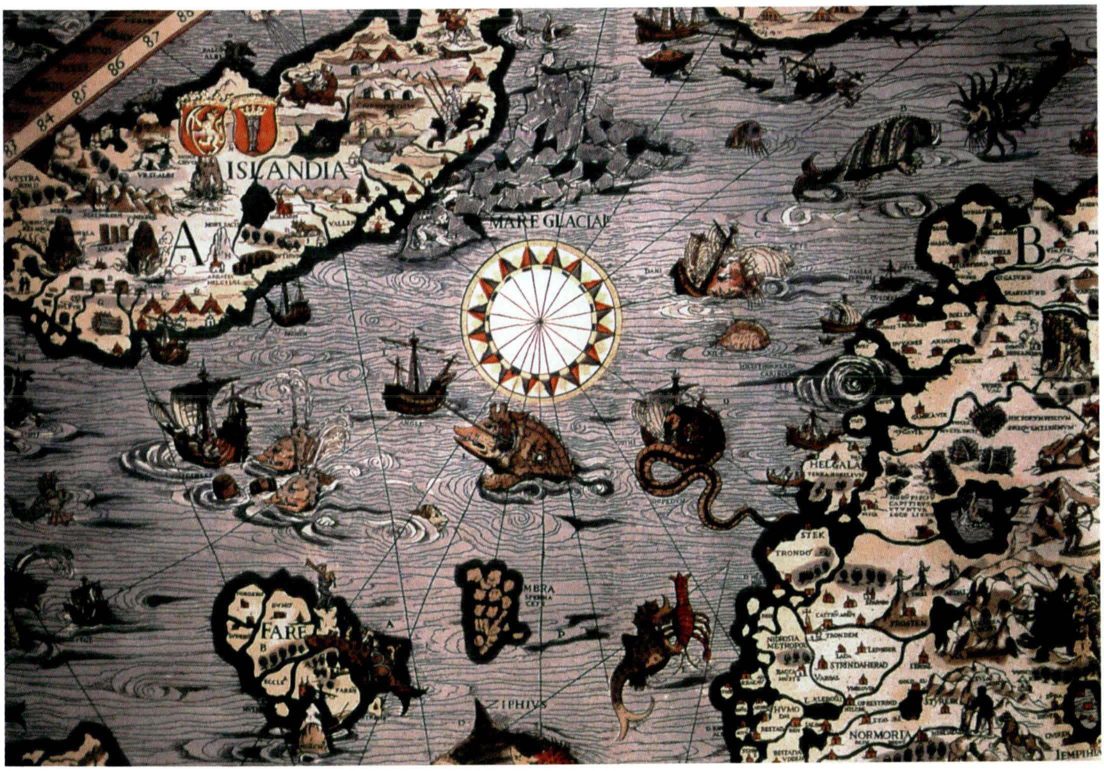

5 Map of Scandinavia, 1539, published to accompany Olaus Magnus, *A Description of the Northern Peoples*.

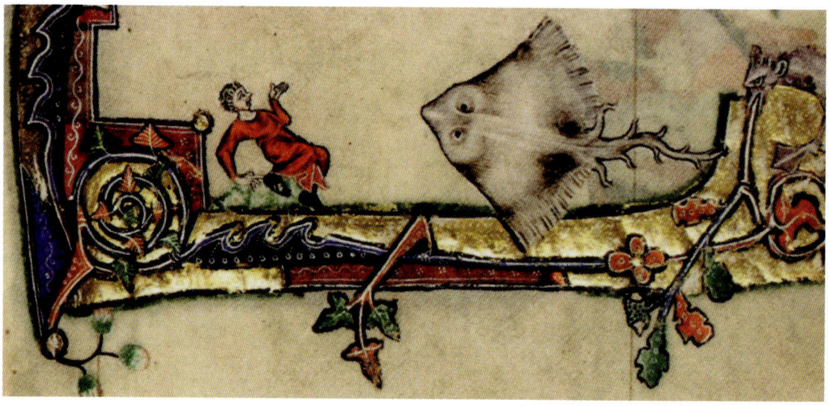

6 Skate and terrified man from the Macclesfield Psalter, early 14th century.

When depicting fishes as they appear under the sea artists struggled, until comparatively recently, from a lack of all the usual facilities necessary for them to make a good picture. A painting is made up of a subject, the foreground and background and surrounding objects. It was not possible to dive deeply into the ocean for first-hand observation nor could the artist stay under water long enough to make visual reminders and reference notes of what he had seen. There was also a problem with models. The choice of fish subjects depended on local availability. Marine species differed in the Mediterranean ports from those of the Atlantic, as well as according to the seasons. Fishes move station for the purposes of breeding and when not breeding may be found in seas hundreds of miles away. The artist was dependent on where the fishermen operated and at which time of year.

Once suitable specimens had been obtained there was the difficulty of arranging them in positions that might be deemed lifelike. Artists could only have imagined what the fishes looked like while swimming in the sea. Propping them up into suitable positions might only have been rudimentary. Another problem is the fleeting nature of colours and the fact that many hues fade quickly after death. Fishes could be kept wet and glistening by having water poured over them, but this did not make up for the serious loss of actual colour. The artist had another considerable difficulty: how to create a convincing underwater seascape? He could only try to emulate landscapes, with high and low areas. Imagined plants would give a greater sense of reality, besides using whatever marine objects could be found on the seashore or had been brought home by sailors, such as shells and pieces of coral. Ideas about water's refraction of light may have been known to them by seeing a spoon in a glass of water, but what effect it had on the fishes in the sea probably never even crossed their minds. Waves, or the effect of ripples, were crudely and mechanically depicted in early pictures. Tintoretto and John White solved how to paint the sea in their own way, and similar black parallel lines overpainted with blue in a mechanical fashion became the norm (illus. 10 & 11).

A naturally occurring but strange phenomenon is the characteristic of some fishes to change colour as they die. Red mullet (*Mullus surmuletus*) is reddish-brown during the day, but at night the stripes break up into a marbled pattern. The colour is at its brightest just before death, and the Romans had living specimens taken to the table to watch the changing brilliant iridescent hues as they died. It is a southern species, seen round the southern coasts of Britain where it is sometimes landed, and a valued food fish.

A more spectacular example is the coryphene, a species that has been repeatedly mistaken for a dolphin. It is a most beautiful and interesting fish, inhabiting warm seas in the Mediterranean and the Indian, Pacific and Atlantic Oceans. When seen in the sea it looks like burnished gold and silver as it gambols round a ship for long periods. Old mariners' stories of dolphins having lovely and changing colours actually refer to coryphenes. Dolphins are blue-black and grey in colour and are mammals, not fish, but the coryphene, like a dolphin in appearance except for its brilliant colours and lacking a snout, is a genuine fish. Mariners spotted them leaping into the air while chasing flying fish, one of their favourite foods. Since coryphenes were regarded as good eating, sailors cut strips of glittering tin into a crude resemblance of flying fish, attached them to hooks and dangled them in mid-air, where the coryphene seized them. The coryphene's wonderful colours grew brighter during its death struggle

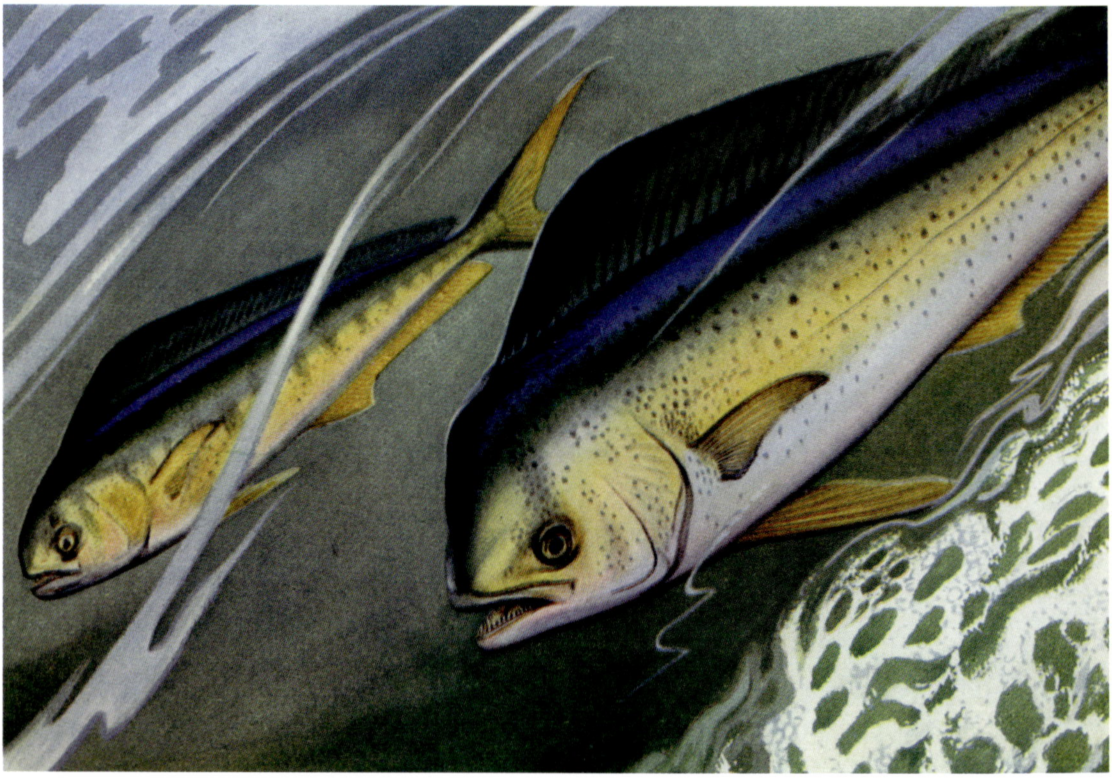

7 A. Fraser-Brunner, *Coryphaena hippurus*, watercolour, reproduced in B. Vesey Fitzgerald, *Game Fish of the World* (1949).

which led to some cruelty when sailors' inflicted a slow death on them in order to enjoy the spectacle. In old maps of the oceans there are often pictures of dolphins – or are they coryphenes?

Alec Fraser-Brunner studied fishes from a diving bell, a glass-bottomed boat and in an aquarium. He said that painting fishes in the diffused light makes them appear unfamiliar to anglers, who usually see fishes with the side turned upward to the rays of light. He also pointed out that in the living fish there is no bright highlight on the corner of the eye, for this appears only when light rays pass through air and fall upon the wet surface of the eye when the fish is out of water. Particularly pertinent to the coryphene were his remarks on the manner in which

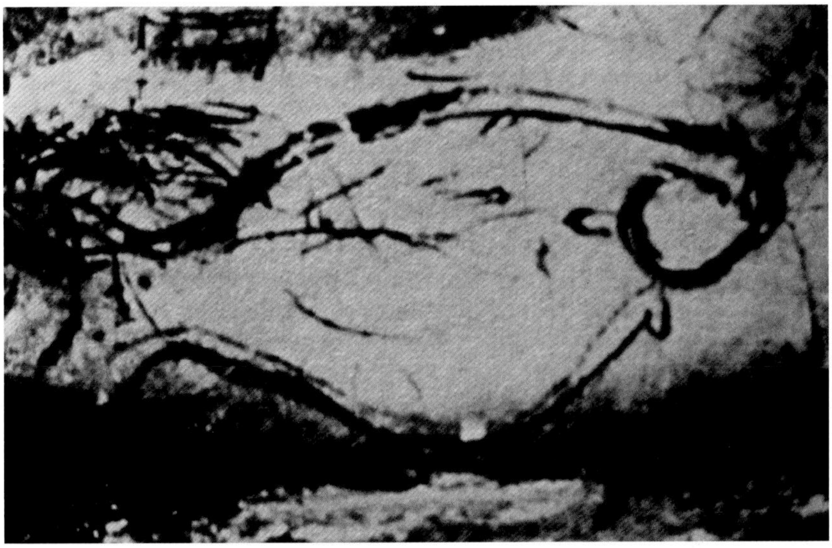

8 Palaeolithic cave painting from La Pileta, Malaga.

fishes' colours intensify as an emotional response or change completely when faded after death. The artist has to decide in which state to paint the coryphene. Ought it to be shown in its normal, relaxed, colourful state, or with the colours intensified when in an emotional state, or the even deeper shades of green, blue, gold and silver as it dies? Thought by some to be among the most beautiful fishes in the ocean the coryphene also is unequalled when hooked for its leaping, skittering, flashing runs and fighting resistance up to the last second. In addition it is one of the greatest delicacies on the table.

In terms of habitat, marine fishes have been divided into three main categories, shore, pelagic and deep sea, whose zones overlap considerably. Shore fishes are never far out to sea and swim along the coast at depths no greater than 180 to 245 metres (600–800 feet). Pelagic fishes are found far out to sea, usually above 245 metres, and being active their oil is dispersed throughout their bodies. They tend to swim in shoals near the surface, like herring and sardines. Demersal, or deep-sea fishes, live below depths of 245 metres, on or near the seabed, for instance, flat fish that spend much of their time lying on the seabed and doing little swimming. Consequently they need little muscle and their flesh is delicate and white, with nutritious oils concentrated in the liver. This group includes haddock, halibut and cod, which feed on invertebrate marine animals.

Scientists have divided fishes into two main groups: 20,000 species of fishes with bony skeletons and around 600 species with cartilaginous skeletons (sharks and rays). Only a few species, like eels, salmon and sturgeons, are able to move freely between fresh and salt water. The richest area, with the greatest number of different species of marine fishes, is in the tropical Indo-West Pacific region from east Africa across to northern Australia and the Great Barrier Reef and associated islands, with some 9,000 species. In sharp contrast, British species available for sea angling number a mere 120.

The earliest pictures of fish were painted onto the walls of caves by Palaeolithic man but not in sufficient detail for us to be able to define their species. A fish on the walls of a cave at La Pileta, Malaga, Spain, is thought to have been painted 25,000 years ago. The Egyptians painted many fishes, but they were river species. Their hieroglyphics included countless small fishes, such as the grey mullet. Fishes in river scenes are recognizable as barbel, perch, wrasse, carp and blenny. Mosaics provide us with a number of the earliest pictorial representations of recognizable sea-fish species, one of the most interesting being a Pompeian mosaic in the Naples museum showing several different Mediterranean species.

We look to Christian art for the earliest paintings in oils, for in the fifteenth and sixteenth centuries the Church ruled that only religious subjects could be painted in churches. It was easy to enforce this rule because it was mainly the clerics who could afford to commission artists for paintings to embellish their churches. Monarchs and noblemen also paid artists for pictures and they ordered a wider range of subjects, including classical subjects, but most were careful not to incur the wrath of the Church by straying outside those decreed. So for early fish paintings we have to search for biblical scenes involving fishes. These are few. In the Old Testament was the story of Jonah being swallowed by a great fish, while the story of Tobias and the Angel features a fish, but greater opportunities for artists were provided by the fifth day of Creation.

9 A second-century BC mosaic found in the House of the Faun at Pompeii, now in the Museo Archeologico Nazionale di Napoli. It depicts species available from the Bay of Naples and beyond into the Tyrrhenian Sea. In the centre is an octopus, and on the left are red and grey mullets, electric rays, dogfish, wrasse, a moray eel and sea bream. The right-hand side shows sea bream, scorpion fish, dogfish, squid, murex (the mollusc that supplied the Romans with their Tyrian purple dye), a painted comber and sea bass.

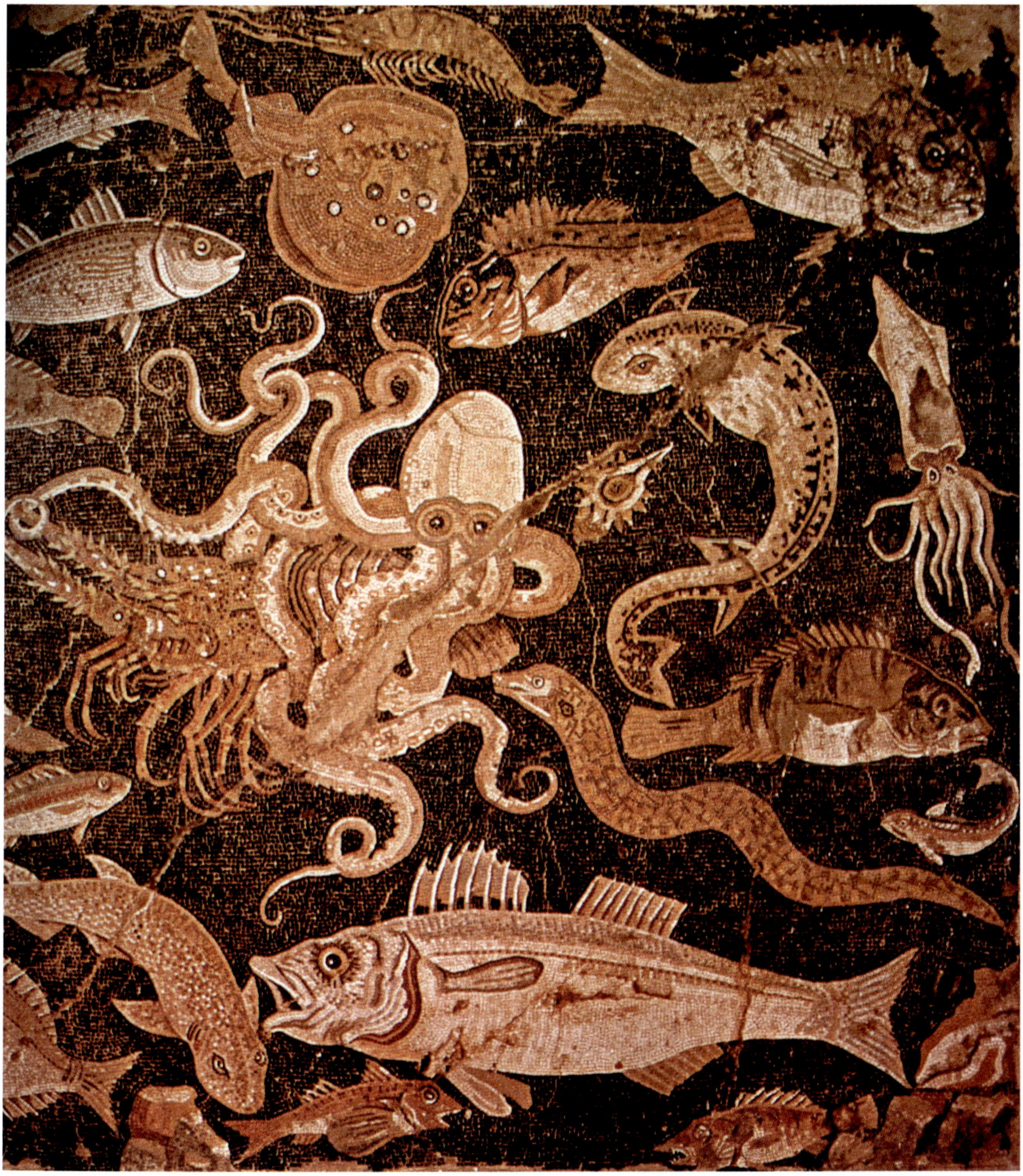

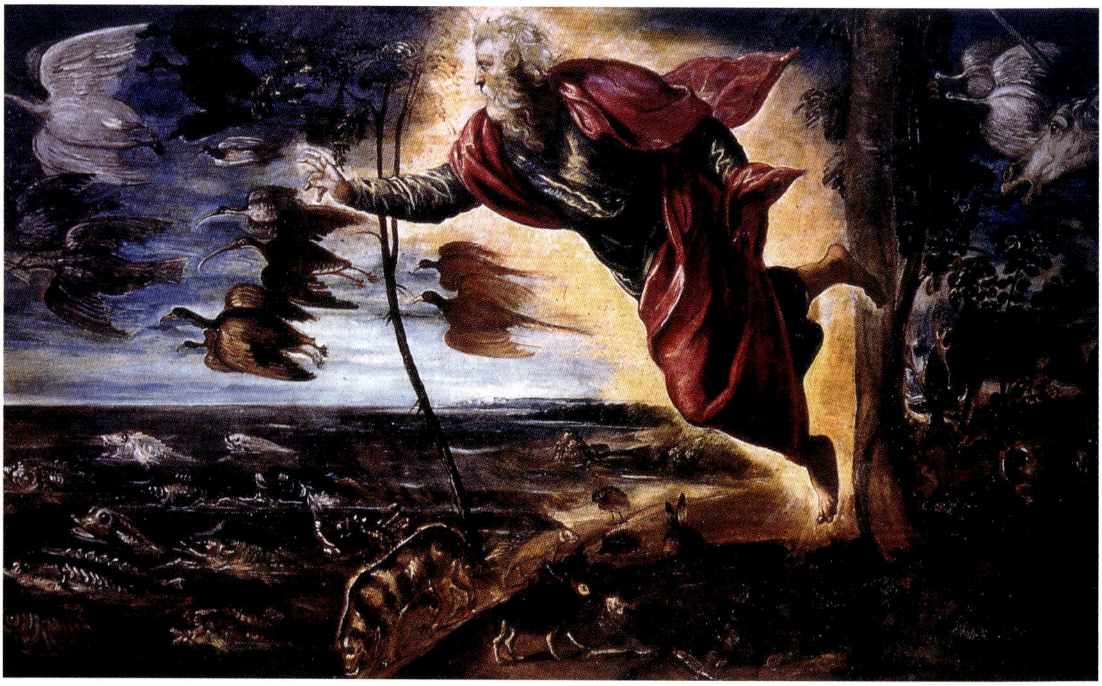

10 Jacopo Tintoretto, *Creation of the Animals*, *c.* 1551, oil on canvas.

The New Testament offers as subjects the Miracle of the Loaves and Fishes by the Sea of Galilee, where the two small fishes are usually invisible, the Tribute Money and the Miraculous Draught of Fishes. In addition there are several occasions when Jesus ate fish with his fishermen disciples. The fish subsequently became a Christian symbol, from the Greek word for fish, *Ichthys*, an acronym for Jesus/Christ/of God/the Son/Saviour.

Appropriately, one of the earliest oil paintings of these subjects portrayed God creating the fishes. The Venetian artist Jacopo Tintoretto (1518–1594) painted in churches around that city, including five pictures of God creating the animals, of which only four survive. One in the Gallerie dell'Accademia, Venice, shows the Creator causing 'the waters to bring forth abundantly the moving creature that hath life, and fowl that may fly above the earth in the open firmament of heaven' on the fifth day of Creation (Genesis 1: 20). Tintoretto has painted a deep sea, densely

THE famous flying fish that so astonished early seamen sailing in warm seas derives its name from leaps into the air and a horizontal 'flight' (though no fins are flapped and it cannot turn) through the air, before dropping back into the sea. The phenomenon is usually seen at night or early in the morning. When the fish accidentally landed on deck they provided a very tasty meal for sailors. About thirty species are known, mainly in the Mediterranean but also in the North Sea and the Pacific Ocean. An Atlantic flying fish, *Cheilopogon heterurus*, is occasionally seen in northern European waters. The straight, low-flying Exocet missile took its name from the scientific label of the flying fish, *Exocoetus volitans.*

packed with fishes, and has painted it to look like a watery element. Most of the eleven fishes of various species are half in and half out of the water. Where light penetrates the dark sea it is possible to see the dark dorsal bodies and lighter bellies of the fishes underwater.

Not long after Tintoretto, an English artist of lesser talent was in America, painting Native Americans while they were fishing in the seas around the coasts of North Carolina and Virginia. John White was sent by Sir Walter Raleigh, governor of Virginia, in 1585 to record in drawings the people, topography and natural history of the country. He made separate watercolours of the 'lookdown' or moonfish, groupers, grunt, soldier-fish, dolphin, flying fish, remora and trigger-fish. He also drew several species of fishes in the sea in a composite picture showing Native methods of fishing by day using a dipnet and spear and also by night when there was a fire in the canoe. There is also a 'holding-pen' made of nets. The fish species are those found in the shallows between the mainland and the Outer Banks where catfish, a hermit crab, burrfish, king crabs, skate or ray and also perhaps a sturgeon can be seen. Hammerhead sharks are recognizable. This extraordinarily shaped shark, with its huge head bearing one eye at each extremity, may grow up to 5 metres (15 feet), feeding mainly on fishes. Attacks by this species would have made the fishermen in this picture wary of it. White painted the blue sea smoothly in the shallows, then used a slightly darker blue with grainy ripples to show the deeper water.

A surprising number of early printed maps had small pictures of fishes, dolphins, whales and other sea creatures (not always the monsters of Magnus's map, illus. 5), painted in the oceans where they had been seen. Frequently unidentifiable and fanciful, nevertheless they were charming

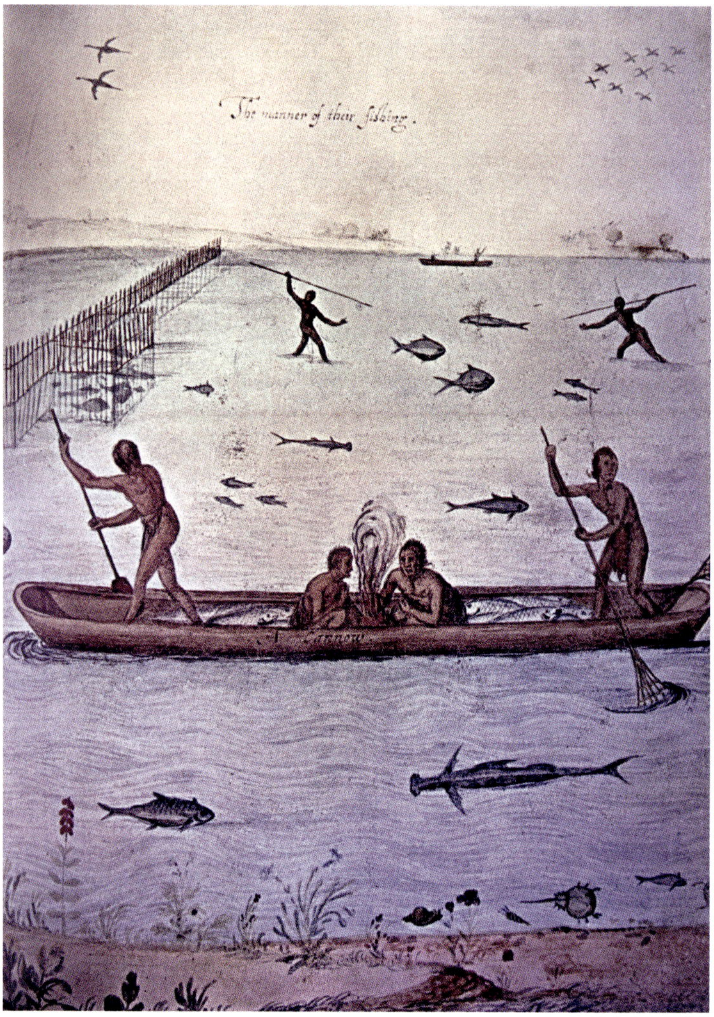

11 John White, *Indians Fishing*, 1585, watercolour.

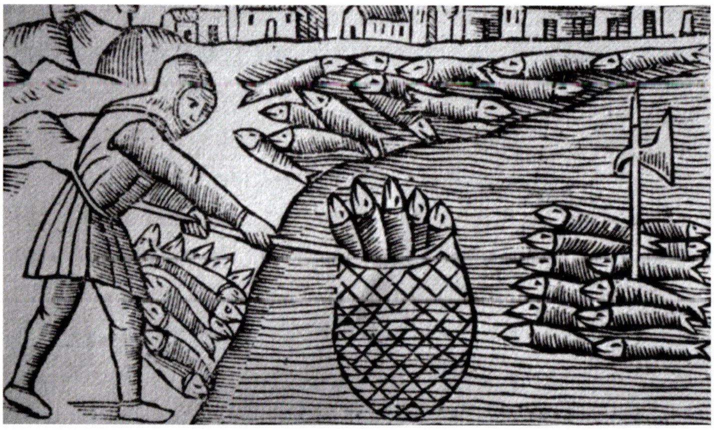

12 Olaus Magnus, woodcut of fishing for shoals of herring, *A Description of the Northern Peoples* (1555). The Swedish historian included this woodcut to emphasize the importance of the herring in Swedish history. It conveyed the idea of the fishes' fecundity and plenitude to the benefit of Swedish fishermen.

COD (*Gadius morhua*) is the largest member of the cod family Gadidae and may grow up to 2 metres in length. There are some thirty species of this marine family in cool European waters. They may occur from the shoreline to depths of 600 metres (220 feet) down the continental shelf. Cod schools gather in spawning grounds in huge numbers after migrating considerable distances. Related species include haddock, whiting, pollock, rockling and ling. Burbot is the only cod fish living in fresh water, but it may be extinct in Britain.

additional points of interest. Two species of fishes in one of John White's maps of Virginia from Florida to Chesapeake Bay, painted in the 1580s, are clearly recognizable as puffer fish and flying fish.

Fish featured largely in monastic fare and monks encouraged fishermen to venture out to sea to bring them their favourite food. Cod, with herrings, were the mainstay of the medieval fish diet, and the fish industry was given a huge impetus by the Catholic Church. The imposition of fasting during Lent and on Fridays became a source of great profit for fishermen and fishmongers. The first reference to 40 days of fasting is the fifth canon of the Council of Nicaea of 325 and the only meal during Lent, eaten in the evening, was meatless, fishless and without butter or eggs. This prohibition against fish in Lent was removed in the Middle Ages; then Fridays throughout the year were decreed as being meatless, and this is when fish became the basis of the Friday meal. The poor had to find the cheapest fishes available and with the discovery of huge shoals of cod and herrings in the Atlantic their problem was partially solved. However, the shellfishes that were gathered in enormous quantities all through the Middle Ages were more affordable. Oysters were priced at 2 pence a gallon in 1298, in 1491 at 4 pence a bushel and were cheaper than other kinds of fishes and crustaceans.

In the fifteenth century British and Continental European fishermen ventured further afield to work the Icelandic waters for cod. Cod live only in the cold waters of the North Atlantic, sometimes being found in vast numbers on the banks or shallows of Iceland and Newfoundland. At this time Basque fishermen searching for whales, landed in Newfoundland and discovered cod in fantastic numbers.

The area of 37,000 square miles between North America and the deep Atlantic, the Grand Banks, is where the cold polar seas of the Labrador

Current move south to meet the warmer North Atlantic water above a raised marine plateau. Here plankton and other single-celled organisms occur in such density that millions of fishes gather to feed. The earliest recorded European fishing voyage to this area was made by French sailors in 1504, but it is suspected that there were earlier expeditions. Soon the Portuguese, Scandinavian and British fishermen were active, most of them in search of cod. The Portuguese salted their fish on board and then took it home to be sun-dried, a practice they still carry out today. The British salted their catch on the spot, returning home months later with it stored in the hold to be packed in barrels for sale.

The most important item in the salt-fish trade was the herring. The Baltic and North Sea swarmed with herring in the fourteenth and fifteenth centuries while the strict observance of fish on Fridays and during Lent was enforced. Vast quantities of salt were required to get the fish back to port and then transported across the country to inland towns and villages.

Winslow Homer's *The Fog Warning* (called originally *Halibut*, or *The Halibut Fisher* by Homer, but altered later), was painted in 1885. It shows a fisherman in a dory, one of a small fleet of boats that were carried by large schooners to the Grand Banks. The dories fanned out to fish halibut in the deep waters, and fish lie in the stern of the dory. The schooner crew kept a lookout for the dense fogs that were common over the Grand Banks and constantly sounded warnings when fog was looming on the horizon. The fog warnings guided the dories back to their ship before they were enveloped and lost. In this painting a dark bank of fog obscures the lower portion of the sky. The fisherman in the dory, looking towards the large sailing vessel on the horizon, must row swiftly back to the schooner in order to escape the approaching fog that could cost him his life. Homer has painted a powerful image of the dangers of fishing the heavy seas of the Grand Banks and the brave fishermen who ventured out into these waters.

Elizabethan fishermen set off for the Grand Banks in February or March, taking provisions for themselves and salt for salting the cod on board before drying it. At the end of summer, when all their salt was used

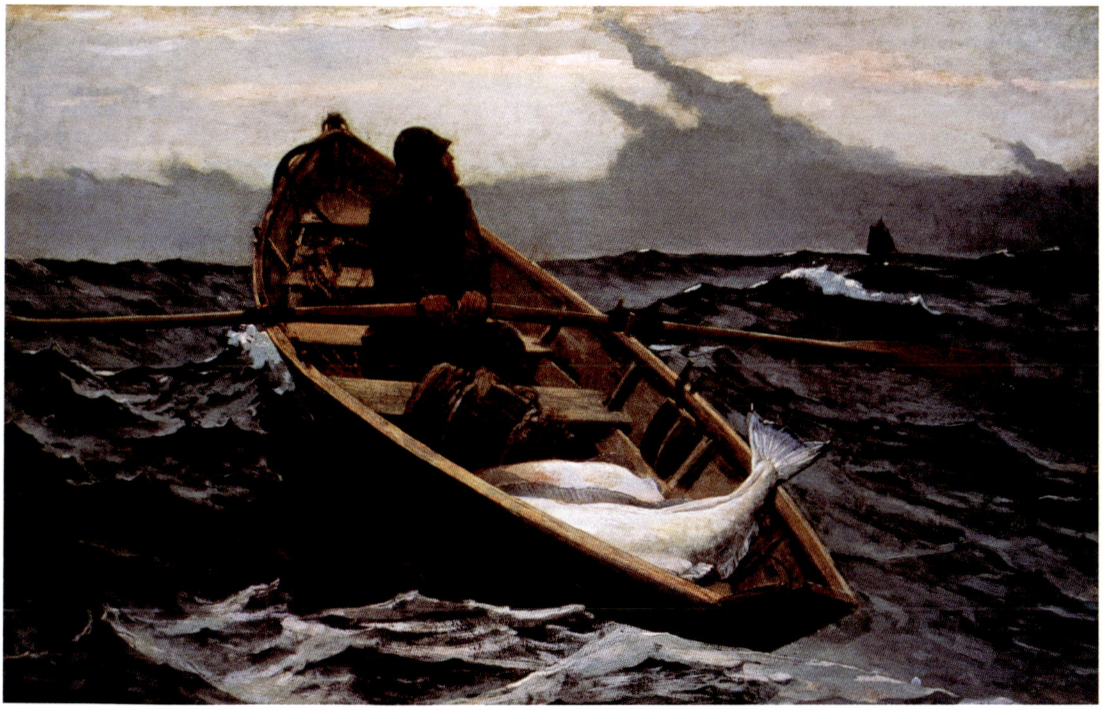

13 Winslow Homer, *The Fog Warning*, 1885, oil on canvas.

up, they set sail for home. Salting the fish preserved it for the months spent at sea and the long voyage home. Immediately after they had been caught, the cods' heads were cut off, they were opened and cleaned, then salted and stowed flat in the hold of the ship in beds 4 or 5 metres square, head to tail with a layer of salt between each layer of fish. After three or four days, when the water had drained off, they were moved to another part of the vessel and again salted and stored, either as before or in barrels of salt. This cod, on arrival home, was called stockfish, a term that applied also to similarly treated pollock, whiting and milwell.

The origins of salting fish are obscure, though both Egypt and Spain had thriving exports of salted fish in pre-Classical times and Roman Gaul was famous for its salted and smoked hams. Roman soldiers were paid part of their wages as salt allowance (Latin *salerium argentinium*), hence the term 'salary'. One of the main reasons the Romans were so interested in the Holy Land was for the opportunity to extract salt from the Dead Sea.

Salt varied in quality according to the three sources from which it was taken. The commonest was sea salt obtained either by natural evaporation

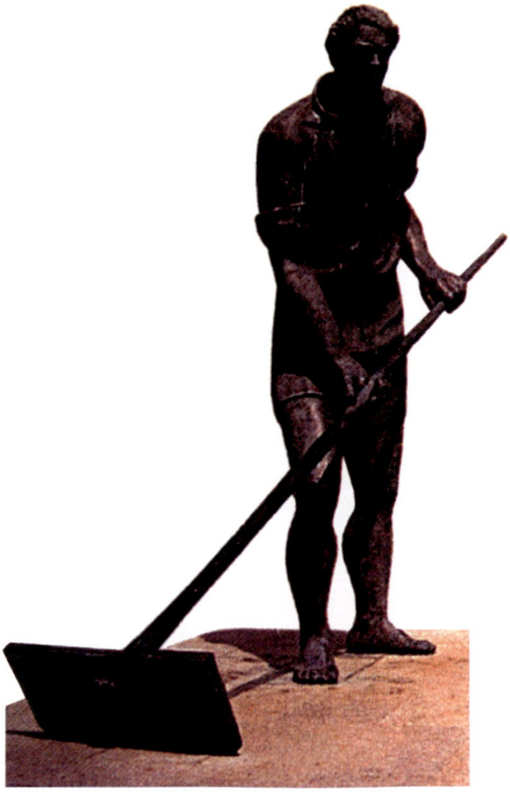

14 Statue of a salt worker in the town centre of Alcochete, Portugal. Salt was used to preserve fishes, including pilchards, for export.

of seawater or by boiling it down in artificial pools and pans. This contained many impurities and was not sufficiently strong to preserve the fish. Salt from natural springs, known as brine salt, occurred where water seeped through rocks. The saline content is higher in brine than in sea salt, but it is scarcer and therefore more expensive. The purest and most highly valued salt was rock salt, mined then reboiled with seawater to increase its saltiness. A deep seam of rock salt lies at a depth of 160 metres (500 feet) below the surface stretching from Ireland (where half a million tonnes per annum is now mined at Carrickfergus near Belfast) to Russia. The most famous of the European salt mines, the thirteenth-century mine at Wieliczka in Poland, is now visited by tourists.

Indications of where salt was produced in Britain from early times remain in some place names. Salt, a village in Staffordshire, was named from a salt pit or salt works. Saltburn indicates a place by a salt stream, as does Saltfleet. Farmsteads or villages of salt workers or merchants are indicated by Salterforth and Saltfleetby, Lincolnshire. Places where salt was found or kept include Salter, Lancashire, and Salterton (Budleigh and Woodbury, both in Devon). Flourishing salt industries grew up on the coast and in Worcestershire and Cheshire where there was a valuable salt mine at Winsford. Salt was so vital for preserving and flavouring food that it was the one commodity that everyone bought, even though for centuries cottagers and villagers were otherwise self-sufficient. When heavy demands were made on salt producers for the purpose of salting fish at sea, all sources of salt were used to capacity and further sources sought. The long Essex sea coast of tidal marshes was used for salt extraction from the Iron Age and there were 45 pans listed for this county alone in the Domesday Book in 1086. The delightful town of Alcochete in Portugal overlooking the Tagus estuary has saltpans that

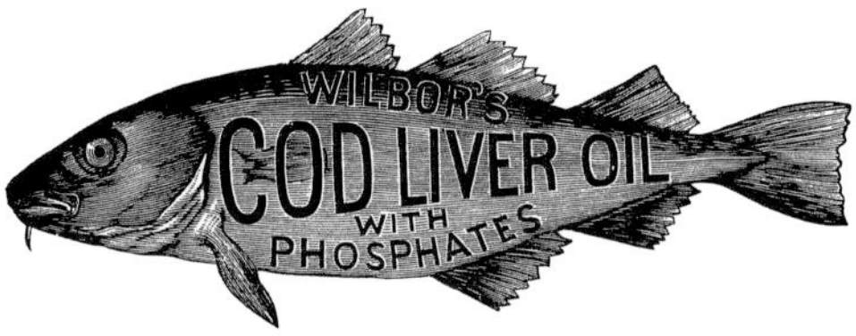

15 A Victorian advertisement for cod liver oil.

can still be seen. In the town centre there is a large statue of a salt worker. In every country locations where salt could be found naturally were carefully guarded and exploited.

Salted cod is no longer eaten in any quantity in Britain, though it features in many Continental recipes that are still very popular. The discovery and exploitation of new fishing grounds off Dogger Bank in the North Sea meant that fresh fish could be taken ashore, first to Barking close to the Thames estuary, later to the northern ports of Hull and Grimsby. Floating cod chests kept them alive and fresh until transported to market. In the mid-nineteenth century, when supplies of ice became plentiful, the cod could be sent by rail and the ports of Hull and Grimsby flourished.

It was long known that cod liver oil was good for making candles. It took a lot longer to find out that the oil has medicinal properties. This came to light by accident in 1815 when Cossacks ate some candles and found them beneficial. The oil is obtained by pressing the fresh cod livers

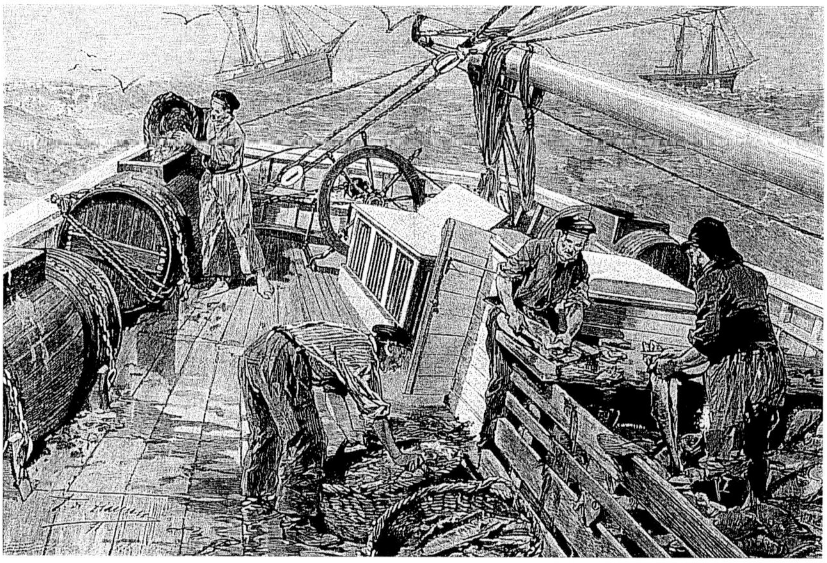

16 Newfoundland cod being sorted into enclosures on board ship. Wood engraving from *The Graphic* (1891).

at a temperature of about 85 degrees Celsius (185 Fahrenheit). The oil is a valuable source of vitamins A and D.

Cod has been important to us for so long that it is one of the few fishes to have its own biography (*Cod*, by Mark Kurlansky) and to have caused Great Britain to have taken up arms in 1976 over fishing quotas. This conflict was with Iceland, which has the second largest cod fisheries after Newfoundland. Cod, formerly one of the most abundant and cheapest fishes, has declined in numbers to such an alarming degree from overfishing that now it is one of the most expensive. Canada banned fishing for cod in its waters in 1996 because the stocks were so depleted. The teeming millions of cod on the Grand Banks almost disappeared. The same will happen to the cod in European waters if strict measures are not taken to enable them to recover.

If cod was thought of as being the wholesome and harmless mainstay of northern hemisphere inhabitants, sharks worldwide were the fish species most dreaded by fishermen and divers alike. There are some 400 shark species found throughout the oceans of the world, about 35 of which have the capability to attack human beings. Though the most feared species of fishes by mariners, relatively few shark attacks on humans lead to fatalities. Modern research suggests that shark attacks are attempts to repel rivals from their territory. Telling that to a diver who has seen the film *Jaws* will do little to calm him, especially if a 6.5-metre (20-foot) great white shark looms out of distant deep water. This is the species most frequently seen in paintings and photographs. Equally fearsome are the oceanic, whitetip and tiger sharks. Despite the awe and fear they inspire sharks have been exploited as game fish for sport and as a source of leather, oil and protein, to the extent that some are now endangered, such as the great white, tiger and hammerhead sharks.

A real-life drama at sea was painted by the American artist John Singleton Copley. *Watson and the Shark* was a record of a tragic accident that occurred while Brook Watson, a fourteen-year-old sailor, was swimming in Havana Harbour. He was attacked by sharks and one leg was so

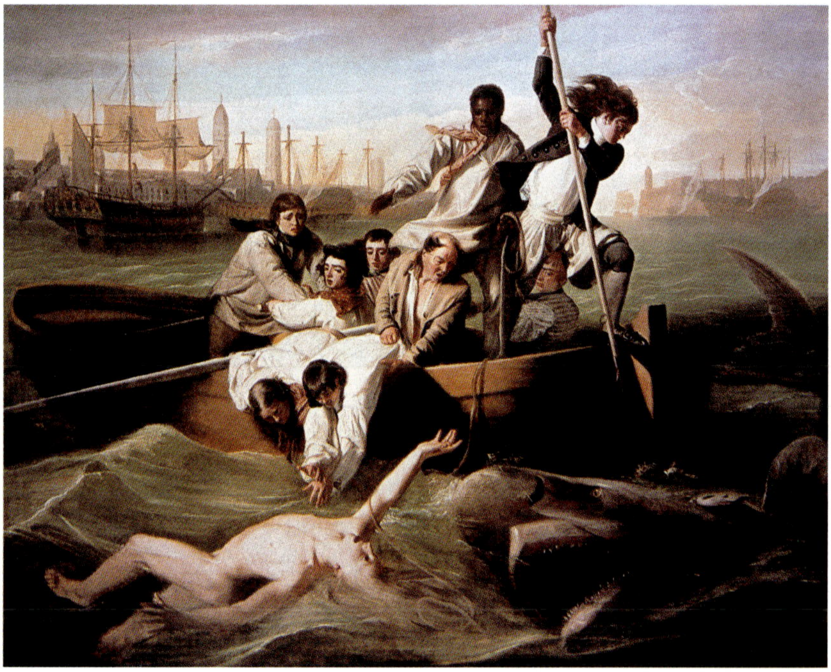

17 John Singleton Copley, *Watson and the Shark*, 1778, oil on canvas.

badly wounded that it had to be amputated below the knee. Watson survived the ordeal and made a career in the navy and then in politics. He was elected Lord Mayor of London for 1796–7 and made a baronet in 1803. Copley recreated the scene years later after meeting Watson in London.

The latest development in man's chequered relationship with sharks has been pioneered by Jacques Cousteau's grandson Fabien. Shark watchers have used a cage or a remote camera underwater, but Fabien uses a submarine so close in appearance and movement to the great white sharks that live off Guadalupe, close to Baja California, that they have accepted it and behave normally in its vicinity. Powered by a silent pneumatic mechanism that waves the tail from side to side, the 4.5-metre (15-foot) submarine looks and behaves like a medium-sized great white. More ominously, researchers at the Pentagon are experimenting with 'remote-controlled' sharks to exploit their natural ability to sense delicate electrical gradients and follow chemical trails left by ships, using electrode implants to turn the sharks into 'stealth spies'.

The urge to explore underwater is as old as mankind. Commercial gain was a strong motive, first for pearl and sponge divers and later to explore what mineral wealth lay in the depths of the sea. Pearl divers searching for oysters had operated for centuries off the coast of Sri Lanka. They and divers in the Mediterranean seeking sponges could hold their breath for two and a half minutes and dive to a depth of 10–12 metres (30 feet). It took until the 1940s for scientists to find the means to enable divers to go deep down into the sea with little more equipment than the pearl divers, unencumbered by lines to the surface.

Man needed to descend deep into the oceans on occasion for military and salvage purposes. Curiosity was also a potent force, and the wish to enjoy new recreational experiences including hunting. Probably the earliest image of men underwater is a relief of *c.* 885 BC of Assyrians in the Euphrates, breathing in air from inflated airbags. Herodotus told the story of a diver called Scyllis who was employed in the fifth century BC by the Persian king Xerxes to recover sunken treasure. Aristotle, the Greek philosopher, mentioned a crude

PEARL oyster (*Meleagrina fucata*): pearls are not obtained from the true oyster family but occur in pearl oysters of the family Pteriidae. Pearls are formed when a small particle of sand or other impurity is trapped within the shell and so becomes coated with a nacreous substance that is secreted to form the shell layers that make up mother-of-pearl to produce a natural pearl. Pearl oysters, six to seven years old, are brought to the surface by divers, placed on the ground to die and putrefy, then examined for the presence of pearls. Cultured pearls are induced by inserting a small particle of mother-of-pearl into oysters, mainly the warm-water species of *Pinctata*.

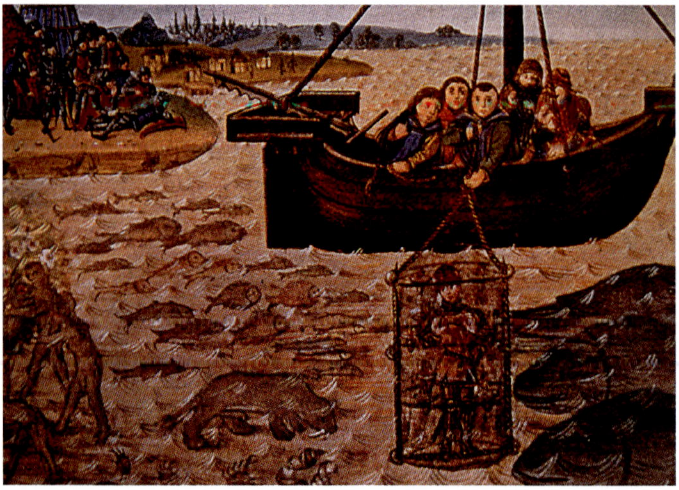

18 Medieval depiction of Alexander in his diving bell; unknown source.

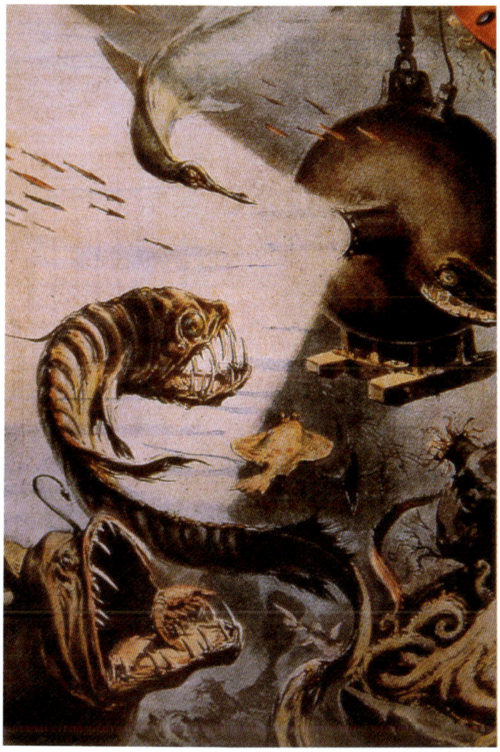

air-supply diving bell in 360 BC. Alexander the Great used divers to remove obstacles that had been sunk in the harbour at Tyre, which he had taken after laying siege to it in 332 BC. It is claimed that he went underwater himself in a glass barrel to check on his divers' work. This episode has been painted several times, some of the pictures being notable for the number of fishes that the artists imagined had gathered round Alexander to take a good look at him.

Diving bells with compressed air trapped inside the inner apex were first referred to in 1531. Interest never waned in experimenting with equipment and ideas for remaining underwater for longer periods over the next 400 years. It was not until 1934, when William Beebe and Otis Barton descended for half a mile in a tethered sphere, that the hitherto unknown world of bizarre, luminous creatures in the murky waters so far down was revealed. Otis Barton called his invention a benthoscope and dived off the coast of Ceylon (now Sri Lanka). The painting of this venture shows flat fishes and a human skull on the seabed with shells, coral and swimming pipefish.

19 Otis Barton in his benthoscope, *c.* 1930.

There were many experiments with diving dresses and helmets, and even a submarine that took trips down to 5 metres (15 feet) in the Thames in 1620, but it was not until technology and necessity combined during the Second World War that the means to dive deeply, unencumbered by heavy equipment and a line back to the surface, was finally found.

Up to this point the fishes in underwater paintings are incidental to the main interest, which is the divers and their equipment. Diving in order to see fishes was a new idea in the late 1960s, and learning to snorkel, scuba dive (with aqualungs, i.e. with cylinders on the back) and go down in bathyscaphes with the intent to paint fishes came still later.

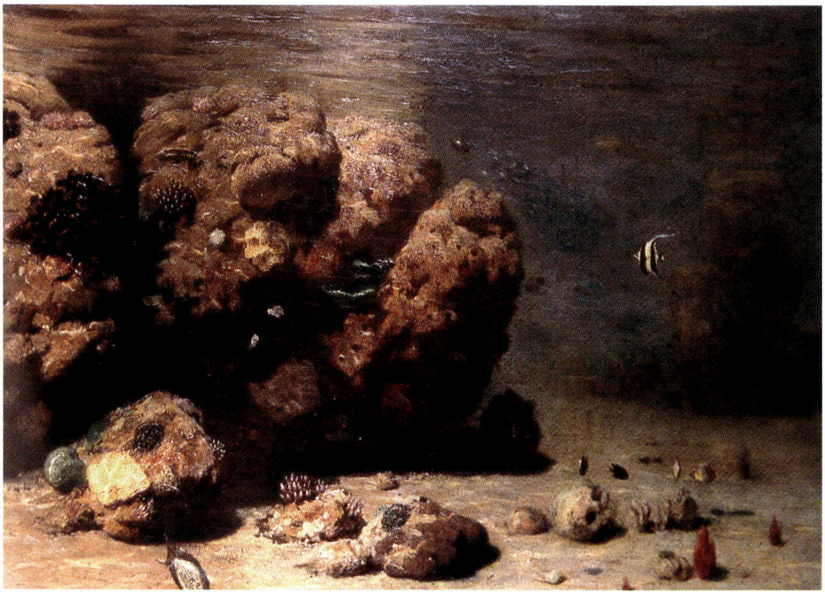

20 Eugen von Ransonnet-Villez, an Austrian diplomat, traveller and inventor of a diving bell, painted this small picture in 1864. It is one of the earliest paintings to successfully show fishes in an underwater marinescape.

Much of this is owed to Jacques Cousteau who first brought the underwater world teeming with brilliantly coloured fishes to the public on television screens in the 1970s. His programmes were designed to concentrate on the underwater scenery and animal life. In 1943 he and Émile Gagnan began to develop a modern scuba (*s*elf-*c*ontained *u*nderwater *b*reathing *a*pparatus) allowing divers to stay underwater for extended periods. In 1948 a Swiss physicist made the first untethered craft, a bathyscaphe, in which his son Jacques soon after took it to the deepest point attained in ocean exploration. Jacques Piccard made the deepest dive up to 1960 (10,920 metres/35,797 feet), to find new fishes and other hitherto unknown and unseen deep-sea life.

Once all this technology was in place and available to people other than naval officers, geologists, archaeologists and marine biologists, artists could, at last, go down to see for themselves what exquisite flora and fauna lay deep in the oceans. They then wanted to record and produce pictures of the beautiful underwater world of the tropics, a wealth of new species not previously painted. Aids to this enterprise were the camera and flash lighting. Colour photographs are the basis of most modern paintings of marine fishes. Water has an effect on the quality of the light, colour, distance, refraction and distortion, and the sea is a moving element with currents and wind agitation. Underwater photography of fishes requires as much patience as photographing birds. The moment a shot is lined up the fishes tend to dash off, just as birds take flight in the air. The multiplicity of skills required to paint living pictures of fishes underwater has meant that there are very few skilled practitioners of this genre.

Since the 1970s hundreds of additional species of fishes have been painted. Patrick Chevailler of Palm Island has been one of the most successful artists painting tropical fishes and evocative underwater scenes. The most colourful saltwater fishes are found in warm waters, precisely those areas where divers prefer to operate. Their colours rival those of birds such as birds of paradise, hummingbirds and peacocks, while their fanciful designs beggar description. They are found in the Caribbean, the Indian Ocean and the South Pacific where they live in crystal-clear waters, darting among corals with gently swaying anemones for companions. Painting them underwater may not be possible except in a submersible and so photography, especially colour photography, was the answer for would-be painters of underwater scenes with fishes.

Current artists who are painting exotic fish species, scenes on coral reefs and in deep water, are few in number. Among British artists are John Dronsfield and Bas. However, there are more American artists at work in this field, for example, Ben Saturen, Suzie Zimos, Elaine Estern, Donna Schaffer; and the Canadian Ming Ma. These artists revel in the brilliant, scintillating colours of the fishes and the varied structures of the reefs with their bright corals.

In America Stanley Meltzoff (1917–2006) has long been considered to be the master of underwater realistic painting. Among the younger generation of American marine artists, Richard Ellis is outstanding. Keith Shackleton is among the best twentieth-century British painters of marine scenes. He painted an example of a swordfish 'flying' out of water, complete with a powerful rendering of deep water and sea foam. His comments accompanying his painting were: 'Swordfish do this and do it often when they are hooked. This one was not. Its motive, shared by several others

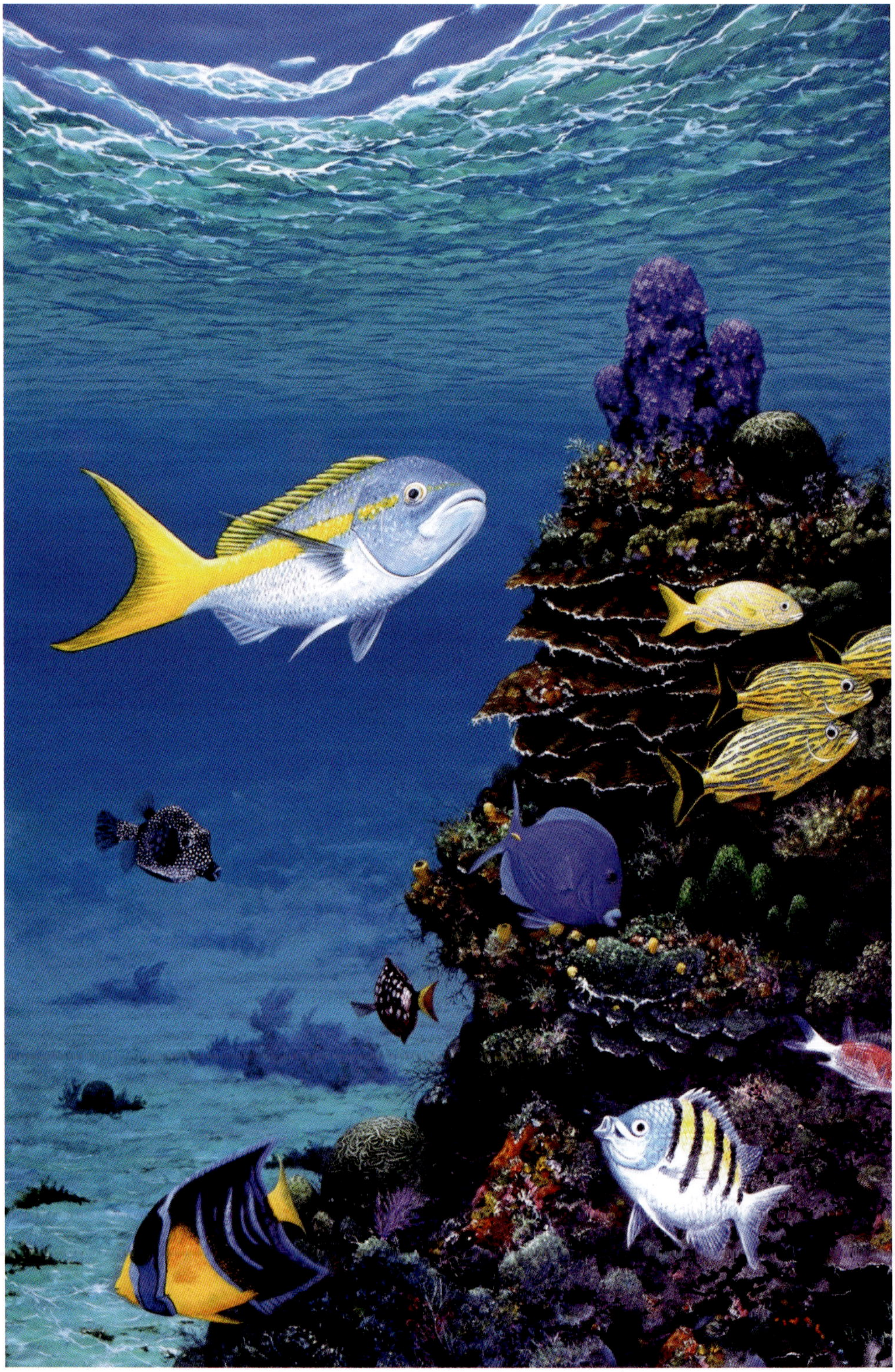

22 Paul André Robert, *Pterois volitans, Scorpion Fish and Amphirion percula*, watercolour reproduced in *Wonders of the Sea: Life in the Oceans* (1937). The scorpion fish inhabits the reefs of the Indian Ocean where it is much dreaded by fishermen, as its dorsal spines have poison glands. The striped *Amphirion percula* uses sea anemones as a natural refuge at any sign of danger.

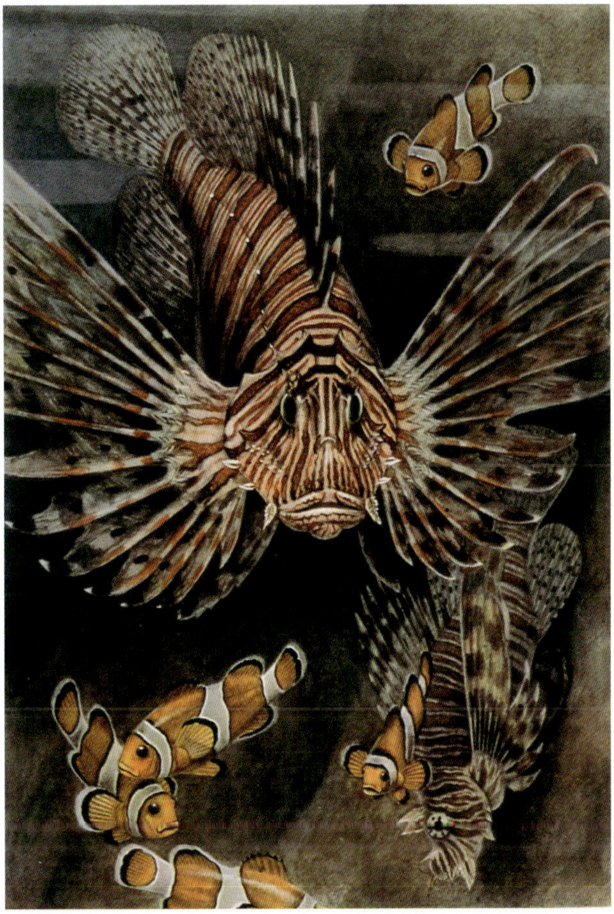

23 Stanley Meltzoff, *Snappers, Sport, Mullet, Blackfish, Stripers at Elberon, Autumn*, 1974, oil over acrylic on canvas.

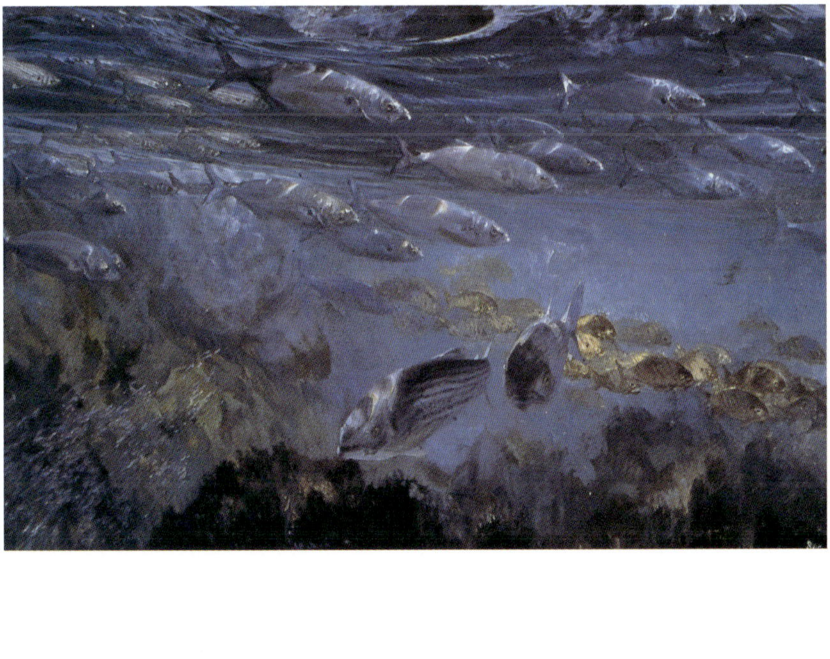

opposite: 21 Patrick Chevailler, *Smith Reef*, *c.* 2000, oil on canvas.

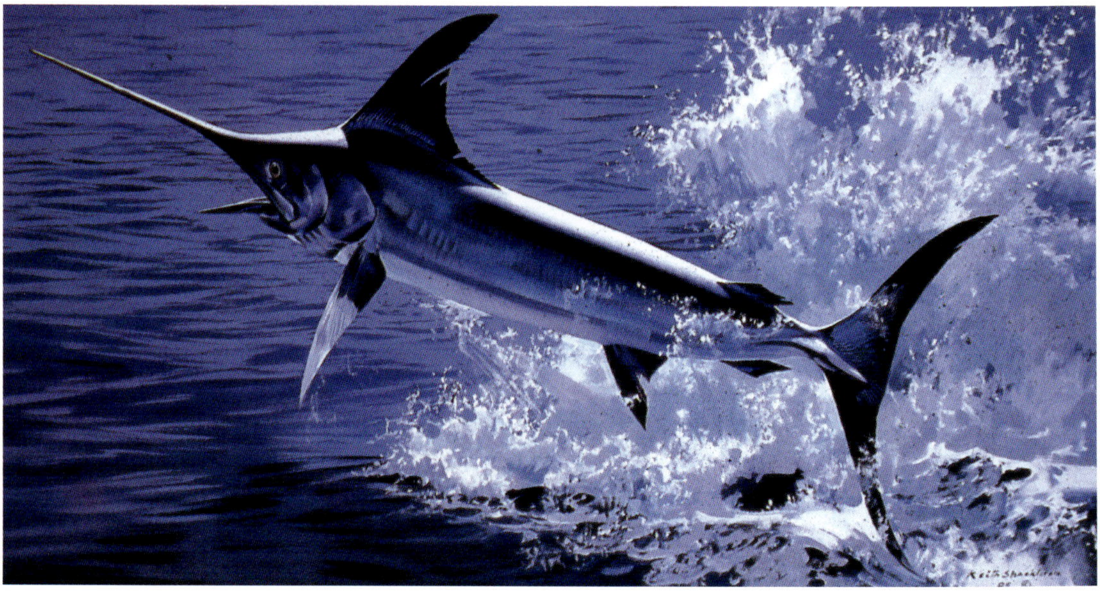

24 Keith Shackleton (*b.* 1923), *Swordfish*, oil on canvas.

25 Ernest Henry Griset (1843–1907), 'The denizens of the deep enact a war dance in preparation for their attack on some divers', printed in *Little Folk* (1883).

that day, could have been the itch of dermal parasites, it could have had some special hunting value, or it could be, as it certainly looked, [to] have stemmed from sheer exuberance. In the right places and on those flat, hot days it is not a rare sight, and characteristic behaviour for many of the different bill-fish species.' Deep water and sea foam are skilfully painted.

Sea angling in Britain has attracted far fewer participants than freshwater angling and hardly any artists record this form of the sport. In the United States of America the situation is very different. Americans are mainly interested in marine big-game fishes and their heroic battles with the larger species while hooking and landing them. They commission artists to record their epic fights. It may be that this tradition was begun by their earliest and still most famous American artist of angling subjects, Winslow Homer. He was concerned with the commercial fishermen's struggles against the elements – fog and huge waves – while fishing on the Grand Banks (illus. 13). Just before the Second World War it was the sport of sea angling for large fishes like tuna and marlin (close relatives of swordfishes) that became more particularly an American form of sport. Men in small boats were depicted

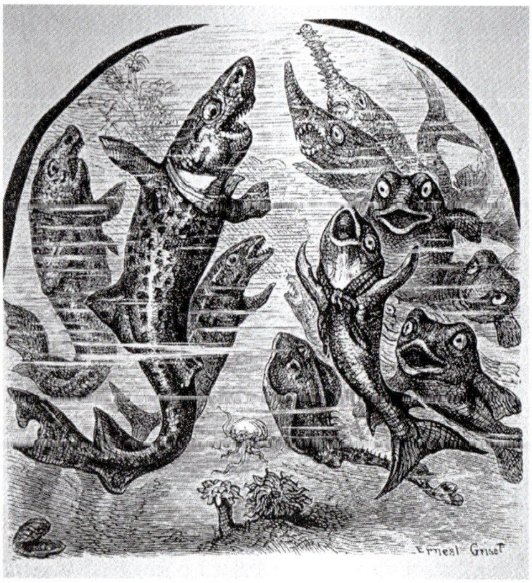

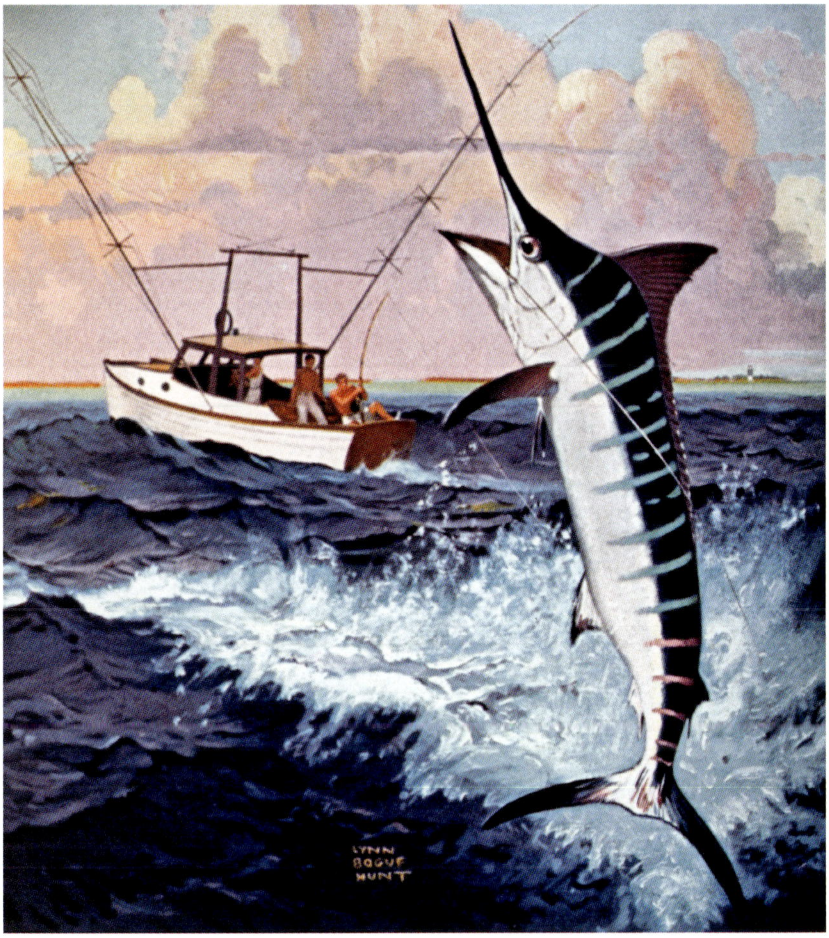

26 Lynn Bogue-Hunt, *Striped Marlin*, *c*. 1923, gouache. The large fishes – tunny, marlins, sharks, bonitos and wahoo – that once terrified ancient mariners are now among the world's most sought-after gamefish. The striped marlin *Tetrapturus audax* has a maximum weight of 480 pounds (220 kg). Their spectacular leaps may be seen off the coasts of Chile, Mexico, California and New Zealand.

holding a rod and line on the end of which huge marlin, sharks and tunny fish were leaping out of the sea in a spectacular bid to escape the hook. Once back on land, unlike English eighteenth- and nineteenth-century gentlemen anglers who liked to have their portraits painted by the river with their freshwater catches lying on the bank, American sea anglers prefer to have a photograph taken of themselves holding up their prize catch full length. A ruler alongside records the exact size of the fish. The angler is more important than the fish in this most robust form of the sport.

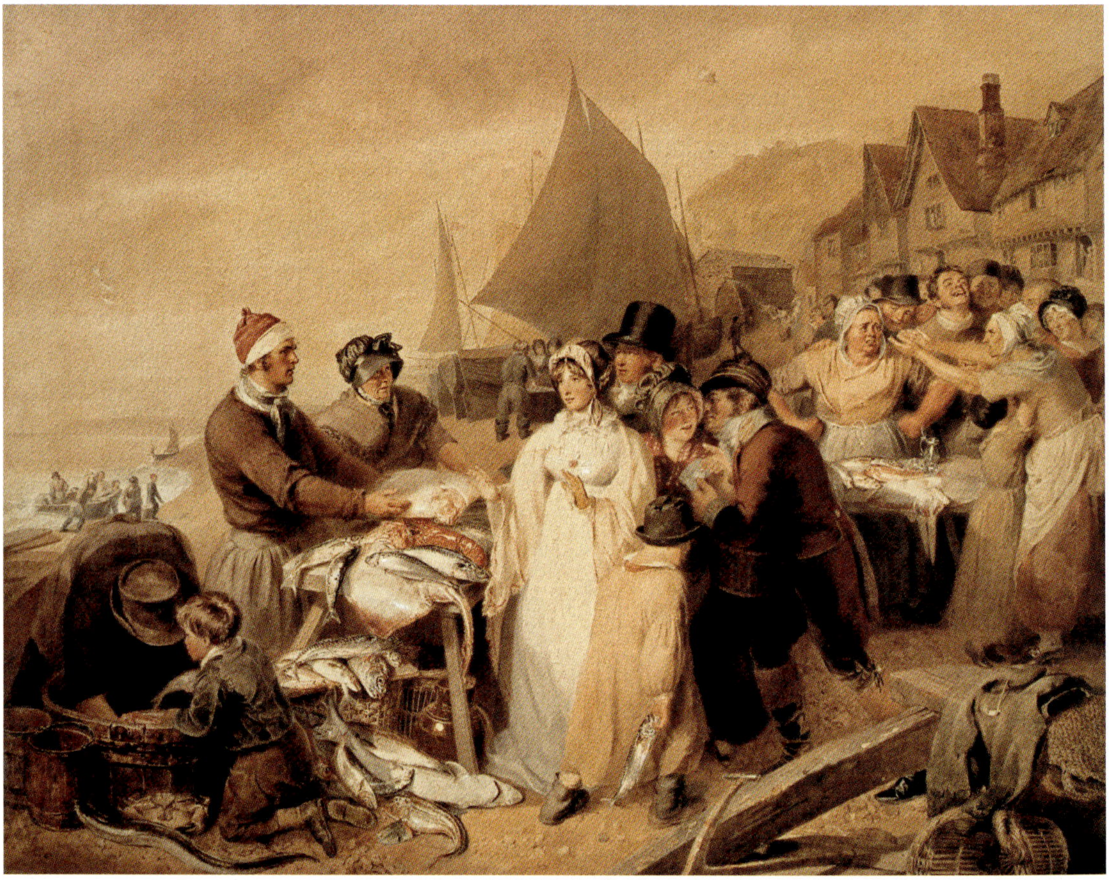

27 Thomas Heaphy, *Fish Market, Hastings*, 1809, watercolour.

two
Fish on the Beach

Paintings of beach scenes evoke memories of walks along the tideline and alert all our senses. We can hear the gentle lapping of the waves nearest the shore, with the roar of the surf behind. We can smell the tang of salt and seaweed in the air. The colours around us are not flat but sparkle in the sunshine. The sand glitters, the water glints and the big sky is luminous, albeit hazy, where it meets the sea on the horizon. We are reminded of the tactile pleasure derived from picking up shiny pebbles and dipping our fingers into rock pools. All these recollections make pictures of beach scenes popular. To include fish on the beach in the painting is an added bonus.

Artists could choose to pile the fish neatly in an artistic arrangement from fish deposited on the beach; paint a fisherman's catch as emptied out from his basket haphazardly onto the beach; or make a completely false but imaginative arrangement from fishes bought in the market. The most likely modus operandi was to sketch fishes as and where obtainable and then make a composition on canvas in the studio. Judging how the artist had compiled his group of fishes in these canvases is but one of the intriguing conundrums for the viewer to solve, given certain clues in the picture.

Today we may stroll along a beach and enjoy only leisure activities there, but in the past beaches were humming with activity. Women were waiting for boats to come in and there were people employed on all jobs related to handling the landed fish, also drying and conserving the catch. Many local fishermen drew their boats onto the beach in coves and inlets, rather than move on to a harbour. They offloaded their fishes straight onto the beach and sold them there. When large vessels stood out to sea, small rowing boats went out to them and collected the fish. Again the fishes were sorted on the beach and sold to waiting customers, while others were packed into barrels and baskets for transportation inland.

When painting such scenes most of the artists worked in oils, but Thomas Heaphy (1775–1835), who was one of the first British artists to paint a beach scene, worked in watercolours. He exhibited his picture *Fish Market, Hastings* at the Old Watercolour Society in 1809 (illus. 27). He had trained in London, first as an engraver, and then entered the Royal Academy Schools in 1796. As a painter he concentrated on picturesque genre scenes and commanded high prices for them. *Fish Market, Hastings* is among the earliest British paintings of a scene with fishes using full watercolours.

In the foreground of Heaphy's painting a boy is assisting a woman to pack fishes into a barrel on the left, and a jacket and clay pipe lie on the right. A lady and gentleman are present at the main fish stall. She is rejecting a large flat fish being offered to her by the fisherman. Her maid is being propositioned by a well-turned-out man in a chestnut brown coat. Two fishwives (one of them with a child clinging to her skirts) are quarrelling, to the amusement of male bystanders. In the background boats are drawn up onto the beach. Among the fishes are eel, mackerel, lobster, dogfish and gurnard, with a lobster.

Several episodes in the life of Jesus took place in and on the water of the Sea of Galilee, because his disciples were fishermen. The story of the Miraculous Draught of Fishes was set on the shores of this stretch of water in the Holy Land that had three names in the New Testament, the Sea of Galilee, the Sea of Tiberias and Lake Gennesaret. It is an inland freshwater lake fed by the river Jordan.

Fish featured largely in the account of the third appearance of the risen Christ to His disciples. Peter, Thomas, Nathaniel, James and John the sons of Zebedee, and two other disciples had decided to go fishing. Having fished all night and caught nothing, a man standing by the lake called to them to cast their net on the right side of the boat. They proceeded to catch more than they could draw into the boat so

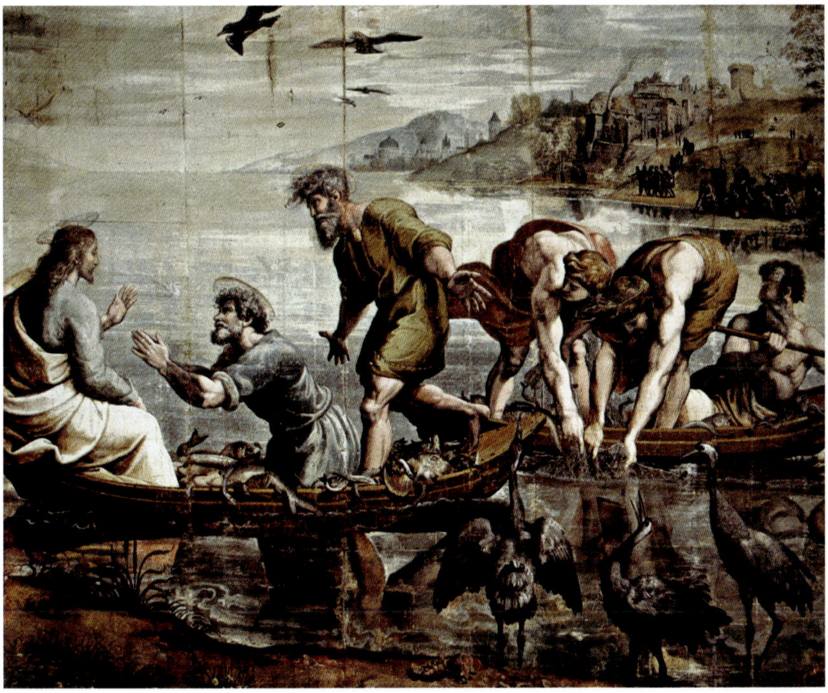

28 Raphael, *The Miraculous Draught of Fishes,* 1515–16, tempera on paper mounted on canvas.

manoeuvred it in close to the shore. John then recognized the man on the shore as Jesus and told Peter, who quickly pulled his coat around him and jumped into the water in his eagerness to reach Jesus. The other disciples followed in a small boat, covering the 200 cubits (a cubit is approximately 46 to 56 cm) by dragging the net with the fishes. When on land again they saw a fire of coals with fishes cooking and some bread laid beside them. Emptying the net of its large fishes they counted 153 and marvelled that the net was not broken. Jesus then said, 'Come and dine', and handed them fish and bread.

The most famous painting of this *Miraculous Draught of Fishes* is by Raphael, whose cartoon for a tapestry of this subject intended to be hung in the Sistine Chapel is now in the Victoria and Albert Museum, London. Raphael has placed Jesus in a boat in the water; in the nets a mixture of marine and freshwater fishes (rays, eels and a dogfish) can be seen. Less well known is Konrad Witz's picture of 1444, showing six disciples in a boat near the shore, a net half drawn out of the water containing clearly painted fishes with other fishes in the shallow water.

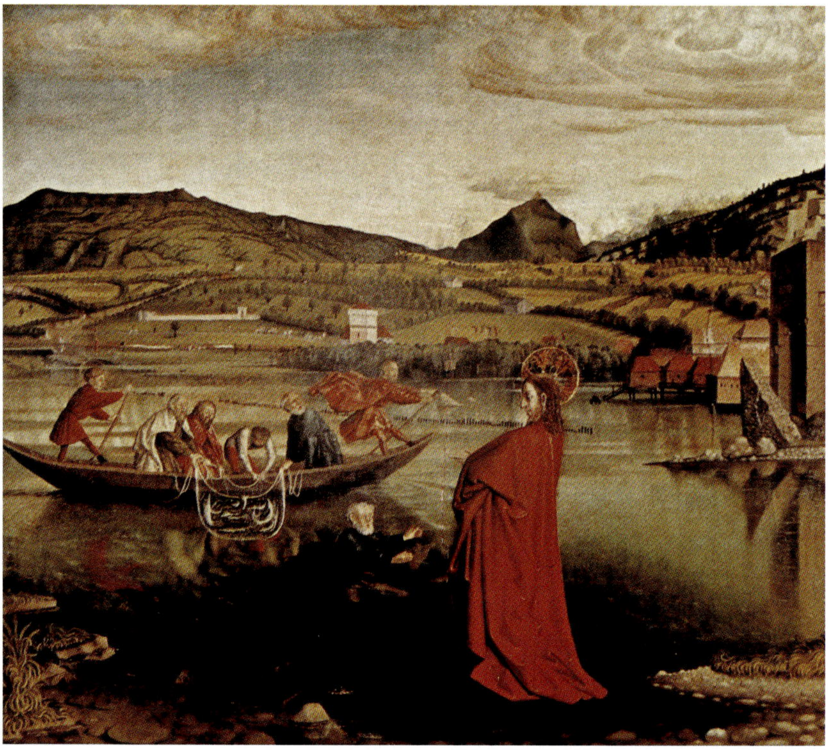

29 Konrad Witz, *The Miraculous Draught of Fishes*, 1444, tempera on wood.

30 *The Miraculous Draught of Fishes*, 12th century, detail from a ceiling in the church at Zillis, Switzerland.

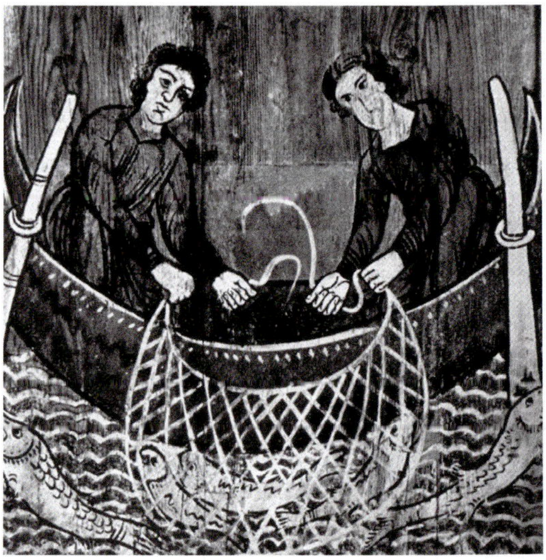

This depiction is closer to the biblical account with Jesus standing in shallow water near the shore. The colours are vibrant and the figures sharply drawn.

There are other versions of this moving story of the fishermen disciples' meeting with their risen Lord, such as the large oil painting in Brussels by the Flemish artist Caspar de Crayer (1582–1669) which has a good, detailed variety of fishes.

Another biblical episode records a taxman demanding taxes from Peter and Jesus – only a small amount but they had no money with which to pay. Jesus told Peter to go to the shore and catch a fish, in whose mouth he would find a coin. Peter retrieved the coin as instructed and paid their tax. In 1426–7 Masaccio painted a fresco nearly

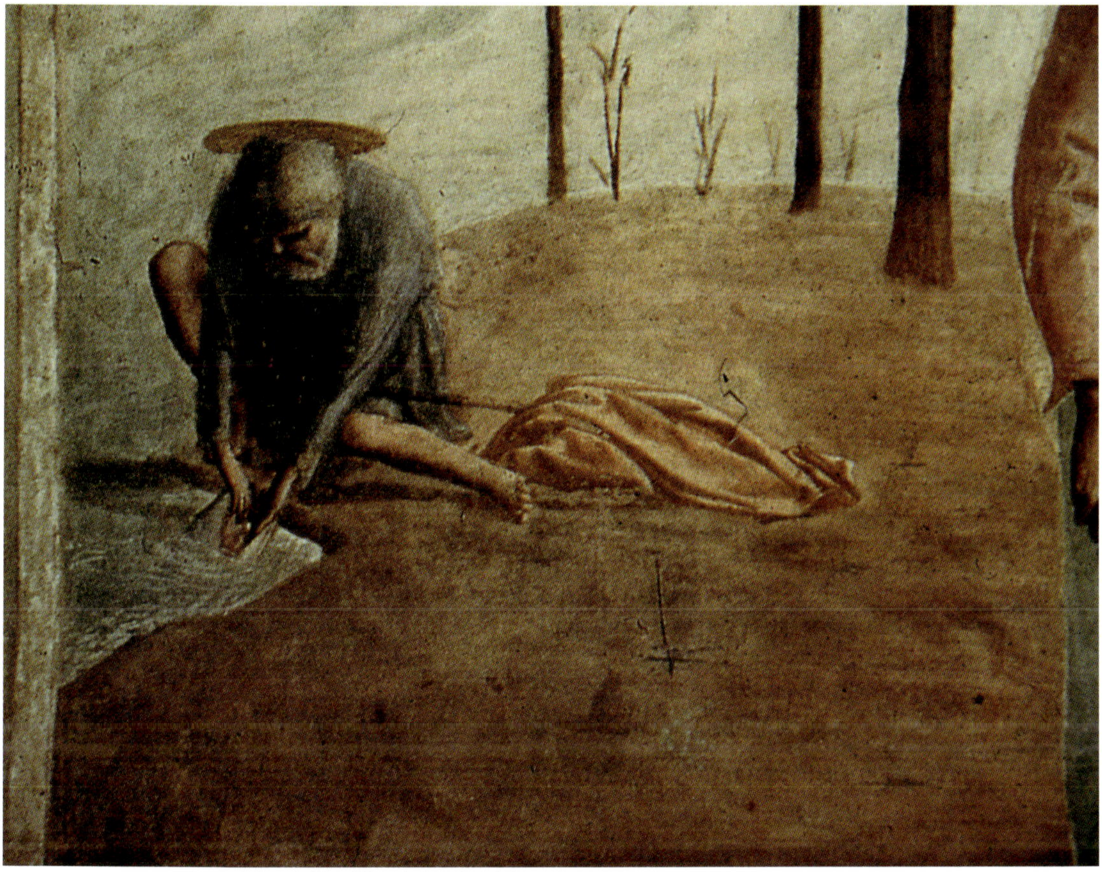

31 Masaccio, *The Tribute Money*, detail, *c.* 1426–7, fresco.

6 metres long and divided into three parts, to tell the story in its various stages. In the centre Christ is instructing Peter to catch a fish and on the left (see the detail here) Peter is taking the coin out of the fish's mouth. On the right Peter is handing over the coin to the tax collector. Traditionally, the money extracted by Peter was believed to have come from a dory. The dory or John Dory is one of our ugliest inshore marine fishes. It is a sad-looking fish with downturned mouth, and spiky because of the spiny dorsal fins from which long filaments trail. It has associations with the Greek god Zeus and with St Peter. Sacred to Zeus, it was named *Zeus faber*. Its most distinguishing feature, apart from its ugly face, is a large black spot ringed with yellow in the middle of its body. This is said to be the thumbprint of Peter who lifted it out of the Sea of Galilee to extract a coin that was used as tax money. John Dory is a salt-water species and

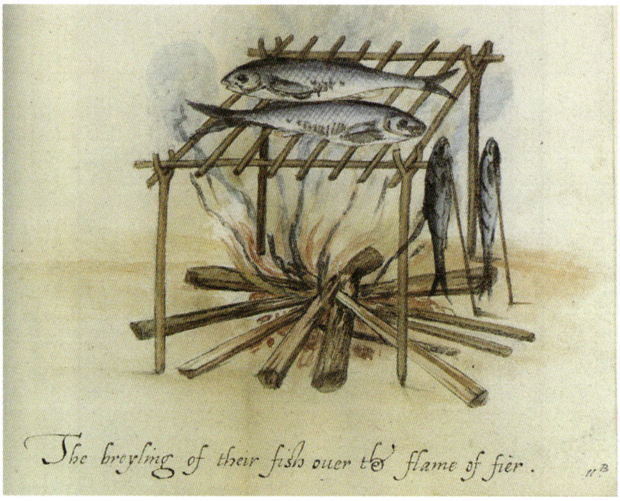

32 John White, Native Americans 'Broyling of their fish', 16th century.

33 Dumont d'Urville, *Voyage de la corvette 'L'Astrolabe'*, 1833. Sailors from *L'Astrolabe* share a catch of fishes with Aborigines at Jervis Bay, New South Wales.

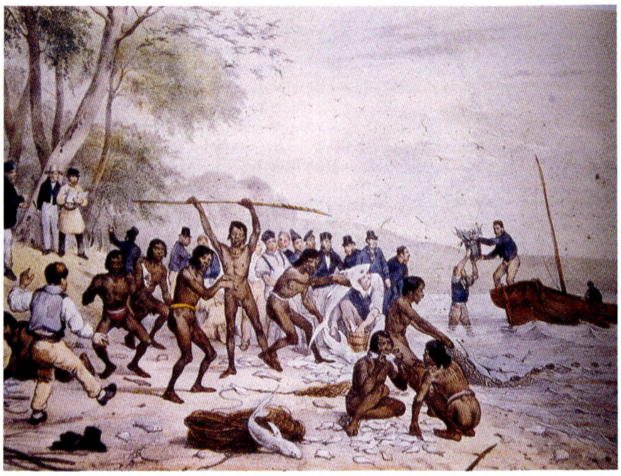

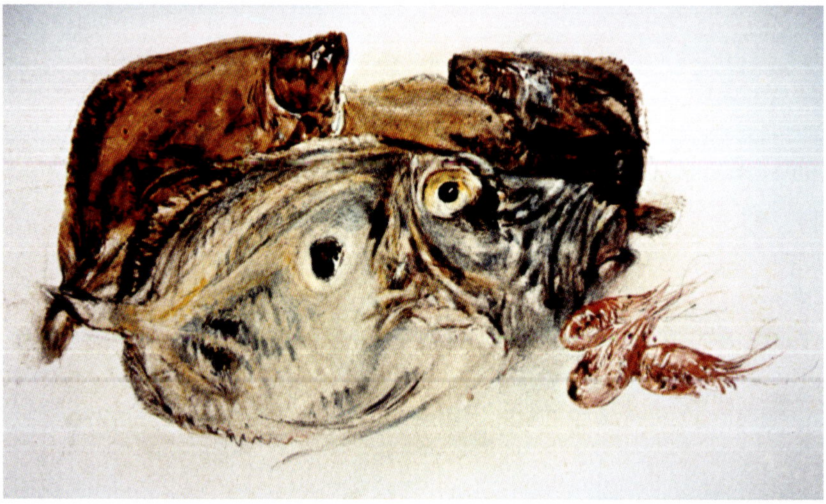

34 J.M.W. Turner, *Study of Fish*, *c.* 1820–30, watercolour.

so not likely to be found in the freshwater lake, the Sea of Galilee. J.M.W. Turner found its ugliness attractive in a perverse kind of way and made a careful watercolour study of one, along with a plaice, and added a touch of colour with shrimps.

Jacob Jordaens called his version of the story the *Miracle of the Obol, or Tribute Money*. The obol in ancient Greece was the sixth part of a drachma in weight or money. In the Middle Ages the word was applied to various small coins, such as the English halfpenny. A beach scene where Jesus finds Peter and Andrew fishing with a casting net at the Sea of Galilee, and calls to them: 'Follow me and I will make you fishers of men', was imagined by Caravaggio, who painted it in oils between 1603 and 1606. This painting was recently discovered in Britain in the Royal Collection. Peter is carrying a large fish by some twine threaded through its mouth. A fish is sometimes used as Peter's symbol in paintings in preference to keys.

These fishermen, like those the world over, knew that the best way to eat fish is fresh from the sea. The barbecue on the beach with newly brought-in fish tops all gastronomic delights. One of the first scenes of a fish barbecue appeared in John White's book about the newly colonized land on the east coast of America in 1585. He had been sent out by Sir Walter Raleigh to record the people, their lifestyle, the animals and plants, in order to judge the potential for establishing a population of settlers there. White painted a watercolour of two Native Americans beside a fire on the beach, cooking fish or 'broiling' them. Two other fish are being gently smoked or dried at the side of the fire.

When the British arrived in Australia at the end of the eighteenth century they discovered tasty mullet, bream and snapper with crustaceans, reef clams and mud oysters. John William Lewin (1770–1819) was the first professional British artist to emigrate to Australia and scored another 'first' with this painting in oils. It is a still-life, *Fish Catch and Dawes Point, Sydney Harbour*, painted about 1813. Lewin assembled this pile of fishes, including a snapper upside down by the basket and two parrotfish, some thirteen years after he arrived in Australia, using sketches of the

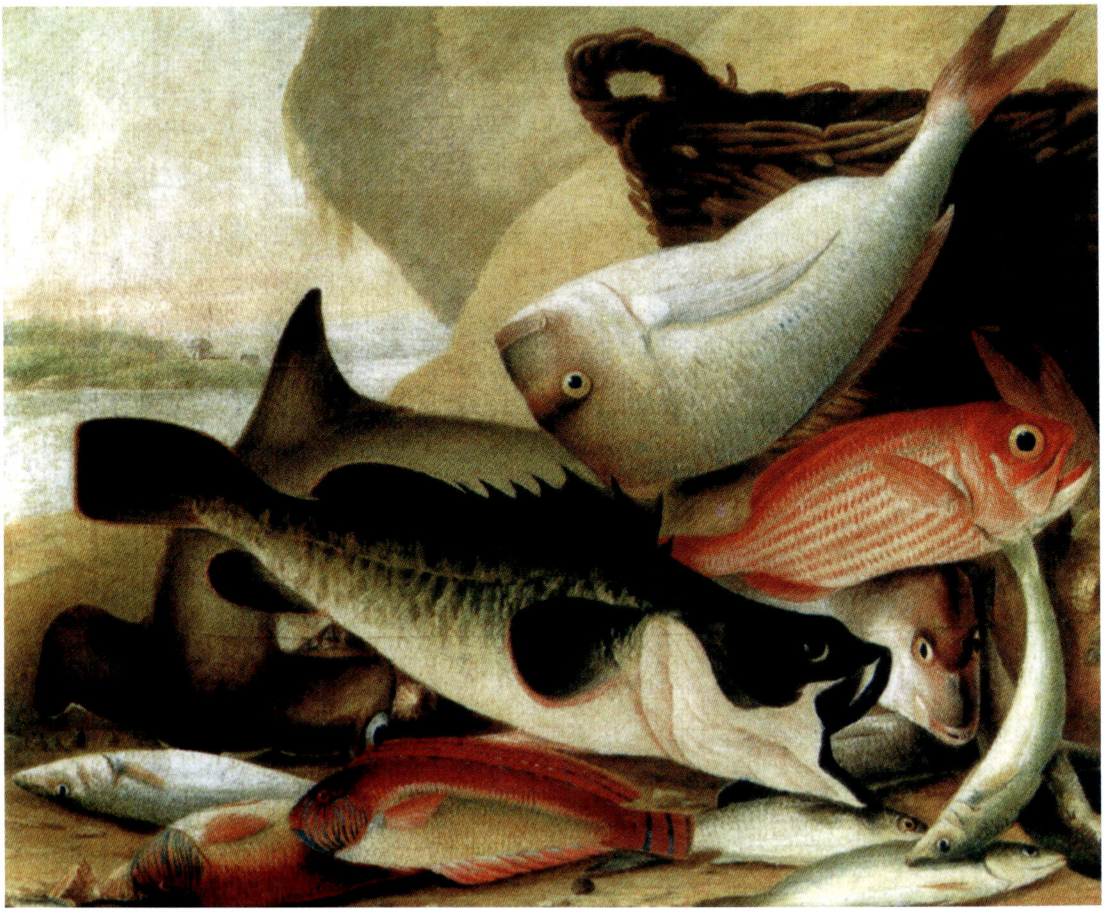

35 John William Lewin, *Fish Catch and Dawes Point, Sydney Harbour*, *c.* 1813, oil on canvas.

fishes done at various times before bringing them together on the canvas. The original sketches are conserved at the Linnean Society in London.

We cannot see what the Aborigines are cooking in the early painting of a beach barbecue they shared with French sailors from *L'Astrolabe* at Jervis Bay, New South Wales, in the early 1830s (illus. 33). One sailor is busy in the background recording the scene. The sharks in the foreground are small and one hopes the Aborigines warned the French of the dangers posed by large ones in Australian waters.

European scenes of fishes on the beach are rather more sober affairs than the early American and Australian pictures discussed above. In seventeenth-century Continental Europe, artists underwent rigorous training before they were allowed to practise as master painters. In order

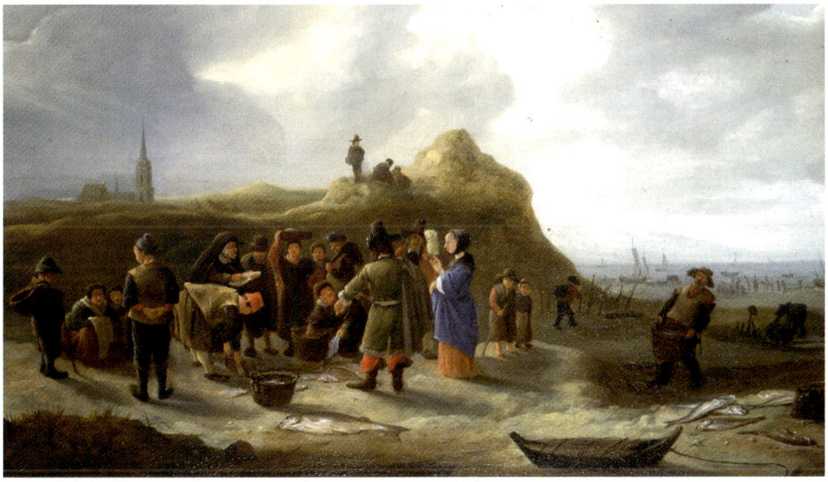

36 Jan Steen (1626–1679), *Fishermen and Figures on a Beach Inspecting their Catch of Fishes*, oil on canvas.

to set up a studio, Dutch, Flemish and Italian artists had to become members of the Guild of St Luke. While serving their apprenticeship they learned drawing and painting in watercolours and oils, composition, perspective, chiaroscuro (light and shade), how to paint different textures and the use of colour. At the end of as many as seven years of apprenticeship they had to produce a 'master-piece' to demonstrate that they had truly mastered all these techniques. Consequently, many of the artists chose to paint a still-life because they could demonstrate their ability to handle fruit and flowers, fur, feathers and fish scales, metal, glass and fabrics such as carpets and tablecloths. These were often set against a small landscape or seascape in the background. Young Dutch and Flemish artists establishing their reputations and trying to attract patrons found that small-scale pictures were popular with the new merchant class whose homes were not on the grand scale of kings and cardinals for whom artists had formerly worked. The great heyday of still-life pictures occurred during the seventeenth century in the Low Countries, Italy and Spain, when such rigorous training produced truly versatile master painters.

The dominance of the Low Countries' economy ended around 1700 due in part to the breakdown of the rigid guild system. Politically,

THE SAYING 'Fish eat fish' was a well-known aphorism in the Dutch Republic as an allusion to the rich devouring the poor. Artists made moralistic images to illustrate it and Pieter Brueghel portrayed great traders absorbing smaller enterprises.

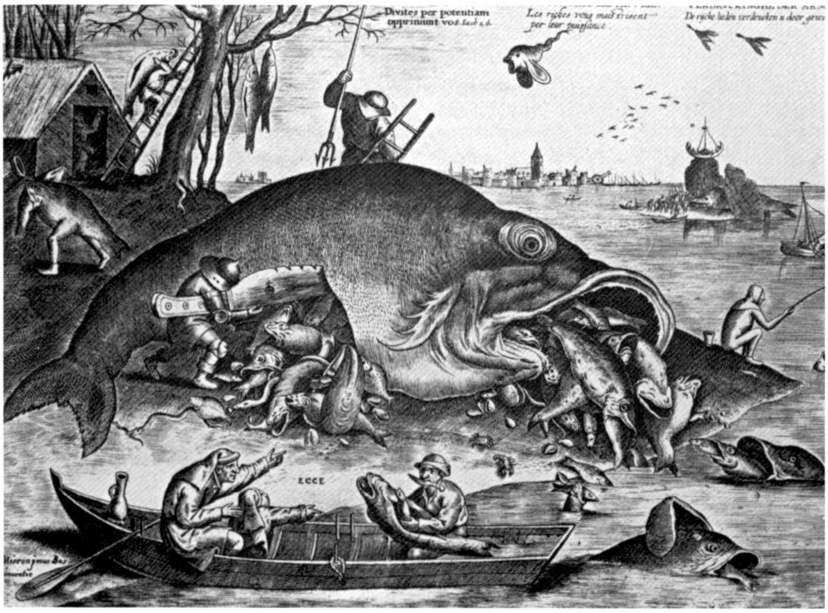

37 Pieter Brueghel, *Big Fish Eat Little Fish*, 1556, engraving.

the growing might of the French king Louis XIV (1643–1715) and the emerging imperialism of Britain combined to challenge the supremacy of the Dutch at sea. While the fashion for natural history pictures and domestic interiors prevailed, the careers of such famous artists as Rembrandt and Rubens blossomed. Their fellow artists in Italy (including Caravaggio) and Spain also painted hundreds of high-quality canvases from which it would be possible to collect a great number of remarkable fish paintings. Outstanding Low Countries painters of fish on the beach include Pieter van Noort, A. van Beyeren, Van Duijnan and Jan Steen.

Jan Steen's *Fishermen and Figures on a Beach Inspecting their Catch of Fishes* shows the various activities following the landing of a catch onto the beach from small rowing boats that have fetched the catch from the larger ships lying offshore (illus. 36). A man is straining to carry a heavy basket of fishes while another is rolling a barrel up the beach. A well-dressed man is directing a woman placing fish into a basket while another woman, her basket already packed and lifted onto her head, stands in the background

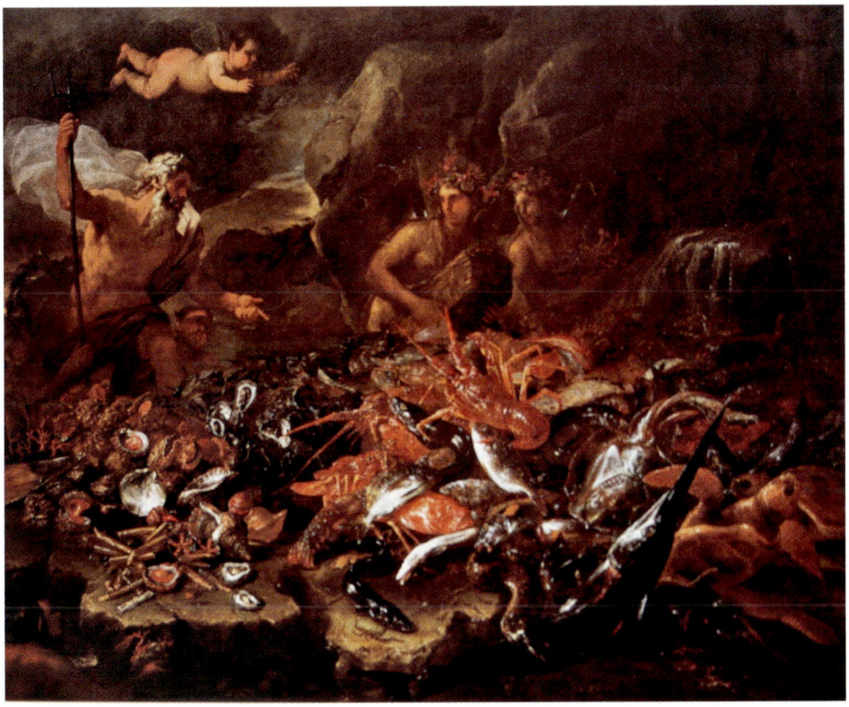

38 Giuseppe Recco and Luca Giordano, *Marine Life with Neptune and Two Nereids*, *c.* 1680, oil on canvas.

waiting to go round houses and streets selling fish. There are several discussions about the catch between interested spectators. A large cod lies in the foreground and a flat fish can also be seen on the ground.

Willem Ormea (1611–1665) painted *Fish on a Dune*, a scene of the Miraculous Draught of Fishes, with Jesus in a red cloak pointing to a boat in the centre. Just as Bont's background was painted by another artist, Ormea employed one to put in the background, in this case one of the artistic Willaerts family. The rather stiff cod, imposing sturgeon, gurnard, exotic empty shells and live crabs in the foreground feature regularly in Ormea's many coastal landscape pictures.

For an impression of a huge landscape/seascape with an extraordinary collection of fishes in the foreground it would be hard to rival Jan van Kessel's *Fishes on the Seashore*, yet this painting in oil on copper is only 18 × 28 cm. It is signed and dated 1661. Jan van Kessel was born in Amsterdam in 1626 but worked and died in Antwerp (1679), where there was a flourishing fish market and industry. A large skate dominates all the other species packed into this small area.

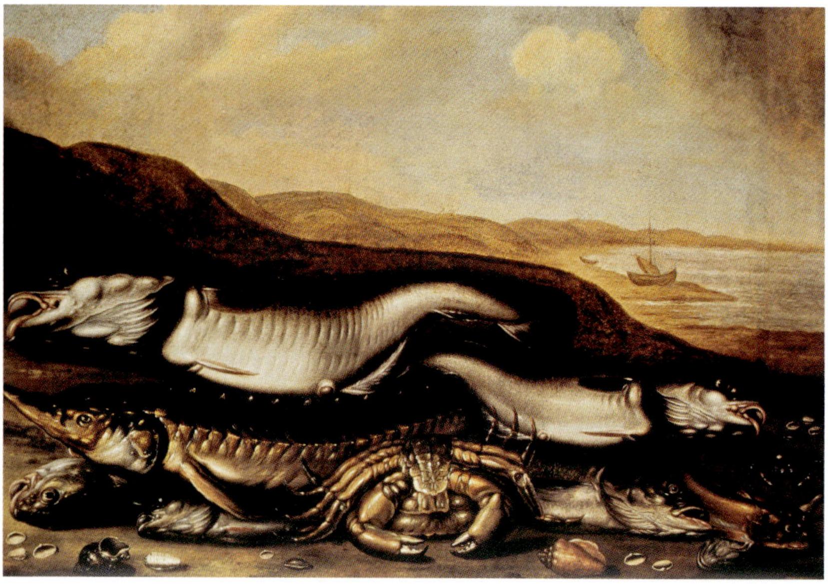

39 Willem Ormea, *Fish on a Dune*, *c.* 1660, oil on canvas.

40 *Fish on a Beach, with the Miraculous Draught of Fishes*, *c.* 1625, oil on canvas, artist unknown.

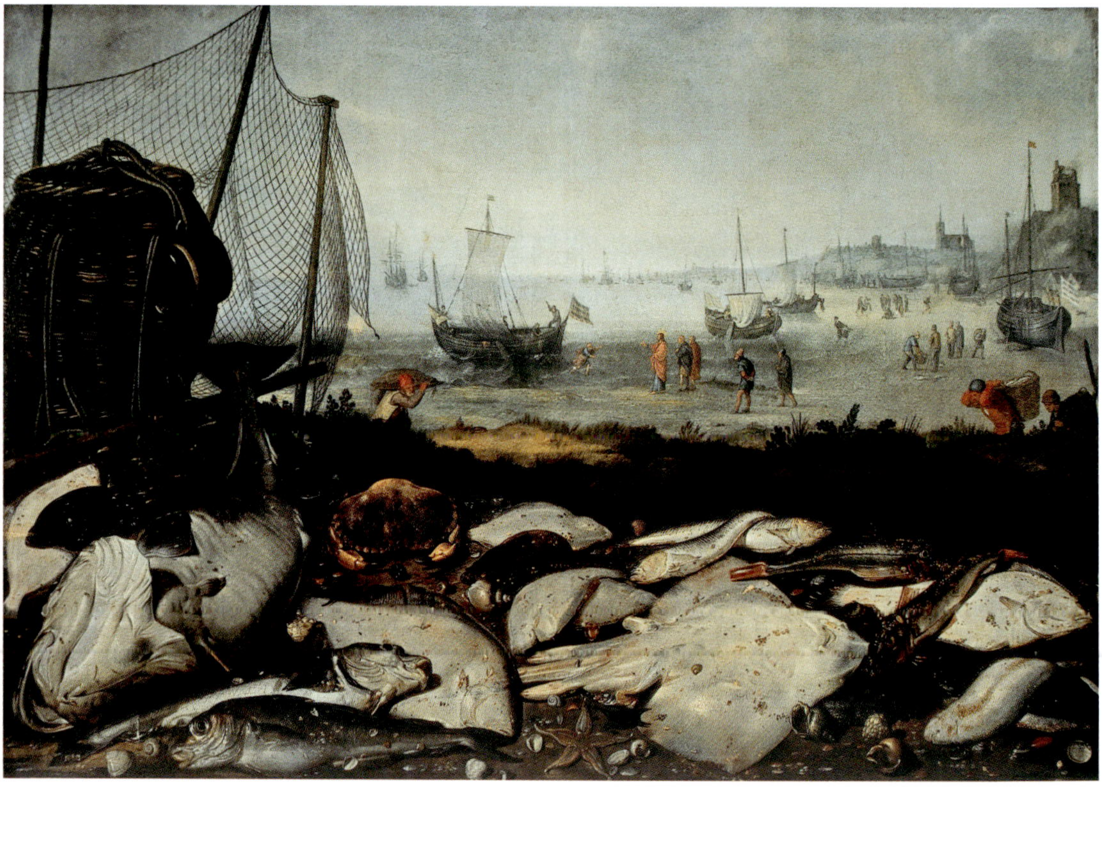

41 Jan van Kessel, *Fishes on the Seashore,* 1661, oil on copper.

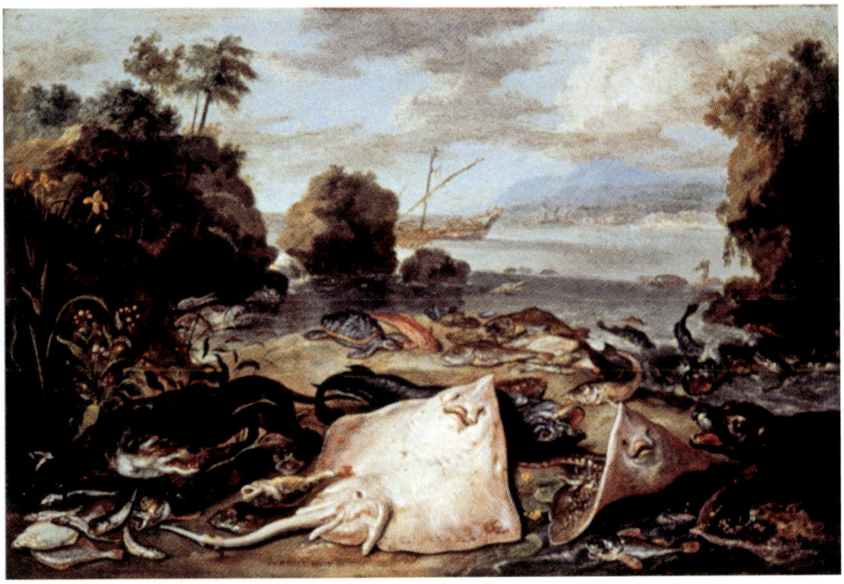

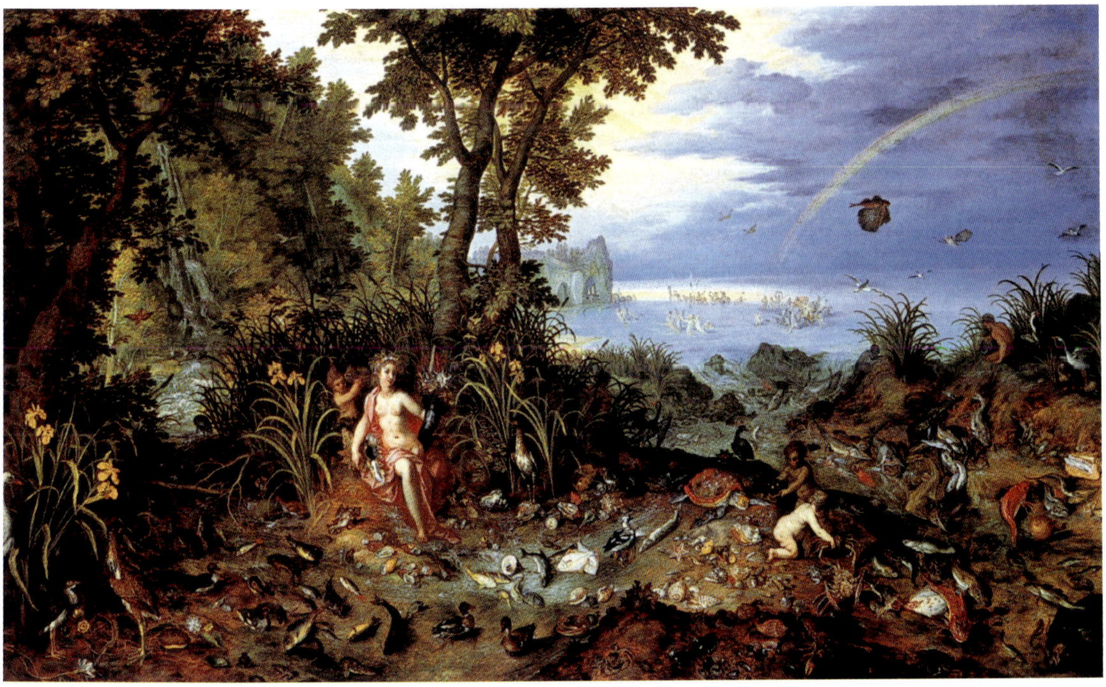

42 Jan Brueghel the Elder, *The Element of Water*, 1611, oil on copper.

The fashion for painting a series of pictures representing the seasons, five senses, twelve months or four elements was popular in the Netherlands throughout the seventeenth century. Jan Brueghel the Elder (1568–1625) painted a series based on the four elements, earth, fire, air and water, of which two, in oil on copper, *The Element of Air* and *The Element of Water*, signed and dated BRVEGHEL 1611, were sold at Sotheby's in 1993. His son, Jan Brueghel the Younger (1601–1678), also painted the four elements, again in oil on copper, 47.7 × 77.5 cm, all four of which are now at Kingston Lacy, Wimborne Minster. The younger Brueghel's picture of the element of water does not show the sea creatures in water, as one would expect, but laid out on the beach for inspection by a sea-nymph (or is it Venus herself with her cupids?). All kinds of fishes, shells, crustaceans and a turtle demonstrate what riches the element water (in this case seawater) supports.

The Greek philosopher Empedocles (fifth century BC) was interested in biology, medicine and physics. He discovered that air is a substance, distinct from empty space. He went further, and proposed the theory that air, with fire, water and earth, were the four elements from which all substances were composed. Today we still speak of fish being in their natural element when swimming in water and even refer, as an analogy, to someone feeling awkward when out of his usual environment or occupation as being 'like a fish out of water'.

In Italy in the seventeenth century several artists painted fishes, especially members of the Recco family. There are numerous paintings by the father, Giuseppe, whose very large seascapes and shore pictures with seafood were appreciated by royalty (he was knighted by Charles II of Spain) and the nobility. He joined the painters' guild in 1665 and signed some of his paintings between 1666 and 1691. Recco had a daughter, Elena, who excelled at fish painting and went to Spain to paint at court. Another Recco, Nicola Maria, may have been one of Giuseppe's twelve children but her work is inferior. Working on the grand scale, an oil on canvas measuring 2.3 × 2.9 m, Giuseppe Recco

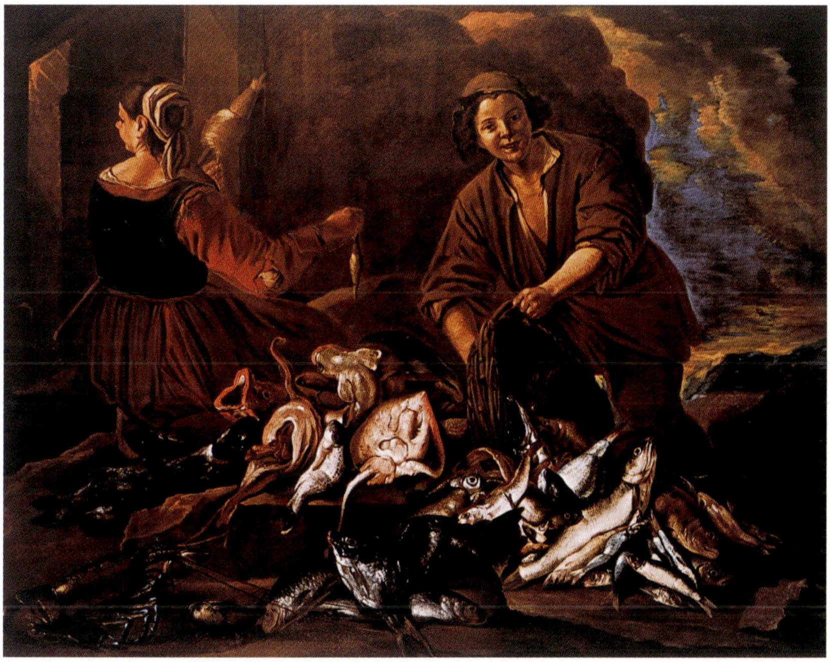

43 Giacomo Francesco Cipper 'Il Todeschini' (1664–1736), *Fish against a Country Background with Girl Spinning and a Young Fish Vendor*, oil on canvas.

included seagods in his *Marine Life with Neptune and Two Nereids*, painted about 1680 with the help of Luca Giordano for the figures (illus. 38). A swordfish and crustaceans are predominant in this composition. His work is similar to that of a contemporary Italian artist, Giovan Battista Ruoppolo.

Gaetano and Gerolamo Cusati also worked on a large scale, filling the foreground with fishes just caught and thrown out of a boat pulled up on shore in their *Fishes*. Sorrento Angelo Maria Crivelli (known as Crivellone) worked for the court in Parma and filled a circular canvas (now in a private collection) with large and small fishes, *Still-life of Fish*, which he signed.

Giacomo Francesco Cipper, better known as Il Todeschini, painted during the first half of the eighteenth century in the Bergamo region. He portrayed poor Italian peasants in realistic situations, like the two in *Fish against a Country Background with Girl Spinning and a Young Fish Vendor*, one spinning while the other tips out a basket of fishes on the beach, hoping to sell them before nightfall. She will sort them and display them for local villagers. They were probably fish caught surplus to requirements

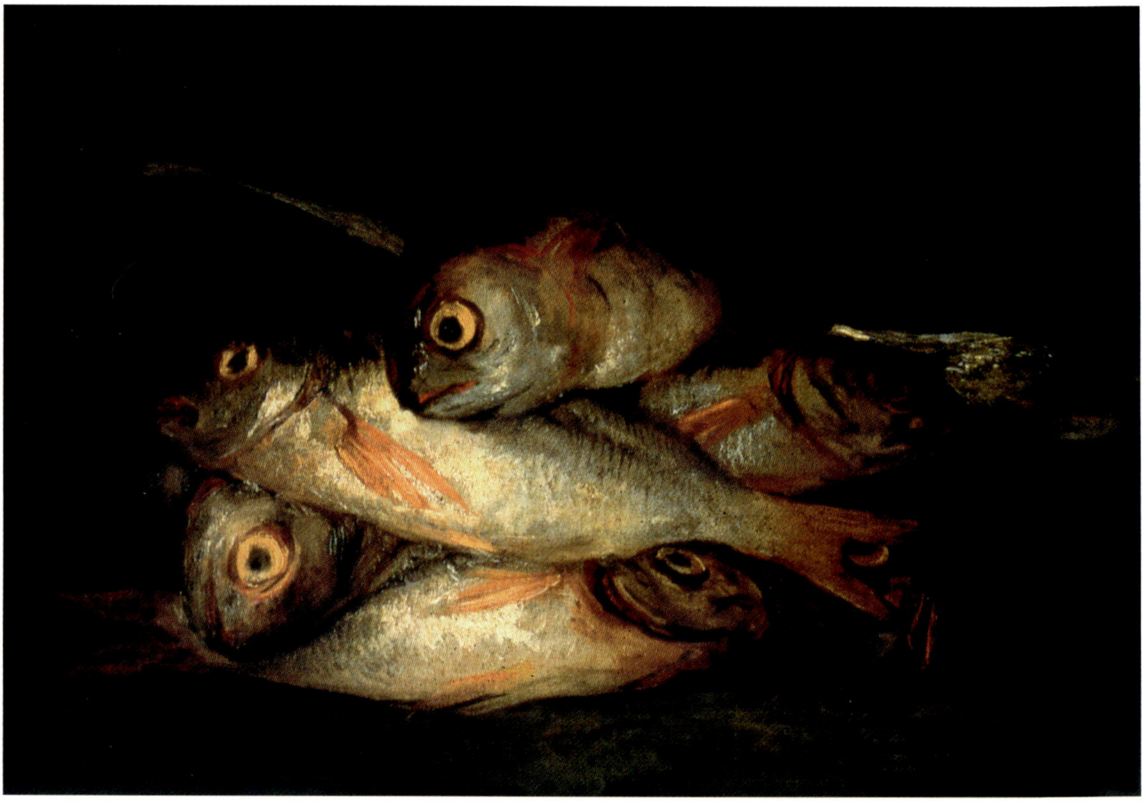

44 Francisco Goya, *Still-life with Golden Bream*, *c.* 1808–12, oil on canvas.

by some fisherman who has gone off to market his choicest fishes elsewhere. She has a motley collection of octopus, lobster, skate and half a dozen small fishes.

Two Spanish paintings of fishes on the beach were executed at a much later date. *Still-life with Golden Bream* by Francisco José y Lucientes Goya (1746–1828) is masterly in its composition, painted with the usual Spanish neatness and economy of their typical *bodegóns*. (The Spanish word *bodegón* was originally applied to the Spanish still life genre pictures of figures and foodstuffs by Velázquez (illus. 90), adapting the word *bodega*, a humble public eating place.) This has the added interest of being a night scene on a beach where moonlight glints across the five wet scaly bodies

BREAM inhabit rivers, lakes and brackish seawater. Golden sea bream (*Pagrus aurata*) are beautiful to look at and to eat, the finest of all the sea breams. They have a gold spot on each cheek and a golden crescent in the middle of the head. The ancient Greeks and Romans considered it a fish for feasts and it was sacred to Aphrodite, goddess of love. Black sea bream (*Spondyliosoma cantharus*) spawns along the Sussex coast in May.

compactly arranged and is reflected in their large eyes. This bream, *Pagrus/Sparus aurata*, is called 'golden' from the gold spot above and in front of the eye, and a golden crescent in the centre of the head. It lives in the Atlantic Ocean along the coasts of Europe and Africa, but is mostly found in the western Mediterranean.

Still-life with Shipwreck, by José Gutiérrez Solana (1886–1945), is an unusual subject painted at a later date. A Spaniard is sorting fishes on a beach with a fishing boat in the background. Some favourite fishes, red mullet and sea bream or bass, are in the foreground and will be sold for good prices. This apparently calm scene with a man at work is belied by the title of this painting. Is he retrieving a lost catch?

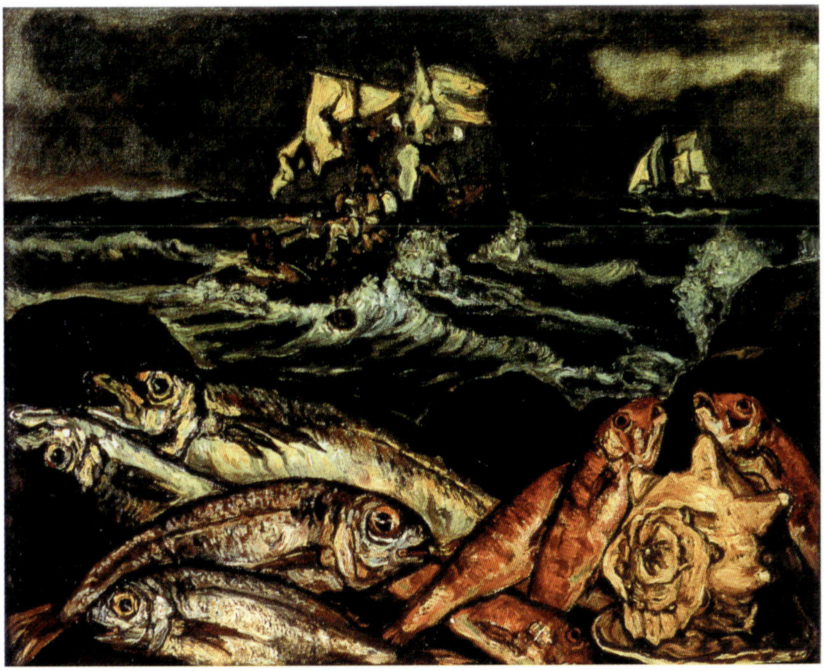

45 José Gutiérrez Solana, *Still-life with Shipwreck*, detail, *c.* 1917–20, oil on canvas.

French fish paintings (other than studies of separate species) are scarce, but there is a magnificent canvas by a relatively unknown French artist, painted in the nineteenth century. Francois Germain Léopold Tabar (1818–1869) was primarily a painter of wide canvases depicting historical battle scenes and landscapes. His painting of fishes on a beach with a village behind and a seascape to the left shows his mastery of a large open vista. In addition to the skate, mullet, bream and crayfish, a basket of mussels is featured.

In Britain a group of Victorian artists was attracted to the special light, beautiful scenery and atmosphere of Cornwall, and in the 1880s began to paint direct from nature out of doors – then a novel idea – around St Ives and Newlyn. Stanhope Alexander Forbes (1857–1947) was one of the most talented of the Newlyn painters. *A Fish Sale on a Cornish Beach*, now in the City Museum and Art Gallery, Plymouth, is one of a series of paintings depicting the life of fishermen of this region. He painted out of doors, attracted by the wet sand and the groups of figures reflected

46 François Germain Léopold Tabar, *Fish on a Beach with Fishing Village and Boats*, *c.* 1850, oil on canvas.

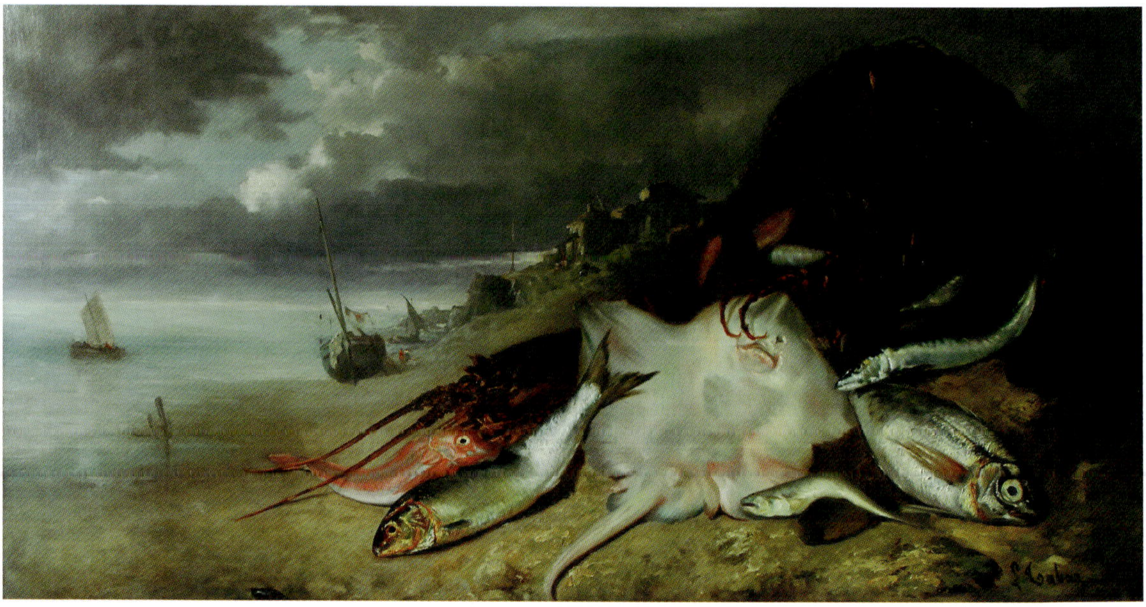

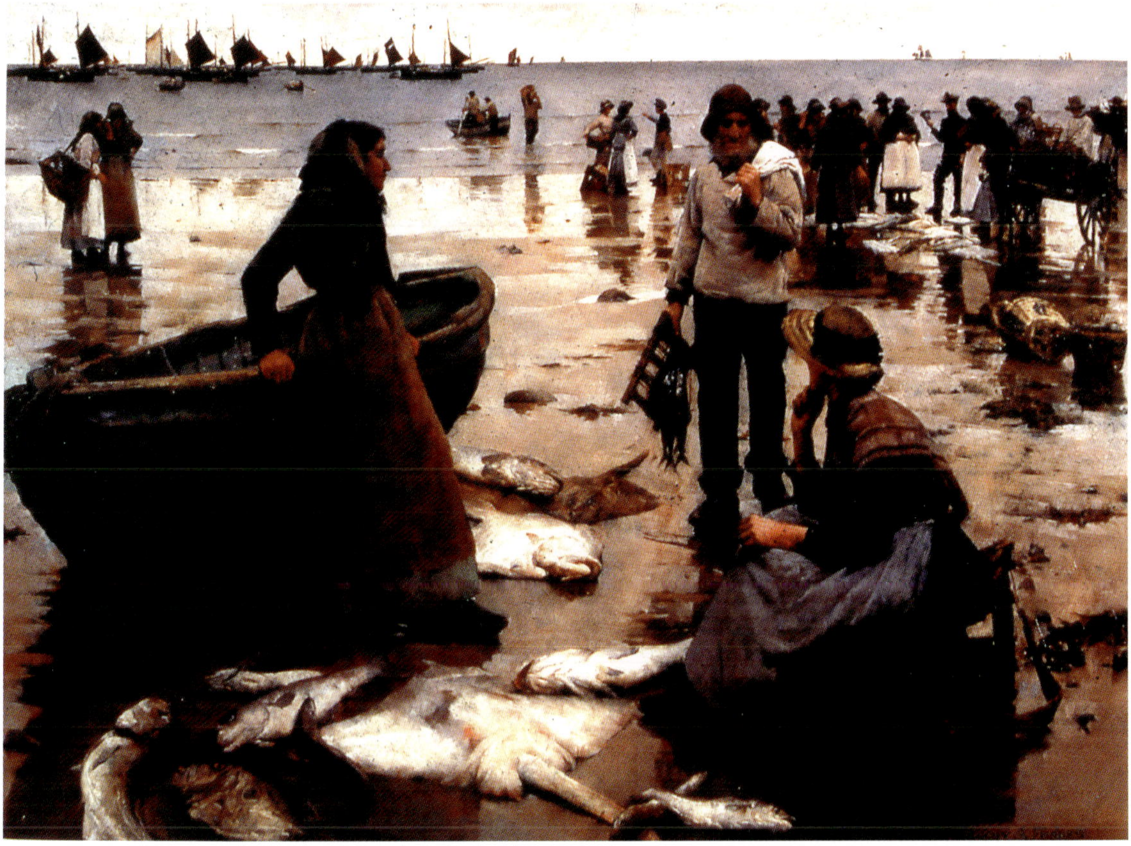

47 Stanhope Alexander Forbes, *A Fish Sale on a Cornish Beach*, c. 1884, oil on canvas.

on its shiny surface. It is a calm morning following a successful night at sea and shows the various activities after small fishing boats are beached or the fishes have been brought in by rowing boats from larger vessels, called drivers, standing offshore. The fish was ferried to shore by boys aged ten to fourteen years old, in small rowing boats. A bell was rung for the barter of the fish to begin. Forbes showed some fish being sold and others being put into a waiting cart to move the fish to market, or being packed into barrels and baskets. The fish may be mackerel, which is fished all round the coast of Cornwall, centred on Newlyn. The mackerel taken in the autumn were salted in great numbers. First

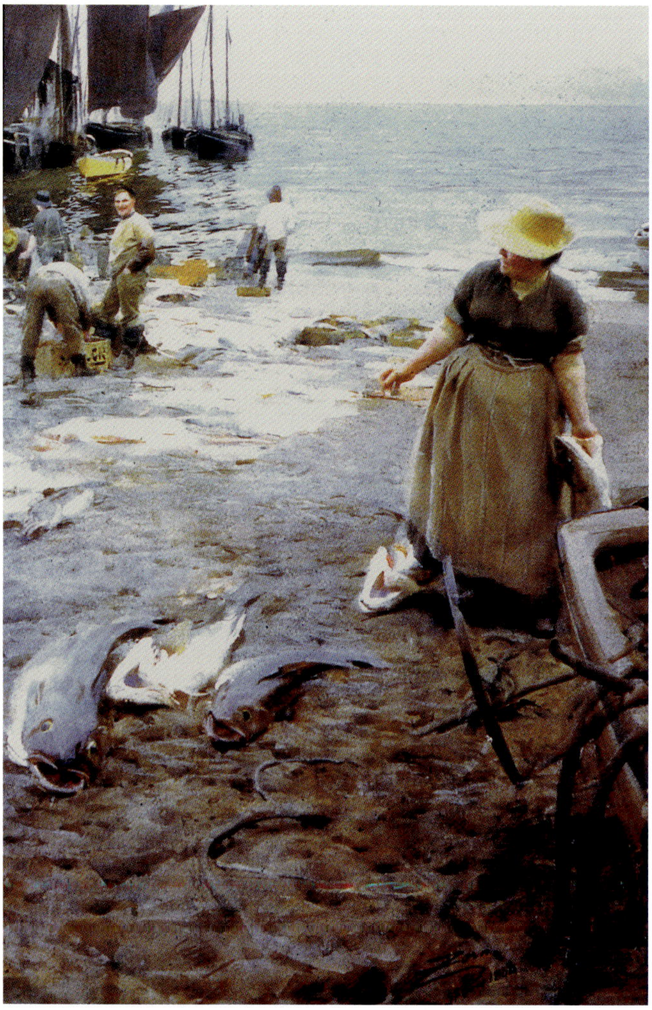

48 Anders Zorn, *Fish Market in St Ives*, 1888, watercolour on paper.

trawlers, then steam drifters, replaced the fleets of sailing drivers, but their increased efficiency has seriously depleted the stocks of mackerel. A study for this painting, signed and dated 1884, was sold in 1993 at Sotheby's.

British artists at St Ives were joined by foreign painters, the most famous being the Swede Anders Zorn (1860–1920). He visited the art colony there in 1887 and painted St Ives harbour in twilight, as well as the fish market. In *Fish Market in St Ives* he included a fishwife on the shore presiding over the haul of giant cod, probably deposited by the boats in the background. He brought cool, fresh Nordic colours into the Cornish light, producing a unique view of fish being landed and sold on the beach. This was one of his first oil paintings and won him a medal when exhibited before being purchased by the French Government; it now hangs in the Louvre.

Charles Napier Hemy (1841–1917) painted a scene of men handling a haul of pilchards from a bulging net. The scene is probably Falmouth, where Hemy lived from 1883 and had a yacht. He was one of the outstanding marine painters of the second half of the nineteenth century. In Cornwall's maritime history the pilchard (a mature sardine), though a small fish, figures largely. Until the early twentieth century, vast shoals appeared in mid-July starting southwest of Land's End. An oily fish, it does not transport easily, so was smoked or salted down. Women

49 Charles Napier Hemy, *Pilchards*, 1897, oil on canvas.

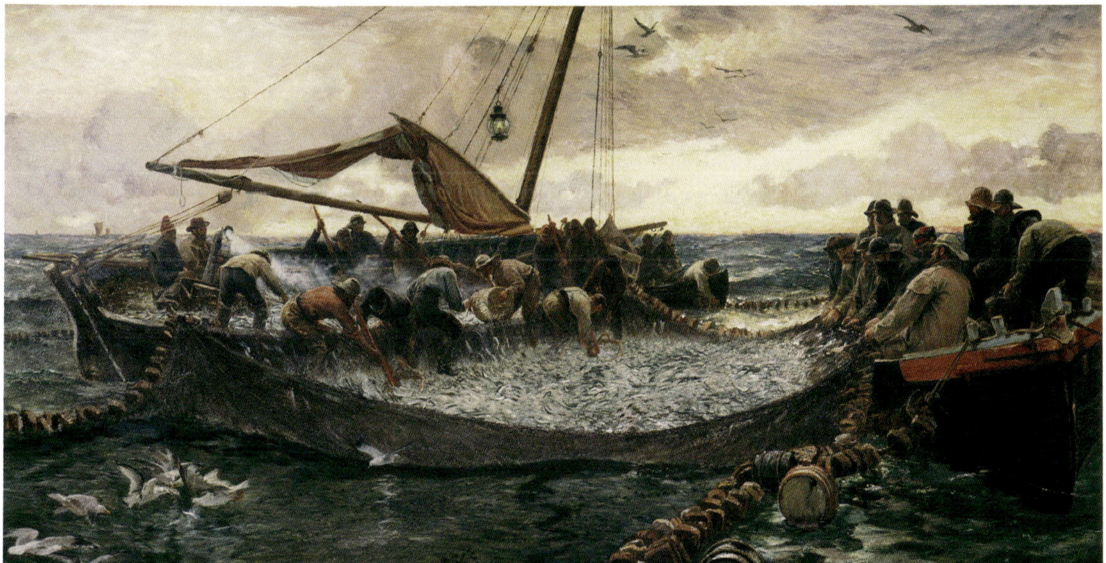

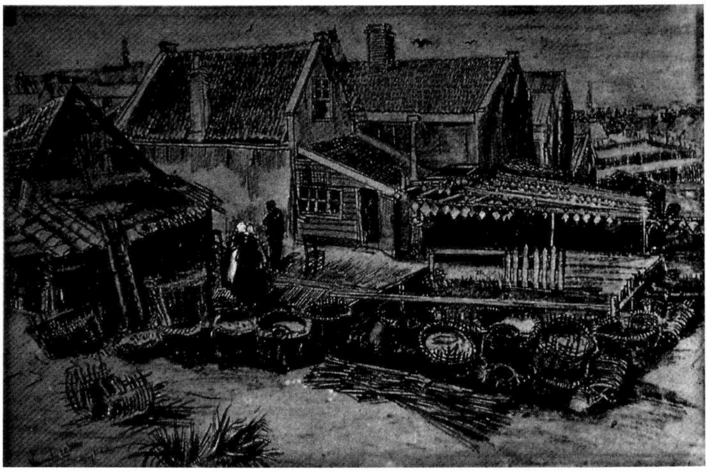

50 Vincent Van Gogh, *Fish-drying Barn at Scheveningen*, 1882, pencil, pen and brush.

PILCHARD (*Sardina pilchardus*) is an oily European sea fish like the herring, but smaller, thicker and rounder, only common off Cornwall at its northern limits, where it may be numerous in warm seasons. Its maximum length is 25 cm (10 inches).

A sardine is a young pilchard, commonly tinned in oil head to tail, giving rise to the saying 'packed like sardines in a tin', i.e. crowded closely together. Sardines were the first food to be canned when a canning factory opened in Brittany in 1834, processing the sardines that abounded on the Breton coast. For years these were the best sardines, but they have almost disappeared. The young are now fished off Portugal and canned as sardines.

and children gutted, smoked and then packed the pilchards into barrels before they were exported to France, Spain and Italy. Nearly every port along the Cornish coast once had a salting cellar; the only remaining one, in Newlyn, closed in 2005. Hemy showed the pilchards being fished from boats gathered round a seine net paid out round a shoal before tying the ends so that they could not escape. A smaller net had been dropped into the shoal and the fish scooped up in baskets to transfer into the boats. Hemy watched the fishermen at work off the Cornish coast for many years.

Van Gogh drew a detailed pen, pencil and brush study of a *Fish-drying Barn at Scheveningen*, a seaside resort near The Hague, in May 1882. Only 28 × 44 cm, it is now conserved at Otterlo in Holland. Van Gogh made a series of drawings and watercolours of views from his window and during his walks while staying at the resort in 1882. The perspective in this drawing is complicated and the artist used a rectangular wood and iron frame constructed with wires drawn from the corners to help him capture the perspective lines of the landscape. Here herring have been gutted and hung to dry from the eaves of the barn. The barn was open, allowing cold, breezy air to dry the fish. The end result would not be very palatable, needing plenty of hot butter and mustard to make it more tasty.

Smokehouses were a common sight on many quays in the past. Originally, any surplus fishes were smoked, but some species were more popular than others, particularly haddock, herring and salmon. The Porthleven drifter fleet was among the major three fleets (along with Newlyn and St Ives) part of whose catches was smoked. The smokehouse at Porthleven is still active, smoking salt-cured mackerel. The finest smoked haddock is finnan haddock, dried on the seashore and smoked over fires of seaweed, green wood, turf and peat, named after a Scottish village, Findon, where the special smoking process originated. Arbroath smokies, haddock, are still smoked in backyards of the village houses. Salmon and trout are also smoked. Herrings, split and gutted but with the head and tail left on, were smoked and became known as kippers. Seahouses in Northumberland is reputedly the first place where herrings were smoked (by John Woodger in 1843) for kippers, although other towns will disagree with this. Once a means of preserving fishes, it is now an alternative for even tastier forms of some species.

In a strange reversal of roles, instead of a man taking fishes out of the water and placing them on the beach, there once was a great fish that spewed a naked, indigestible man out onto the beach. The story of Jonah is told in the first two chapters of the book of Jonah in the Old Testament. A prophet, he was sent by God to the sinful city of Nineveh to announce its destruction. Jonah did not want to go and tried to escape on a ship, but God sent a storm and Jonah had to admit to the sailors that it was his fault the storm was endangering their lives, and asked to be thrown overboard. He was swallowed by a great fish, prayed for deliverance, and after three days and three nights (foretelling the period Jesus would remain in the grave) he was spat out on dry land. When

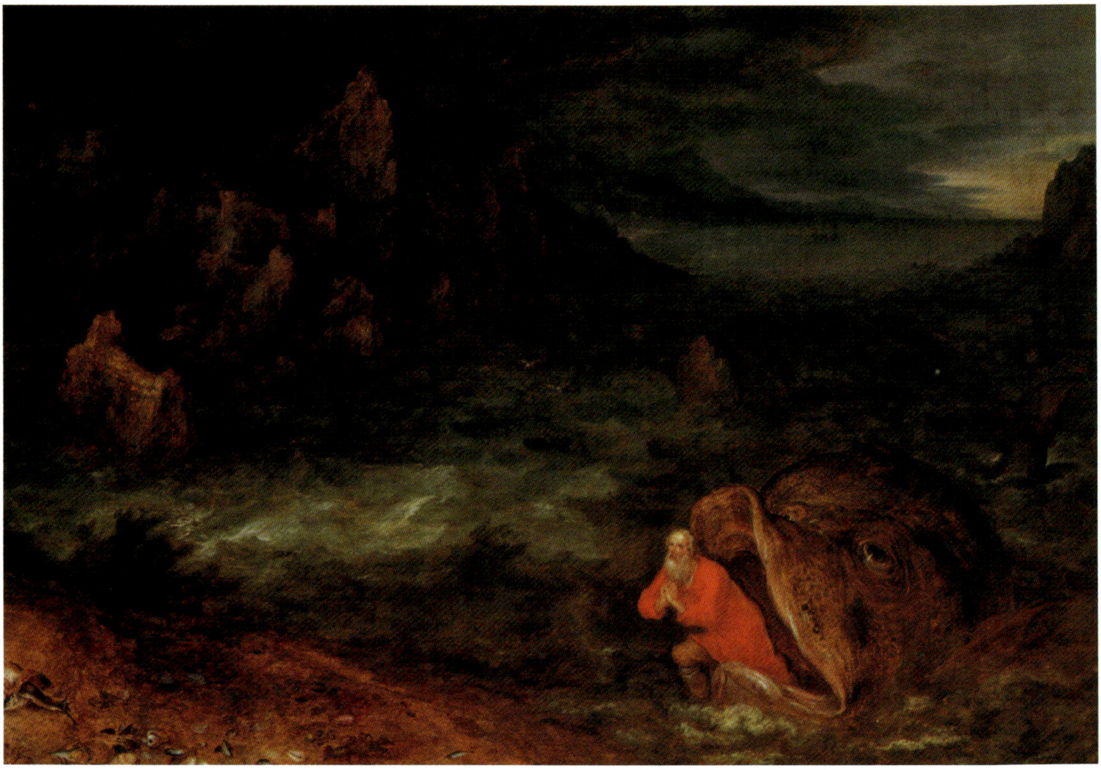

51 Jan Brueghel the Elder, *Jonah Leaving the Whale*, c. 1600, oil on panel.

Jonah obeyed and took the message to the people of Nineveh, they repented. Consequently, God did not destroy the city, demonstrating that He cares for all people, including non-Israelites.

Whether Jonah was swallowed by a great fish or by a whale has long been debated by zoologists. This was of no concern to the early artists who illustrated the story. Jan Brueghel the Elder painted an imaginative gigantic fish of sufficient size to swallow a man.

three
Fish in the Market

For hundreds of years, the manner of selling fish was simple. Without the benefit of refrigeration or any speedy means of transporting fish inland, the day's catch was sold on quaysides or on the beach by individual trawlermen, fishermen just returned from a day's fishing, or their wives. Small fish markets were found only in coastal towns at the docks because moving fish inland, other than salted or dried, was impractical except in the coldest weather. While one of the most nutritious and easily cooked foods, fish is also one of the most perishable and difficult to keep in a fresh condition.

The fish market stall attracted local artists to paint the bustling, colourful scenes there. Some artists concentrated on the general market scene, others on the vendors and purchasers, while many found the enormously attractive and colourful fishes offered for sale an irresistible challenge. Capturing the different colours, shapes and above all the gleaming wetness and shine on the fish gave life and eye-catching appeal to the picture. Before the days of photography, replicating the brilliant hues of a fish with paint was the only way to preserve them, given that colour in fish is very fugitive, vanishing with great rapidity after death.

Painters quickly realized the opportunity for a kaleidoscope of colours that fishes afforded. Even the smallest touches of red gave dramatic accents to a composition that immediately caught the eye. Lobsters, salmon cuts, red fins and the occasional completely red fish (such as the red snapper, red mullet, the ocean perch, also called a redfish, and pink shrimps) provided plenty of excuse to indulge in the spectacular. Other colours, blues, greens and silvers, provided similar potential effects and could be arranged on the canvas accordingly.

Fishmongers often formed associations or guilds. In London by the middle of the twelfth century there were two: the stock fishmongers who dealt mostly in dried fish and the salt fishmongers who handled imported salted and pickled fish, including herrings, cod, eels, whiting and mackerel from the Low Countries and the Baltic. Selling fresh fish caught off the Kent and Essex coasts was but a small part of the trade. In 1536 the two guilds joined to form the Worshipful Company of Fishmongers, and one of the most important duties of the company officials was to ensure that only fresh and unadulterated fishes were sold. Based in Fishmongers' Hall in the City of London it is one of the few remaining guild companies that still performs its original function.

In London fishes were sold at fishmongers' stalls in open markets. Billingsgate Market, famous both for its fishes and bad language, has been in operation for many centuries, although it has now moved from its original location. Billingsgate and Queenhithe were the two main wharves where fishing vessels moored to land their catch. The first recorded toll regulations for the market date from 1016. A drawing of the market made more than five centuries later in the reign of Elizabeth I shows sheds, with ships moored, traders carrying fish and a fishwife offering fish for sale. To this Elizabethan Billingsgate was brought cod from Newfoundland for

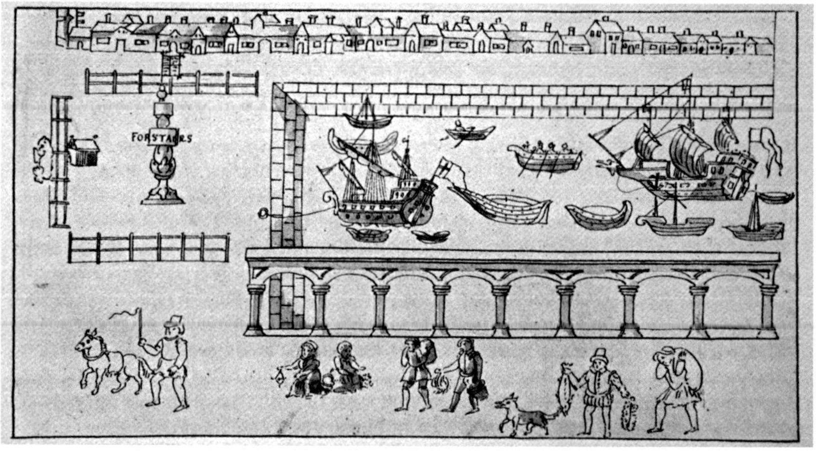

52 Detail from a drawing of London made in 1598, showing the fish market at Billingsgate.

the first time by West Country fishermen who salted them at sea. Pickling in brine was another method of preserving the fish, including anchovies brought from the Mediterranean, salted mullet, herrings and whitefish.

Despite the wonderful opportunities for British painters to see all kinds of fishes and colourful market characters, none appears to have painted the familiar but perhaps too lowly scenes. On the Continent it was very different. During the sixteenth century many of the European port cities rose to a prominence they had not previously enjoyed. Antwerp increased in importance in the fifteenth century when its harbour was expanded to take 2,000 vessels at anchor, which made it the largest port in Europe. Also the most important banking centre, the wealth in trade made the town very prosperous. The rise of a rich merchant class brought about many changes, not least in the type of paintings that were wanted. Paintings were needed to decorate the many ostentatious houses that were being built and these quickly became physical demonstrations of the wealth and success of their owners, who developed a taste for records of the everyday things around them. Interior and domestic scenes, views of markets, taverns, people working or playing music, became favourite subjects, attracting artists to Antwerp to supply this need. These paintings were a celebration of the wealth and prosperity that Antwerp was enjoying, while representing a significant departure from the portraits and religious images that had previously dominated art.

Artists were dependent on patrons and painted what the customer required. Among the growing community of successful artists there were painters of fishes, of fruit and vegetables and of flowers, besides scenes involving the sellers and buyers. Seeking a niche for himself, or trying to outdo a rival in order to attract a patron, was a strong motive, but it is obvious that many of the artists at work in the sixteenth and seventeenth centuries in the Low Countries delighted in the pictorial possibilities that such subjects offered them.

Artists would have sketched the fishes and then assembled an array of different species, a mixture of both saltwater and freshwater, in their paintings. Since the colour of fish fades rapidly and the freshness disappears at an alarming rate, this was the only way a fish still-life with many species could be assembled. It was akin to flower painters making detailed studies of the different flowers in their seasons and later assembling a completely artificial bouquet in their picture.

Some fish paintings reflected the vogue for a series or group of pictures, like the four paintings by Brueghel the Elder of the fish market, the fruit and vegetable market, the meat market and poultry market now in the National Gallery, London. Another set represented the four elements, fire, earth, air and water. Such matching series of pictures were very popular during the seventeenth century with patrons. Pieter Boel (1622–1674) found the subject 'water' the ideal excuse to paint fishes. His picture, *Still-life of Fish on a Quay*, is not a typical fisherman's catch, rather a collection of fishes chosen for the subject 'water'. He painted a mixture of freshwater and marine fishes: trout, gurnard, carp, burbot, ray, lumpsucker and whiting.

In Dutch and Flemish market scenes of the period, men are always in charge of butcher's stalls, but women frequently preside over fruit and vegetable stalls and are invariably present on fish stalls, sometimes alone. Women in Scandinavia were employed in the unpleasant job of gutting fish, and statues of fishwives have been put up in their memory on the quays in a number of Scandinavian cities. In the Netherlands also there are statues of fishwives, for instance in Utrecht. The fishwives were regarded as lowly workers and their ability to hold their own in arguments by using invective was notorious. This reputation is commemorated in the English language down to the present time when 'speaking like a fishwife' is regarded as a term of disapproval. In the Netherlands and other parts of Europe the voice of a fishwife is similarly regarded. If, in order to make a profit, they had to negotiate with the fishermen on prices for the catch, their sharpened wits and equally sharp tongues are understandable. Nevetheless, their prominence in the business of fishmongering is a curious feature of a period when one could take for granted male domination in

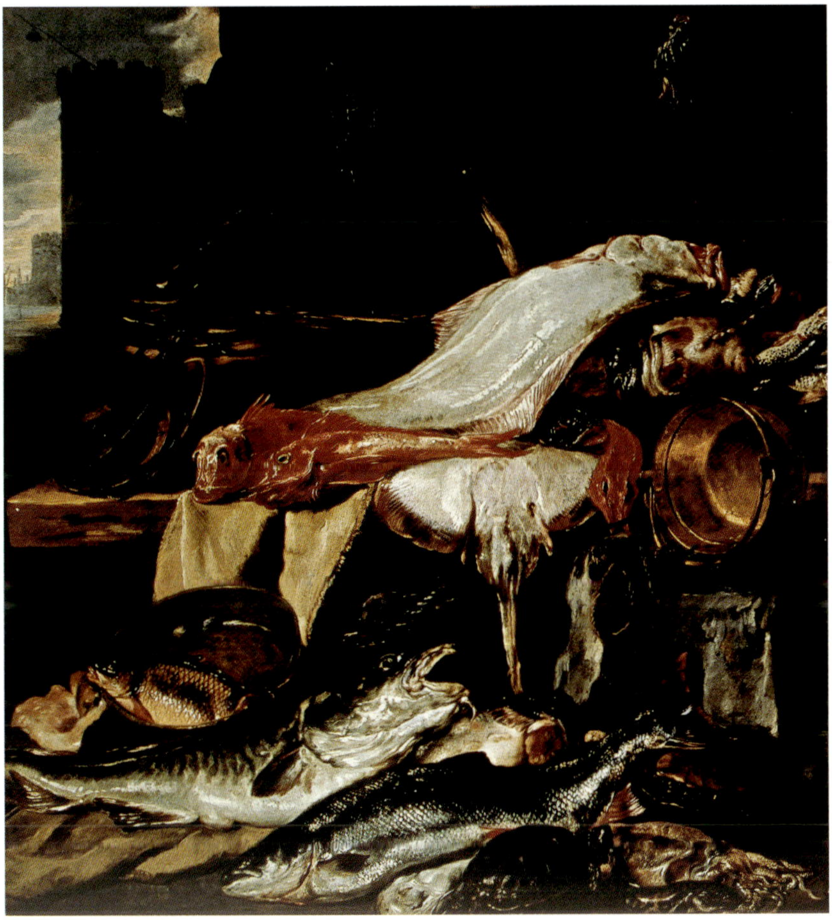

53 Pieter Boel, *Still-life of Fish on a Quay*, c. 1660–65, oil on canvas.

other trades and any workplace. Perhaps the fishwife was a consequence of dividing the labour in a trade where speed of sale was essential. The men were responsible for catching the fish, their wives for selling it before it went bad.

In fish paintings the amount of fish shown as being sold varied considerably. The early Flemish and Dutch fish-stall painters, Aertsen, Beuckelaer, Jordaens and Snyders, also Adriaen van Utrecht, painted an abundance of both fishes and varieties. Later artists, Cuyp for example, were more interested in the people involved in the fish-buying transactions. The Italians Passarotti and Ceruti were as concerned with the fish sellers and buyers as with the fishes; consequently there are fewer species shown in their work. When the British began to paint markets in the nineteenth century they were almost wholly concerned with the architecture; the people and the fishes served merely as devices to enliven the large buildings. Anyone wanting to know what fish were eaten will find more guidance in the early Dutch and Flemish pictures of market stalls (and scenes on the beach) than anywhere else in fish art.

Amsterdam-born Pieter Aertsen (1508–1575) gravitated to the prosperous city of Antwerp where he painted numerous market scenes, including a fish market. He was probably the first still-life painter to paint fishes as a subject. Although the exact date of his *Market Scene* is uncertain, it is thought that most likely it dates before he left Antwerp to return to Amsterdam in 1556. This is the only known fish painting by Aertsen. He included skates/rays, gurnard, cod and other smaller fishes.

Aertsen taught his nephew Joachim Beuckelaer (active 1560–74) to paint while they worked together in his studio, and Beuckelaer successfully produced similar market scenes in Antwerp. His several market stalls with fish, birds and vegetables were presided over by buxom wives and male traders. One, of a fish market, was from a *Four Elements* series, representing water, and had a small illustration of the Miraculous Draught of Fishes in the background. Initially he adhered to the old tradition of painting biblical scenes, as dictated by the Catholic Church, but this was gradually ignored so that the biblical scene shrank to a small area at the rear of the picture, before disappearing altogether. Beuckelaer's *A Fish Market* of 1570 includes a large variety of fishes displayed in shallow cane baskets. A deeper tub may have held water to keep the fish fresh, or been a measure, like a bushel, for the traders. *A Fish Market* is now in the National Gallery, London, but similar paintings by Beuckelaer can be seen in Ghent, Antwerp, Hull, Dieppe and Naples. He was a very proficient painter and his pictures are sought after for their celebration of the rich variety

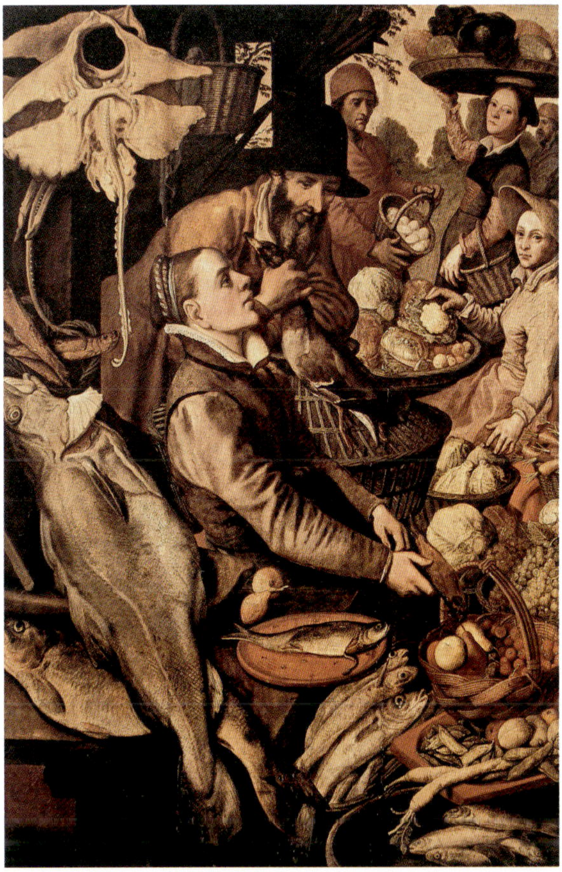

54 Pieter Aertsen, *Market Scene*, *c.* 1555, oil on panel.

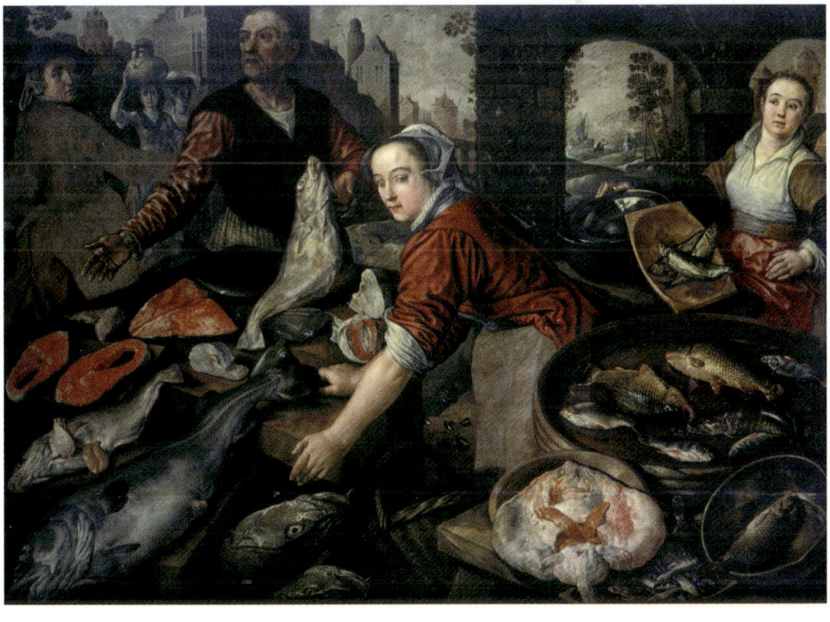

55 Joachim Beuckelaer, *A Fish Market,* 1570, oil on canvas.

of fishes coming into the port at Antwerp. This painting features a thorn-backed ray, sprats, cod, salmon, herring, carp and perch.

The work of Frans Snyders (1579–1657), also of Antwerp, is represented in many of the world's great galleries; he is perhaps most famous for his pictures of the hunt and its aftermath. Among his favourite subjects, however, was the fish market and he took this particular genre to a very high standard. His paintings were widely admired by his contemporaries, both artists and customers. When he was thirty he returned from a period

THORN-BACKED ray (*Raja clavata*) is found in cold and temperate waters, lurking on the bottom of the seabed waiting for prey to pass by. It lives along almost all the coasts of Europe and along the Atlantic coast of Africa. The thorns are small dermal spikes and larger spines on the back along the midline of the body and down the long tail. Of the many rays and skates, this is thought to have the best flavour.

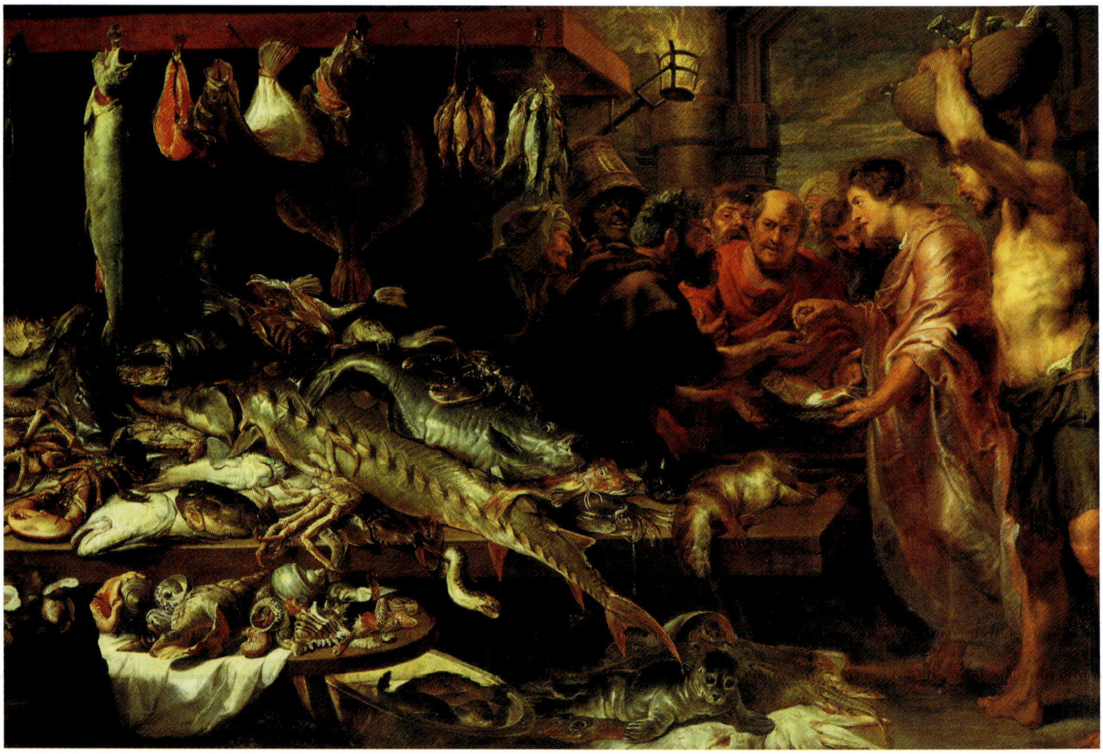

56 Frans Snyders, *The Fish Market,* in collaboration with Anthony van Dyck, who painted the figures, *c.* 1618–20, oil on canvas.

STURGEON (*Acipenser sturio*) appear in several Dutch paintings of the seventeenth century but are now extinct in Dutch waters. It was a royal fish, the property of the crown in medieval England, not allowed on any table other than that of the king. Always rare, it was occasionally caught in the Severn, Thames and Tyne. Pepys dined on sturgeon on 26 April 1662 with the mayor at Southampton; it had not been seen there for twenty years before that. Some live entirely in fresh water but most are anadromous, migrating to rivers to spawn.

Caviare is the roe from 25 species of sturgeon, three of which produce most of the world's caviare: beluga sturgeon produces beluga caviare, Russian sturgeon produces oscietra caviare and stellate sturgeon produces sevruga caviare. Born and growing up in freshwater estuaries before moving out to sea, the females take 20 years to reach maturity but are long-lived and may grow up to 6 metres (20 feet) long. They can lay 3,000–4,000 eggs.

in Italy just in time to take advantage of the 1609 armistice in the conflict that had raged between the Netherlands and Spain since 1579. The Antwerp fisheries were no longer held in check by Spanish dominance at sea, and the wide range of different species on display in some of Snyders's paintings is a reflection of this unrestricted access to the sea for the Antwerp fishermen. In *The Fish Market* a sturgeon lies at the centre as a focal point, surrounded by cod, wolf fish, lampreys and hanging up behind salmon and a turbot or brill.

The folding of large flatfish and holding the two ends together with twine for ease of carriage is a feature often seen in these paintings of fishes. Shoppers either placed the fish in flat woven baskets, in a fish bucket or carried these flat fishes home through the streets by the twine. Paper was not used to wrap up shopping for it was far too expensive. Less frequently seen on the stalls are the seals that appear here on the low table and on the floor. At this period seals, porpoises and whales were common elements in the diet in the Lowlands and also in England.

Snyders was only one of many Dutch and Flemish artists who went to Italy. Painting in Antwerp owes its progressive Baroque dimension to him and to fellow artists such as Adriaen van Utrecht (1599–1652) and Jan Fyt (1611–1661) who spent time studying in Italy. Adriaen van Utrecht settled in Antwerp after completing his work as a journeyman in 1625. He was a rival of Snyders and their work influenced each other. Van Utrecht was of particular importance when he introduced a variety of motifs into his still-life paintings that were essentially his own. His earliest dated pictures, from the years 1627 to 1630, show that he had

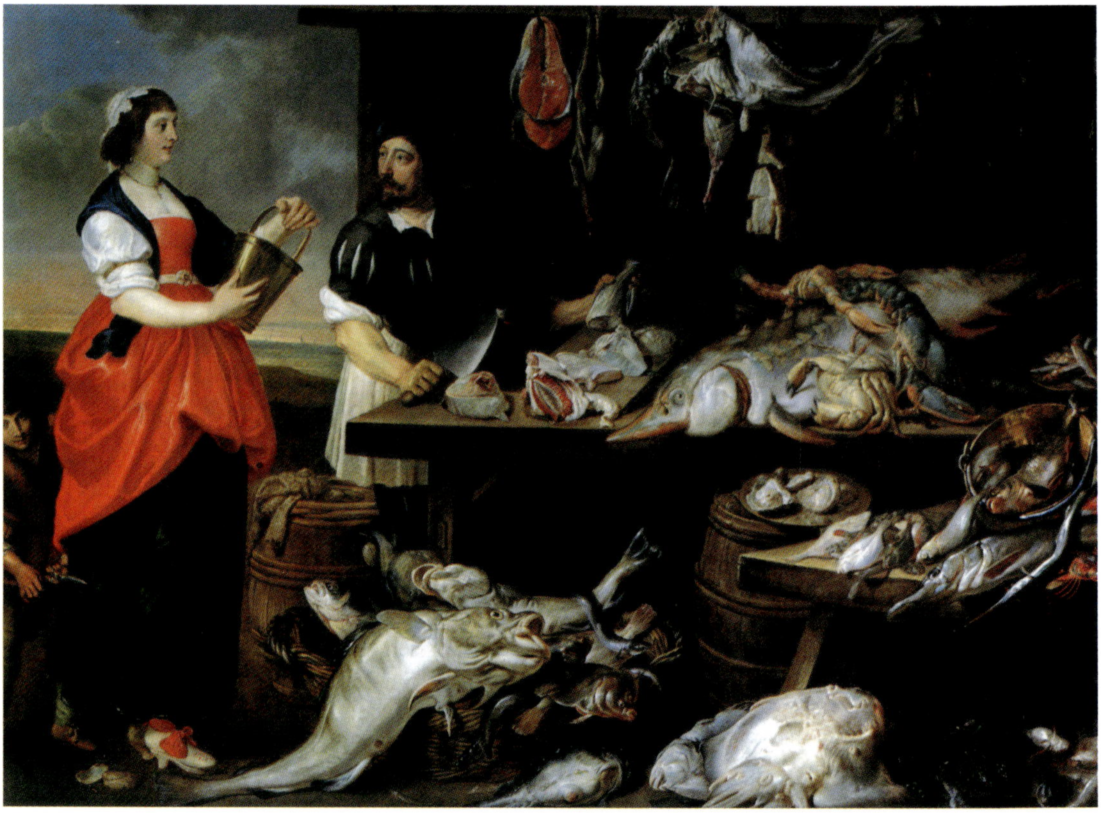

57 Adriaen van Utrecht, *A Fishmonger's Stall*, *c.* 1640, oil on canvas.

seen a more advanced stage of still-life painting in Italy. He took back with him from the south a preference for strong light falling from the side. In *A Fishmonger's Stall* of around 1640 the brightly dressed customer holds up her brass bucket to the fish seller who is chopping at cod, while a boy steals her purse. Among the wealth of species in this painting are sturgeon, roach, flounder, carp, herring, garfish, pike, gurnard, lamprey, lumpsucker and rays.

The Thirty Years War ended in 1648 with the signing of the Peace of Münster. One of its agreed terms was that the Scheldt would be closed and this meant the financial ruin of Antwerp. It was not until 1795 that the estuary was reopened and Antwerp regained some of its prosperity.

The Dutch benefited from the decline of Antwerp. Until the thirteenth century the site of Amsterdam was occupied by a small fishing community, but from the late fourteenth century it became increasingly prosperous in the Baltic trade. By the sixteenth century it was an important commodities market. From 1578 the inhabitants of the Netherlands sided with Calvinists against the Roman Catholics and their prosperity continued to increase until in the seventeenth and eighteenth centuries. Amsterdam was the banking capital of the world. Part of its wealth was derived from the trade of the Dutch East India Company, established in 1602. Another source of new wealth, after years of inadequate supplies of food, was the increase in food production from improved agricultural practices. The Protestant Dutch artists were also free of the Roman Catholic clerics who had been their patrons for so long. Artists now turned to painting what they saw around them, home interiors and natural objects like flowers, fruit, vegetables and fishes, which all proved immensely popular subjects with their secular patrons.

A good proportion of Dutch wealth depended on the herring fleet. Herring were not only the staple food but also the export of salted herring brought in substantial revenues. An earlier, fortuitous discovery or invention helped to make the northern provinces rich. In 1384 a Dutchman, Willem Beukels, chanced on the way to preserve herrings more efficiently. Previously, herrings had been packed whole in barrels of salt, and those in the centre frequently rotted. Beukels gutted them before salting, which increased the area exposed to the salt and thus their preservation period so that ships could stay at sea longer and travel further afield. It was about this time that, for some unexplained reason, the herring cooperated with the Dutch trawlermen by shifting their spawning ground from the Baltic to the North Sea.

The Treaty of Münster of 1648 recognized the sovereignty of the United Netherlands and this led to their Golden Age, politically and commercially, during the rest of the seventeenth century. Their artists flourished too, including fish painters, because so many newly rich citizens

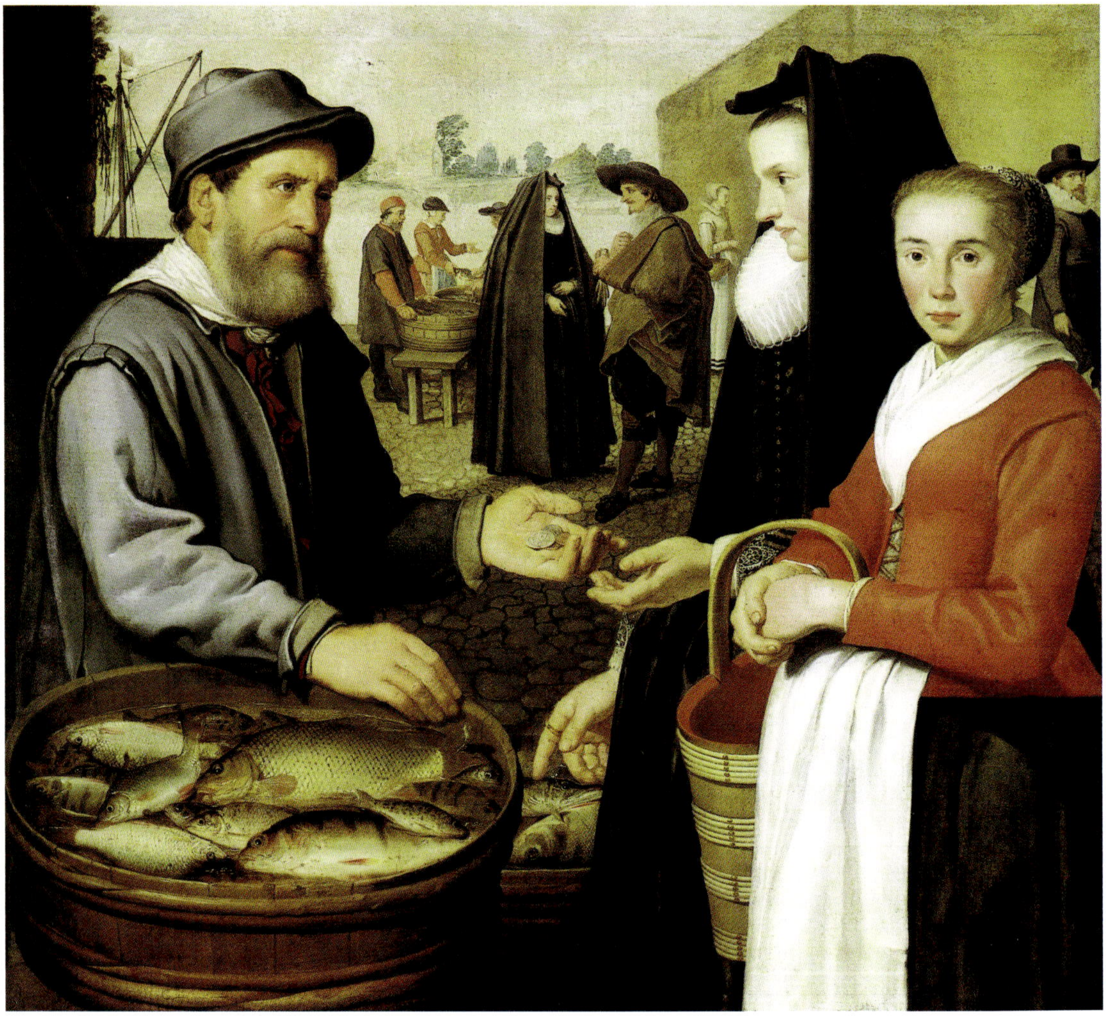

58 Jacob Gerritsz. Cuyp, *The Fish Market*, 1627, oil on canvas.

wished to own paintings celebrating their prosperity built on sea trade. The prosperity was not limited to the immediate vicinity of Amsterdam. Jacob Gerritsz. Cuyp (1594–1651/2), father of the more famous Aelbert Cuyp, lived in Dordrecht, which lies on the Oude Maas, one of the busiest waterway junctions in the Netherlands, linking Antwerp in Belgium with Rotterdam, and was carrying on a brisk trade, as paintings of the seventeenth century portray. Cuyp was a good figure painter and his sensitive portraits of the fishmonger and the woman buyer with her maid in his *Fish Market* focuses on them rather than the fishes in the basket under his arm. The maid stares uncomfortably out of the picture while the fishmonger pays more attention to her than to her mistress. It has been suggested that he may be a self-portrait. The artist has been more careful with his portrayal of this male figure than with the two women.

Most women in these paintings go to market with a woven shopping basket over their arm (an exception being the overdressed woman in the van Utrecht picture), like the Cuyp maidservant, but in Pieter de Hooch's painting of a scene in a wealthy household the maid holds a brass bucket of the correct size and dimensions for carrying fish. Having purchased the ingredients for dinner this Dutch maid took the fish home in the bucket. Here she presents it for her mistress to inspect the choice and quality of the fish she had purchased (illus. 59).

Hendrick Martensz. Sorgh (*c.* 1610–1670) of Rotterdam specialized in market scenes with a lively bustle around the stalls. One of his paintings shows a white stork; the inclusion of a bird of this species is significant, for white storks were encouraged to help clean up the market by eating the offal, discarded fish heads and other waste. White storks nested widely throughout the Netherlands, often encouraged by local people who provided poles surmounted by baskets or old cartwheels on top of which the storks could build their bulky nests. This friendly relationship with the Dutch still persists and, in addition to the poles, storks are also allowed to nest on top of chimneys.

The Haarlem painter Adriaen van Ostade (1610–1685) is chiefly celebrated for his images of peasant indoor life, but one of his best paintings is an outdoor scene, *The Fishwife,* painted in 1672. The viewer becomes the customer while the fishwife stares uncompromisingly out of the picture plane as she prepares to deal with the expected order. In her left hand she raises the head of one of her four haddocks, while the right grips a large knife in a very purposeful manner. The cutting capacity of the blade is fiercely emphasized by the sharply severed salmon lying at her left elbow. A small crab and a group of flounders or plaice are all she has left for sale as evening closes in.

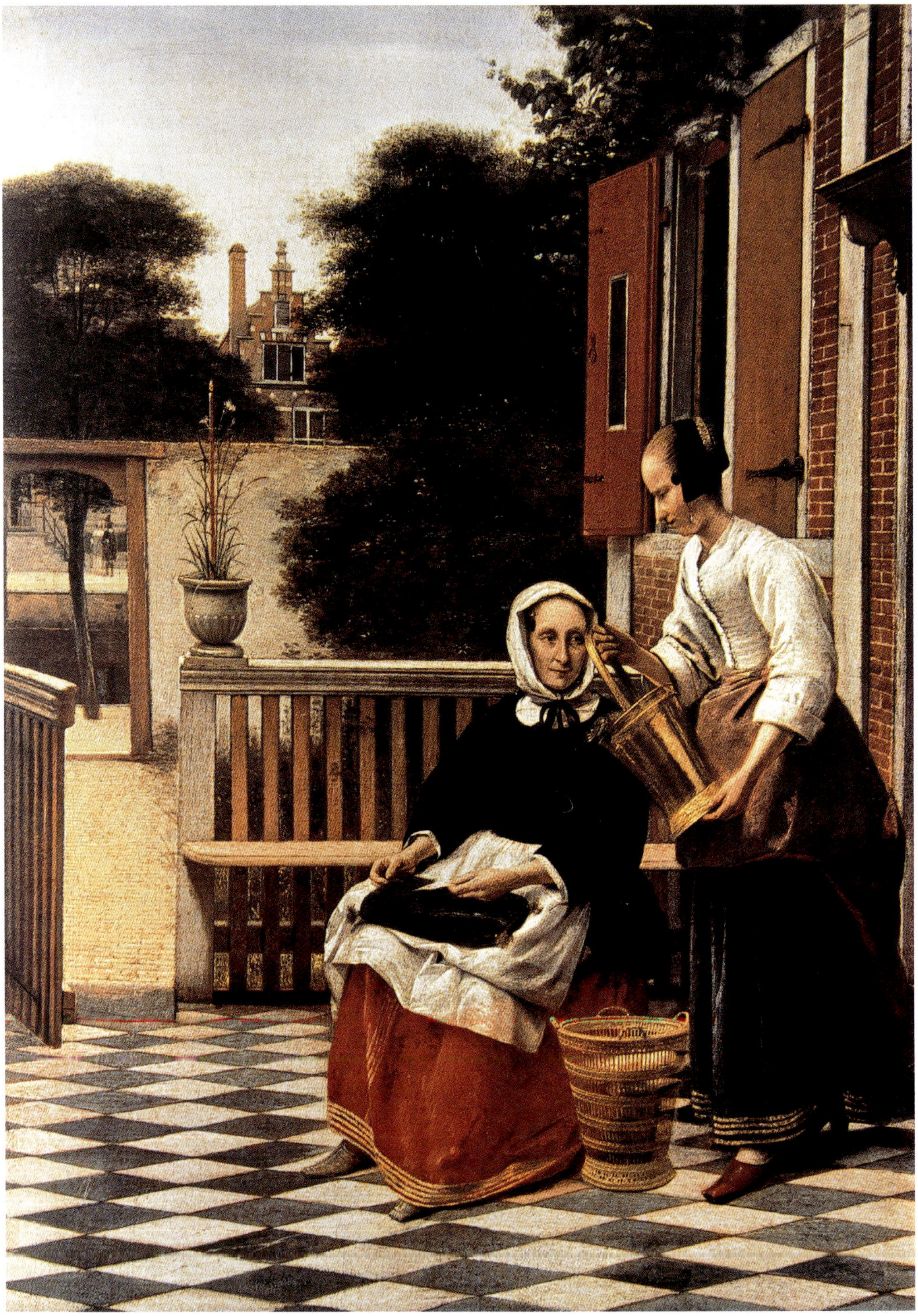

59 Pieter de Hooch, *Woman and Maidservant in a Courtyard, c.* 1661, oil on canvas.

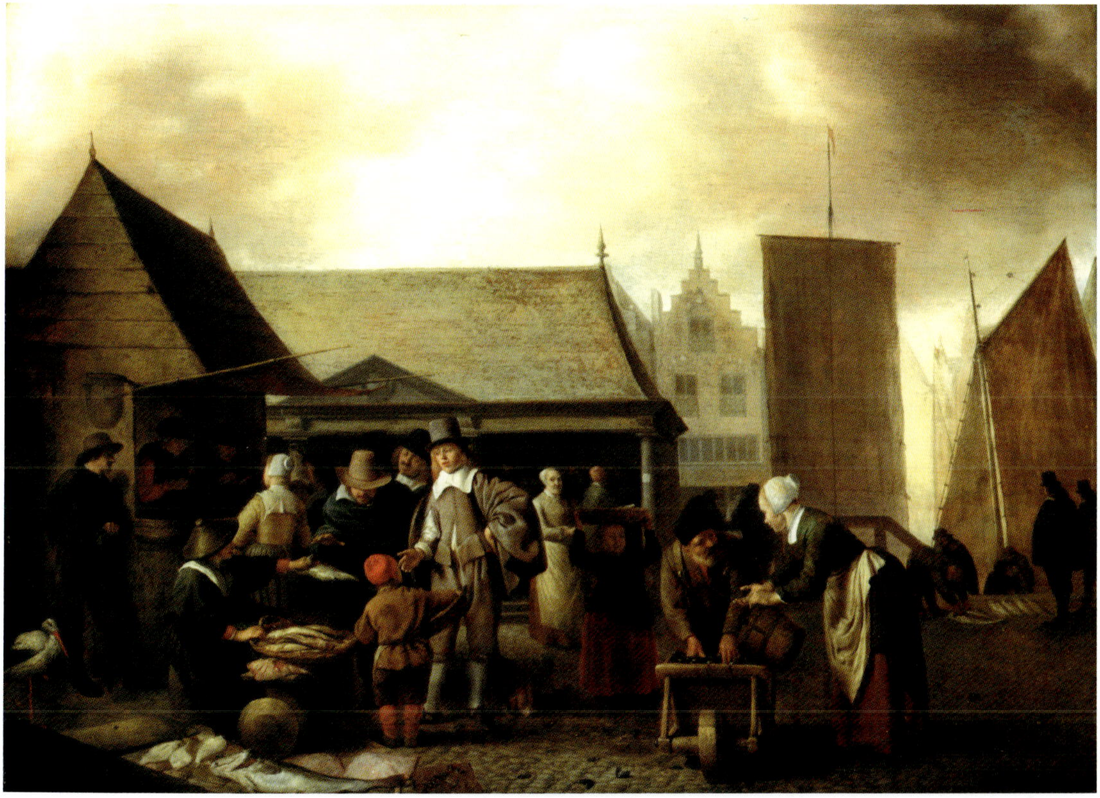

60 Hendrick Martensz. Sorgh, *The Fishmarket*, *c.* 1649–50, oil on canvas.

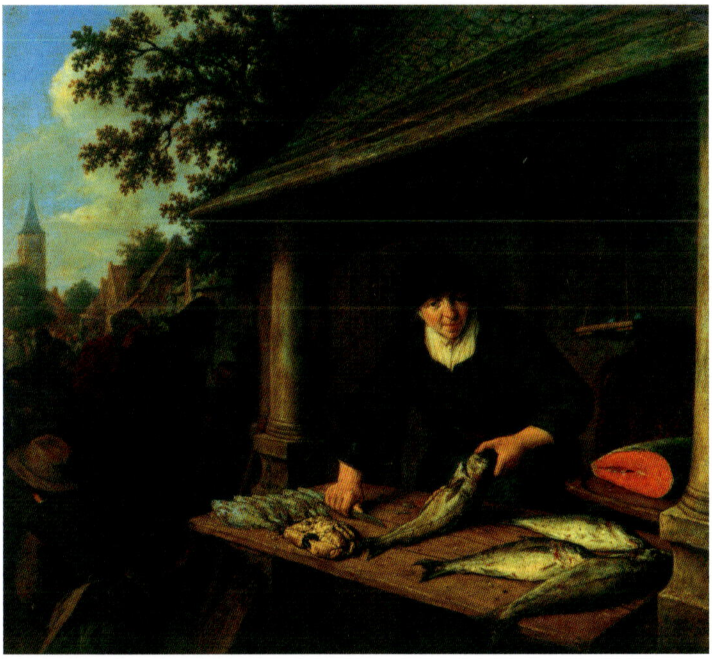

61 Adriaen van Ostade, *The Fishwife*, 1672, oil on canvas.

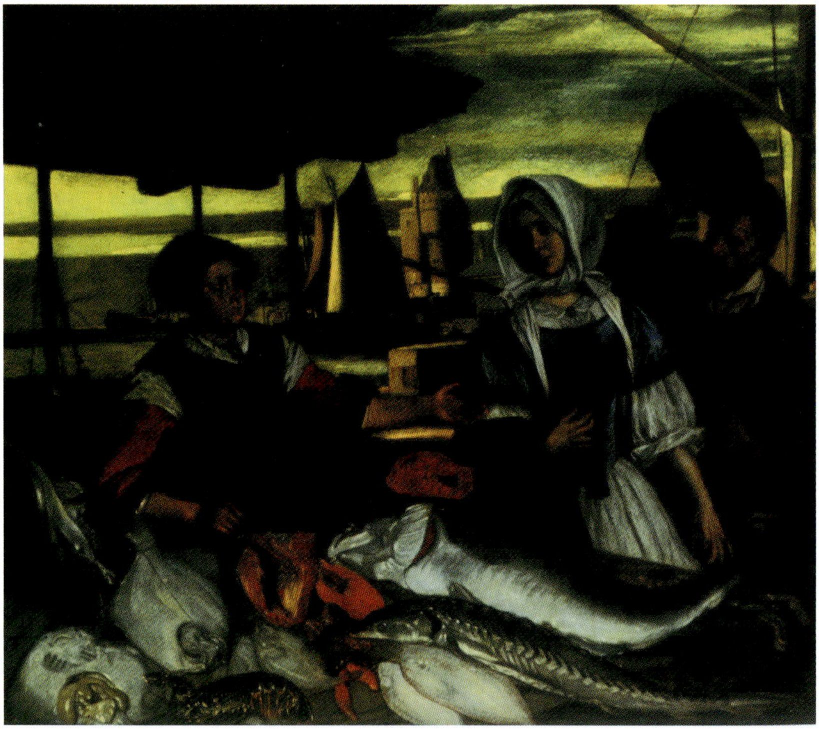

62 Emanuel de Witte, *Fish Market at Eventide,* 1672, oil on canvas.

Emmanuel de Witte (1617–1692), a Dutch master of Alkmaar, painted *Fish Market at Eventide* when he was in Amsterdam in 1672. Here, the background is much darker. Markets operated as and when the tide and boats came in and a boat is seen close behind the stall. A well-dressed couple pose as customers for the fishes, which are more expensive species than usual. Apart from the colourful cuts of salmon there is a prominent sturgeon next to two soles and a large cod, with rays, a flounder or perhaps plaice and the (difficult to identify) brill/halibut/turbot group. The lady of the house is to be seen purchasing fishes in several Dutch and Flemish market scenes. De Witte also painted a *New Fish Market in Amsterdam* in about 1662. The market may have had a new site but he included the same old open shacks with tattered awnings that provided no more protection for the fish sellers.

There were other Flemish and Dutch artists who painted in the fish market, supplying the merchants of coastal towns and inland cities with pictures of local scenes. Two notable Flemish painters were Frans Ykens (1601–1693) and Pieter Snyers (1681–1752). These artists were among the last to paint great fish scenes during the Dutch and Flemish Golden Age of painting.

Although the Italian influence had been so important to many painters from the Lowlands, hardly any Italian painters painted fish markets. An exception was Bartolomeo Passarotti of Bologna (*c.* 1529–1592) whose undated picture is a very early example of a fish painting, perhaps the first in Italy. His picture of a man and woman with a fish stall was one of a series of three, *The Fish Shop*, *The Butcher's Shop* and *The Poulterer's Shop*. The fishmonger handles a carp; nearby there is a lobster, a fish head, turtles in a basket and a collection of exotic shells in another basket.

Around a century and a half later Giacomo Ceruti of Milan (1698–1767) painted *Boy with a Basket of Fish.* This picture was overlooked for many years. It was once in the royal collection at Parma and went to the Palazzo Pitti in Florence in 1861. There it was inventoried without any attribution and has only recently been ascribed to Ceruti. The Italians had long enjoyed fish from the Adriatic, the Mediterranean, the marshes and lagoons. In Venice the fishmongers were well organized in medieval times: all fish to be sold had first to be taken to the 'tallpole' in the centre of the markets at San Marco and Rialto to be valued and duty paid before it was put on sale. The fishmongers' stalls were inspected daily and any stale fish removed and destroyed, by law. The sellers were not permitted to sprinkle the fish to keep them cool or freshen them up, but they found a way round that particular law. Two of them would start quarrelling, the dispute led to fighting and one would knock the other to the ground, at which point bystanders would fetch pails of water and throw them over the prostrate fishmonger, conveniently spraying it over his fish at the same time. This was a ruse at least a thousand years old, for a Greek writer, Athenaeus, had revealed the trick in a book (about 23 learned

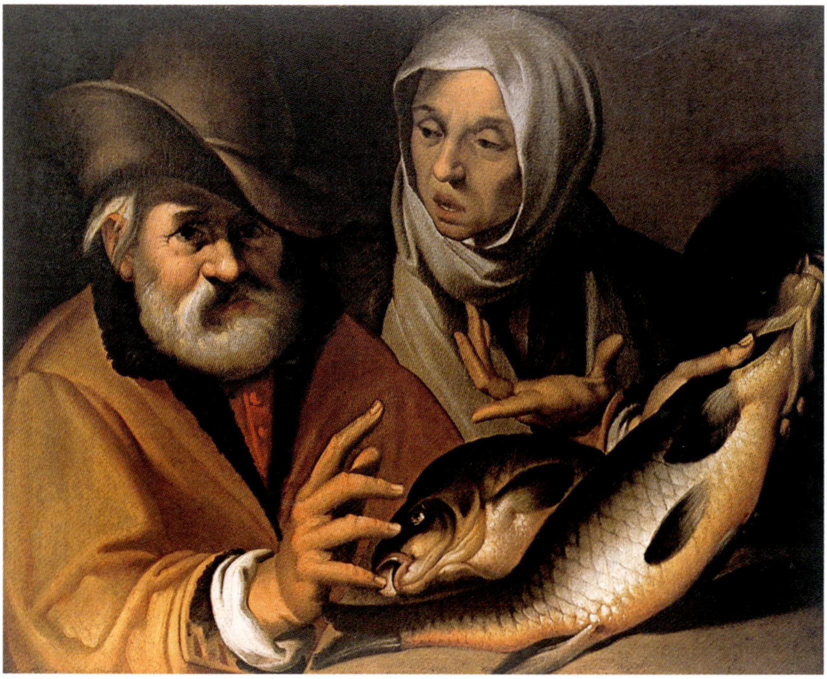

63 Bartolomeo Passarotti, *The Fish Stall,* detail, *c.* 1580, oil on canvas. Passarotti painted several versions of these two sellers, with different fishes on their stall.

64 Giacomo Ceruti, *Boy with a Basket of Fish,* *c.* 1735, oil on canvas.

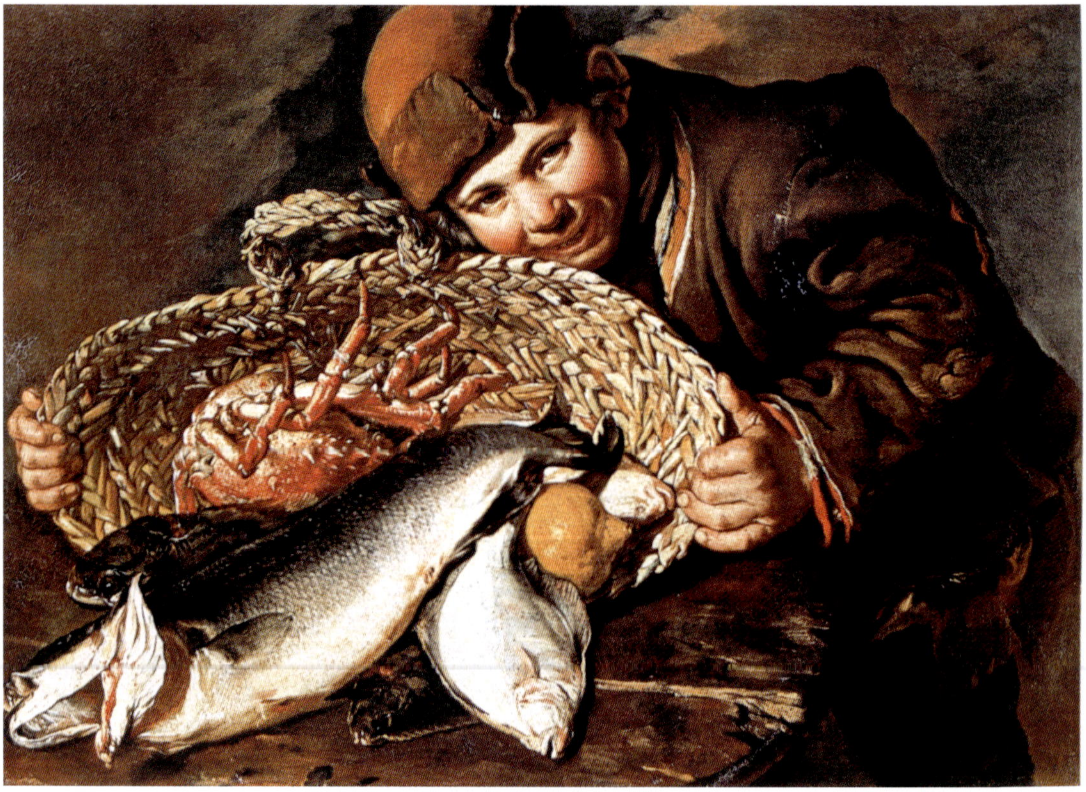

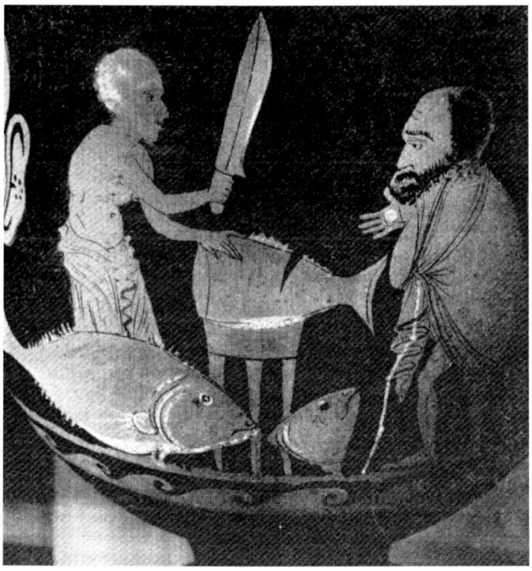

65 A Greek fishmonger topping and tailing a tuna. Detail from a 4th-century BC krater (a large two-handled bowl for mixing wine) from Lipari, Sicily.

connoisseurs of dining, *The Deipnosophists*) written about AD 200.

Similar rules were maintained in London's Billingsgate where the Worshipful Company of Fishmongers took a prominent part in maintaining standards and preventing bad fish being sold. The sale of unsalted fish was forbidden after the second day and fish could only be immersed in water twice. The restrictions meant that various means to keep fish fresh were devised. In the seventeenth century fish and other seafoods, especially expensive turbot and lobsters taken near Tynemouth and destined for the London market, were kept alive in rockpools, then transferred into water-filled wells in the ships that took them to Billingsgate. Such holding operations were unavoidable because the market in London fluctuated, operating only six days a week.

Some fishmongers sent orders to their customers by delivery boys. In a scene painted by William Hogarth, one meets with a mishap on the way. A windy day in the 1780s caused mayhem in St Paul's Churchyard, London, with hats and wigs blowing off, people getting in one another's way, and an unfortunate errand boy falling full length and spilling the contents of a tray of fishes.

New technology in the nineteenth century transformed the marketing of fish. First, ice was used for transporting fish overland to market. Ice was not, at first, carried on fishing vessels, so they had to continue to land their fish daily. From Elizabethan days fleets had fished Newfoundland waters for cod but salted their fish for the long voyage home. Ice was to provide the means by which fleets could stay at sea longer and return fresh fish in good condition to port. The revolution for the Scottish salmon industry and the English fishing industry came from China. For years the Chinese had been storing ice in ice houses along coasts and estuaries. Chinese fishermen drew their supplies of snow and ice from these storehouses and used it to pack their catch to keep it in a perfect state of preservation until they could offload it in dock.

In 1785 a Scottish servant of the East India Company, Alexander Dalrymple, on leave in England, met George Dempster, a fellow Scot and Member of Parliament for Perthshire burghs and former director of the East India Company. Dalrymple happened to mention the Chinese fishermen's habit of carrying ice on their boats to preserve fish and that they employed the same method to carry the fish packed in ice inland, once it had been offloaded. Dempster was sufficiently impressed by Dalrymple's description that he immediately wrote off to his salmon supplier in Scotland, a Mr Richardson. Though slightly sceptical, Mr Richardson experimented by packing freshly caught salmon in boxes filled with pounded ice and sending them on a six-day voyage to London. They arrived in perfect condition, with swift consequences, especially after George Dempster had a letter published in the *Scots Magazine* narrating how the salmon had remained fresh. It did not take long before the Scottish salmon trade was transformed, with large sales of salmon in London from fish caught around Aberdeen, Montrose and Inverness, not only in the cold months of the year but in summer too. The new steamboat service in the 1840s regularly carried salmon in ice from Scotland to London, and the railways from the 1850s onwards further speeded up delivery and provided more carriage capacity.

The demand for ice soon outstripped supply, but the story of the enterprising Essex farmer organizing his neighbours for miles around Barking to flood their fields in winter is another milestone in the history of fish marketing. This supplemented ice from the American Wenham Lake ice business that had started shipping ice to Britain in the mid-1840s, followed by bought-in Norwegian ice. The manufacture of artificial ice was the next innovation and with that came refrigeration and refrigerated ships that brought new species of fish from all round the world.

Ice played another role, this time after the fishmonger had sold the fish to the housewife. Ice houses had been known in Denmark since 1564 and in London Charles II had a 'Yeoman of the ice houses' in the 1660s. Once the king started a fashion the aristocrats followed suit and stately-home owners were soon having ice houses dug in their grounds. Several may still be seen today. Large houses frequently had more than one ice house, usually built a little distance from the house. These were somewhat inconvenient and ice stores built into the basements of houses were preferred, particularly after the 1850s. Houses in towns in close proximity to railway stations constructed large iceboxes in their cellars that could be replenished frequently from ice depots.

From the early 1800s new market buildings were erected in Britain's main towns. Fishmongers had stalls within these new market buildings, but for many years this was only possible on the coast, as at Plymouth. It was not until the middle of the nineteenth century that large catches could be transported from European and British ports to inland markets. The transformation came about by the combination of steam used for speeding up shipping transport and the building of railways.

Until 1850 Billingsgate Market consisted only of an open space by the dock dotted with low booths and sheds. A row of wooden houses with a square in front provided salesmen and fishmongers with some shelter during the hours they carried on their trade. The porters' round 'bobbing hats' were named after the charge they made (a 'bob', i.e. one shilling, or 5 pence in today's coinage) to carry the fish from the wholesaler to the retailer. In 1850 a new Billingsgate wholesale fish market, with a tall central tower, was built to replace the old sheds. It soon proved inadequate and another attempt was made with a larger building in 1874–7. That also eventually proved inefficient as well as inadequate and a new building costing £11 million on a new site was opened in 1982. The old bell that was rung to announce the beginning of trading each day was transferred to the new site and signalled trading there from 19 January 1982.

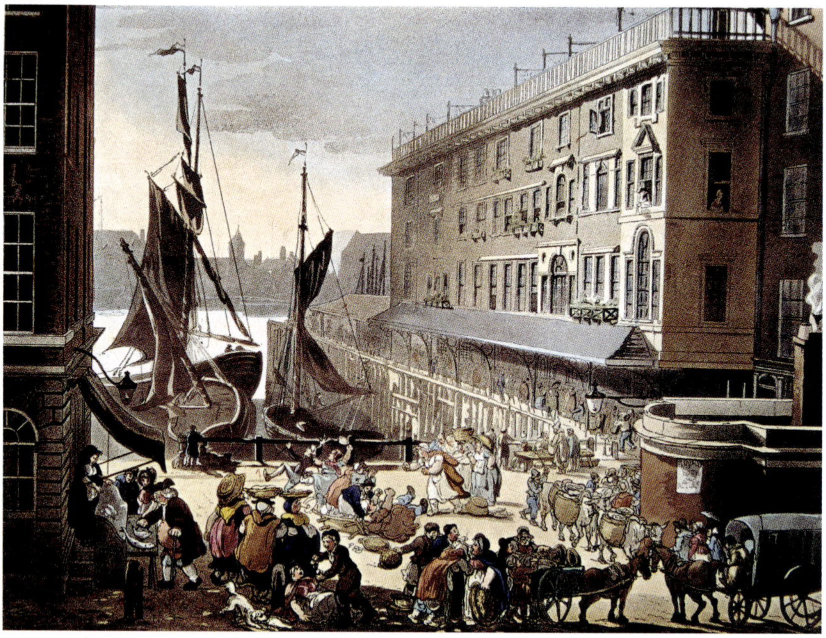

66 Thomas Rowlandson's view of Billingsgate Fish Market, London, 1808.

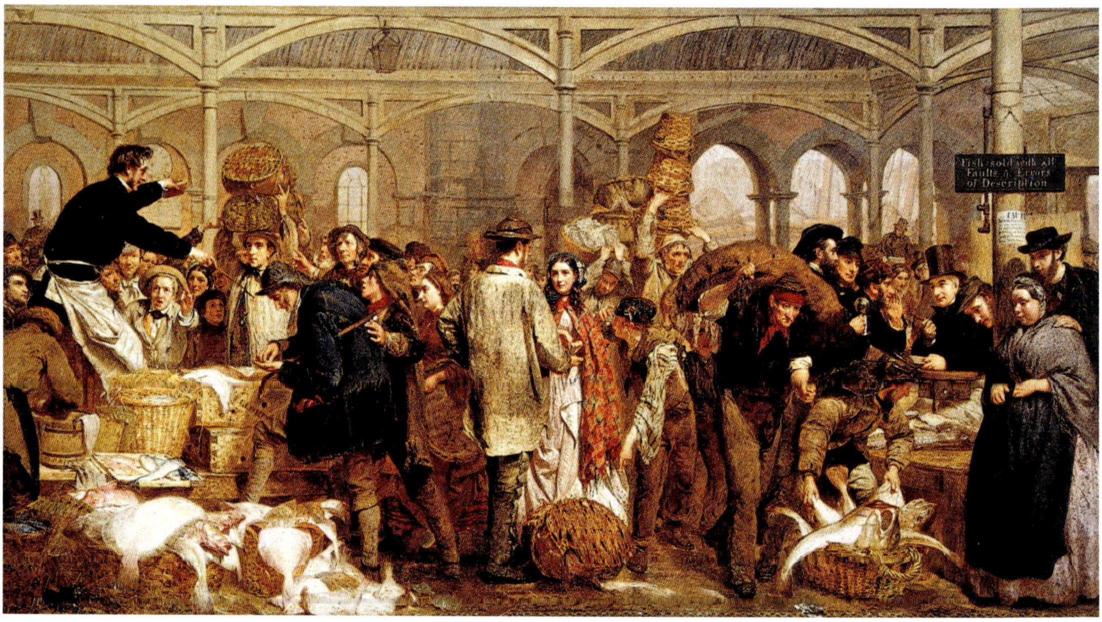

67 George Elgar Hicks, *The Interior of Billingsgate Fish Market at 6 a.m.*, 1861, oil on canvas.

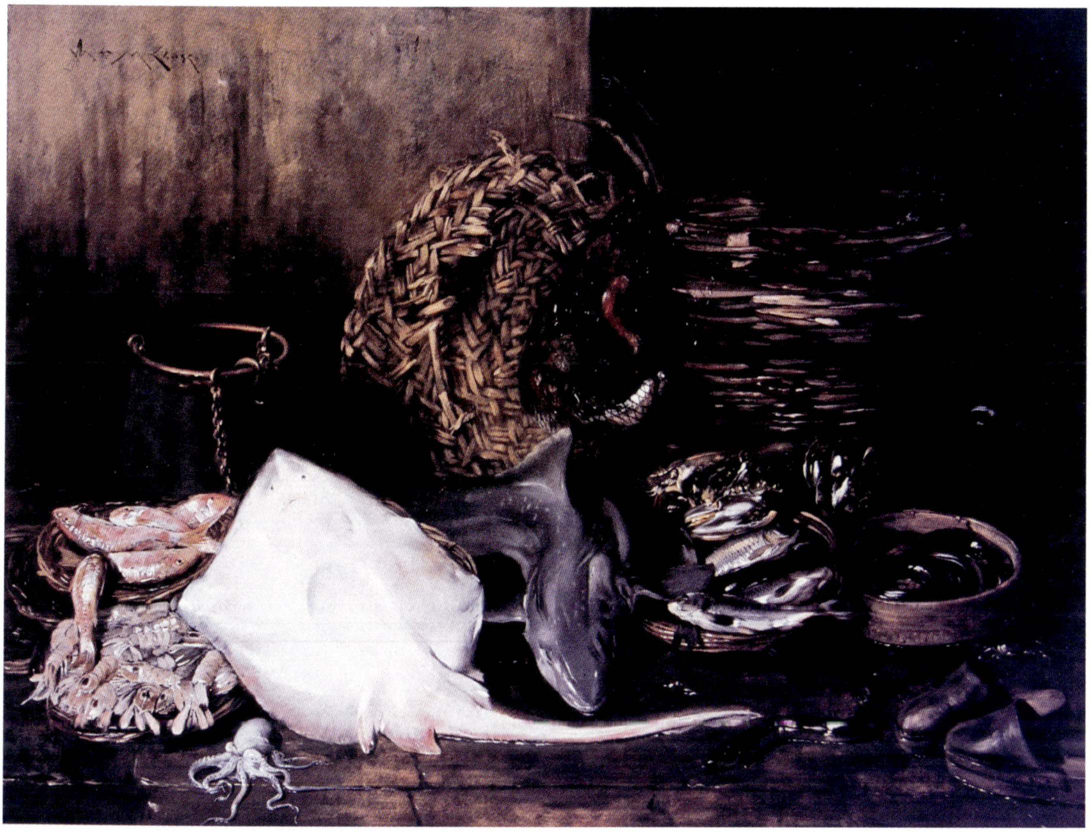

68 William Merritt Chase, *A Fish Market in Venice (The Yield of the Waters),* 1878, oil on canvas.

Unlike the Netherlands and Belgium, where the flourishing markets had inspired artists to record their wares, British artists were disinterested. It was not until the nineteenth century that they turned to recording fishes, but these were large ones caught in rivers and laid on the bank by the newly affluent sportsmen from the towns as well as the country. The enthusiasm for angling and paintings of angling scenes drew in artists who then had to learn to draw and paint fish realistically.

The nineteenth-century American artist William Merritt Chase (1849–1916), who was trained in Munich before returning to America, painted *A Fish Market in Venice* in 1878 and several kitchen pieces in the style of the old Dutch masters. A rare example of a twentieth-century painting of a fish market hangs in the Fishmongers' Hall, London. This is a very lively scene of Billingsgate Market, painted by order of the court of the Fishmongers' Company in 1973 by Hector McDonnell.

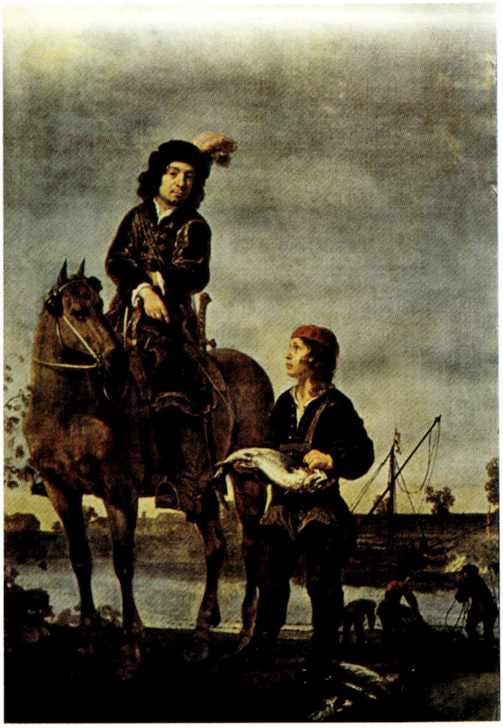

69 Aelbert Cuyp, *Equestrian Portrait of Pieter de Roovere*, detail, *c.* 1650, oil on canvas.

A new kind of marketing was introduced in the twentieth century. It was the next step from using ice to pack around fishes to preserve them. While Clarence Birdseye (1886–1956) was in the Arctic about the time of the First World War, working as a field naturalist for the United States Government, he noticed that freshly caught fish dropped on the ice froze solid almost at once. He realized that this was a possible way to transport fish and to market it in that condition. It took years of experimentation to freeze fish on a commercial basis and it was not until 1925 that he succeeded. Two years later he had processed almost 1 million lbs of frozen fish, and then went on to freeze meat, poultry, fruit and vegetables. So it was frozen fish that led the way to a new product, frozen food. Once on the market and in shops the customer needed their own freezer at home in which to keep the frozen fish. Several attempts to produce home freezers were made but it was not until the 1940s that cabinets were used widely in the United States. It took a further twenty years before refrigeration technology allowed freezer cabinets to become reliable kitchen appliances all over the world. A boost to Birds Eye sales during this period was provided by the introduction of their fish fingers in 1955, leading to marketing whole frozen meals. Birds Eye is now a household name, synonymous with frozen food, but few know that it all started with an observant field naturalist called Clarence Birdseye seeing fishes lying frozen on the ice in the Arctic.

Street pedlars were familiar figures in towns and villages across Europe. Dutch artists have given us some delightful pictures and the English also recorded the appearance of pedlars, their baskets and what fish they carried around as they took them directly to the doors of their

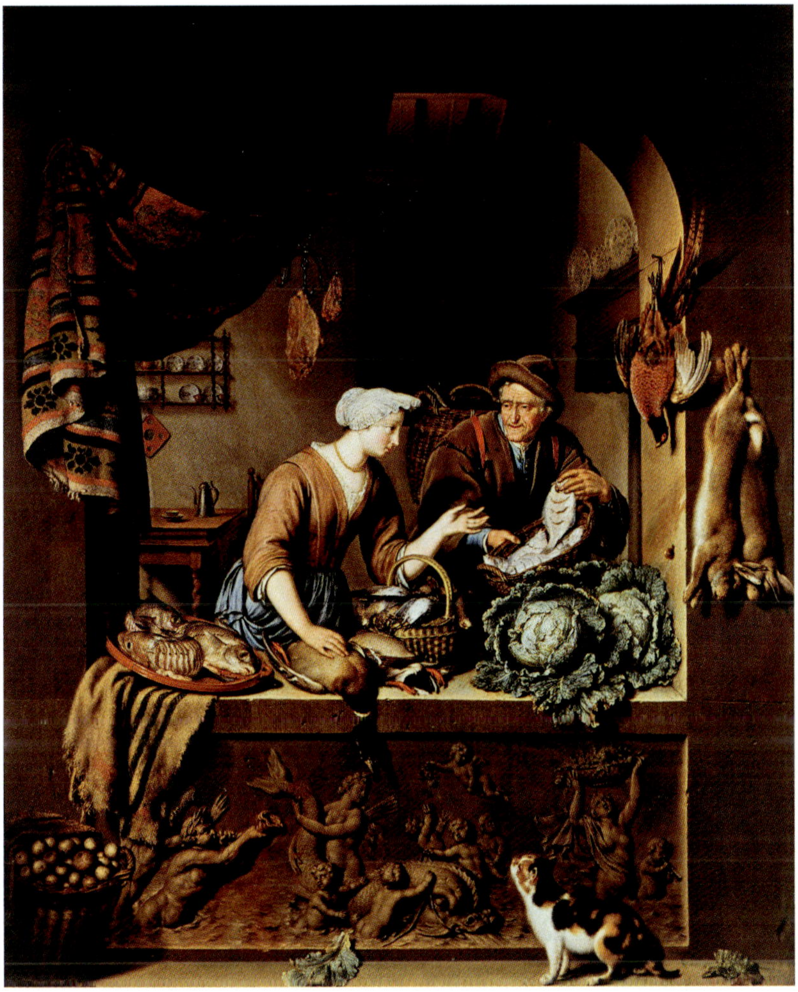

70 Willem van Mieris, *A Woman and a Fish Pedlar in a Kitchen*, 1713, oil on canvas.

customers. Aelbert Cuyp (1620–1691) of Dordrecht, son and pupil of Jacob Gerritsz., painted a portrait of an elegant horseman in one of his beautifully observed serene landscapes. This same horseman appeared in several of Cuyp's paintings and is here used as the means to show the fish pedlar offering a large fish to a potential customer. It is a beautiful painting, though completely artificial in its compilation.

Willem van Mieris (1662–1747), the Dutch painter of *A Woman and a Fish Pedlar in a Kitchen*, signed it along the top edge on the left and dated it *Anno 1713*. The painting is enlivened by the inclusion of a cat, a device employed by several Dutch painters of fishes such as

Alexander Adriaenssen's *Still-life of Fish with a Cat*, *c*. 1640–45, in the Museo del Prado, Madrid). The cats added a touch of life, of mystery and a slight menace. Mostly, only their faces are visible in some dark area of the painting, eyes large and glinting. We know that however well fed, the chance to steal a fish is irresistible to a cat. The lurking presence in the paintings conveys the impression that the cat knows it is stealing and will be chased away if spotted. The sense of guilt may be part of the seventeenth-century artists' intentions, a moralistic statement of sin and corruption, like the flies depicted on fruit and caterpillars on flowers in still-lifes. The Mieris marmalade cat may just be curious – or can it smell fish? Is it about to spring onto the stall? This is not only a delightful painting of an open kitchen where different kinds of food are sorted and cleaned before being transferred to a larder, but one of the best marmalade cats to appear in any painting. The luxurious carpet is a tour de force of texture painting and the Chinese blue and white ceramics on the shelves are indicative that this maid works in the kitchen of a very wealthy household.

An engraving of a fish stall in Birmingham Market Hall of 1870 shows a woman transferring fish from a stall into her wheeled basket before setting out on her rounds. Fish pedlars, taking fishes in baskets from door to door, had a harder time trying to sell their wares in a short space of time than stall holders, but she probably had regular customers and knew what quantity she could dispose of before nightfall.

Selling at the door was shown by Francis Wheatley (1747–1801) in his painting *New Mackerel*. Weymouth fish market sold mackerel at a penny halfpenny or two pence each in August 1782, about the time this was painted and then stipple engraved. Mackerel were taken to London and sold by street sellers from fish purchased at Billingsgate and put on carts. Being oily fish and particularly perishable they had to be sold quickly.

MACKEREL (*Scomber scombrus*) is one of the most brightly coloured of our sea fish, with its bluish-green iridescent wavy zigzag bands on the back. It is found in the North Atlantic, the Mediterranean and the Black Sea. Economically, it was very important in European countries, despite being one of the most difficult fish to transport and market because it is very oily so deteriorates rapidly.

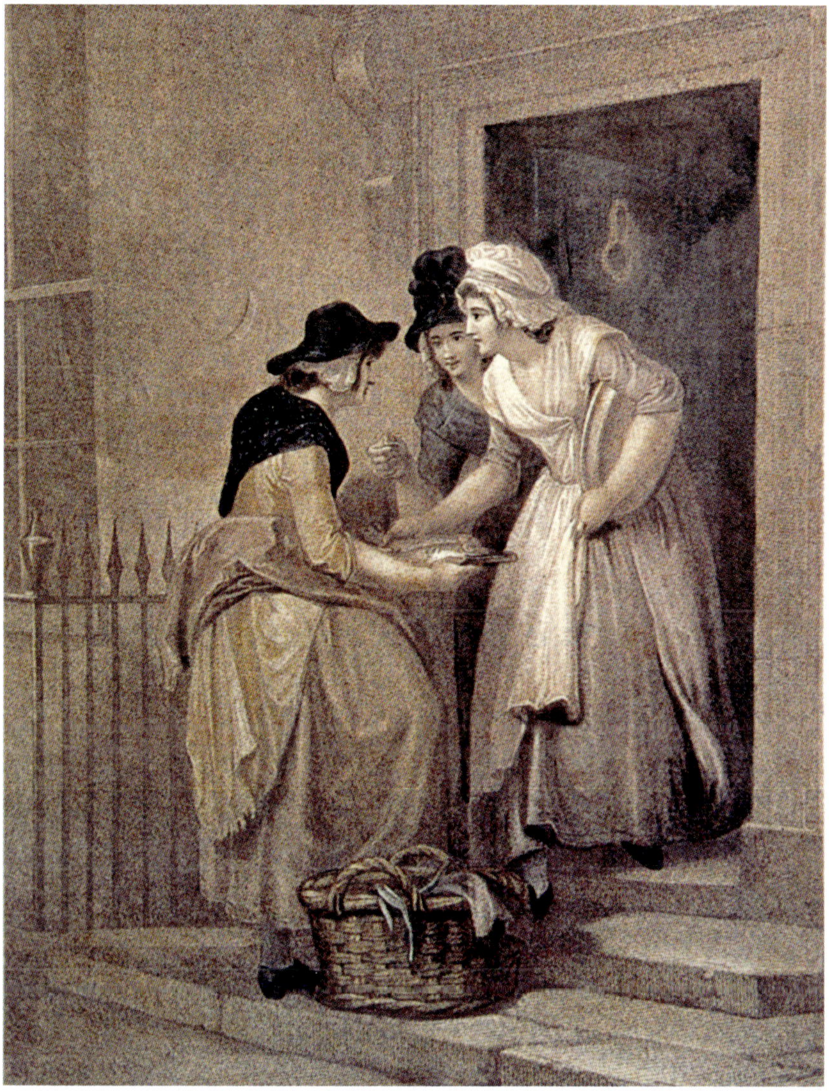

71 Stipple engraving after the painting by Francis Wheatley, *New Mackerel*, *c.* 1780.

They were the one fish that could be sold on Sundays (even in Scotland), but only before and after divine service, by Act of Parliament in 1536 and for many years afterwards.

For those who could not afford to buy paintings, prints made after paintings were pleasant and cheap substitutes. The *Cries of the City of London* were favourite prints throughout the eighteenth century. They had first been issued in 1697 using Marcellus Laroon's drawings of 74 street sellers and hucksters. New editions were issued in the childhood of the famous English painter and engraver, William Hogarth (1697–1764), who painted a picture of *The Shrimp Girl* in the 1740s that looked back to this earlier tradition. Her wicker platter of shrimps, on which the measuring jug can be seen at the front, is balanced on her head. If this had been painted by a Dutchman a century earlier there would have been a pile of shrimps visible on top of the basket, but in this English painting there is not one to be seen.

Fish pedlars on the London streets continued to cry their wares, noisily competing one with another. John and Thomas Bewick illustrated Henry Mayhew's *Cries of London*, including sellers of cockles, flounders and dabs, and mackerel, but the Bewicks were more interested in the street seller than her wares. Only in one engraving, of *Fresh Fish*, were any fishes visible in the basket on her head.

The poor waited until Saturday night when the traders were selling off their perishable goods at reduced prices. Henry Mayhew described the scene when the market became more of a fair in character:

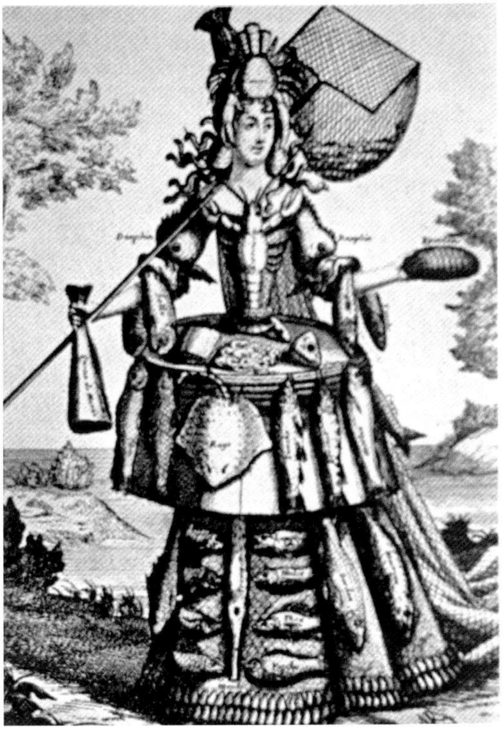

72 *Fancy Dress for a Fish Seller, c.* 1774, engraving, artist unknown.

> There are hundreds of stalls, and every stall has its one or two lights; either it is illuminated by the intense white light of the new self-generating gas-lamp, or else it is brightened up by the red smoky flame of the old-fashioned grease-lamp. One man shows off his yellow haddock with a candle stuck in a bundle of firewood; his neighbour makes a candlestick of a huge turnip, and the tallow gutters over its sides.

In 1850 the Billingsgate supply of fish was sold three ways. One third went to the London fishmongers, one third was dispatched to the country and the remaining third was bought by the street sellers. Fanning out from Billingsgate the fish pedlars carried baskets of the cheaper kinds of fish, plaice, herrings, sprats, mackerel, shrimps, whelks, cockles, winkles and red herrings. Barrows laden with baskets of fish, donkeys pulling carts and fish girls with baskets over their arms all offered fish for pence. They were measured in saucers (whelks), in pints (shrimps) or singly as one plaice for three pence or herrings at four for one penny.

Once fish could be moved safely around the country, fish shops could open in any town, relying on the railways to bring them fresh supplies daily. A Swiss animal painter who lived and worked in London, Jacques-Laurent Agasse, painted *A Fishmonger's Shop* in 1840. An errand boy is setting out on delivery with a tray of fishes on his head, while customers choose their purchases. On the slab are some herrings or mackerel in a tray, a sea trout, sole, skate, cod, shrimps in a glass bowl, turbot, red mullet, carp and pike. Hanging up on hooks on the shutter are turbot and eel fish or monk fish. Lying on the pavement are salmon, flounders or dabs and eels in a tray. Shops like this one could display expensive fish and cheaper fish, catering for clients across the social spectrum.

THE lesser spotted dogfish, *Scyliorhinus caniculus*, a type of shark, which grows to a maximum of 1 metre (3 feet) long is eaten in Britain under the name of rock salmon or is used as bait. Sharks have a cartilaginous skeleton, lacking true bones. As recently as 1976 a new 5-metre (16-foot) long shark was discovered off Los Angeles, at a depth of approximately 300 metres (1000 feet) and named megamouth.

The British are famous for their fish-and-chip shops, with battered cod or haddock deep-fried, served with chips (fingers of deep fried potatoes). There were fried-fish sellers before the chips were added; about 300 of them in London alone in the 1860s. It is uncertain who first had the idea of adding the chips but fish-and-chip shops started to become popular in the decade 1864–74. It is a quick and easy-to-eat meal, cheap and wholesome – except for the deep frying. Favourite fish used today are cod, haddock, skate and 'rock salmon' (dogfish).

The Children's Book of Shops (*c.* 1900) depicts a shop with an aptly named proprietor, Mr Shrimpton. The shop is situated near the shore and women bearing baskets on their heads are bringing the fish up from the boats docked there. Simplistic it may be, but the barrels, buckets and tables keeping the fish off the floor show how fish was marketed at this period, with a timeless scene of a lobster intriguing a young boy.

Today, fishes are flown into Britain from many parts of the world. It would not be possible to meet the demand for fish in the markets had

73 Jacques-Laurent Agasse, *A Fishmonger's Shop*, 1840, oil on canvas.

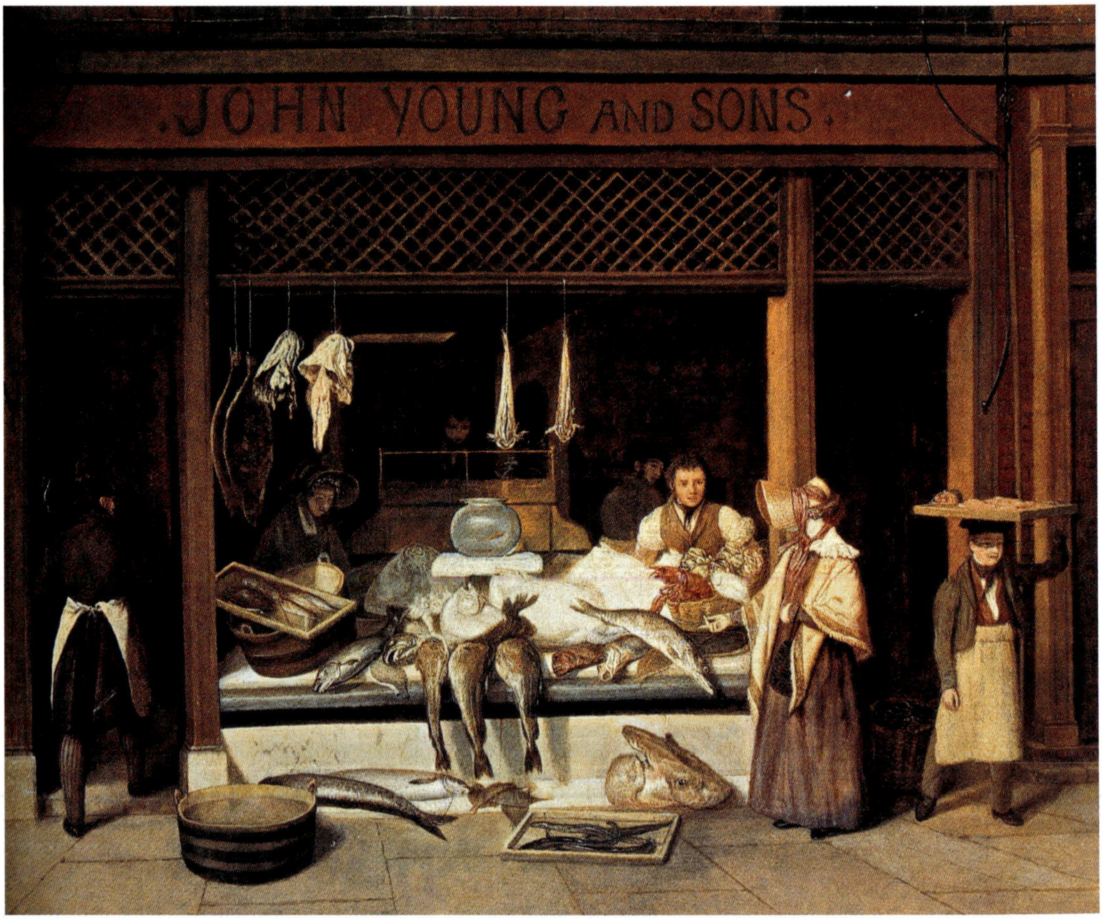

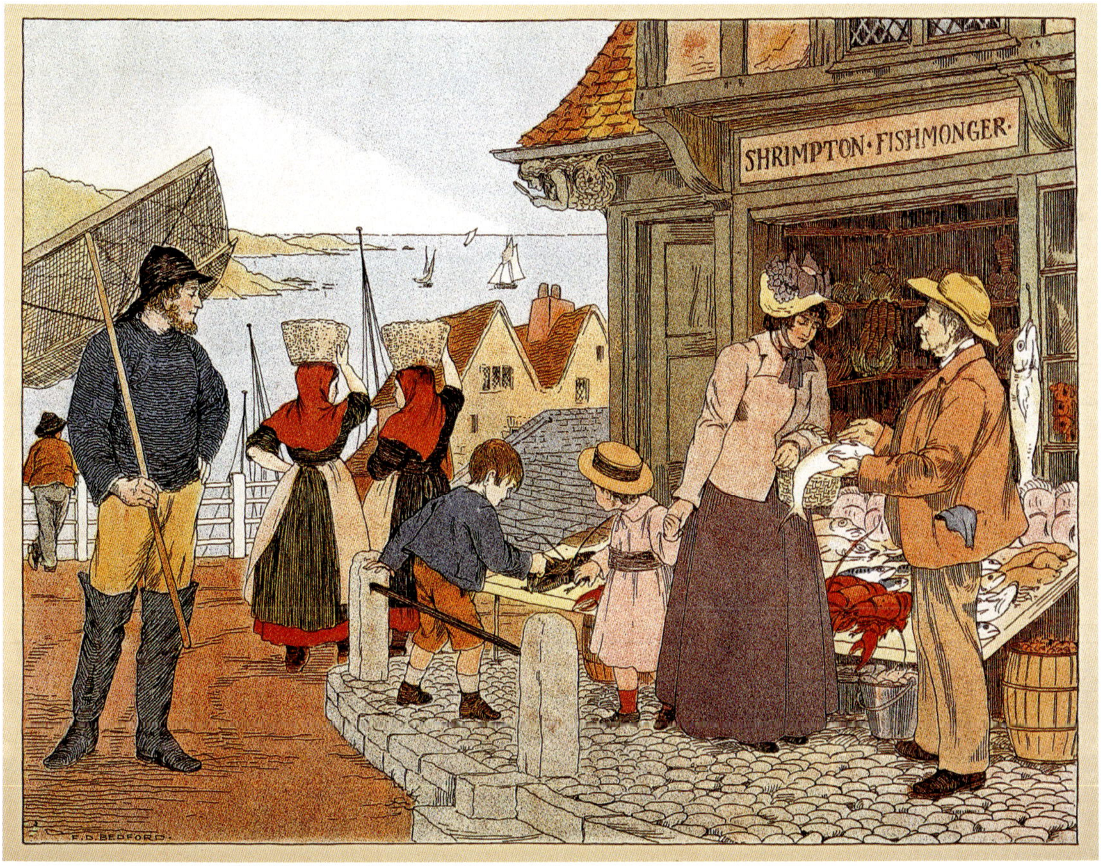

74 F. D. Bedford, 'Mr Shrimpton the Fishmonger', *c.* 1900, chromolithograph from *The Children's Book of Shops*.

we to rely on fish caught in home waters. With herring now so scarce, it is easier to buy snappers and other exotics in London markets. However, we can visit markets all over the country – indoor or outdoor – and buy fish from fishmongers. We have fish shops and fish stalls on local markets and fresh fish straight from a local port are carried by vans and itinerant fish sellers. Numerous books on fish cookery leave us in no doubt as to the nutritional value and delights to be had from eating fish. But the best way to buy fish is still to greet an incoming boat and get it straight from the sea or, better still, go and catch it for oneself.

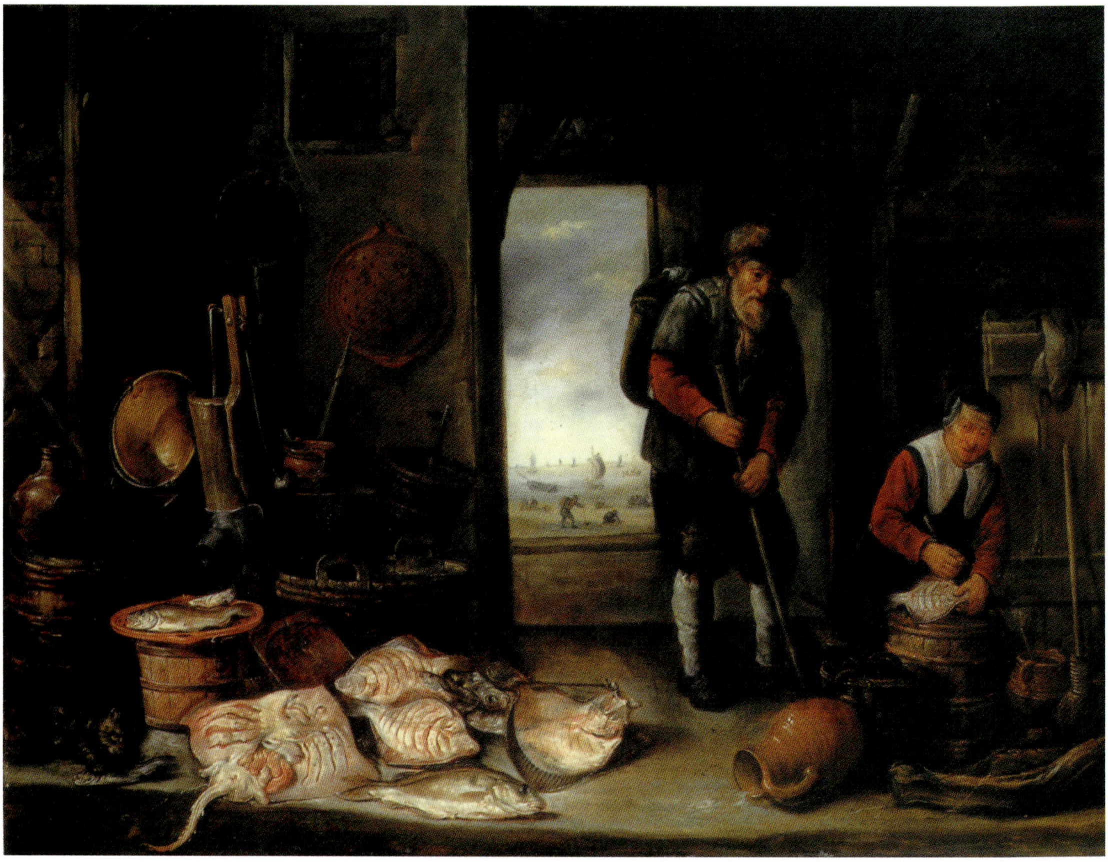

75 Pieter de Putter, *A Fisherman's Interior, c.* 1650, oil on panel.

four

Fish in the Kitchen

The moment that fish are put into the shopping basket, the responsibility for preventing their decay is transferred from the fishmonger to the cook. Today, fish is put straight into the refrigerator. Before houses had refrigerators it was taken to an ice box in the cellar and before that it was placed in the coolest part of the larder or kitchen and cooked as quickly as possible. In seventeenth-century Dutch paintings of kitchen scenes fish is nearly always dumped on the floor. The stone floors in clean households were washed down with buckets of cold water daily. Putting the fish on the floor not only had the advantage of its being in the coldest place in the kitchen but also it could not taint any cooking surfaces such as the wooden tables. Fish on the floor would, no doubt, be a great temptation to the household cat. In several kitchen-scene paintings a dog stands near the fish as though guarding it against thieving cats.

Pieter de Putter (*c.* 1600–1659) painted several pictures of fishes. This fisherman's cottage interior shows the different ways in which he preserved the quality of the fish he had caught. The place is littered with barrels and cooking implements, fish (rays, haddock and one of the family turbot, brill or halibut) on the floor and barrels to hold oysters, salted fish and water in which fish were kept and cleaned. The woman is preparing a plaice.

Studies of one species of fish in a kitchen scene are rare but Pieter van Noort (1602–post-1648), a Dutch artist who specialized in, and was famous for, his fish paintings, chose five plaice in various positions. Mrs Beeton wrote that plaice was found in the Baltic and the Mediterranean and abundant on the coast of England: 'Its flesh is inferior to that of sole and, as it is low-priced fish, it is generally bought by the poor.'

PLAICE (*Pleuronectes platessa*) is a favourite flat fish with large orange/red spots on the upper side of the body, white underneath. It lives in the Mediterranean, Baltic, Atlantic and Barent seas, feeding almost exclusively on shellfish that it crushes with powerful teeth. Plaice is less expensive and blander in taste than Dover sole (*Solea solea*), which is one of the finest sea fishes for eating.

In medieval times kitchens were often separate buildings, kept away from the main house because of the fire risk. The kitchen buildings had high roofs to allow the smoke, steam and cooking smells to drift up and out through roof vents. Even at that early period there was a separate scalding house where fish were descaled and their entrails extracted in tubs in a trough. Rushes covered the floors to capture any bits dropped and were irregularly swept out. Elizabethan kitchens were on the ground floor behind the main hall and had a wet and a dry pantry attached. The salted and fresh fish (sometimes packed in seaweed) were kept in the wet larder. After salting, the smoky chimney was used to cure the fish. Being fond of pies, the Elizabethans ate their fish, such as lampreys, sturgeon, ling and cod, liberally laced with dried fruit and spices, packed into pastry cases. The hard pastry case was returned to the kitchen after the contents had been spooned out onto the diners' trenchers or plates at the dining table.

76 Pieter van Noort, *Plaice,* 1621, oil on panel.

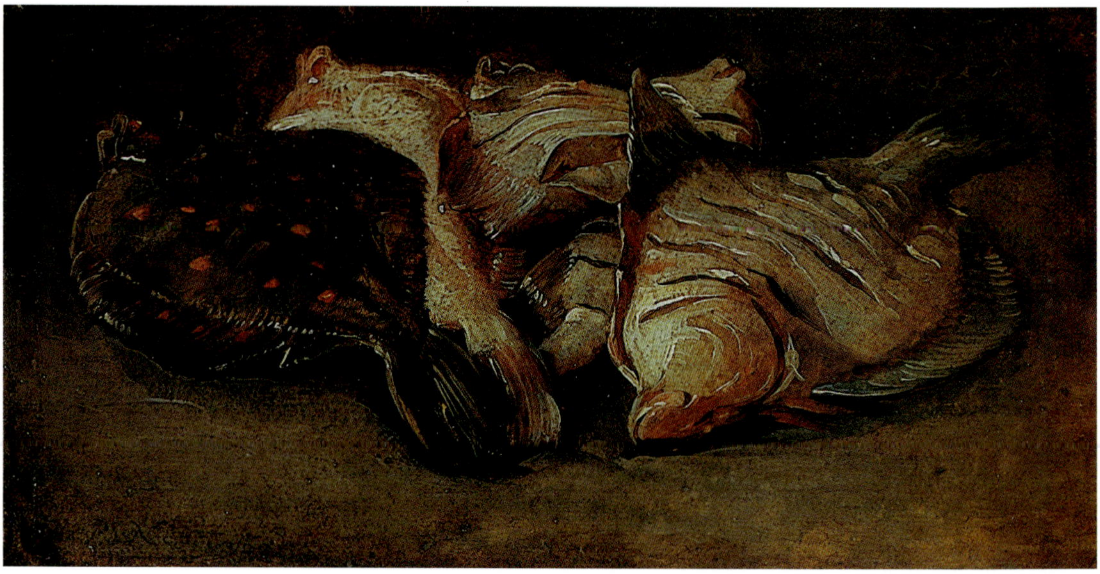

For centuries, large houses had separate larders for wet foods and another for dry foods. The larder took its name from *lardarium*, a process by which joints of meat were potted into huge containers and covered with lard. By excluding the air the meat could be kept for weeks. On a much-reduced scale this idea was used for potted fish in small dishes that were then sealed with melted butter. The larder would also house huge barrels containing hundreds of herrings and oysters. Slate and marble slabs provided places for fish to be laid out, then covered with a cloth to keep away the flies. These slabs were regularly scrubbed with chloride of lime to disinfect them. In large establishments there was also a *salsarium* where fish and meat were salted. Small quantities of salt were kept dry in the main kitchen in a hole in the wall near the fireplace.

Occasionally, larger steaks of fish were hung on circular metal rings near an open window where a cool breeze kept the suspended fish fresh. In summer the scent from the fish and the open window would invite flies into the kitchen if the window were not screened in some way. Metal rings suspended from the ceiling feature in Dutch, Flemish and Spanish paintings. David Teniers the Younger (1610–1690) clearly shows the suspended metal ring and the fish placed on the floor in his *Kitchen Scene*. This is really an allegorical painting about the four elements. The artist is present, dressed as a falconer, who with his bird personifies the element air. The burning hearth represents fire, while the fishes and fishermen and other sea creatures represent water. Earth is the dogs and game and the gifts of the earth, the cabbage and apples. It is most unusual to have all four elements in one composition; usually artists painted a series of four canvases.

Another kitchen scene, painted in 1605 by one of the earliest Dutch still-life painters, Joachim Uytewael (*c.* 1566–1638), shows many (though not all) cooks busily engaged in preparing a meal. The little dog is too idle to chase the cat that has one fish under a paw while it looks greedily at another, larger, one. The scene is chaotic, like the pile of fishes on the floor.

Where larger quantities of fish were to be prepared for cooking, the best place was an outhouse or barn. Savery, Cuyp and Rubens painted

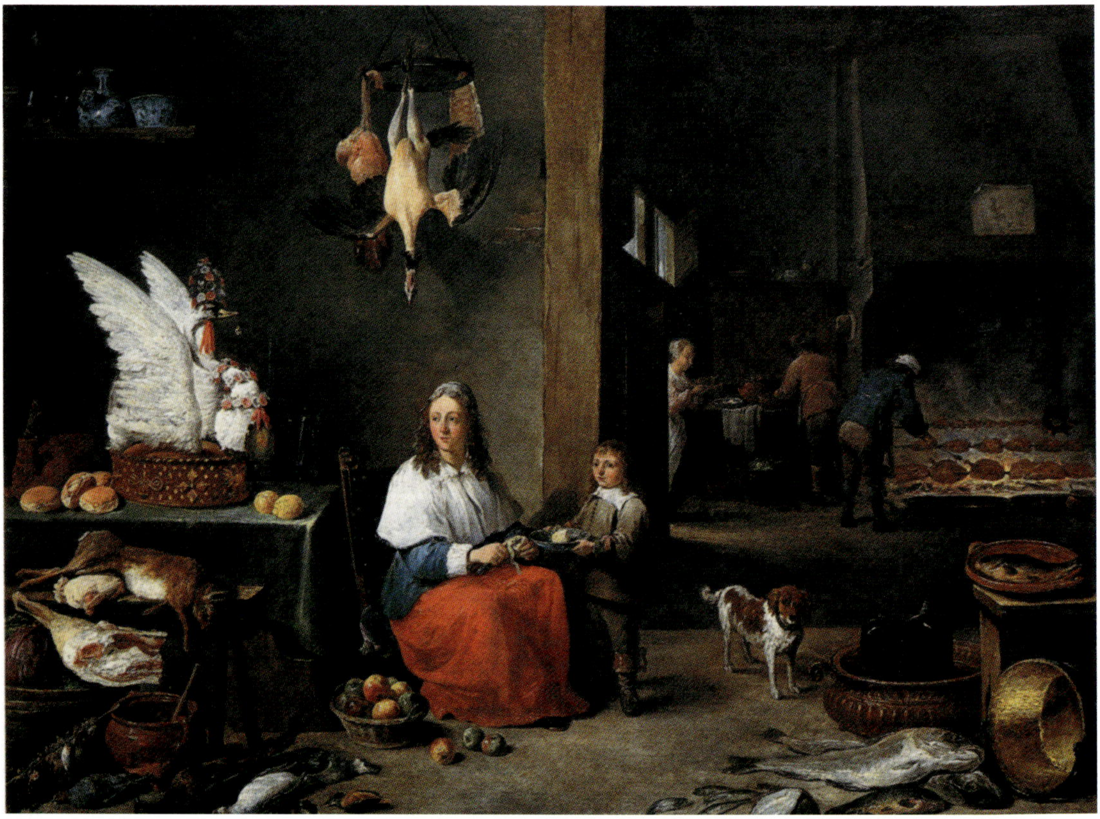

77 David Teniers the Younger, *Kitchen Scene*, 1644, oil on copper.

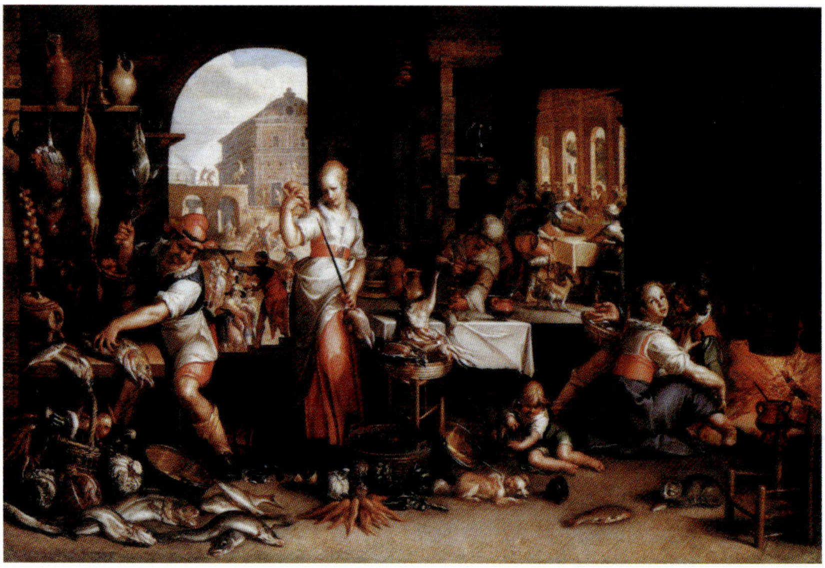

78 Joachim Uytewael, *Kitchen Scene*, 1605, oil on canvas.

Dutch stable and barn interiors, showing them housing not just cattle, farm implements and farm produce, but also providing the cook with preparatory areas for food. These cool places were an adjunct to the kitchen and all its activities, where fish could be kept away from other foods, gutted and descaled and made ready for the cooking pot.

Very few paintings show the preparation of fish, but Justus de Gelder (1650–1707/24) depicted a young woman cleaning fish under the watchful eye of her mistress in a painting of about 1675. A brass bucket on the table beside the maid suggests that she has just returned from the market, carrying the fish home in the traditional manner in a bucket. The pike may be about to be cooked in the cauldron (using the skimmer to lift it out when ready) or grilled on the grid hanging on the wall behind her. As in the de Gelder picture, several other paintings show kitchen utensils that were used in the preparation of fish, such as pots and pans, but above

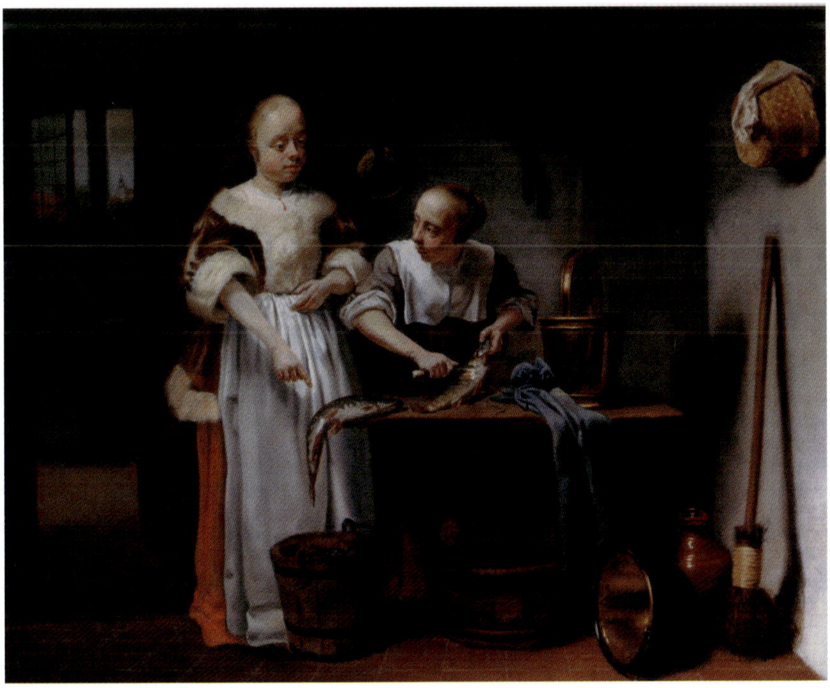

79 Justus de Gelder, *Cleaning Fish in a Kitchen*, *c.* 1675, oil on canvas.

all in Dutch paintings the presence of skimmers is noticeable. Numbers of fish rest on skimmers in the raw state, and these round or oval flat brass sieves were used to lift cooked fish that needed careful handling so that they did not break up. Among the earliest fish paintings, those by Clara Peeters executed between 1607 and 1630, there are several examples of copper fish lifters resembling elongated fish slices. The curved and perforated turner was also used to flip the fish over during cooking. Clara Peeters was one of the originators of Dutch still-life painting whose work shows considerable quality. She is thought to have been born in Antwerp in 1594 but little is known about her life; her biographer, Pamela Decoteau, could not establish her dates of birth and death, but detailed some 107 works attributed to or signed by Peeters between 1605 and 1621. The first were painted when she was in her teens, and the fish paintings of

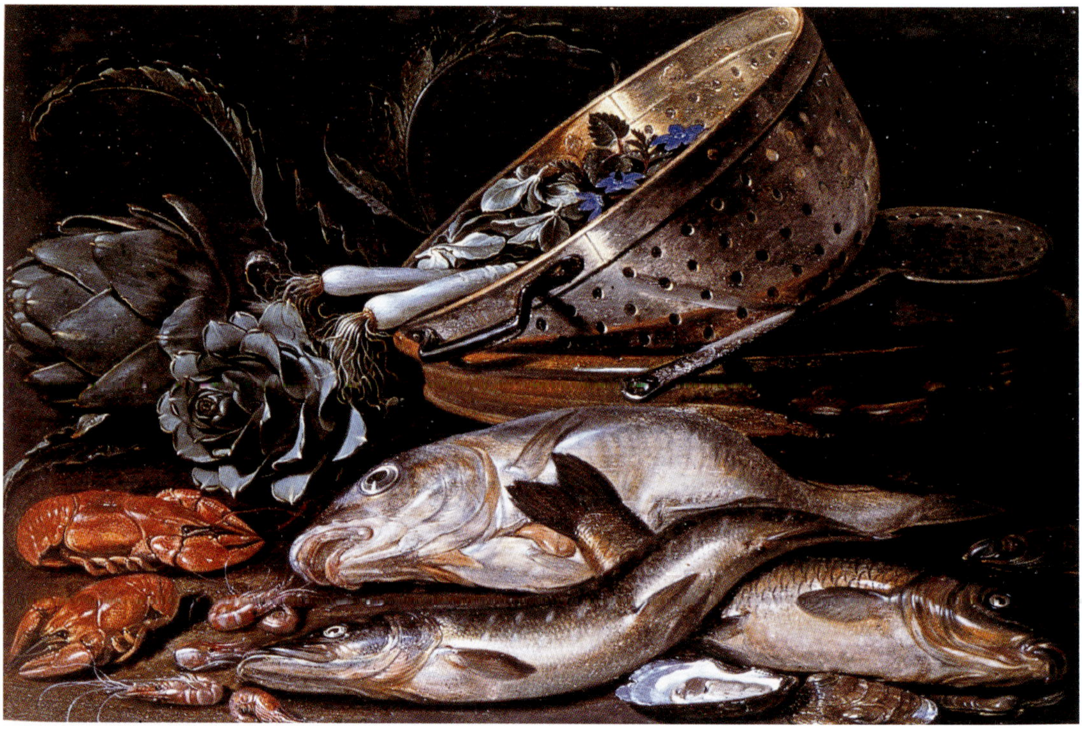

80 Clara Peeters, *Fish*, 1610, oil on panel.

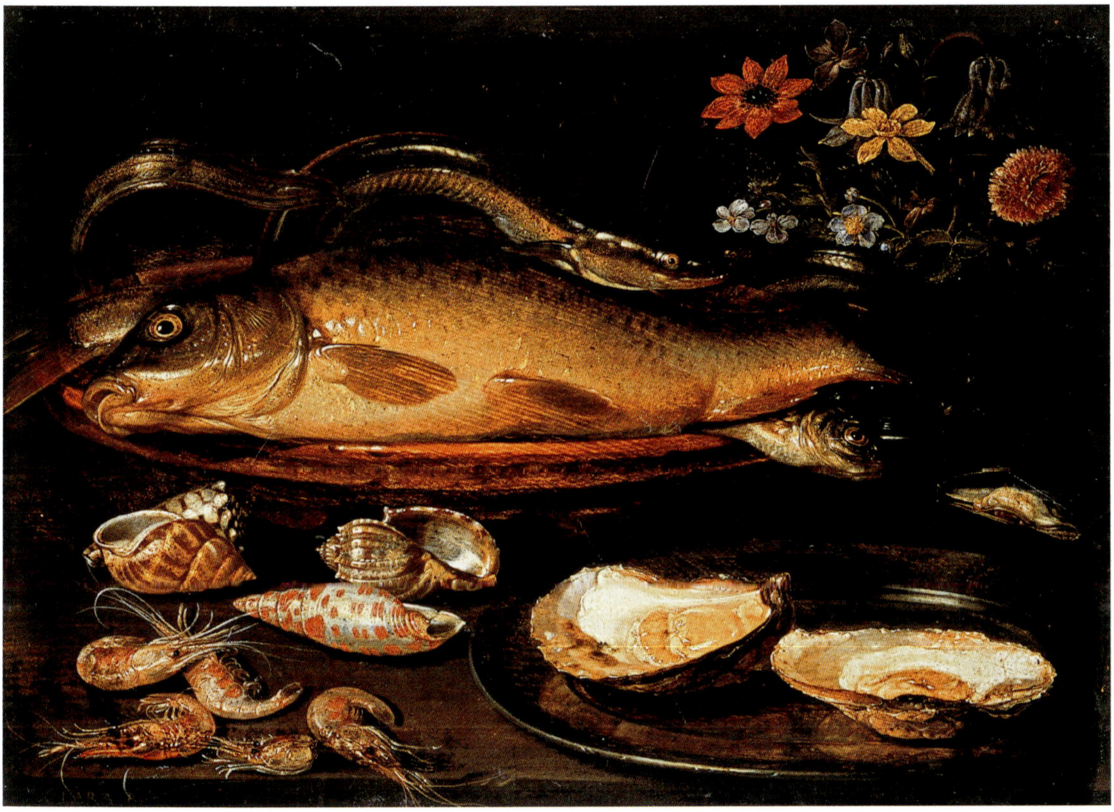

81 Clara Peeters, *Fish Still-life with a Bouquet of Flowers*, 1615, oil on panel.

1607–9 were among the earliest. Living in Antwerp gave her a choice of both marine fishes (cod, ling, herring) and freshwater species, which would have been available at the market. *Fish*, *c.* 1610, demonstrates her skill with light falling on the colander and artichokes, the wetness of the fishes and subtle use of reds across the foreground. Her fish paintings prior to 1611 predate by several years most of the Dutch paintings of fish. She chose a mixture of freshwater fishes, carp, pike, roach and eels, and shellfish, shrimps, crayfish and oysters from estuaries to include in *Fish Still-life with a Bouquet of Flowers* of 1615. This painting springs another surprise. Incorporating a bunch of flowers in a fish and shell painting was a novel idea. Clara Peeters clearly had an independent mind and spirit.

In 1700 in England, as elsewhere in Europe, kitchen equipment was simple, usually made locally by the blacksmith, the whitesmith or a potter. After steel knives and choppers began to be manufactured especially for kitchen use, the pounding of fish to a pulp with pestle and mortar gave way to chopping it up into small pieces and cooking it in different ways. Several new methods of cooking fish then evolved: baking, braising, frying, grilling, roasting, steaming or, if it was to be cooked whole, poaching in a fish kettle. This all necessitated the manufacture of newly designed pots, pans, dishes and glasses.

Seventeenth-century Dutch paintings frequently showed these brass and copper sieves and dishes, earthenware bowls, jugs and plates. However,

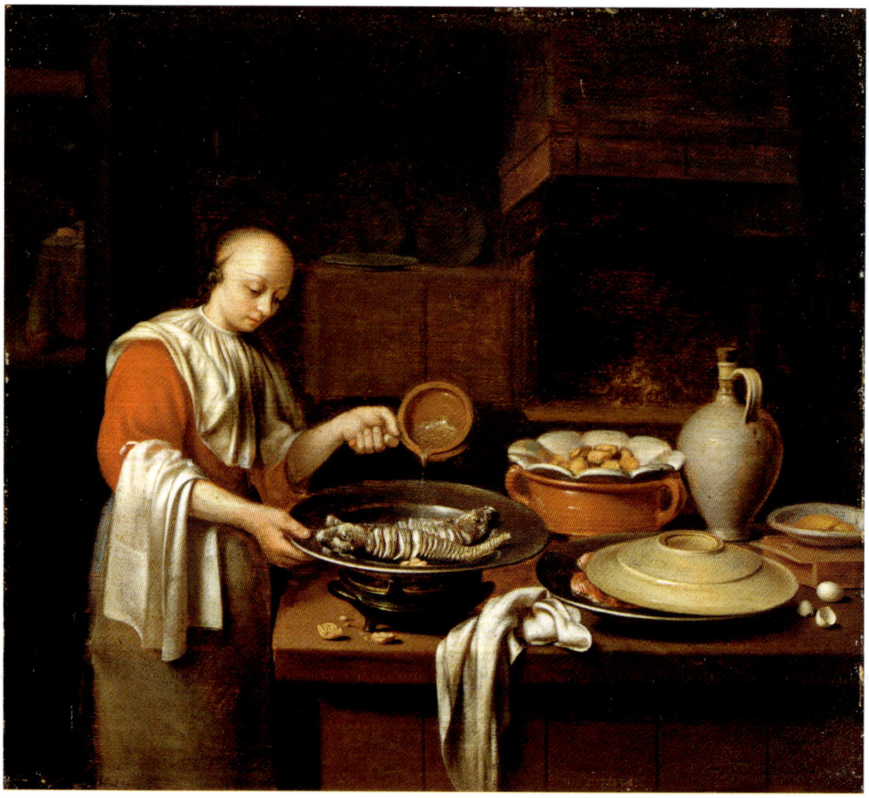

82 Reinier Covijn, *Woman Cooking Fish*, oil on panel.

83 John Ainslie, *Joseph Florence, Chef to the 3rd, 4th and 5th Dukes of Buccleuch*, 1817, oil on canvas.

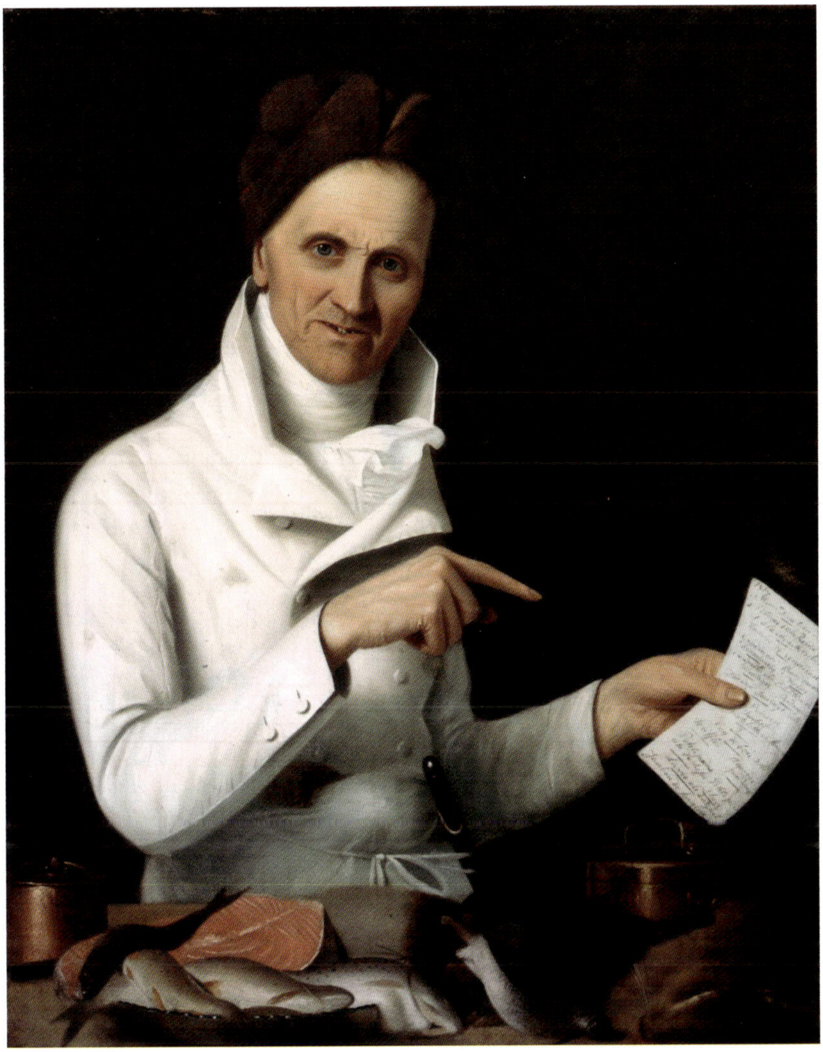

hardly any of the still-life fish paintings show the fish actually being cooked. An exception, *Woman Cooking Fish*, in Dordrecht Museum, is by Rieneir Covijn (*c.* 1636–1681), an obscure Flemish artist who painted peasant interiors while working in Dordrecht. The woman is using a flat pan and is pouring oil from a dish held in her left hand.

Early kitchen-scene paintings show women in charge of the cooking. Most households employed women cooks, but after Charles II returned to England from exile on the Continent the fashion for employing a French chef became established in aristocratic English houses. Throughout the eighteenth century it was fashionable to employ a French male chef and this practice continued into the nineteenth century. The portrait of

TURBOT (*Scophthalmus maximus*) is considered one of the best flavoured fish in the sea and consequently one of the most expensive. It lives at a depth of 20 to 70 metres (65–230 feet), lying on a sandy or rocky bottom in the Atlantic in the far north of Scotland south to the Mediterranean, and is caught in the North Sea. It is scarce and never in sufficient supply to satisfy demand. Alternatives are its close relatives brill (*Scophthalmus rhombus*) and the narrower-shaped halibut (*Hippoglossus hippoglossus*).

Joseph Florence, the Duke of Buccleuch's cook at Drumlanrig, Dumfriesshire, shows him pointing to 'turbot' on a menu. Turbot was also called the 'Pheasant of the Sea' and 'Le roi de Carême'. It was highly regarded as early as the thirteenth century by monks, who referred to it as the 'King of Lent'. Elizabethans boiled it and preserved it fresh in vinegar. In the seventeenth century turbot, with lobsters, were taken near Tynemouth and kept alive in rock pools until they could be transferred into wells of water in the bottom of ships for the London market, and it later became a favourite of Victorian dinner parties. Joseph Florence probably poached a whole turbot in milk to keep the flesh pure white in a special large diamond-shaped copper fish kettle (French *turbotière*) with handles on the points and a grid for lifting it out when cooked. Victorian chefs each had their own special recipe for turbot dishes.

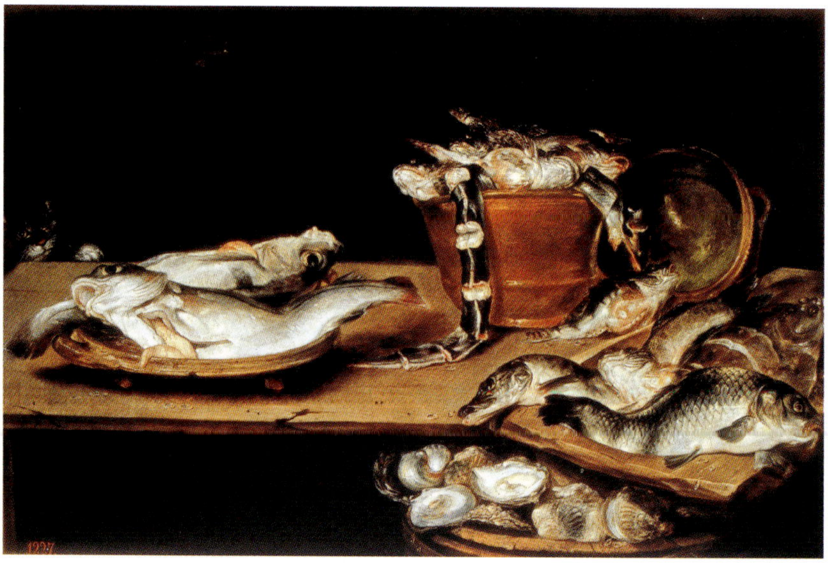

84 Alexander Adriaenssen, *Still-life with Fish and a Cat*, 1640, oil on panel.

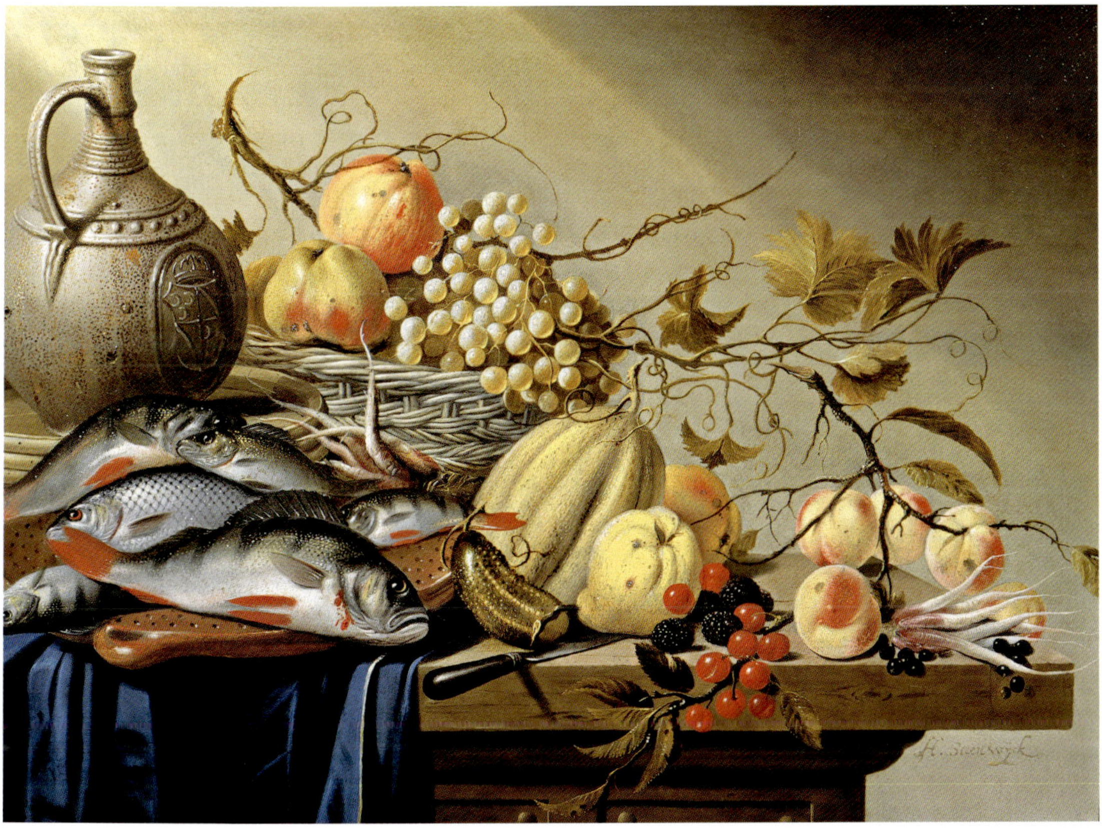

85 Harmen van Steenwyck, *Still-life with Fruit and Fish*, *c.* 1650, oil on panel.

Only families with serious social pretensions employed a French chef with his own staff. The distinctive hat worn by the chef was not *de rigeur* until after about 1845. Other households had kitchens run by women cooks who had worked their way up through the kitchen staff hierarchy. They were blessed with gas stoves from about 1841 and electric cookers from about 1891, with ever-increasing amounts of gadgetry to assist their culinary arts.

Genuine kitchen scenes show the cook and kitchen skivvies preparing the fish or otherwise busy in the kitchen where there are fish present either on the table on platters and drainage skimmers or resting on the floor. Many kitchen scenes, however, are of uncooked fish arranged artistically on a wooden table for the benefit of the artist who wanted to paint a fish still-life, and his assembly of fish was a mixture of whatever species appealed to him and were available. Harmen van Steenwyck (*c.* 1612–1656) painted such a kitchen still-life, placing his fishes on a luxurious piece of cloth which no household would have permitted, in 1650 or at any other time. Alexander Adriaenssen and Abraham van Beyeren both chose a bare wooden table on which to display a collection of fish species. Their pictures, though beautifully painted with a wonderful facility, incorporating several species of fish, copper and brass, nevertheless lack the colour and vivacity of those that have cooks busily at work.

An austere kitchen still-life was painted by a German artist, Christoff Paudiss, who served his apprenticeship in Amsterdam where he became familiar with Dutch still-life. He was regarded as the most brilliant German student of Rembrandt. His *Still-life with Herring* is signed and dated 1660. Besides the herring he included onions, cheese, beer, a Gouda pipe and tobacco, as well as a print pinned to the wall. German kitchen still-life paintings are very rare and this had been inspired by his Dutch connections. Although German painters of this period rarely tackled fish subjects, another exception is now regarded as being eminent in the history of still-life. Abraham Mignon (1640–1679) was highly respected in his life-time when his pictures fetched good prices. He went to the Dutch Republic in about 1659, staying in Utrecht for some years. Technically competent, he was able to incorporate utensils, fishing tackle, flowers or any other decorative object into his compositions. In his *Still-life with Fish and Fishing Tackle* the perforated skimmer has fish sliced ready for the cook.

It was in the kitchen that all those hundreds of barrels of salted herrings and stockfish bought in the market and stored for months had to be made palatable. Stockfish arrived looking like stiff pieces of leather and were just as hard and unappetizing. It took some pounding with a grooved hammer and soaking to revitalize them. 'When stock fish or salted cod was required for cooking', an Elizabethan manuscript said, 'it behoves to beat it with a wooden hammer for a full hour, and then set it to soak in warm water for a full two hours or more, then cook and scour it very well like beef, then eat it with mustard or soaked in butter.' In eighteenth-century England tastebuds were more refined and they wanted to get rid of as much of the salt as possible, so it was 'layered in water 12 hours, then lay it 12 hours on a board, and then 12 hours more in water'. Not until the middle of the nineteenth century did the railways and steamships bring in fresh cod and herrings, and then preserved fish became neither necessary nor popular any more.

There was a use for fish in medieval times that we might not relish now. In medieval kitchens a firm setting jelly was made with the swim-bladders of fish that were boiled until the liquid became glutinous. Calves' feet were boiled separately and the two liquids combined, coloured with dye and poured in layers to set. Different colours were cut into suitable shapes and laid in a shallow bowl over which transparent jelly was poured. When the shapes were cut to resemble fish, the pieces were suspended in a colourless jelly, making them appear to be swimming in the sea. The colourless, odourless and tasteless glue we call gelatine, made from bones and hides and marginally less revolting than the setting fluid from fish swim-bladders, superseded it, but gelatine made from plants – the bark of beech, elder and nut-trees – was known in the early part of the nineteenth century. Jellies, savoury and sweet, were so popular that moulds were made in ceramics and metal, often in the shape of a fish, that were easy to turn out, retaining their attractive shape. Many of Mrs Beeton's elaborate dishes were set in jelly moulds in a great variety of shapes and sizes.

With the cool waters of the northern coast and the warm waters of the Mediterranean providing the Spanish with a wide range of fishes, their coastal villagers ate well on seafood. They even have their own brand of bream, the Spanish sea bream, *Pagellus acarne*, caught in the warm waters off Spanish coasts in the Bay of Biscay and the Mediterranean. This bream is rosy red like the red bream but the black spot is smaller and placed just at the top of the pectoral fin, while the larger black spot on the red bream lies above the fin, level with the eye. Because the bream was so highly regarded most early Spanish kitchen scenes feature it.

Some of the first fish paintings were by Spaniards. In the 1590s, simultaneously, a new genre of still-life emerged in Spain, Italy and

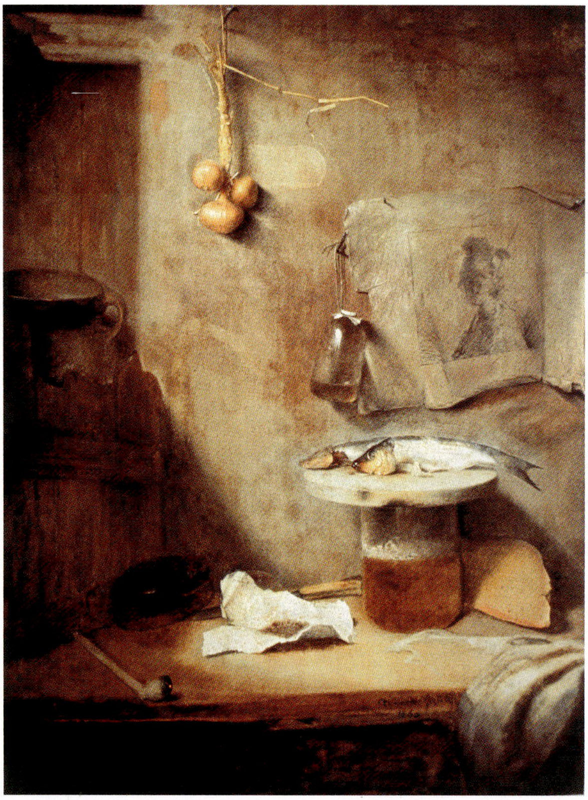

86 Christoff Paudiss, *Still-life with Herring*, 1660, oil on panel.

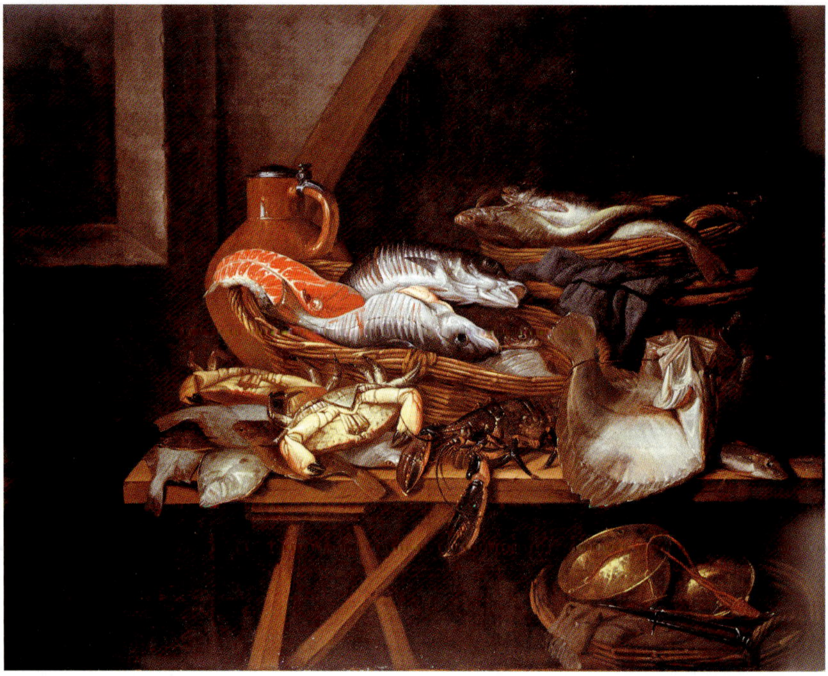

87 Abraham Hendriksz. van Beyeren (*c.* 1620–1690), *Fish and Shellfish in Baskets on a Wooden Table with a Jug and Pot*, oil on canvas.

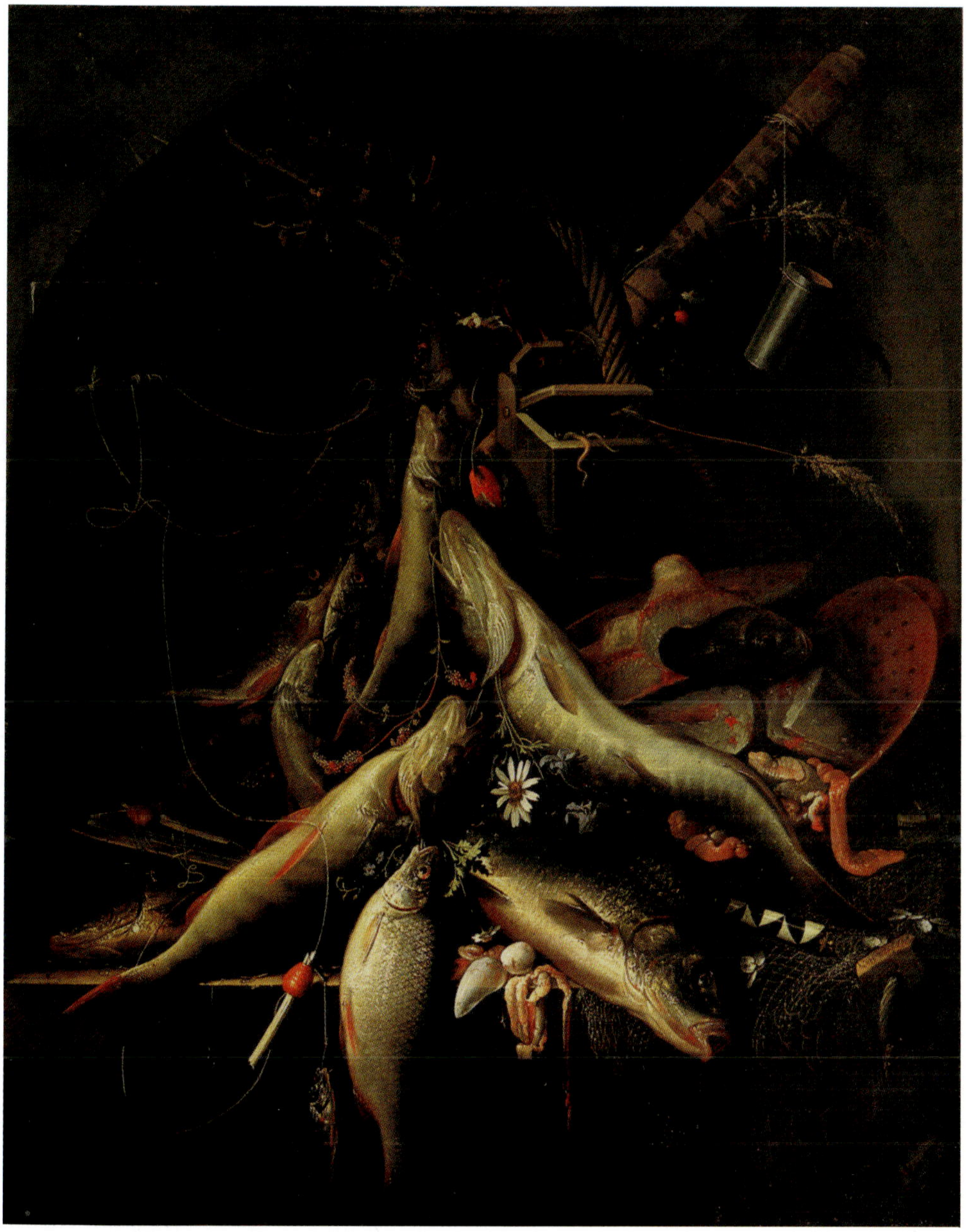

88 Abraham Mignon, *Still-life with Fish and Fishing Tackle, c.* 1675, oil on canvas.

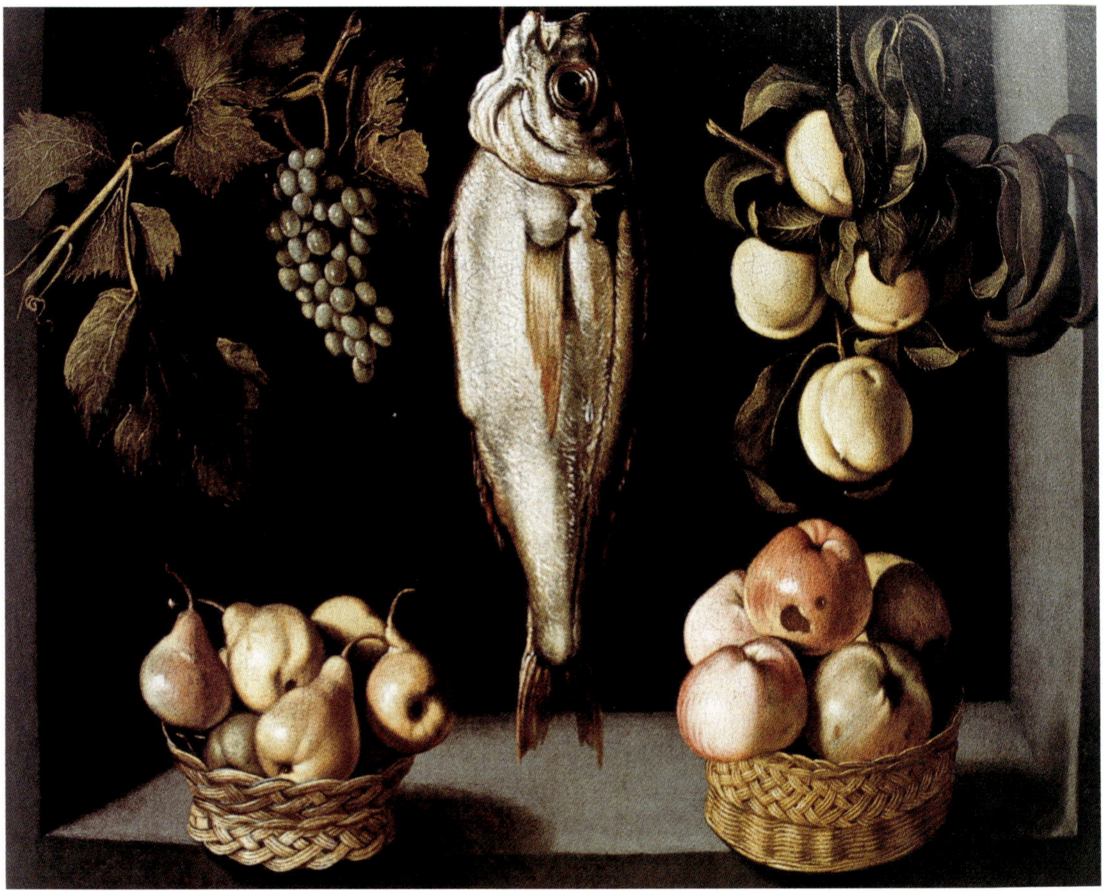

89 *Still-life with Hanging Fish and Baskets of Fruit*, *c.* 1620, oil on canvas, artist unknown.

Flanders. A very early Spanish kitchen scene (with no fish), dated to about 1590, by Vincenzo Campi, is close in style to those of the Dutch artist Aertsen (1508–1575). However, the first Spanish kitchen fish scene dates from about 1615–25 and is by an unknown artist, *Still-life with Hanging Fish and Baskets of Fruit*. The distinctive Spanish arrangement is already present, the elements carefully and neatly spaced, creating the impression that each one deserves to be appreciated individually. The economy of objects in Spanish still-life paintings may be indicative of the poverty of many Spaniards, who did not enjoy the prosperity and corresponding wealth of foodstuffs of their Dutch and Flemish contemporaries.

This painting by Diego Velázquez shows four sea bass on a plate. Velázquez's *bodegóns* were influenced by the Italian still-life pictures imported at this time to Spain. Sea bass was a favourite fish for Spanish tables, along with tuna, monkfish, sardines and mackerel. It is highly valued and regarded as one of the finest and best flavoured of all fishes by anglers and cooks in the East as well as Europe.

Tomas Hiepes (or Yepes, 1600–1674), a painter of flowers, fruits, fishes and wild game, is represented in many Spanish museums and private collections, especially around his native Valencia. His *Still-life of Fishes* is unusually complicated for a Spanish artist, with many more kitchen

TWO species of sea bream are known around the coasts of the British Isles, Black Sea bream and Red Sea bream (*Pagellus bogarevo*), relatively common in the seas to the south and west during spawning migrations. A very good food fish with white tasty flesh, it is occasionally caught by anglers. In the Bay of Biscay and the Mediterranean, Spanish bream (*Pagellus acarne*) form a part of dragnet catches and are also caught by anglers. The exquisite golden bream (*Patrus* or *Sparus aurata*) is the finest of all sea breams, found in the Mediterranean. It was eaten at Roman and Greek feasts and sacred to Aphrodite, goddess of love.

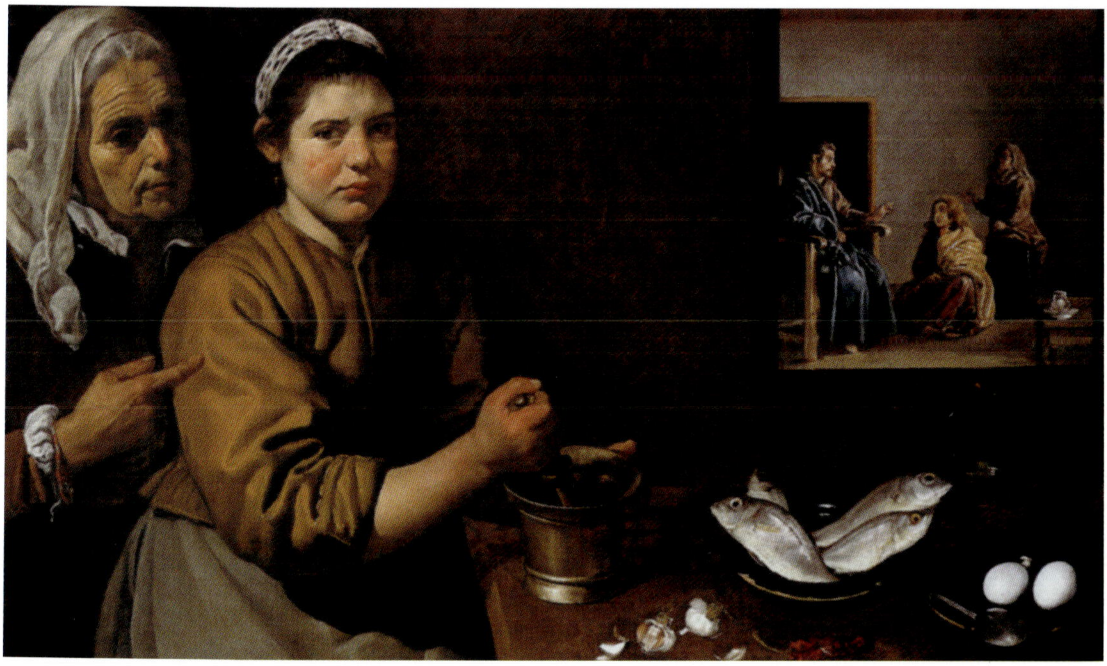

90 Diego Velázquez, *Kitchen Scene with Christ in the House of Martha and Mary*, 1618, oil on canvas.

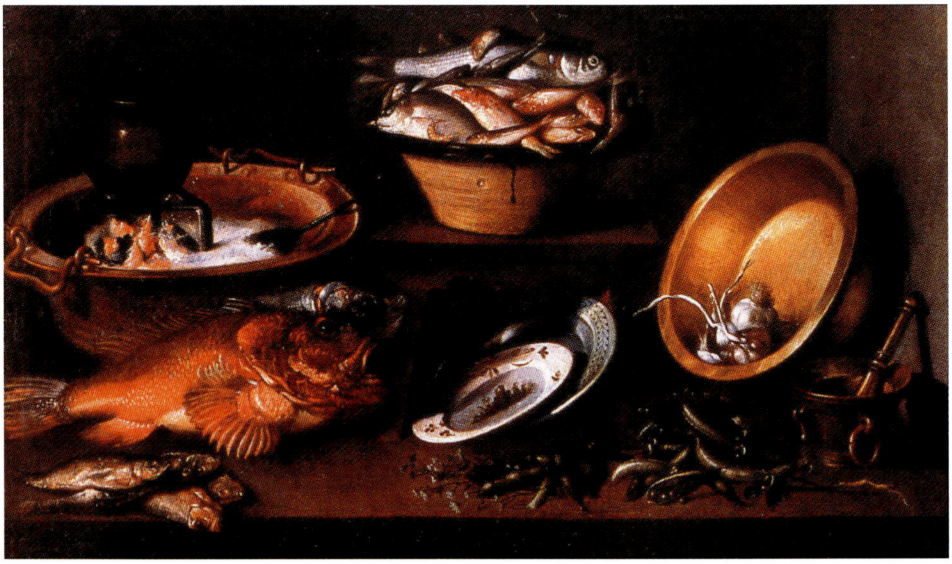

91 Tomás Hiepes, *Still-life of Fishes*, *c.* 1650, oil on canvas.

bowls, dishes, grouped fishes, garlic, and a pestle and mortar than his compatriots put in a picture. Nevertheless, the symmetrical composition with the colours carefully balanced and weighted make it unmistakeably Spanish in character.

Among the biblical scenes containing fish, the least often painted on canvas is that of the boy with the loaves and fishes that he gave to Christ to feed a crowd. In 1622 Alejandro de Loarte painted a large oil on canvas, 2.75 x 4 metres, on this subject that came onto the art market in Madrid in 1992. The boy is standing in front of Christ making his offering of fishes that are clearly visible. Loarte also painted a neat larder scene *Bodegón de Caza con Escena de Cocina* with an eel curled up in a circle and some sardines. The young fish (pilchards) were fished heavily off the Biscay coast and off Portugal where they are now canned as 'sardines'.

In 1795 a British patent was taken out for a process of vacuum-sealed tinplate and the first cannery opened in Bermondsey, London. The British

Navy was supplied with food in cans, then Americans took up canning and shipped their tinned salmon to Britain. In 1834 a canning factory opened in Brittany to process the sardines that abounded on the Breton coast. A Danish artist, Peder Severin Krøyer (1851–1909), visited Brittany after studying for two years in Paris. He went to see the women at work in the Concarneau canning factory and described them in a letter dated 9 October 1879: 'The girls and matrons sit along a long table filled with sardines . . . through some small openings in the roof the sunlight falls and creates a wonderful feeling.' Concarneau was then one of Brittany's centres for the fishing and canning industry with at least 1,200 boats operating out of the harbour and some 13,000 people employed in the process of boiling, salting, bottling and canning the huge quantities

92 Alejandro de Loarte, *Bodegón de Caza con Escena de Cocina,* 1622, oil on canvas.

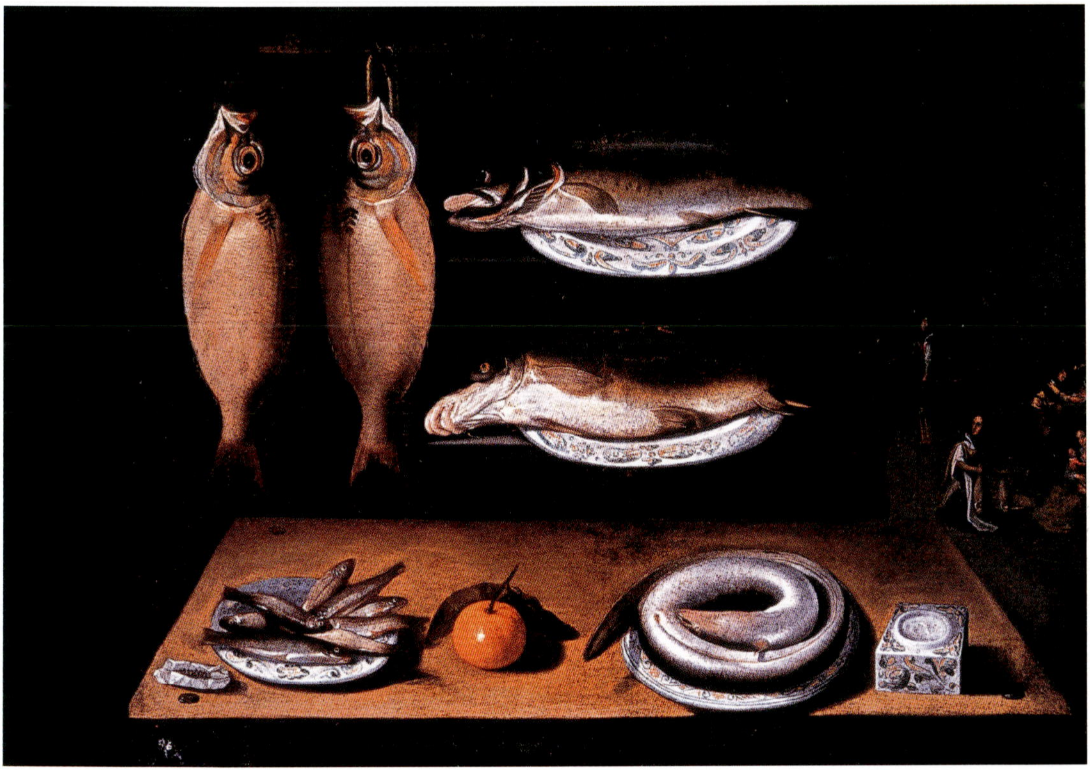

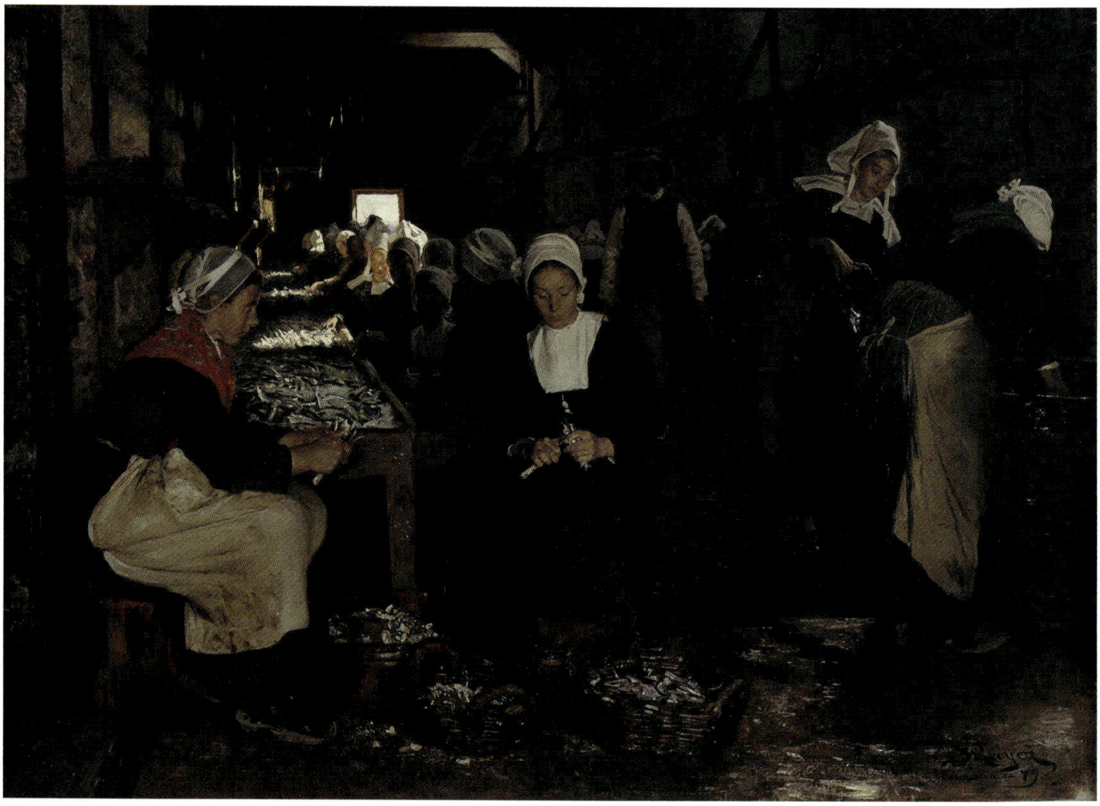

93 Peder Severin Krøyer, *A Sardine Factory in Concarneau*, 1879, oil on canvas.

of fish. Krøyer painted the scene in the realistic manner of the Spanish master he so admired, Velázquez. For many years the tiny Breton sardines were the best but they almost disappeared through over-fishing and now French canned sardines come from north Africa.

It took fifty years after canning of food began for someone to devise a can-opener, using a spike and a cast iron bull's head complemented by curly cast iron tails or wooden handles, first put on the market in 1860 by a manufacturer of bully beef. Until then, incredibly, the instructions on the can label read 'cut round the top near the outer edge with a chisel and hammer'. The first record of a 'tin-opener' in literature occurred in 1884, when they were called 'sardine shears' or scissors, which, it was explained, were 'for cutting open tin boxes'. 'To be packed like sardines' was a term in use in 1917 and 'packed like sardines in a box' in 1922.

A very early, perhaps the earliest, kitchen scene, a fresco from Pompeii painted before AD 79, showed a basket of fish accompanied by asparagus and cakes. The fresco is now conserved in the Museo Nazionale, Naples. The Romans and Italians were very fond of their food, and being surrounded by the sea, ate quantities of fish. By the sixteenth century in Italy kitchens were equipped with free-standing charcoal braziers, with

94 Fresco from Pompeii.

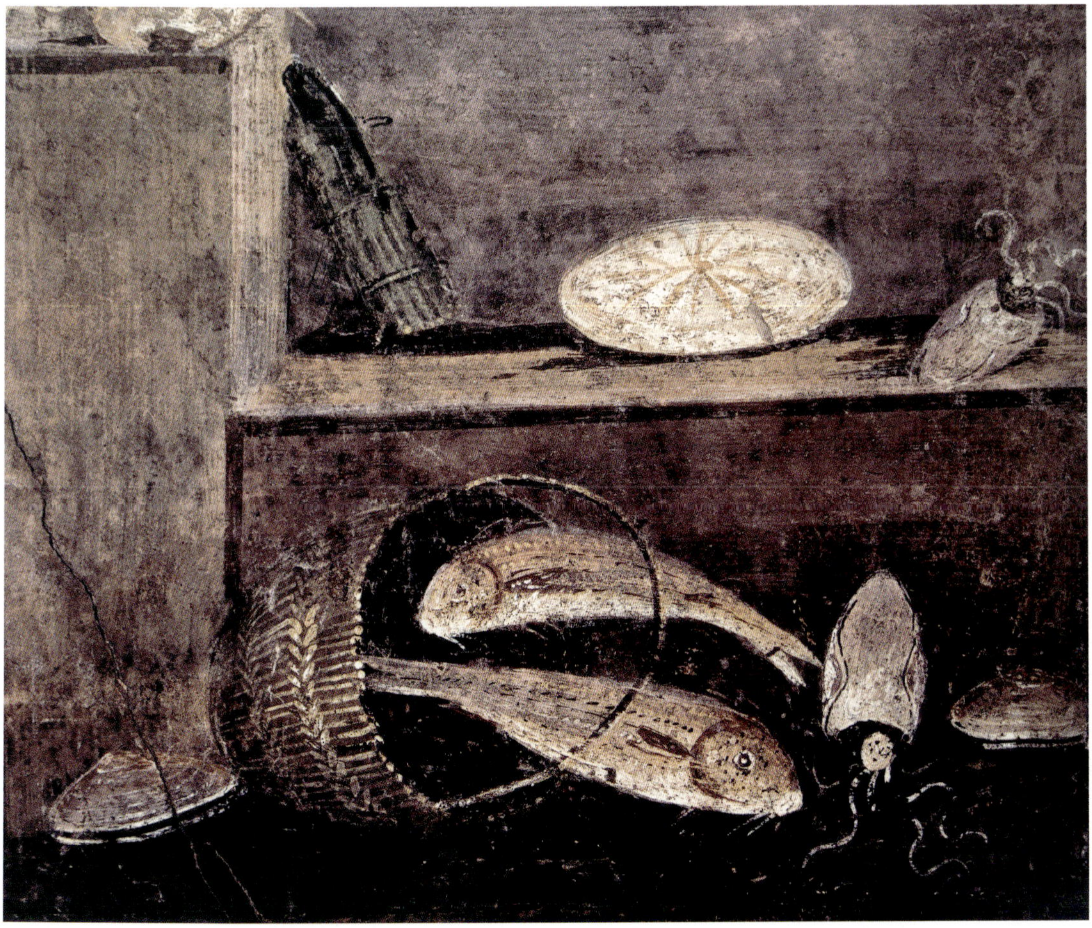

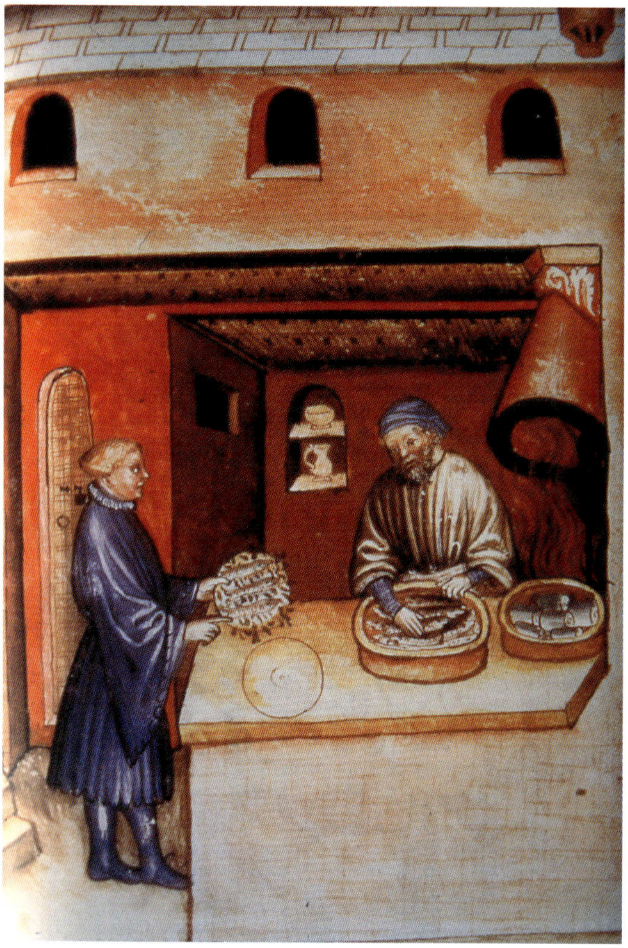

95 Italian kitchen with a cook marinating herrings in vinegar, 14th century.

spits low down for large, whole fish and a grid iron that could be placed over the brazier or on a small fire on the floor carrying smaller fish. A hearth laid on the earth was used for centuries until one built up on bricks made the work less back-breaking, as well as safer for women wearing long skirts.

Italian artists were showing an interest in fish at the same time that Spanish artists began to paint them. The Italians were great fish eaters, having the resources of the Adriatic on the east coast and the Tyrrhenian Sea on the west for a wonderful range of sea fishes, as well as freshwater fishes from the lakes, rivers Tiber and Po and the marshes. Cities on the coast, such as Naples, had an abundance of different kinds of fishes all the year round and thus at good prices. Of all their fishes the sturgeon was the most highly prized for centuries. Golden bream were also favoured, with sea bass, turbot, sole, red mullet, scorpion, octopus and squid and many more. Eels were also widely appreciated, particularly because they could be carried over relatively long distances in grass-filled baskets and could survive for days outside water. Tench were highly regarded and supplied by fishermen from Lakes Como and Maggiore, Tagliacozzo and Vico and Santa Preseda, supplying the large cities of Milan and Rome, but the best were thought to be those caught in the Tiber and Po.

The Italian artist presenting the most species in his paintings was Giuseppe Recco (1645–1695). His canvases are full of exciting species

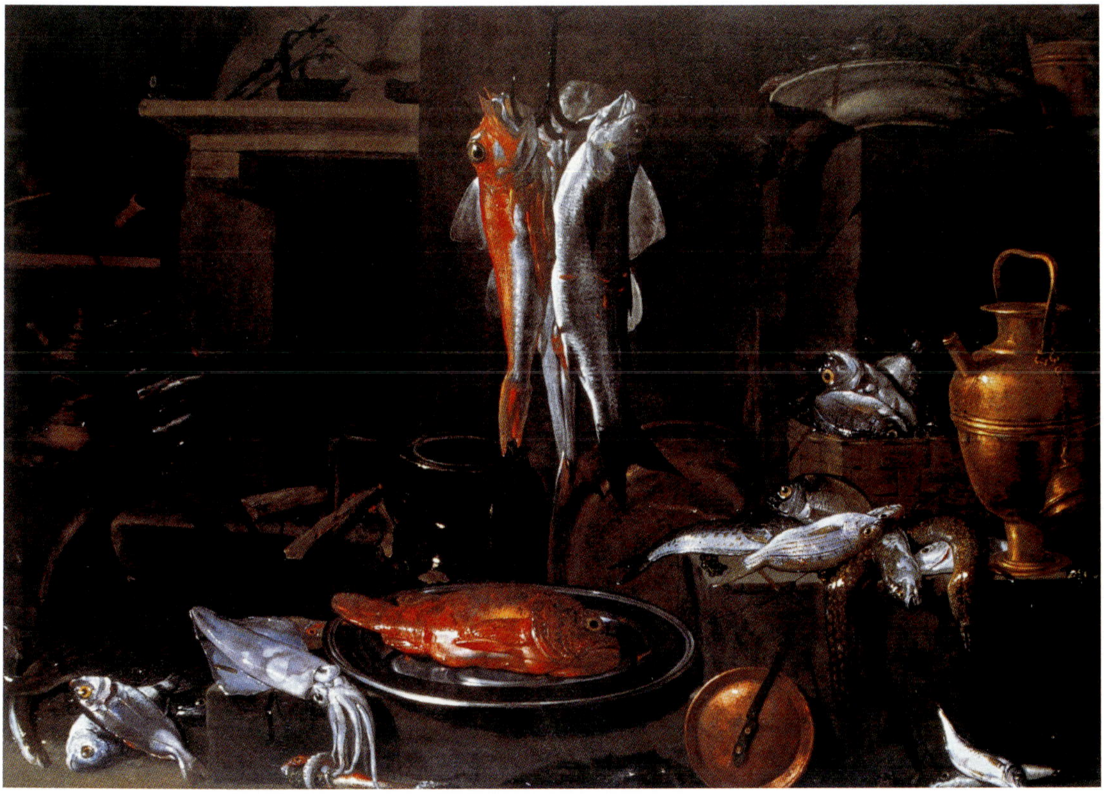

96 Giuseppe Recco, *Kitchen Interior with Fishes*, *c.* 1660, oil on canvas.

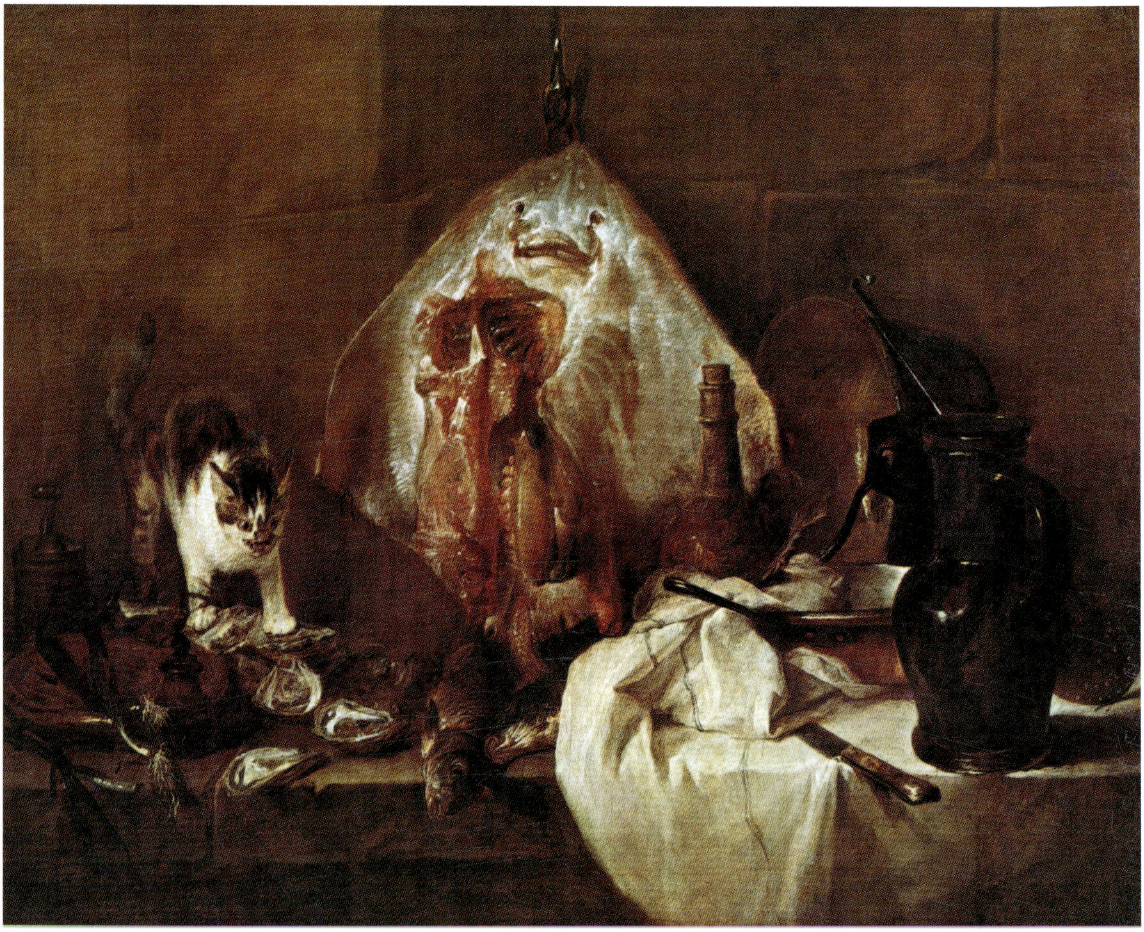

97 Jean-Baptiste-Siméon Chardin, *The Ray*, 1738, oil on canvas.

such as pandora, cuttlefish, skipper, hake, as well as the favourite bream. His kitchen scenes are authentic with fish suspended from hooks hanging from the ceiling, fish on plates and tables, with pans and utensils at the ready for the cook. He enjoyed painting copper bowls, plates and jugs. Born in Naples, his interest in food was typically Neapolitan with fish predominating, though he painted the more expensive fish rather than the oysters and mussels that were the common ingredients of cooking for the poor in this port.

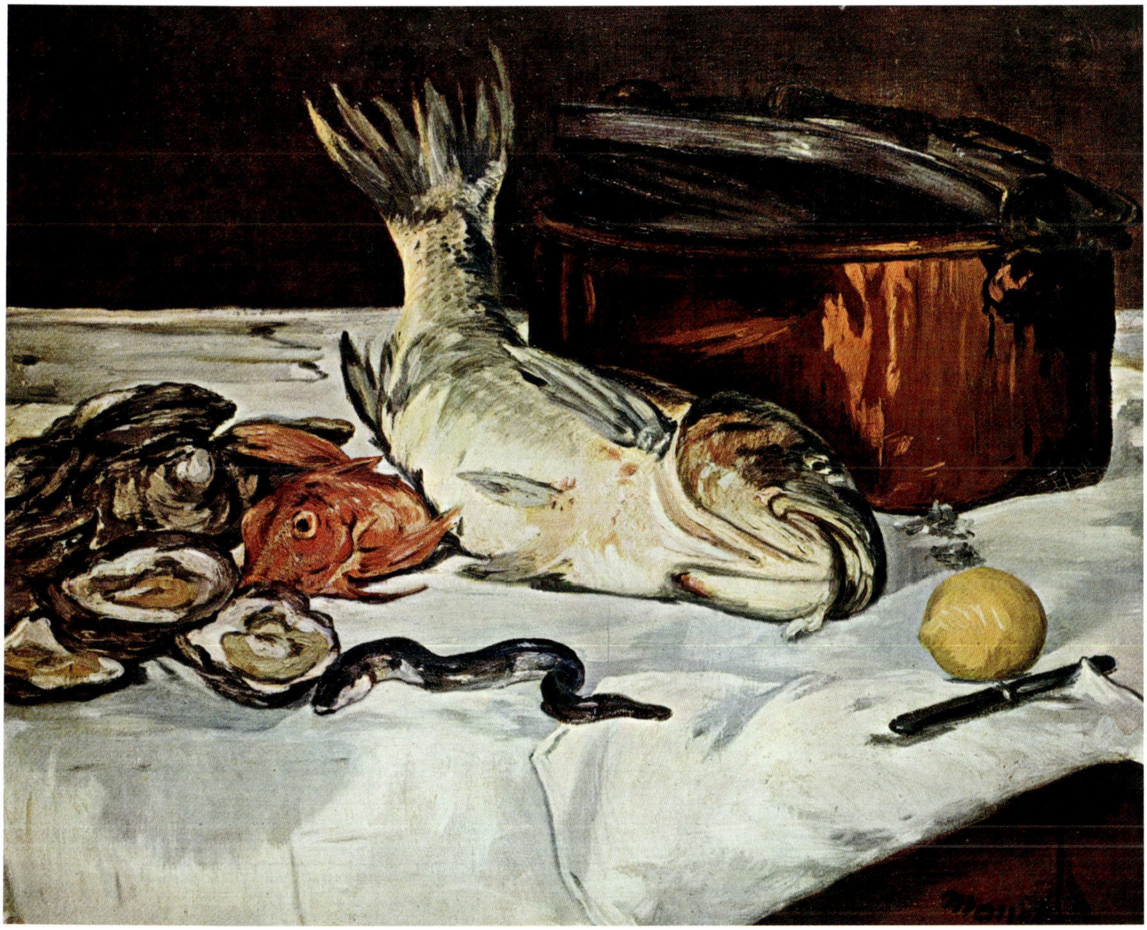

98 Edouard Manet, *Still-life with Salmon, Gurnard, Eel, Oysters and Lemon,* 1864, oil on canvas.

Among the finest still-life painters of the eighteenth century was Jean-Baptiste Siméon Chardin (1699–1779). He frequently painted fish, this painting of a ray being among his earliest and done about the time he was accepted as a member of the Académie de Peinture et de Sculpture in Paris. On the right of the ray are kitchen utensils and on the left an apprehensive cat, back arched and tail twitching as it treads among the carp and oysters. Edouard Manet also painted a salmon with gurnard, oysters and an eel, during the summer of 1864 while he was at

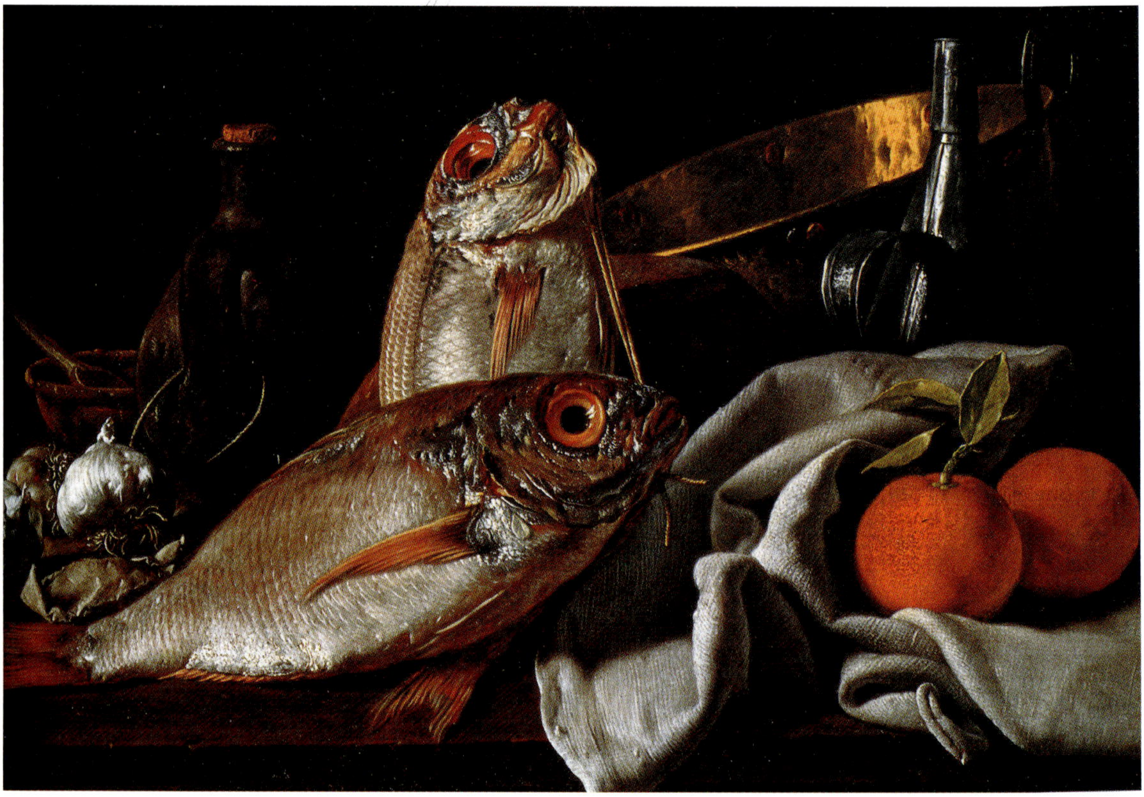

99 Luis Meléndez, *Still-life with Sea Bream and Oranges,* 1772, oil on canvas.

Boulogne-sur-Mer. A cooking pot rests on the table behind the fishes. Five years later Manet gave a lesson on still-life painting to his pupil Eva Gonzalès: 'Get it down quickly. Don't worry about the background. Just go for tonal values.' He recommended rendering the subjects in such a way as to make the same impression on the viewer as on the painter, pointing out that when looking at the whole 'you don't try to count the scales on the salmon . . . you see them as little silver pearls against grey and pink'.

Two important Spanish artists of the eighteenth century returned to the subject of fish and placed them in the kitchen. Luis Meléndez (1716–1780) featured two large bream in his *Still-life with Sea Bream and Oranges*, signed and dated 1772. It was such a beautifully rendered and virtuoso work of art and realism that, by request, he painted it three times. The best-known version hangs in the Prado. He also painted a magnificent steak of salmon with a lemon. His more famous compatriot Goya also painted a salmon steak but was outdone on this occasion.

It was not until the nineteenth century that a British artist took an interest in portraying fishes. The British had been largely preoccupied with portrait painting until the end of the eighteenth century when their attention switched to history and landscape painting. When British artists finally took notice of fish it was only because fishing had become a great sporting activity. That some fish ended up in the kitchen and were worthy of attention for their colour, shape and intriguing wetness seems first to have been noticed by Charles Keene. His limpid, wet fishes look as though they had been laid on the floor in *Still-life with Fish* of about 1860.

Across the Atlantic William Merritt Chase painted *Still-life with Fish*, *c.* 1903, now in the Brooklyn Museum, New York, depicting a large skate/ray and fish kettle.

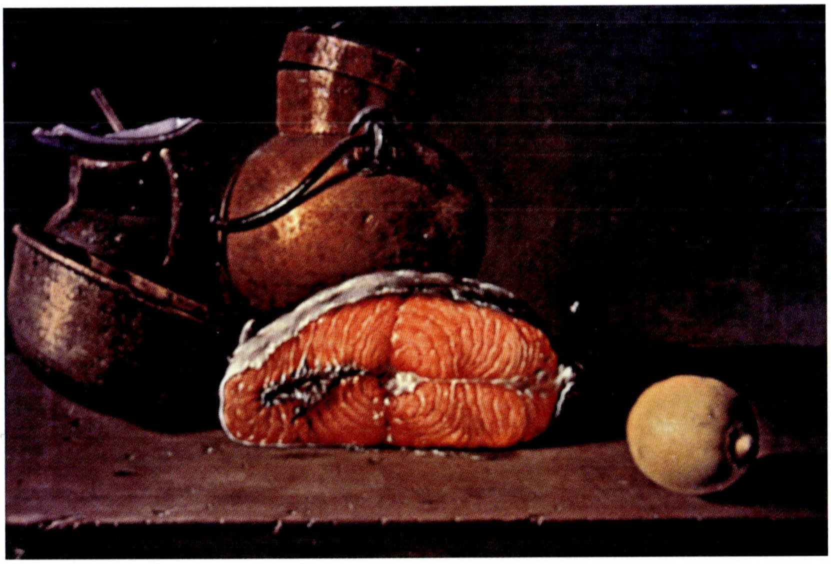

100 Luis Meléndez, *Salmon Slice with Lemon*, 1772, oil on canvas.

However, both British and American artists preferred to portray their fishes lying on a riverbank, so there are very few nineteenth- and twentieth-century kitchen scenes or still-lifes of fishes in the kitchen. A notable exception, Peter Coker (1926–2004), painted the sparse kitchen scene *Fish with Grill*, with some bread, which serves to indicate what is today regarded as a healthy way of cooking fish.

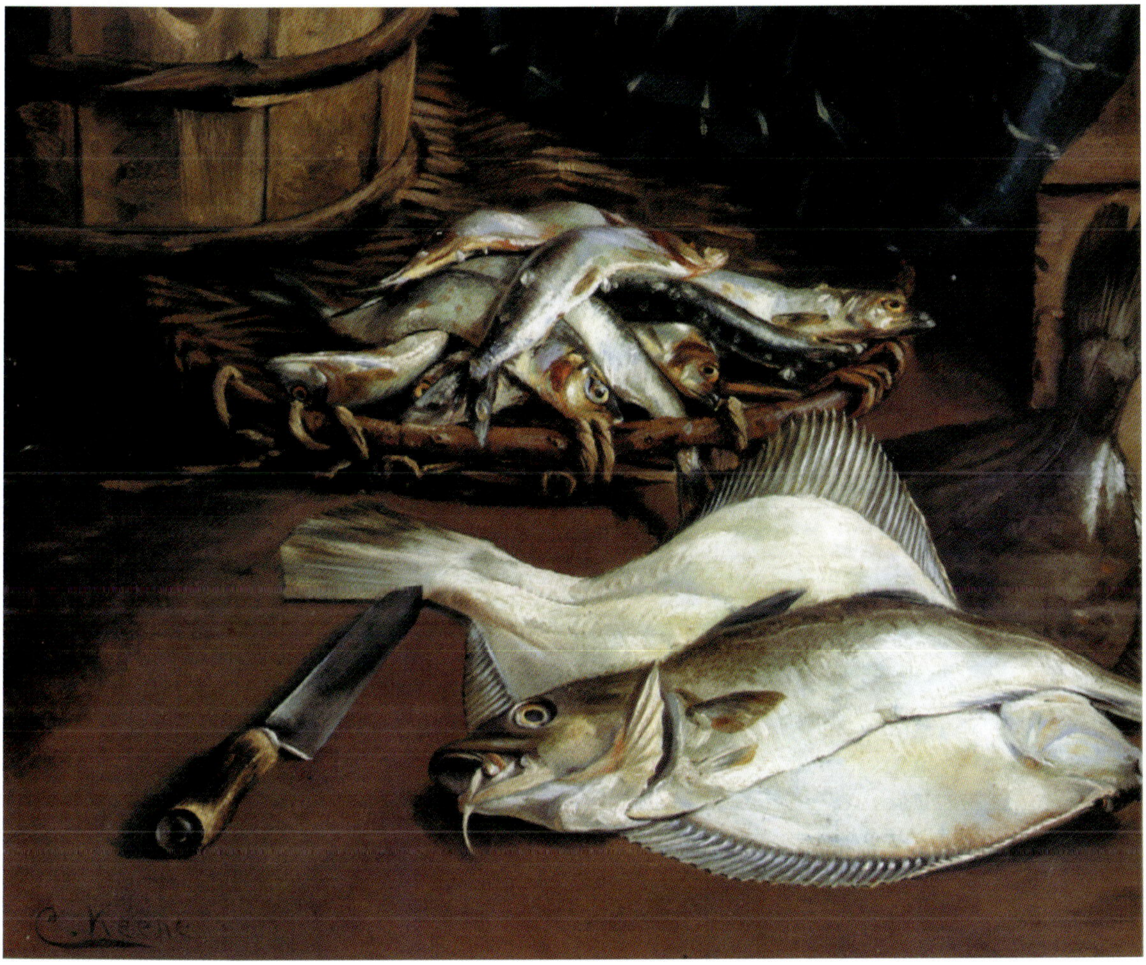

101 Charles Keene, *Still-life with Fish*, detail, *c.* 1860, oil on canvas.

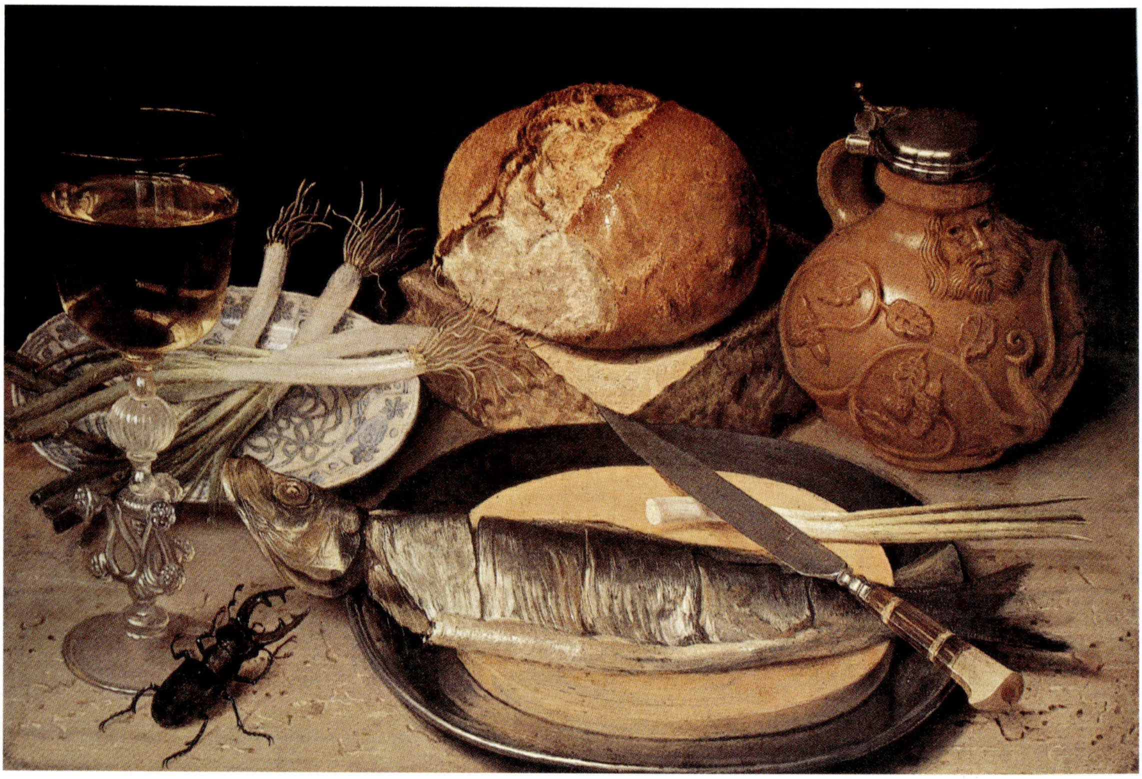

102 Georg Flegel, *Still-life with Stag Beetle*, 1635, oil on panel.

five
Fish on the Table

When fishes were displayed on market stalls they were arranged on a tilted surface. The stone slabs or wooden tables of the stalls were at an angle so that the fish could drain. Coincidentally, the angle facilitated the easy viewing of an attractive arrangement. The market subject included people and backdrops showing other activities giving artists many features and opportunities for lively scenes.

Artists painting fish on the table, on the other hand, mostly painted a still-life scene, devoid of people and movement. Only a few fish would be on the table and those sometimes all the same species. Usually, the fish still-life had a small number of additional, simple elements. The different textures and tonal values, the hard glossy surfaces of metal, glass and earthenware vessels and plates were balanced against the soft material of the tablecloth. Additional colours were provided by onions, lemons, wine or beer and bread. Each object was meticulously painted. The greatest challenge, however, was the flat fish on a flat plate on a flat table surface. The viewer was not standing back, as in market scenes, but now had to be close up to the table, looking down onto it. The painting of the fish on the plate needed to be accurate, more detailed and realistic for this closer, intimate view.

Several still-life paintings of breakfasts show herrings cut with a knife and the knife laid alongside the fish. The knives in the Dutch and German paintings, for example in those of Pieter Claesz and Georg Flegel, were sharply pointed. No table forks were used in the Low Countries or Britain before the late 1600s. The knife was used to spear meat and firm fish and convey it to the mouth. Crumbly food was picked up by the fingers and sauces mopped up with bread. Though very large forks were used in the kitchen for lifting joints of meat, small table forks were not considered proper eating utensils by English gentlemen until the 1680s. This was despite Thomas Coryat, upon his return from Italy, attempting to introduce them. In 1608 he had set out on a walking tour through Paris, Lyons, Turin, Venice, Zurich and finally Strasbourg. He walked for 3,180 kilometres (1,975 miles) and three years later, back in England, wrote *Coryat's crudities; hastily gobled up in five months' travels.* He explained that an Italian could not 'by any means indure to have his dish touched with fingers, seeing all mens fingers are not alike cleane'. No dipping into a dish with everyone else for the Italians (unlike their Roman antecedents)! They had adopted the use of forks instead of fingers, a use learned from the Greeks. At the time Coryat was writing Italians were thought to be very refined in their manners, especially when dining. Despite this Coryat was mocked and given the nickname 'Furcifer' (Italian for forked, Latin *furca*, fork). It took another eighty years for the English and the Dutch to adopt a two-pronged fork to help them eat more elegantly. The three-pronged fork followed soon after. Not until Victorian times were specially designed silver and electroplated fish knives and forks manufactured.

Breakfast

The *ontbijt*, a breakfast or light meal, was frequently depicted in the seventeenth century by Dutch and Flemish artists. Invariably the herring was the main ingredient. The table was covered with a runner and a carefully ironed white damask cloth with its creases running towards the back of the painting. Accompanied by a loaf of bread, an onion and lemon, with a drink in a glass or rumer, it appears to be the simplest of meals and yet in such paintings there lie many interpretations and meanings, both obvious and hidden.

At its most basic, the herring painting represents the poor man's breakfast or the cottagers' meal. Herrings were plentiful and therefore

ONCE 1.3–2 million tonnes of herring (*Clupea harengus*) were caught annually, but this is now much reduced because of overfishing of the young. Members of the herring family form one of the most important of the world's fisheries resources. They live in the North Atlantic and spawn around the coast of Norway. In mid-autumn the waters of the North Sea get colder and the banks of herrings that have spent the summer in Scandinavian waters move southwards. When summer warms the water in their southern habitat they move back north again. A bloater is a whole herring that has been soaked in brine before being cold smoked and is thus raw.

cheap, available all year round, even though salted during part of the year, and entirely approved of by church and state. The state derived so much of its wealth from herrings that everyone was encouraged to eat them. They were a safe, wholesome food, and very tasty into the bargain.

The frugality of the seventeenth-century breakfast contrasts with today's Low Countries breakfast with its array of hams and other cooked meats, cheeses and a variety of breads. The old, sparse breakfast was compatible with the idea of the herring meal being suitable Lenten fare. When the herring in a painting was placed between a loaf of bread and a flagon or glass of liquid, the eucharistic inferences reinforced the impression that the artist was painting a Lenten repast. During Lent fish replaced meat for everybody, though in many poor households it was a basic meal at all times of the year. For impoverished artists, the advantage they derived from the popularity of food paintings was that they could paint the herring, then eat it.

Several paintings show the herring cut into portions, sometimes cleverly retaining the outer contours of the body by slicing it to within an inch of the edge. The herrings in the paintings appear to be raw, or may be processed in several ways, for they are very versatile fish for cooking purposes. They may be eaten raw, cooked fresh, pickled in brine (today most often in the form of rollmops), hot or cold smoked. They have excellent roes both hard (female) and soft (male) and are delicious soused.

Economically they were so important that they had a profound effect on the maritime history of Europe, leading to wars to maintain control over their habitats. Charlemagne (King of the Franks, *c.* 742–814, crowned Emperor of the West by Pope Leo III in 800) founded the fortified port of Hamburg in order to defend the herring fleet. The ports at Bremen,

Rostock and Lübeck formed a group that became known as the Hanseatic League. In the thirteenth century the League ports fought with Denmark over herring fishing rights and Copenhagen was burned to the ground in 1242. The League had stations in several places, including Bruges, Bergen and Novgorod. In 1406 Hanseatic fishermen caught 96 Englishmen fishing off Bergen and bound them hand and foot before throwing them overboard to drown. Only when the Scandinavian countries joined together could the Hanseatic League ports' fishermen be held in check.

The expansion of ports along the Dutch coast, leading to that nation's great prosperity in the seventeenth century, was built on their teeming banks of herring. The Dutch were well aware of the importance of this fish to their economic welfare, for they not only ate quantities of fish but also exported it. For this reason their artists painted the fish with respect and in loving detail to record its vital influence in their lives and that of their nation.

In Claesz's *Fish Still-life,* the fish has been cut into small parallel pieces arranged alternately and set against the edge of the plate to emphasize the herring's original contours. The same method of cutting up herring can be seen in several other Dutch and Flemish paintings. There can be no doubt that this fish has Lenten associations. It parallels the German artist Flegel's still-life of 1635 where the herring has also been cut up, though without any sophisticated pattern or ornamentation. Flegel emphasized the fasting motif more clearly with leeks on the table to show that it was a humble meal. Placed between the eucharistic symbols of bread and wine, evil also is present, in the form of a stag beetle.

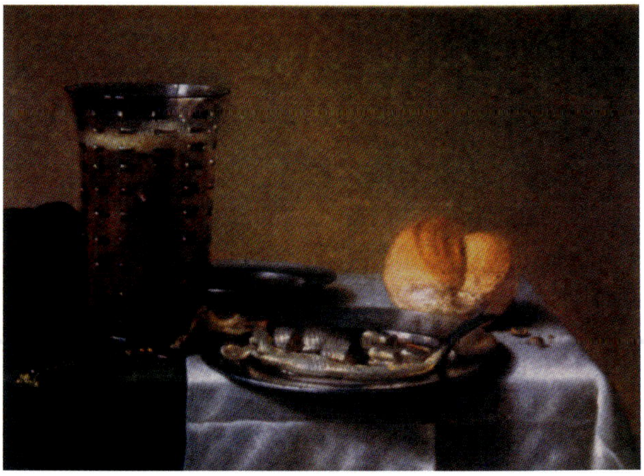

103 Pieter Claesz, *Fish Still-life*, 1636, oil on panel.

Joseph de Bray (*c.* 1630–1664) gave this picture the title *Lof van den Pekelharingh, In Praise of Pickled Herring.*

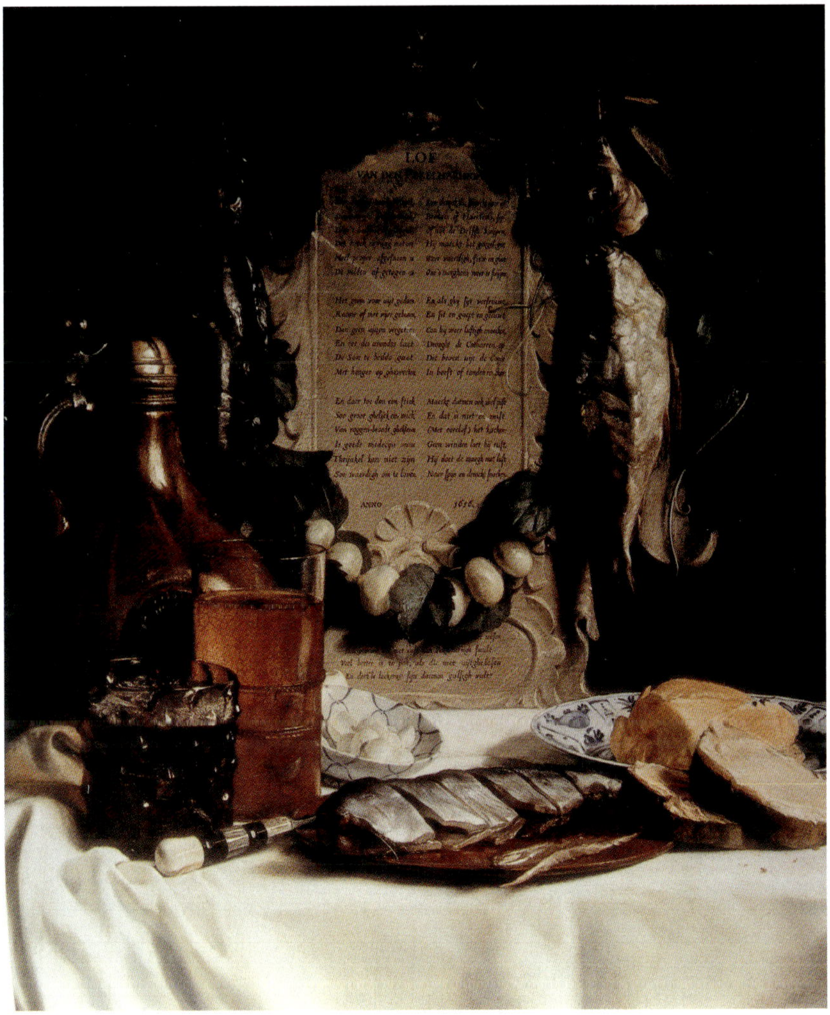

104 Joseph de Bray, *In Praise of Pickled Herring*, 1656, oil on panel.

The tablet in the centre is inscribed with a poem by his uncle extolling the virtues of herring for good health. He recommended eating these oily fish with crisp rye bread and butter, onions and beer.

Britain's herring fleets off the east coast caught thousands of fish during the summer and there was a big salting and pickling industry to process them for travel inland. At first, they were preserved in a very primitive fashion by salting in heaps on the shore without even being gutted. In the fourteenth century the methods of the Dutchman Willem Beukels were adopted: the herrings were gutted and soaked for about

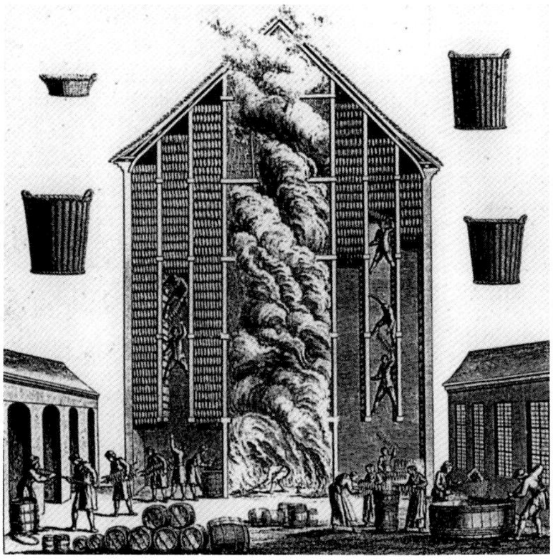

105 Henri-Louis Duhamel du Monceau (inspecteur général de la Marine), *Making Red Herrings*, engraving in *Traité général des pesches* (1760–77). *Making Red Herrings* shows the master smoker who kept up the fire (in the centre) with smokers who withdrew the herrings from the brine and put them to drain in baskets. The women strung them onto wands and handed them to men who hung them in the louvres (on the left). When smoked, they were taken down and handed over to be counted and examined for rejects, before being passed to be packed in barrels.

fifteen hours in brine before being barrelled up in rows between layers of dry salt to produce 'white herrings' that thus became a year-round food resource. Smoking herrings was a development of the same period. The fish were first soaked in brine then hung up and smoked in special chimneys for many hours and finally barrelled as 'red herrings'. The centre of the British herring industry was the Norfolk port of Yarmouth. In 1108, when the town was made a borough by Henry I, the annual payment to the Crown for this recognition was 10 milliards (defined as one thousand million) of herring. Herring pies were also common medieval rents; the city of Norwich was bound by ancient charter to send a hundred herring baked in 24 pies annually to the king, who regarded them as delicacies. The French also prospered on herrings and from Dieppe to Boulogne all the way along the coast boats put in with great catches that were transferred to fishmongers' baskets and taken to Paris.

Eating salted fish created a great thirst and a consequent large consumption of ale. The inevitable result was that there was much drunkenness – especially during that period of fasting and abstinence called 'Lent', when the consumption of salted fish increased considerably while meat was forbidden. The increase in drunkenness during Lent was remarked upon by several authors.

On 12 February 1429 pickled herrings were responsible for a neologism that remains in use to this day. At the height of the Hundred Years War a force under the distinguished soldier and veteran of Agincourt (1415), Sir John Fastolf or Falstaff, was taking provisions, largely in the form of pickled herrings, to the English troops besieging Orleans. They were attacked by a much larger French unit but swiftly drew up a defensive position using the barrels of herrings to build a wall from behind which they shot at the French, eventually getting the better of their attackers.

Shooting arrows from the protection of such a makeshift defensive wall was a battlefield novelty and, taking its name from the Old French *barrique*, Spanish *barrica* meaning 'barrel', the construction became known as a 'barricade'. The encounter itself was forever after called the 'Battle of the Herrings'.

In the Elizabethan period herrings caught in distant waters were, like cod, salted at sea, but the North Sea herring fishery was run by the Dutch and not until early in the nineteenth century did a Scottish fleet develop and later a British herring industry, peaking just before 1914, when around 350 million tonnes were landed annually. Ships fished in early autumn off the coast of East Anglia. The ports of Grimsby, Great Yarmouth and Lowestoft were packed in the early twentieth century by steam drifters.

Kippers were more popular for the British breakfast table. These are whole herrings split and gutted but with the head and tail left on, then smoked.

Luncheon

Luncheon originated in Britain in the late sixteenth century as a snack, usually of bread and cheese, to fill the gap between an early breakfast and mid-day dinner. In the eighteenth century dinner gradually became eaten at an ever later hour, so luncheon moved to mid-day. Jean-François de Troy's painting of an oyster luncheon is a midday meal and a very elegant one. It was painted in 1734 when oysters were plentiful. Large numbers of oysters are being consumed accompanied by champagne from the bottles in the ice-chest. No forks are on the table, only several tongue-slittingly sharp knives about which English travellers complained bitterly – and sorely – when travelling in France. The champagne glasses were rinsed and cooled in the fine porcelain bowls containing cold water.

When Low Countries artists, such as Claesz, Es and Beert, were lovingly painting detailed and realistic pictures of open oysters lying in

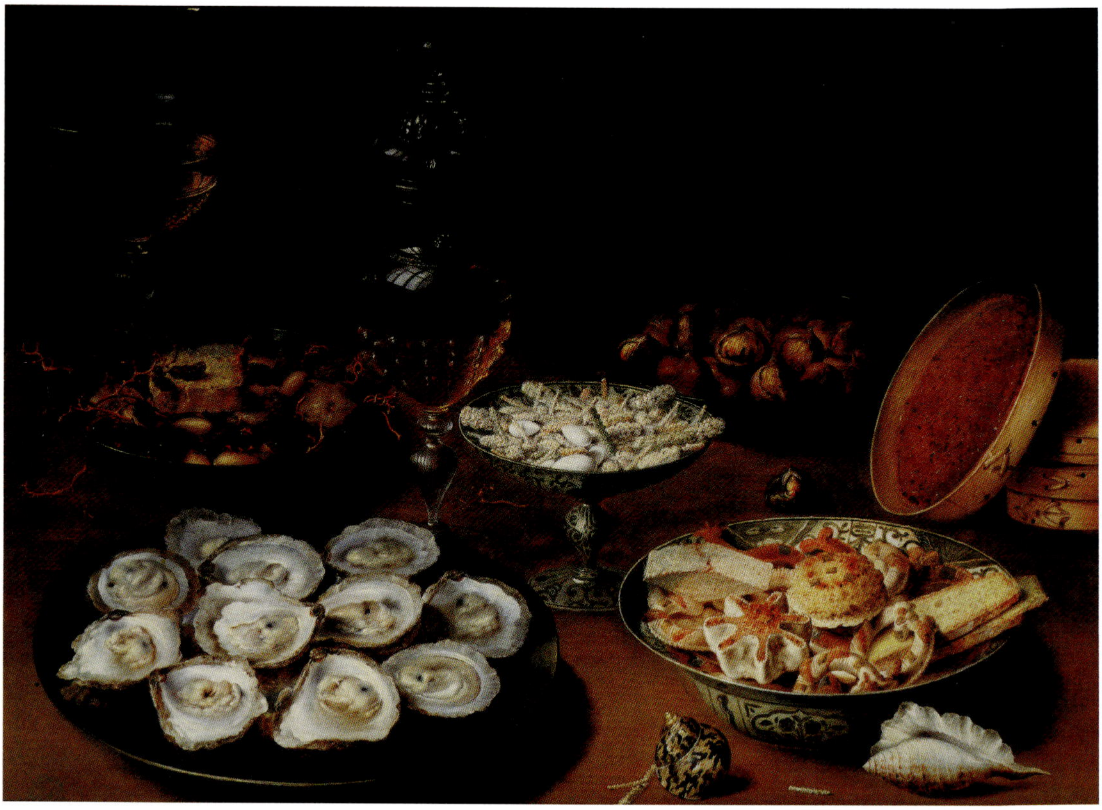

106 Osias Beert the Elder (*c.* 1580–1623), *Still-life: Breakfast with Oysters, and Sweets*, oil on panel.

their shells, the shell had a symbolic meaning that had been given to it in a third-century book about animals, *Physiologus*. Describing the behaviour of animals in 55 chapters, it relates them to Christian doctrine. The shell is symbolically likened to Mary, who gave birth to the 'pearl of great price', Jesus. When Beert and fellow Low Countries artists painted oysters in their shells, they had this innocent meaning. Jan Steen's *Girl Eating Oysters* is a less than innocent Dutch oyster meal. This carries the other symbolic meaning of oysters, that of an aphrodisiac. The sly look of this young lady, and the bed behind her, clearly suggest this other meaning.

There are four EUROPEAN OYSTER species, but most important is the common oyster *Ostrea edulis* from the celebrated localities Whitstable in Kent and Colchester in Essex. Oysters native to Britain spawn in the summer and so are not sold in summer months (months without *r* in the name) May to August. Highly commercial and eaten in vast quantities, they were one of the earliest victims of overfishing, in both Britain and France in the 1860s. They then became prestige food for the rich at one shilling a dozen. The collective noun is a bed or hive of oysters.

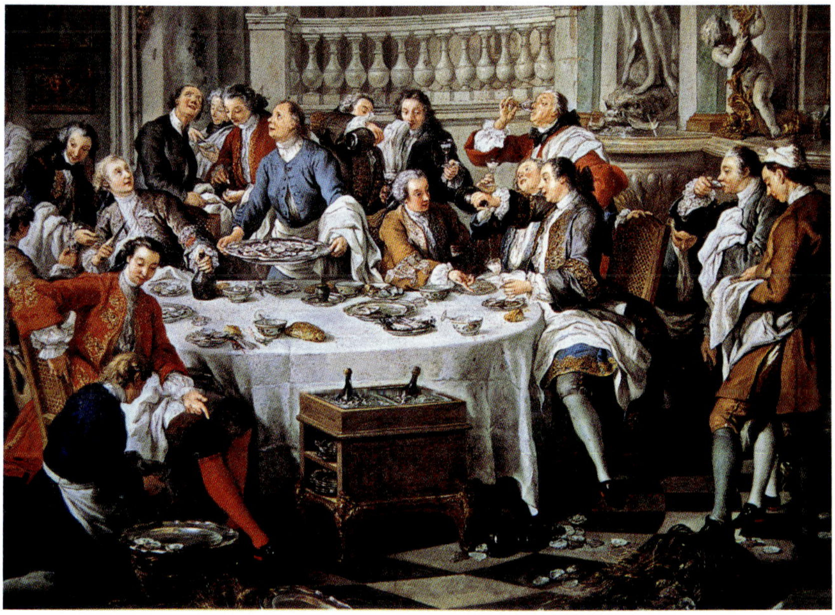

107 Jean-François de Troy, *Oyster Luncheon,* detail, 1734, oil on canvas.

Dinner

Dining out in Roman times involved reclining on one of three couches arranged within reach of a central dining table, which was serviced by slaves from the fourth side. The guests took their own napkins, which they wore round their necks. They ate with the fingers of their right hand (cleaning them on their napkins) while propped up on their left elbows. We know a lot about the fish eaten in ancient Rome and Pompeii from mosaics and wall paintings showing the different varieties on their menus. A fresco found at Pompeii of a still-life with fishes depicts both fishes including red and grey mullets, electric rays, dogfishes, wrasses and moray

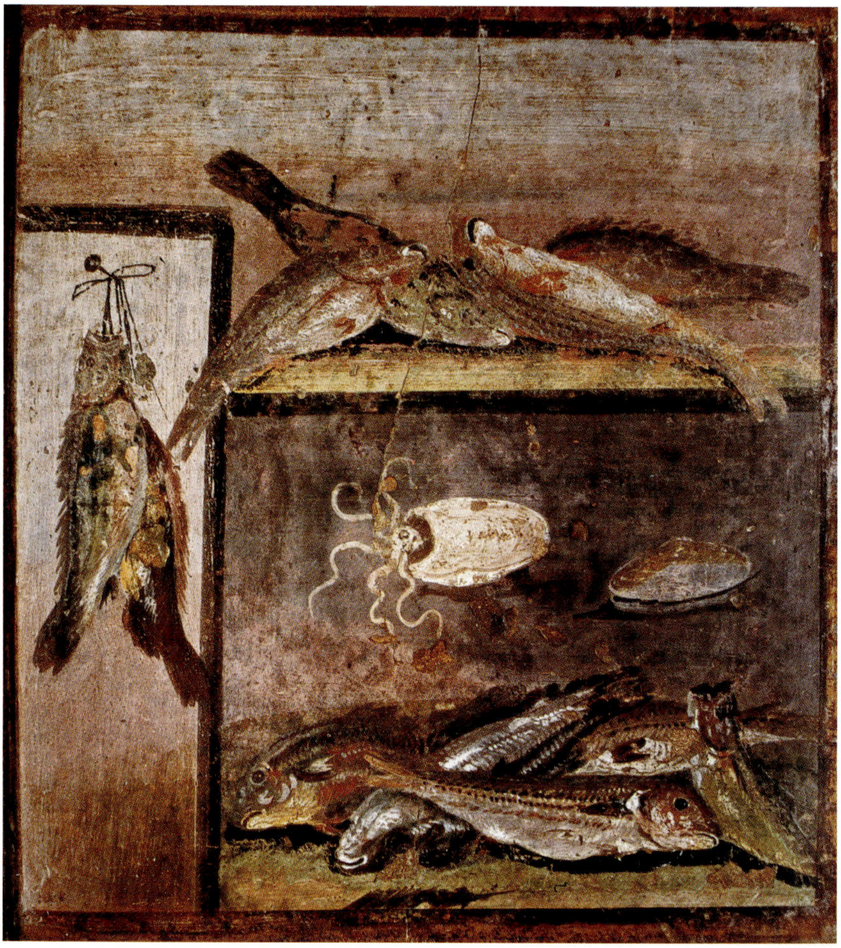

108 Still-life of fishes, fresco found at Pompeii.

eel, and shellfish. From other wall paintings that would decorate a dining room it is clear that clams and cockles, sole, gurnard and squid were plentiful around Naples. In Roman Britain freshwater fishes that were served included eel, dace, perch, pike and carp. Sea fish was popular, as we know from remains of shells of periwinkles, mussels, whelks, cockles and scallops at various sites. Cod, ling, haddock, grey mullet and herring and sea bream were caught, probably with a line and barbed hooks that have also been found on Roman sites.

Until the 1700s an Englishman took his own cutlery with him when he went out to dine. This, for many years, would mean carrying a knife and spoon. For both cook and diner, cutting up food, including

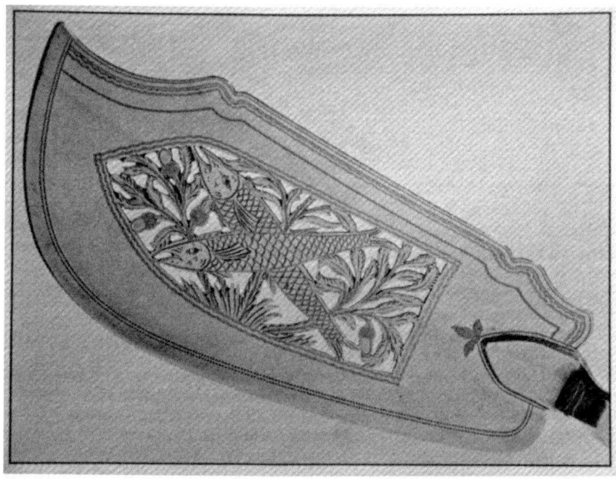

109 Silver fish slice, 1810.

fish, into small pieces and mixing it with fruit and spices to put in a pie was a popular form of presentation. The pie's pastry lid was lifted off and the contents spooned onto individual bread or wooden trenchers (metal plates were used only by the wealthy and only rough earthenware platters and beakers were available before the mid-eighteenth century). The hard pastry case was returned to the kitchen. Most of the population had lost their teeth by middle age, so appreciated soft food such as fish.

After the two-pronged fork was finally accepted, three prongs were the next improvement and, finally, a special fish fork and fish knife, with blades no longer made of steel (for that was thought to rust when used with fish) but silver. The blades now had blunter ends for they were no longer required to spear pieces of food to convey to the mouth. From the mid-nineteenth century the host supplied these separate fish-eaters and would also use a silver server or fish slice. The more elegant fish slice was made in silver and instead of round holes to act as filters, it was pierced with marine patterns, sometimes designs of fish. When made of silver, with silver handles, the fish slice was also used in the dining room to serve the fish.

During the eighteenth century the main meal of the day in Britain lasted from four o'clock in the afternoon until early evening. It consisted of two courses, each with a variety of foods that were arranged on the table symmetrically. The first course was soup or fish and a joint of meat at one end of the table, with side dishes. The second course had two dishes of cooked game and meat at the end of the table, supplemented by cooked puddings. By the mid-nineteenth century this system had been supplanted by a fashion from Russia where each dish was served separately in succession. This method of serving a meal persists today.

The French Impressionists delighted in painting their friends in cafés and at dinner parties, and many dishes of food may be seen in their

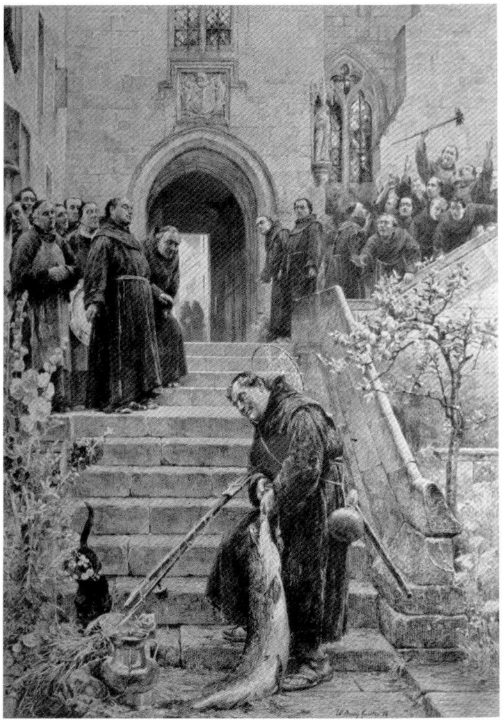

110 Walter Dendy Sadler, *Habet*, etched by L. Muller, 1906, original painting oil on canvas, 1886.

paintings but not sufficiently clearly to recognize the ingredients. There are so many impressionistic dinner parties that it is disappointing that French artists preferred to paint fish as individual studies, for example, Manet's *Salmon, Gurnard, Eel, Oysters and Lemon* (illus. 98) and later Van Gogh's *Still-life with Mackerel*, 1886. In the Parisian cafés of the time Auguste Escoffier was making his name as the father of modern French cuisine. His meal of a first course of soup or melon followed by elaborate fish and shellfish dishes, then a meat or poultry dish with vegetables and finally a dessert, has set the pattern for dining ever since.

A few British artists painted indoor scenes of domestic meals where the food included fish. Tableware now included ceramics in fish shapes. But again there are only indistinct glimpses of the fish on the table. One of the few clear pictures of a fish appears in Walter Dendy Sadler's painting of monks at dinner, *Friday*, but their pike was emphasized in this picture because it had been the subject of two earlier paintings, *Thursday*, when the monks had been depicted fishing on a riverbank, and then *Habet* (Got it!), where a monk was shown carrying the large, newly caught pike. These three were painted during the 1880s when a few Victorian artists re-envisaged monks of medieval times. Sadler's paintings proved to be very popular, mainly because of the strongly individual faces of the monks whose concentration by the river turns into satisfaction and keen anticipation as the pike is carried up the steps to the monastery (in *Habet*) by the monk who had hooked it in the painting *Thursday* (now in Tate Britain). The same monks are seen round the table with the abbot about to carve the pike, and the successful angler is seated two places to the left of the abbot. *Thursday* was painted in 1880 and showed several of the monks by the river, or rather, friends of Sadler dressed in monks' habits. *Friday* was painted in 1882 and exhibited at the Royal Academy, while *Habet* (exhibited at the Royal Academy in 1886) was painted in a different format, the earlier pictures being landscape and *Habet* (present location unknown) a portrait. The set of three prints sold well. *Thursday* and *Friday* were engraved by William Henry Boucher in 1905 and 1904 respectively and *Habet* by Louis Muller in 1906. The detail in the pictures is significant. In *Habet* the steel-rimmed net is carried in such a way as to form a halo round the head of the successful angler. Hollyhocks by the steps were chosen because they were reputedly brought to Europe from the Holy Land in the late sixteenth century. There is an apple tree on the right. Sadler has given the monks two-pronged forks with which to eat their pike but, though he was correct in that early forks were two-pronged, they were not used in England until 150 years after the dissolution of the monasteries. A nice touch is the monastery's black cat coming down the steps to investigate, having caught a scent of fish. These are the kinds of paintings, telling a story, much loved by the Victorians.

111 Walter Dendy Sadler, *Friday*, 1882, oil on canvas.

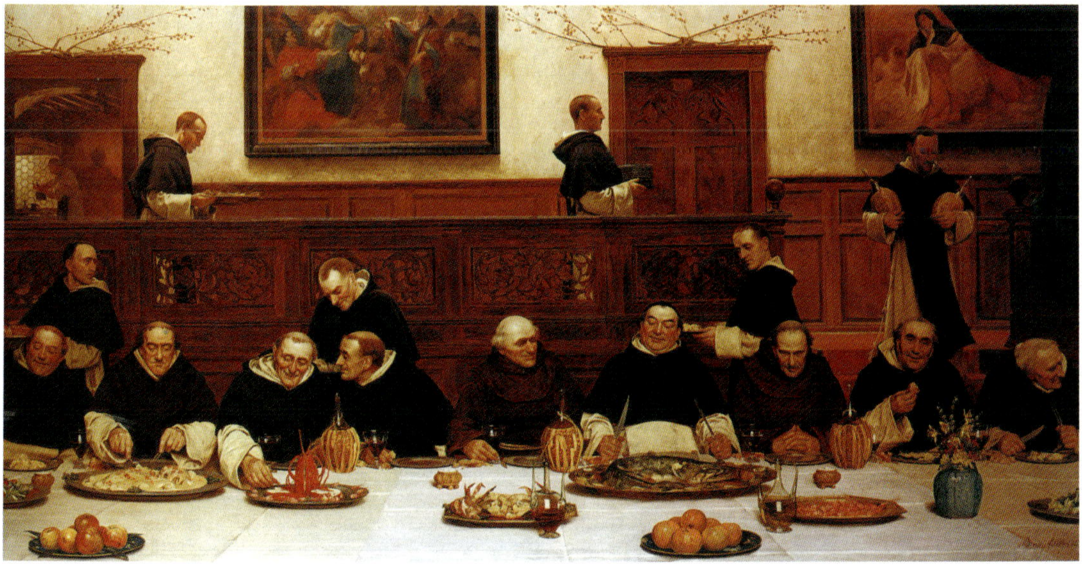

Dinner at home was most likely to be a meal of one species of fish, several of which would be cooked to cater for all members of the family. Willem Hendrick van der Nat painted both a bundle of sprats and loose sprats, with an apple to provide colour. Once very popular, either eaten raw after marinating or fried, this very oily fish is now preferred hot smoked and canned. They are abundant in the Baltic, North Sea and Atlantic. Coarse fishermen use them to entice pike and sea fishermen have caught several species using them as bait, so much so that they have passed into the English language in the proverb 'use a sprat to catch a mackerel', meaning to venture a small expenditure in the hope of a large gain. Lord Mayor's Day in London, 9 November, was known as Sprat Day because it was the opening day of the sprat season. They used to swim up the Thames, where juvenile fish were sold as 'whitebait', a non-existent species name under which the fry of both herrings and sprat were sold. Once so numerous that they were sold at 6 pence per barrel for manuring fields, sprats have suffered greatly from overfishing.

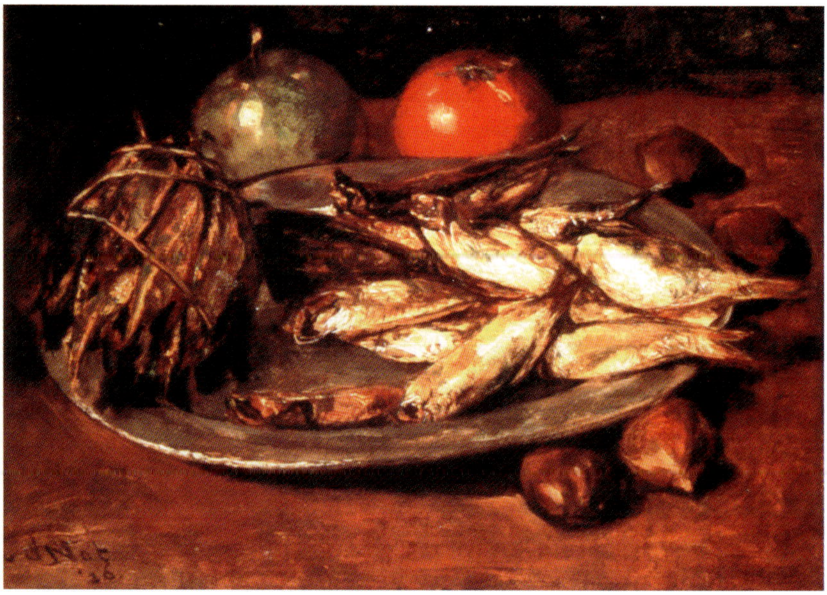

112 Willem Hendrick van der Nat (1864–1929), *Sprats*, oil on panel.

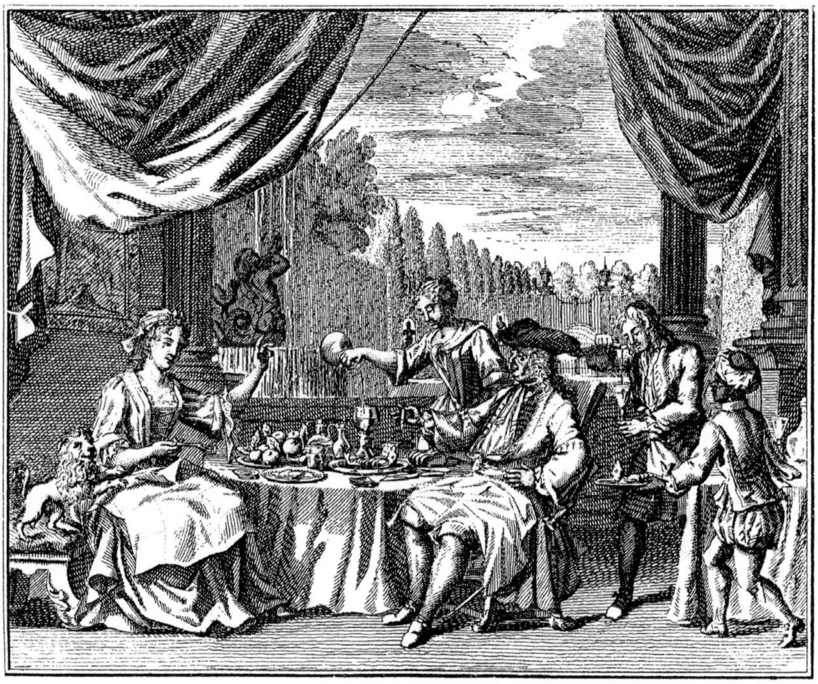

113 *The Herring Banket or Feast*, engraving showing a woman using a two-pronged fork, in the reign of George II (1727–60).

Banquet

By far the most numerous paintings of fish laid out on a table for a meal are banquet scenes. Depictions of exuberant gastronomic delights were greatly appreciated by European patrons and their artists enjoyed supplying them. Painters could indulge in a great splash of colour, a wide range of textures and forms, and include anything edible in a riot of extravagance.

Anyone preparing a banquet would select a quantity of the finest, most colourful and luxurious foods available. For the Europeans of the late seventeenth century, the fishes they would choose would be turbot, sturgeon and rays, but their preference for creating a great impact of colour, shape and flavour would lie with the three crustaceans: lobsters, crabs and shrimps. Lobsters hold centre stage in a large proportion of painted banqueting scenes; the ultimate luxury seafood because of their firm, sweet flesh with a delicious flavour. That these shellfishes were among the most vibrantly colourful examples of seafood when cooked added to the desirability of their inclusion. Artists who recorded banquets,

LOBSTERS are in the order of Decapoda (ten legs), having eyes on stalks and long antennae. They are mainly nocturnal and scavenge dead fish with very large claws or pincers on their front legs and smaller ones on their second and third pairs of legs. The best lobsters live in cold waters. They moult every two years, shedding their outgrown shells. Their colour varies according to habitat, from steel-blue to greenish-brown or reddish-purple. All turn red when cooked.

The European lobster (*Homarus gammarus*) occurs all round British coasts and is caught in lobsterpots. Its life cycle is still only partially known but it is long-lived, twenty years not being unusual, by which time it may be 1 metre (3 feet) long and weigh 5 kg (11 lb). The Norway lobster is smaller, seldom more than 20 cm (8 in); scampi, the Dublin Bay prawn or langoustine is *Nephrops norvegicus* because originally found off Norway but now caught all along the Atlantic coast, in the western Mediterranean and the Adriatic.

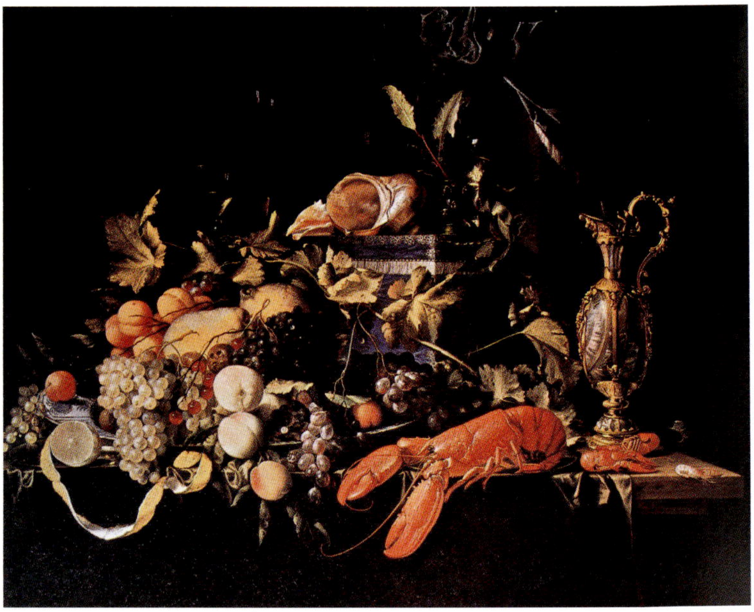

114 Jan Davidsz. de Heem, *Still-life with Fruit and Lobster*, *c*. 1648–9, oil on canvas.

either real or imaginary, nearly all placed a lobster as a focal point and grouped other foods around it. The brilliant scarlet carapace provided the perfect foil for the white, silver or blue-grey tones of other fishes.

Smaller accents of colour, pinkish-red, were provided by shrimps and crabs, occasionally by red fishes such as salmon, mullet or gurnards. Other luxury items of the times were fine fruits, some in baskets, others in valuable ceramic or metal vessels. Rummers of wine added another dimension in texture and colour.

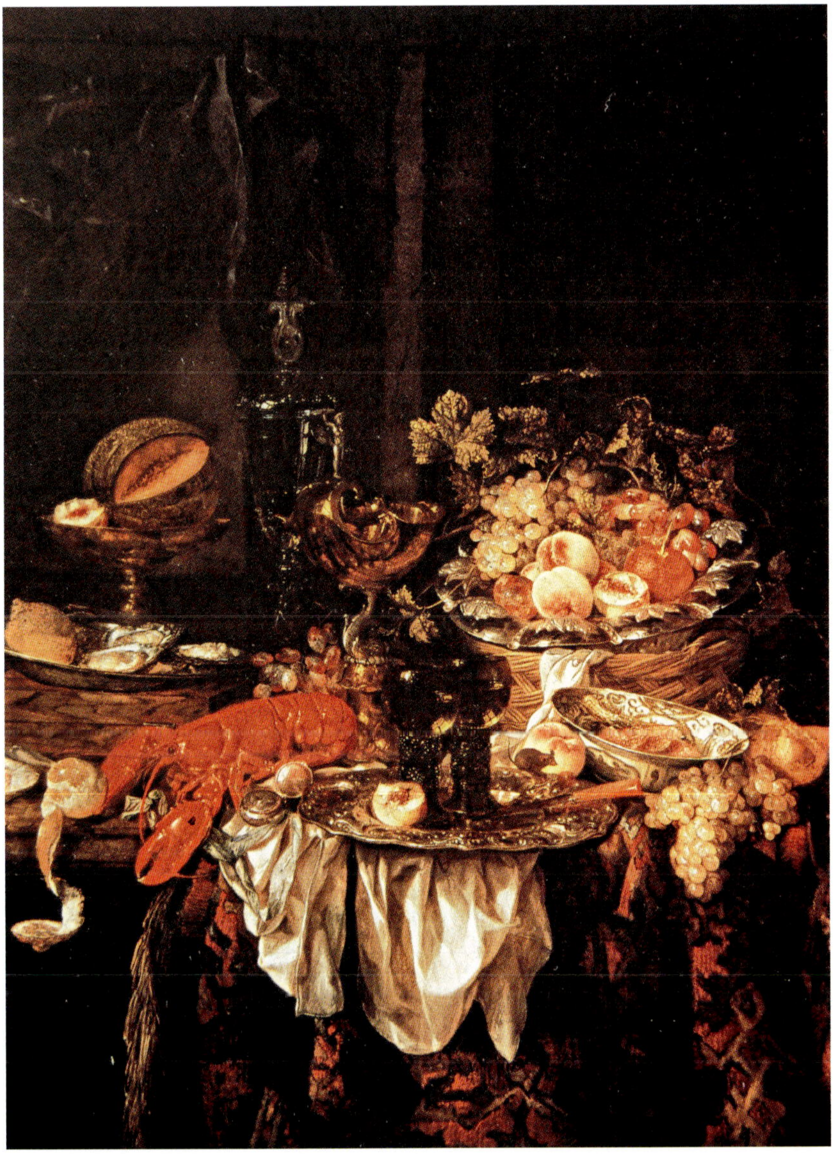

115 Abraham Hendriksz. van Beyeren, *Sumptuous Still-life*, 1667, oil on canvas.

Jan Davidsz. de Heem (1608–1684) moved to Antwerp about 1636 and began to paint increasingly extravagant still-life pictures of flowers, fruit and other foodstuffs, excited by the luxuries that Antwerp afforded a painter. He was responsible for inventing the scene of a table laden with the ingredients for a banquet. This was carried to the last degree of luxury by Abraham van Beyeren of The Hague. In the culture of the aristocracy and middle classes of the seventeenth century onwards the banquet consisted of six to eight courses. The first course was soup and minced meats; the second more bowls of meats; third, big roasts and poultry and game; fourth, small roasts and small birds; fifth, fish and ham, shellfish and turtles, Seville oranges or lemons; sixth, dishes made from butter, ham, eggs, colourful jellies and vegetables; seventh, fruit; eighth, preserves, sweetmeats and confections. Such an array formed the ingredients for a *Sumptuous Still-life* by van Beyeren. A marble-topped table is partially covered by an oriental rug on which are arranged a melon on a gilt tazza and oysters with a lemon on a silver plate. Two of the elaborate containers have fish decoration. The two rummers, filled with white wine, stand on a silver plate decorated with a fish-scale pattern. The gilt beaker with a curling rim and crystal goblet stands on a shell with a foot shaped like a fish. Amid all the splendour a tiny mouse on the edge of a silver dish appears to be regarding a peach as of particular interest for a nibble.

Jan Brueghel the Elder used a collection of ingredients for a banquet for an oil painting. The reason for this wider canvas lies in the title the *Sense of Taste*, for this is one of five canvases illustrating the five senses,

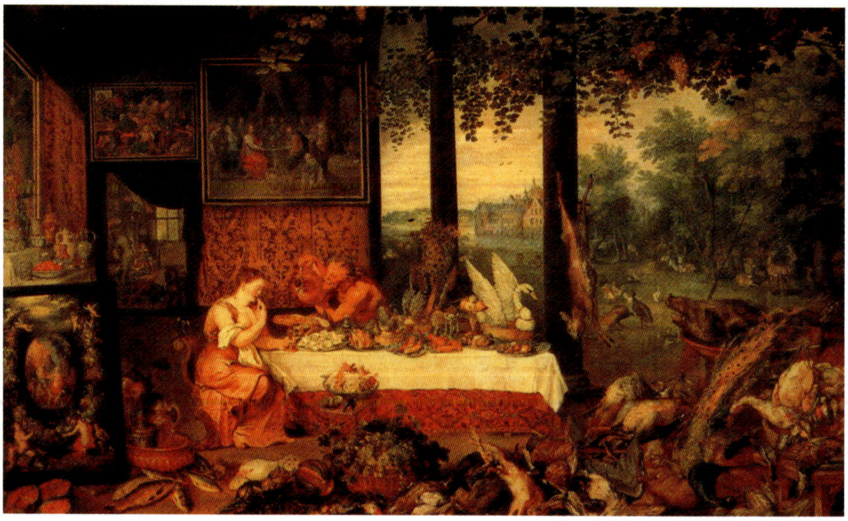

116 Jan Brueghel the Elder, *Sense of Taste*, 1618, oil on wood.

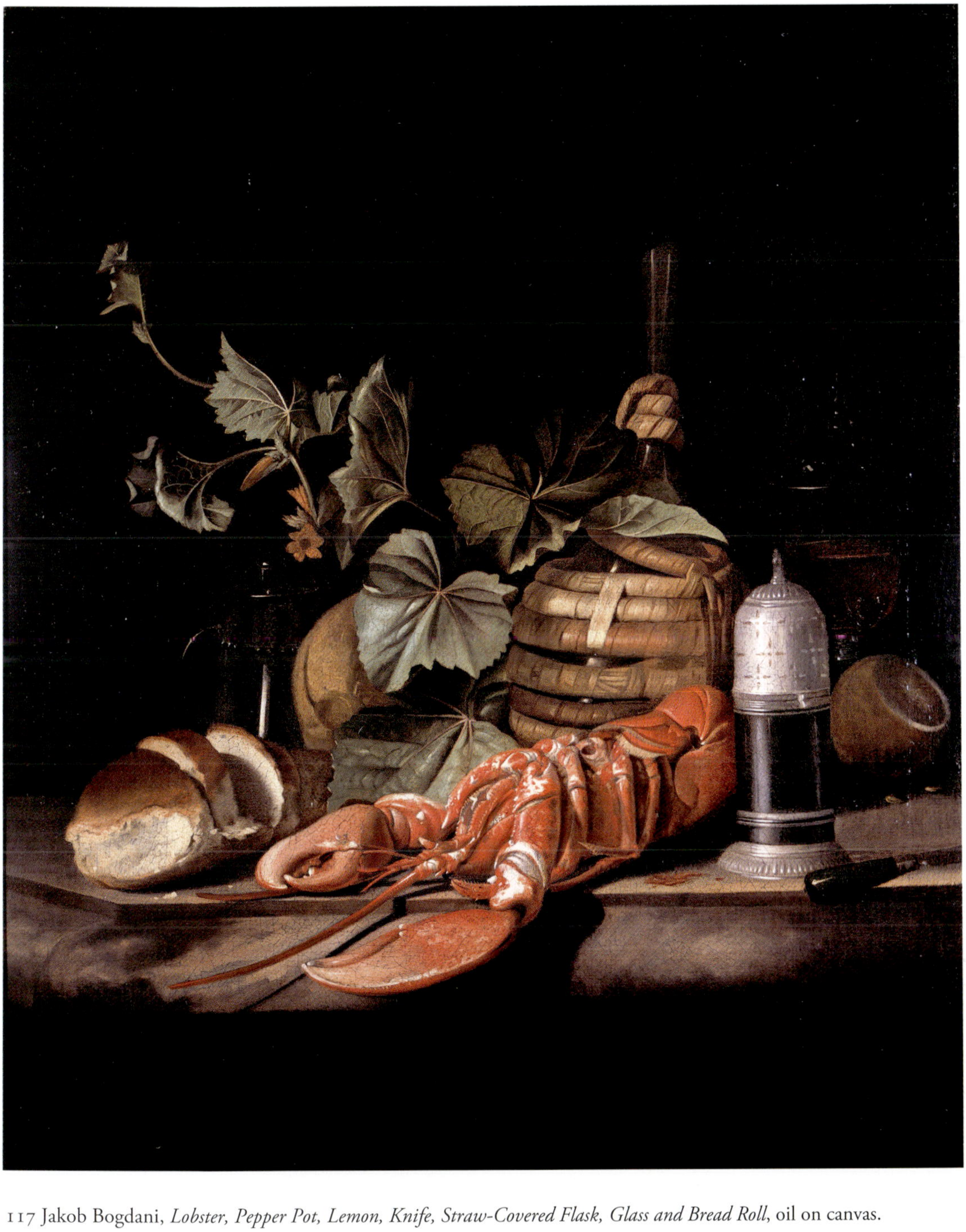

117 Jakob Bogdani, *Lobster, Pepper Pot, Lemon, Knife, Straw-Covered Flask, Glass and Bread Roll*, oil on canvas.

seeing, hearing, smelling, touching and tasting. The white cloth-covered table is laid out with exotic foodstuffs. The uncooked fishes lie on the floor in the left foreground and appear to be less important than the birds, especially the magnificent swan pie that has already been prepared.

Jakob Bogdani (1660–1724) was content with just a lobster seasoned with a lemon and pepper accompanied by wine from a straw-covered flask, with a handy knife.

Supper

The most famous supper in history was hosted by Jesus Christ and attended by his twelve Apostles, the 'Feast of the Passover', which came to be known by Christians as the Last Supper since it occurred just before Christ's death. Apart from unleavened bread and wine we do not know what they ate but, traditionally, whether represented in art as a simple meal or symbolically as the Institution of the Eucharist, or communion, from very early times the fish Ichthys was on the table, and came to symbolize Christ.

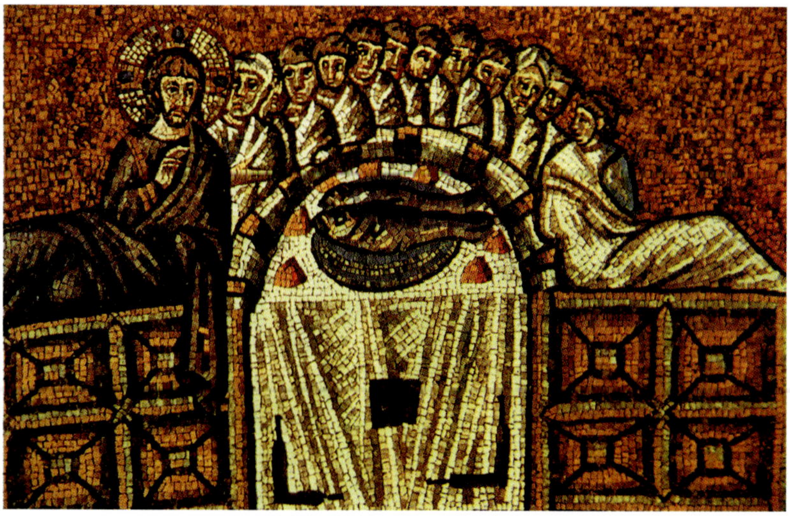

118 A 5th-century mosaic of the *Last Supper* in the Basilica Sant'Apollinare near Ravenna. Jesus and the disciples are reclining, like Roman diners.

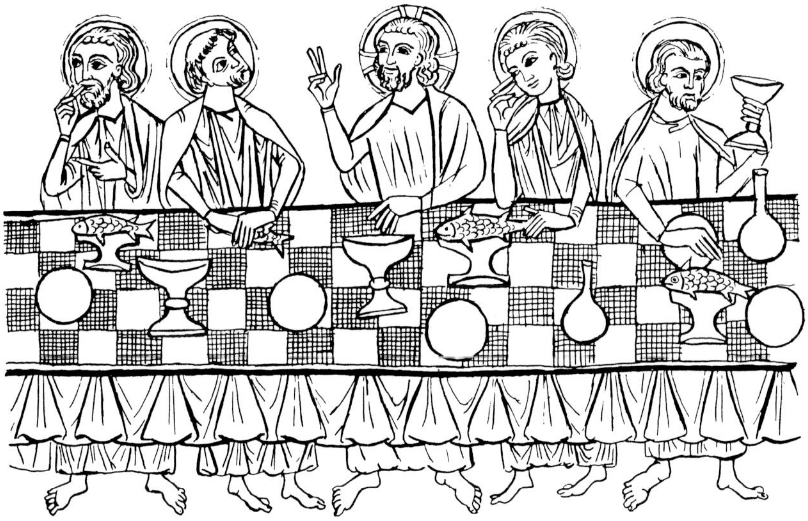

119 A Spanish portrayal of the Last Supper, painted on a 13th-century wood panel. The diners are sitting up to the table, but there is still no cutlery.

A mosaicist working at the basilica of Sant'Apollinare in the fifth century, harboured no doubts as to the ingredients of the Last Supper, nor did the Spanish artist of the painting on a wooden panel illustrated above, done in the thirteenth century. He showed several fishes on plates while the disciple next to Jesus (probably Peter) holds one firmly in his grasp.

Leonardo da Vinci's *Last Supper* of 1495–7 is the painting of this meal that immediately springs to mind. The items of food are not easy to define now, but there appears to be a sliced-up fish on the plate in front of the disciple on Jesus's left hand.

From breakfast through the day to supper time, fishes on the menu in all their great variety are depicted in paintings showing meals awaiting consumption. These pictures confirm that 'Fish is the tastiest, most delicious food that Nature has provided' (Antonio Latini, *Lo Scalco alla moderna* [The Modern Steward], 1692–4). Their appeal to artists was summed up by Sir William Nicholson, who painted fish on several occasions. He said: 'Fish are painted because of the artists' interest in fish and [it is] convenient to put it on a plate on a table.'

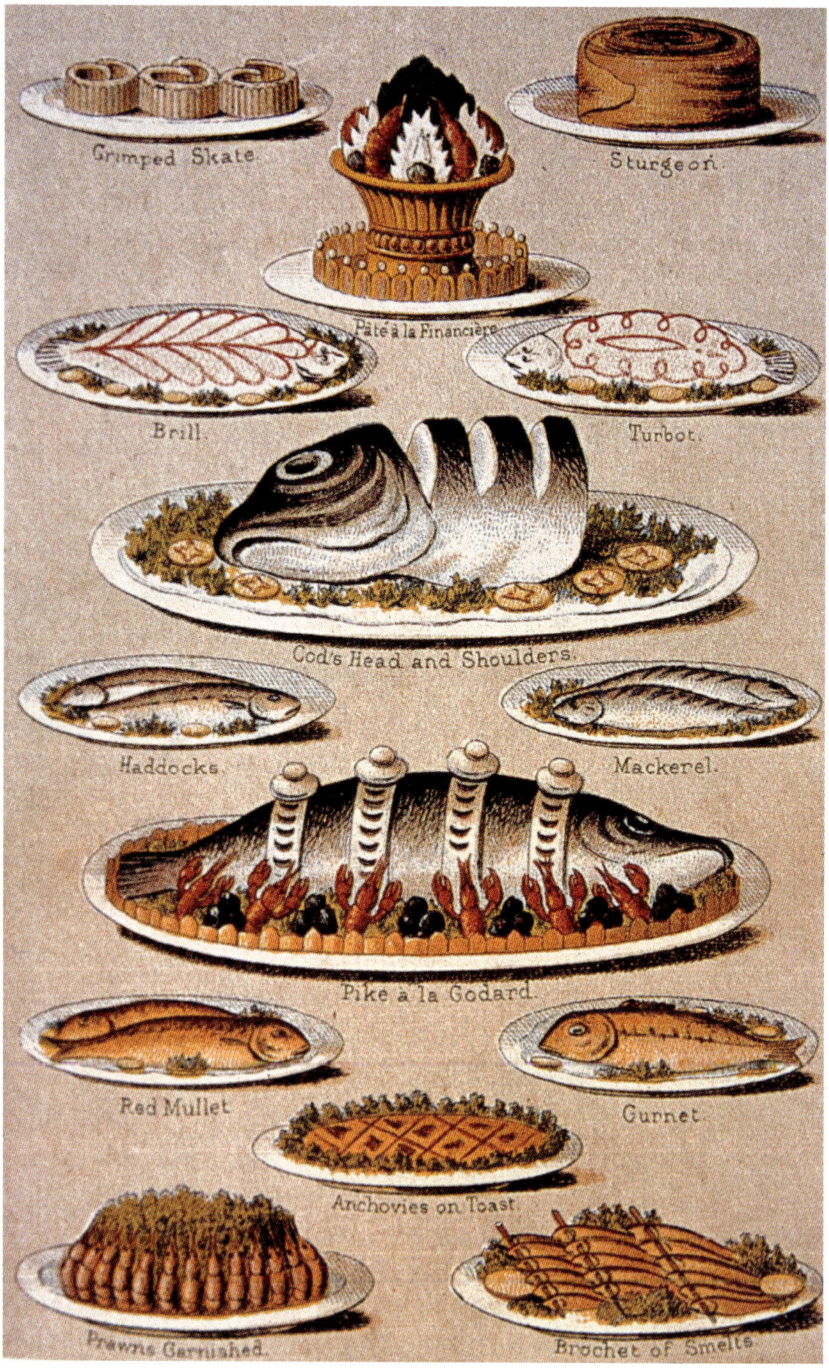

120 Fish dishes from *Mrs Beeton's Book of Household Management*.

121 Sir William Newzam Prior Nicholson, *Fish*, 1922, oil on wood. Nicholson (1872–1949) once played a trick on gallery visitors when he exhibited the painting *Fish* in 1922. He fastened a small piece of actual fish to the back of the picture and stood by to observe what happened. People stood in front of it and sniffed, and believing their eyes could hardly believe their noses. Nicholson said: 'The effect is most interesting.'

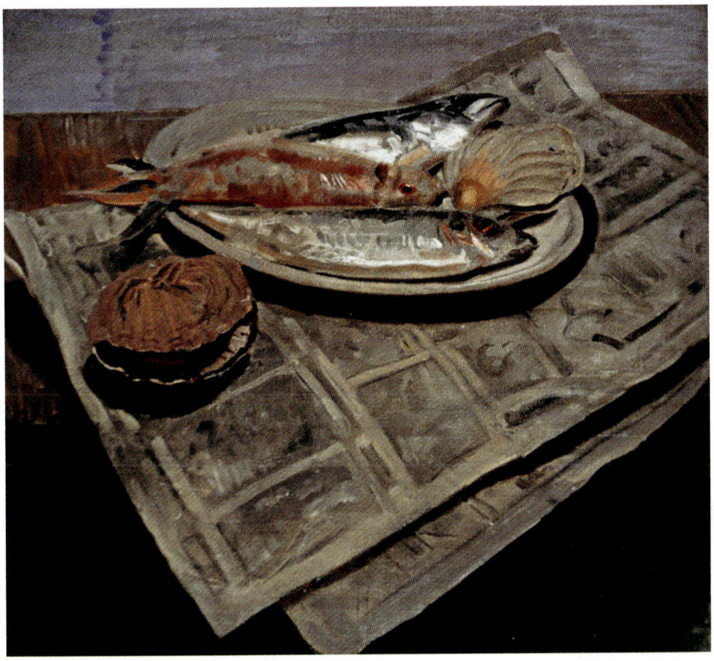

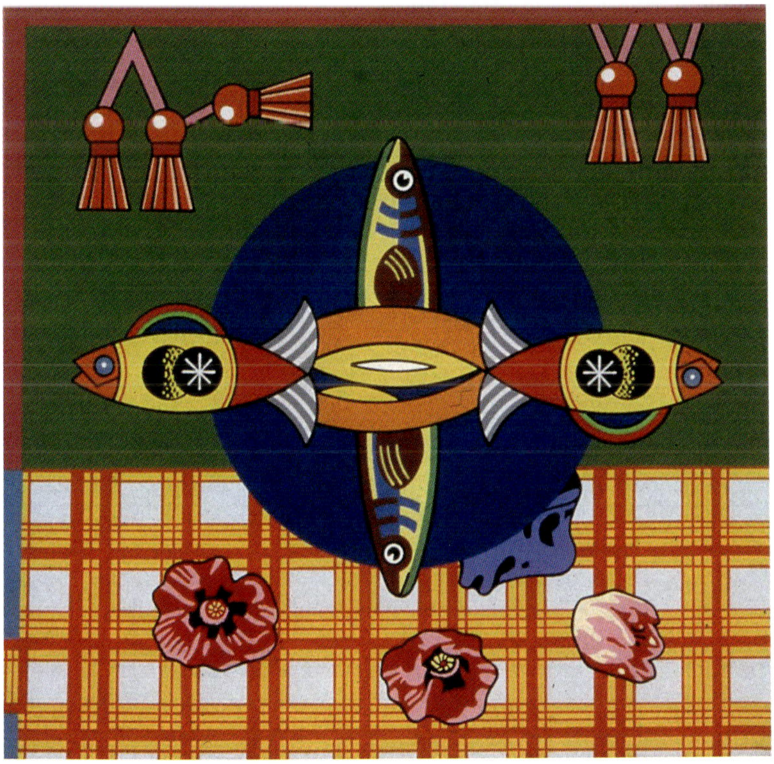

122 Trevor Winkfield, *Still-life with Fish*, 1998, acrylic on linen, 53 × 56 cm.

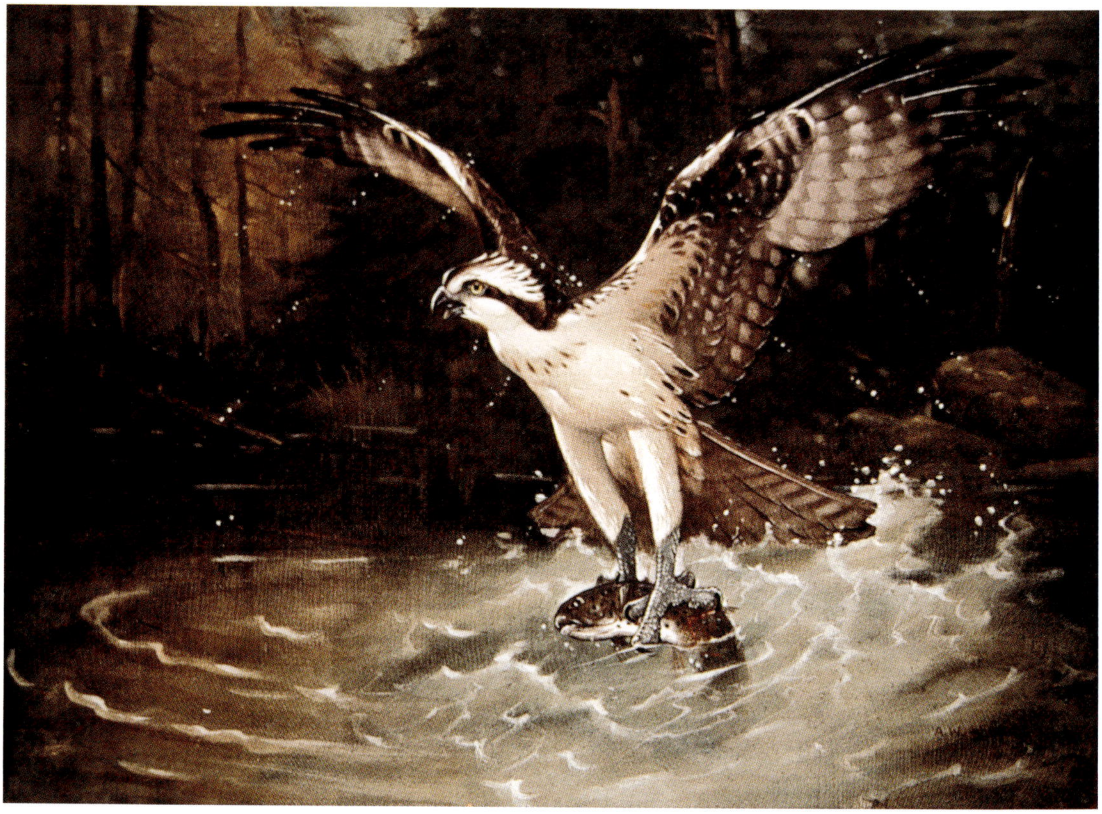

123 Allen William Seaby (1867–1952), *An Osprey with its Prey*, watercolour and bodycolour on linen.

six

Fish in Still Waters

Obtaining a reliable source of fish for food all the year round has always been a problem. In different parts of the world, geography, climate, natural seasonal variation and the disappearance of shoals of fish contributed to alternating states of plenty and shortage. To overcome these difficulties channels and pools were cut leading off rivers and streams. Where there was no access to a river, natural springs were used to fill moats and ponds. These still-water resources supplemented fish from the sea and rivers. In addition, garden pools, aquaria and small fish bowls were created for recreational purposes so that it was easy to see fishes at close quarters.

Inland lakes

Inland lakes or lochs offer fishermen and artists opportunities to observe and enjoy diverse freshwater species of fish. Landlocked freshwater lakes or meres occur at different levels. Mountain lakes can be very deep and cold except in the upper layer near the surface. The vegetation may be poor and the lake will yield only trout and minnows in the upper layers and charr in the depths of the lake. When charr were prolific in Lake Windermere they were potted as luxuries for the London market. Small mountain tarns and corrie lakes are always cold and life is poor, only providing sustenance for small trout and charr if the water is deep enough to withstand freezing to the base.

Lowland lakes have richer marginal vegetation and a greater variety of fishes. Those master fishermen, ospreys, know where to fish for a varied diet in smaller Scottish lochs and English lakes that are rich in minerals

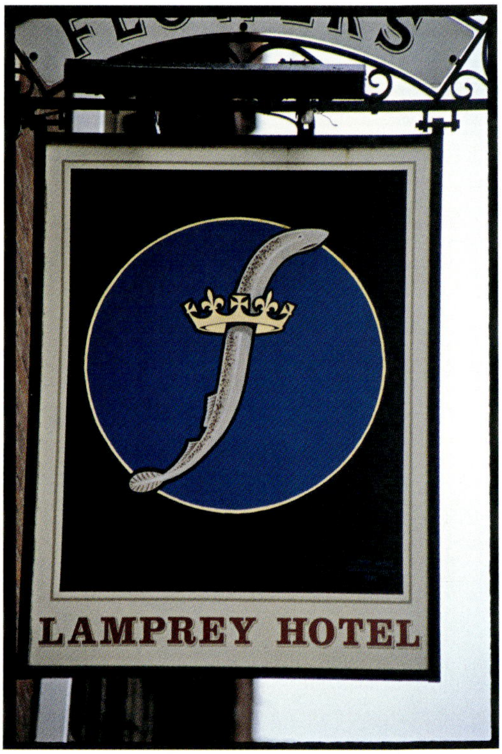

124 Sign of The Lamprey Inn, Gloucester. A crown hangs around the lamprey's neck in reference to Henry I's fondness for lampreys.

and abound with wildlife. The osprey hovers over the water, drops down for a closer look, then dives onto the fish just below the surface, thrusting its legs forward at the last second to clutch the fish in its long curved talons. It does not often miss, and once grasped the slippery fish is held implacably by the pads with their short stiff spicules on the under-surface of the osprey's feet. The osprey takes its prey back to a perch to eat – a clean operation of sighting, catching, landing that takes only a few seconds to complete. An analysis of the diet of a pair of ospreys found that they ate 42 per cent trout (mainly rainbow), 29 per cent perch, 18 per cent roach and 11 per cent pike, of a maximum length of some 40 cm.

Marshes, as well as natural freshwater lakes, were important sources of fishes. Early records of several abbeys exploiting the rich resources of the Fens of East Anglia have been preserved from as early as the seventh century. The low-lying marshes and fens of the Somerset Levels, as well as East Anglia, once yielded an abundance of eels, pike (young ones called pickerel), perch, roach, burbot and lamprey. Burbot (the only species of the cod family occurring in fresh water in Europe) is probably extinct in Britain now. Lampreys were once a favourite fish at court feasts in medieval times and Henry I (*r.* 1100–35) is said to have died from a fever that developed from indigestion after eating a surfeit of lampreys. There are still some freshwater populations of the river lamprey *Lampetra fluviatilis* in Loch Lomond and Lake Ladoga (in Finland, the largest lake in Europe) and it is an important commercial species in Scandinavia. Although called river lamprey, it spends part of its life in the sea. The purely freshwater species, the brook lamprey *Lampetra planeri*, occurs in western European streams where it is used mainly for bait. It is now rare in Britain.

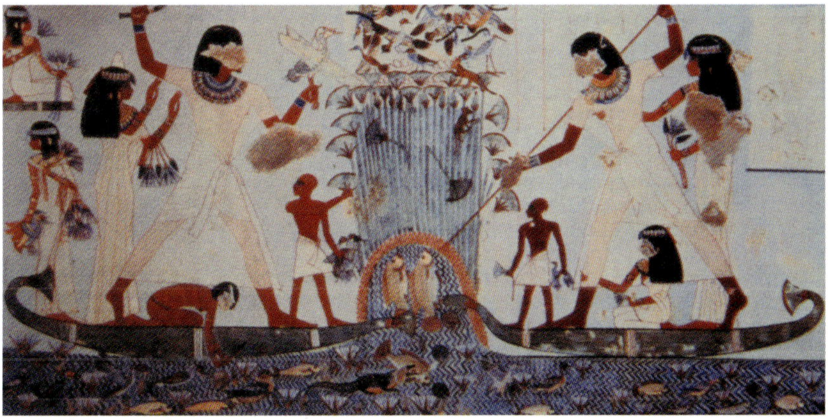

125 A wall painting in the tomb of Menna at Western Thebes showing a man and his family fishing in the marshes, *c.* 1380 BC.

Ponds and stews

Records of men digging out channels from rivers leading to ponds exist from centuries before Christ. In ancient Egypt the four-month-long inundation of the Nile, followed by eight months of drying out of the land, required some control. The water that flowed so providentially at one time of year needed to be channelled and retained for the other part, and that included the fishes in the water. The Egyptians built channels, ditches and pools to collect the water and entrap it. Wall paintings in tombs show these waterworks with the fishes caught in them. Several species of fish are shown swimming in man-made pools. Nile fishes include varieties of blenny, wrasse, Nile perch, catfish and carp, many of which are clearly distinguishable in Egyptian paintings.

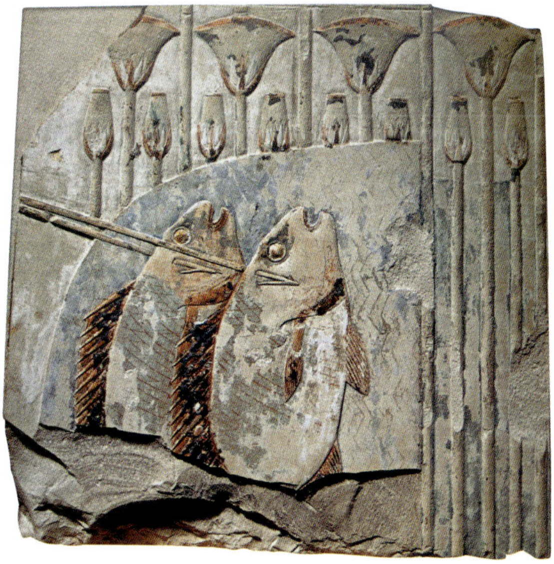

126 A detail from a similar scene in the tomb shows two fishes being speared with a bident.

In Assyria, at Nineveh, a similar system of cutting a channel ending in a pool is depicted in a wall painting, with a fisherman wading in the pool, carrying a basket round his neck. He is fishing with a line and hook. Nineveh, situated by the river Tigris (opposite the present city of Mosul, Iraq), was the capital of the Assyrian Empire until its destruction by the Medes in 612 BC. It was excavated between 1845 and 1851 by Austen Henry Layard

THE CATFISH or wolf fish (*Anarhichas lupus*) is most notable for its barbels, thin filaments on the side of the mouth, resembling feline whiskers, and the sharp spines on its fins. It has large sharp teeth and a very ugly face so it can be sold for food only after the head is removed and it is renamed 'rock salmon'. In some parts of Europe its slimy skin is used to produce a kind of leather, its bones and swim bladder for glue.

(1817–1894) who sent the greater part of the excavated monuments to the British Museum. Layard had this fragment of a bas-relief engraved to illustrate his *Monuments of Nineveh* (1849).

For Europeans who needed fish as part of their diet in order to survive, reliance on sea- or river-fishing was too haphazard. Winds and tides at sea, drought and torrents inland, all put at risk the availability of a fish meal. As early as the first century BC artificial ponds of saltwater for red mullet, moray eels and other fishes were created by the Romans, and aristocrats had them in their gardens. The fishes provided entertainment as well as food for anglers and

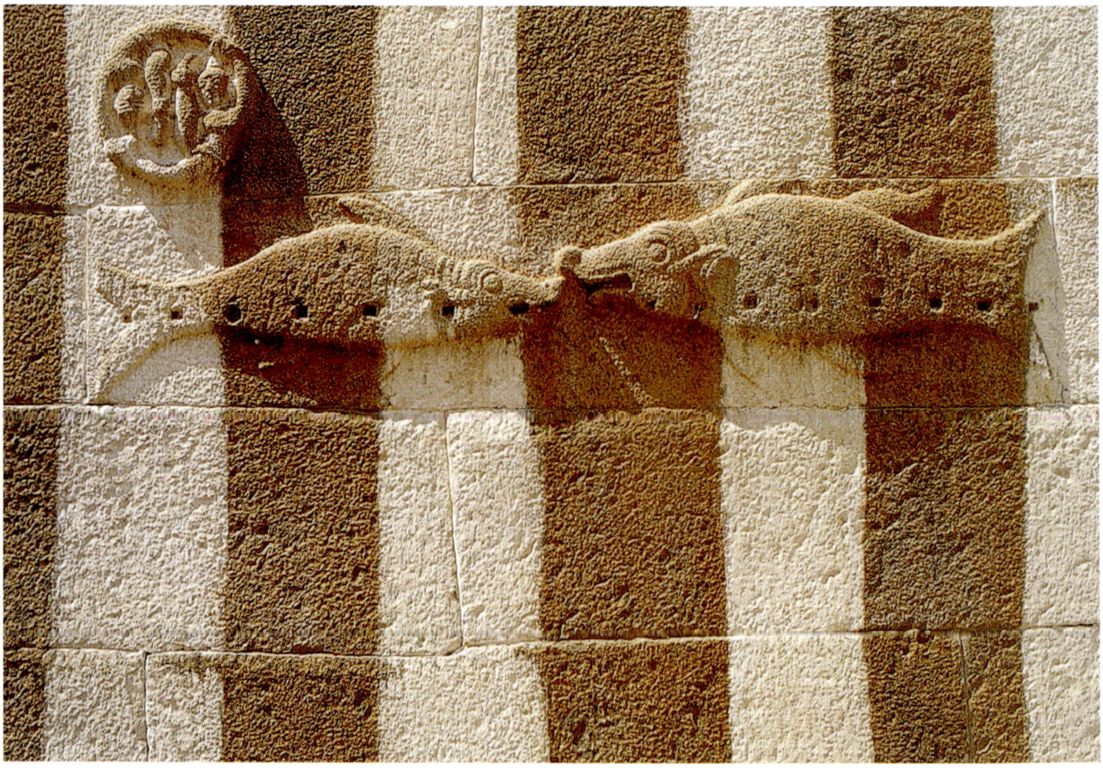

128 From A. H. Layard, *Monuments of Nineveh* (1849). At Nineveh (flourished 8th century to 612 BC), a channel ending in a pool provided fishing for an Assyrian who had a basket slung around his neck.

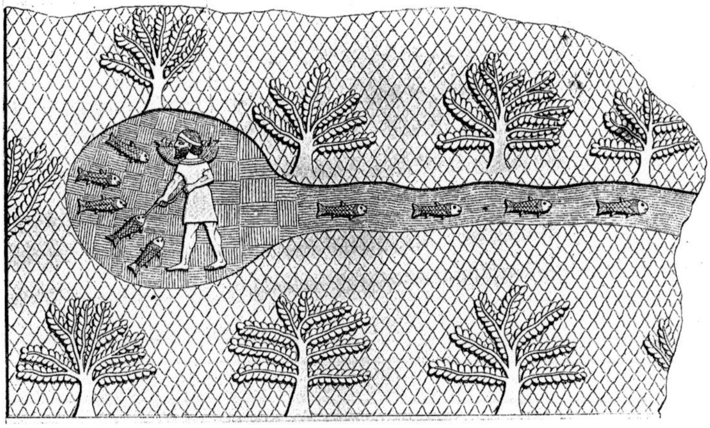

for guests who watched the changing colour of red mullet while dying. Roman freshwater ponds were usually for species kept by artisans for food and profit. The Romans' ponds appear to have had little influence on the British. The word 'fishpool' had entered the British language by about 950 when the Lindisfarne Gospel of John, verse 7, was written as 'in paet fiscpol'. A few monastic fishponds were dug in Britain but they were not used extensively either by monasteries or on demesnes until the second half of the twelfth century.

Before the Reformation in 1530 the added restrictions on a diet imposed on Christians everywhere in the Middle Ages forced countries to look for an adequate alternative source of protein, and that meant fish. Monks ate more sea fish at supper time than freshwater fish, having fishermen employed on the coast to supply their needs. As the monasteries grew in size from the twelfth century onwards monks in Britain solved their dilemma by digging out one or more ponds and keeping fish alive in them. Where there were as many as three freshwater ponds, one was reserved for pike by themselves, one for less aggressive fishes and a third, called a stew, for fish ready to be taken out for the table. Fishes such as tench that had been kept in ponds with muddy clay bottoms remained in the stew for several days in order to clean their flesh of the muddy taste. Some monks enjoyed the job of fishing for their dinner in the stew, though large establishments employed a fisherman for the purpose of netting the stew fishes. The ponds could be stocked with the monks' favourite fishes: carp, tench and eels, initially brought in to stock new ponds from other

127 Relief on granite enclosure wall of a Hindu temple in Vijayanagara, Karnataka, India. The Raghunath Temple was built in the 16th century.

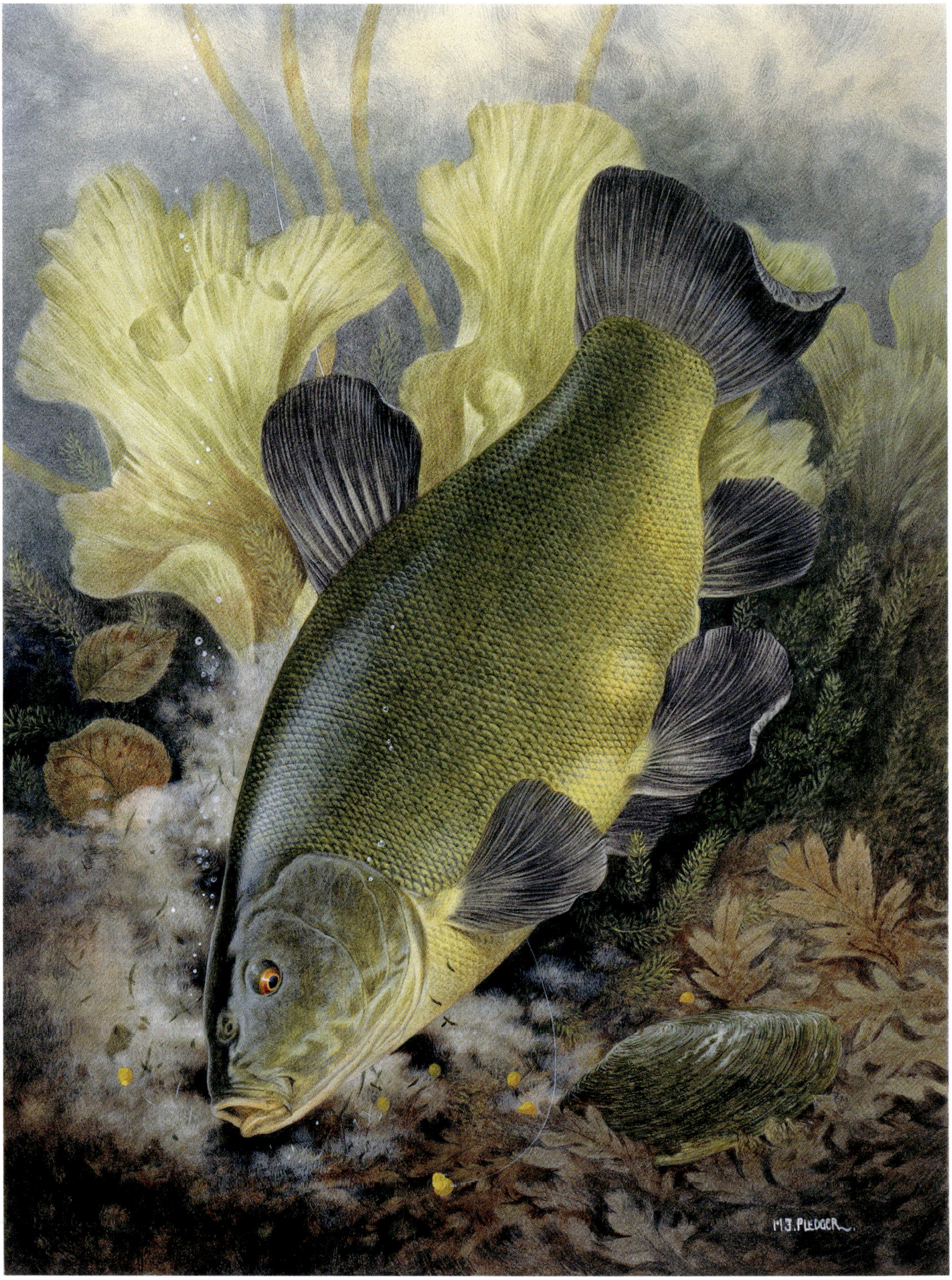

129 Maurice J. Pledger, *Tench Feeding on Corn*, 1998, watercolour.

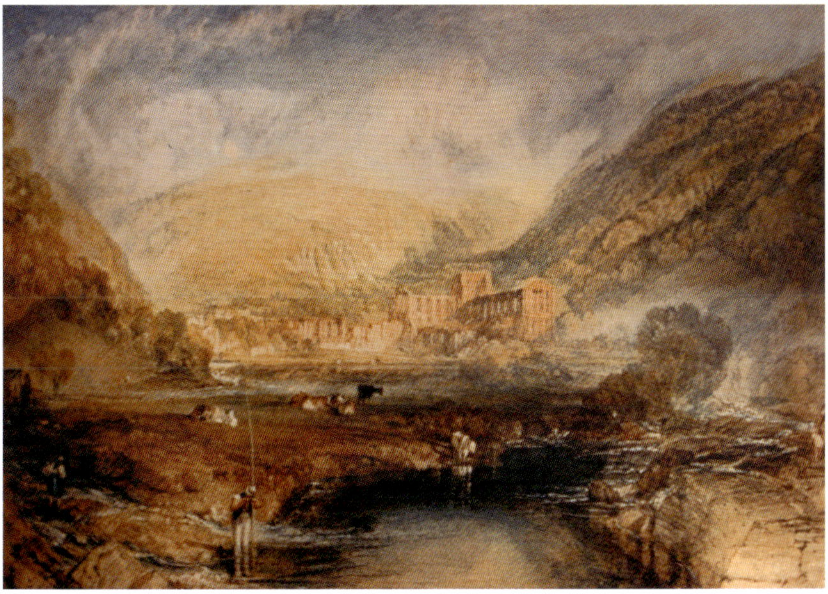

130 J.M.W. Turner, *Rievaulx Abbey*, c. 1825, watercolour.

sources in barrels full of water. Other species kept in ponds were bream, perch, roach, rudd and chub. Acres of land were given over to creating these ponds where the fishes were fattened with boiled corn and other grain before being harvested, somewhat in the manner of today's fish farms.

Apart from food the monks had another use for tench. They are covered in mucus that was used medicinally and gave the fish a nickname 'Doctor Fish'. It was a popular fish in monastery ponds and stews because its white flesh made very good eating. It was kept in a pond with a muddy bottom where it remained dormant in winter. It is now a fish mainly of lakes and ponds, able to inhabit small overgrown ponds where some other fishes would die. For present-day anglers it is a popular symbol of summer, when it is the prime quarry. In Europe, where it is eaten, it is used as a supplementary crop in carp farms.

Monasticism had a long history in Europe before becoming established in England. St Benedict established his rules for simple living in the sixth century and the early abbeys in England followed his example. The Cistercians who built monasteries in England in the twelfth century were also of his order of monasticism. Between 1128 and 1150 Cistercian monks from Cîteaux in Burgundy built no fewer than 35 great houses in England, among them Fountains and Rievaulx abbeys in Yorkshire.

Rievaulx Abbey in the valley of the river Rye is now one of England's most spectacular, romantic ruins in its beautiful landscape setting. It is best seen early in the morning or late afternoon. J.M.W. Turner captured the scene in the early morning while the sun was drying out the mist that surrounds the buildings, encircled by hills. Turner was a keen fisherman and has placed an angler in the foreground, showing him concentrating on tying a fly. The river would have supplied fish for the small newly arrived community of a dozen monks, but Rievaulx in its heyday in the early thirteenth century housed some 140 monks supported by more than 600 lay brethren. This necessitated the construction of fishponds and millponds.

It was not only on monastic lands that extensive systems of channels and ponds were constructed but also on estates and manorial demesnes, especially where there were natural springs. Chains of small lakes were used to breed fishes and move them on to clean water in stews ready for taking by the cook. Besides pike, both trout and perch (which were of a similar voracious nature) were kept in separate ponds, but carp and tench could be kept together. Other freshwater fishes kept in ponds included roach, bream and dace. Thomas Tusser (*c.* 1524–1580), an East Anglian leaseholder who lived in Essex about 8 miles from the Maldon saltings, wrote doggerel verse giving advice in *Five Hundred Points of Good Husbandry* for farmers and landowners. As part of September's husbandry he exhorted the farmer: 'Thy ponds renew, put eeles in stew, To leeve till Lent, and then to be spent.' The ponds had to be cleaned out every three or four years to get rid of excess sediment, encroaching weeds and reeds.

Many monasteries had a pond stocked with eels among other fishes. They were also imported in great quantities from the Low Countries in the Middle Ages and because they were cheaper than most fishes, other than shellfish, were bought by the poor. For centuries they were caught with an eel spear and in woven basket eel traps. Conger eels *Conger conger* are wholly marine and can reach 2 metres (6 feet) in length. They were easily caught and became the staple diet of Cornish cooking and monastic food.

Some of these series of ponds may still be seen (at Canons Ashby, Northamptonshire; Charlecote Park, Warwickshire; Felbrigg Hall, Norfolk, to name a few) but with the end of compulsory fish-eating days in the eighteenth century and improved transport so that fish could be moved around the country and delivered in a relatively fresh state, most of them were no longer needed. Many were altered by successive landscapists, William Kent (1684–1748), Lancelot 'Capability' Brown (1716–1783) and Humphry Repton (1752–1818), who combined them to create large ornamental lakes. These 'natural-looking' lakes were ideal for more species of fishes because of their varying depths and provided their gentlemanly owners with the delights of angling for pleasure, a sport fast gaining in popularity.

Moats, millponds and canals

Moats surrounding houses were built in the twelfth to thirteenth centuries for defence, while later medieval moats were created as status symbols. They were often stocked with fishes as a source of fresh food for the table. Care had to be taken not to soil the moat water, often spring-fed, by flushing foul waste into it from the house. Carp was the favourite fish in the moats but perch were also put in to breed because their flesh was regarded as very good eating. Trammel nets were used to get the fishes out of the moat. Thousands of moats still survive today in England.

The carp is a large group of fish originally found in Central Europe as well as Asia. The wild carp was being farmed for food in Asia by about 400 BC. Carp have been popular subjects for Japanese artists like Ohara Shoson, who painted under several other names including Ohara Shosos

The COMMON CARP (*Cyprinus carpio*) originated from Asia where the Chinese emperors prized them highly both as ornamental pets and as food. Travellers along the Silk Road took them to Europe. By the fifteenth century they had become the staple food of Eastern European Jews, who also cultivated them in pools. The Romans bred carp in artificial ponds and the first monks (in Italy about AD 500) bred them and took their knowledge of fish culture with them across Europe. By the end of the Middle Ages carp were also being kept in estate ponds.

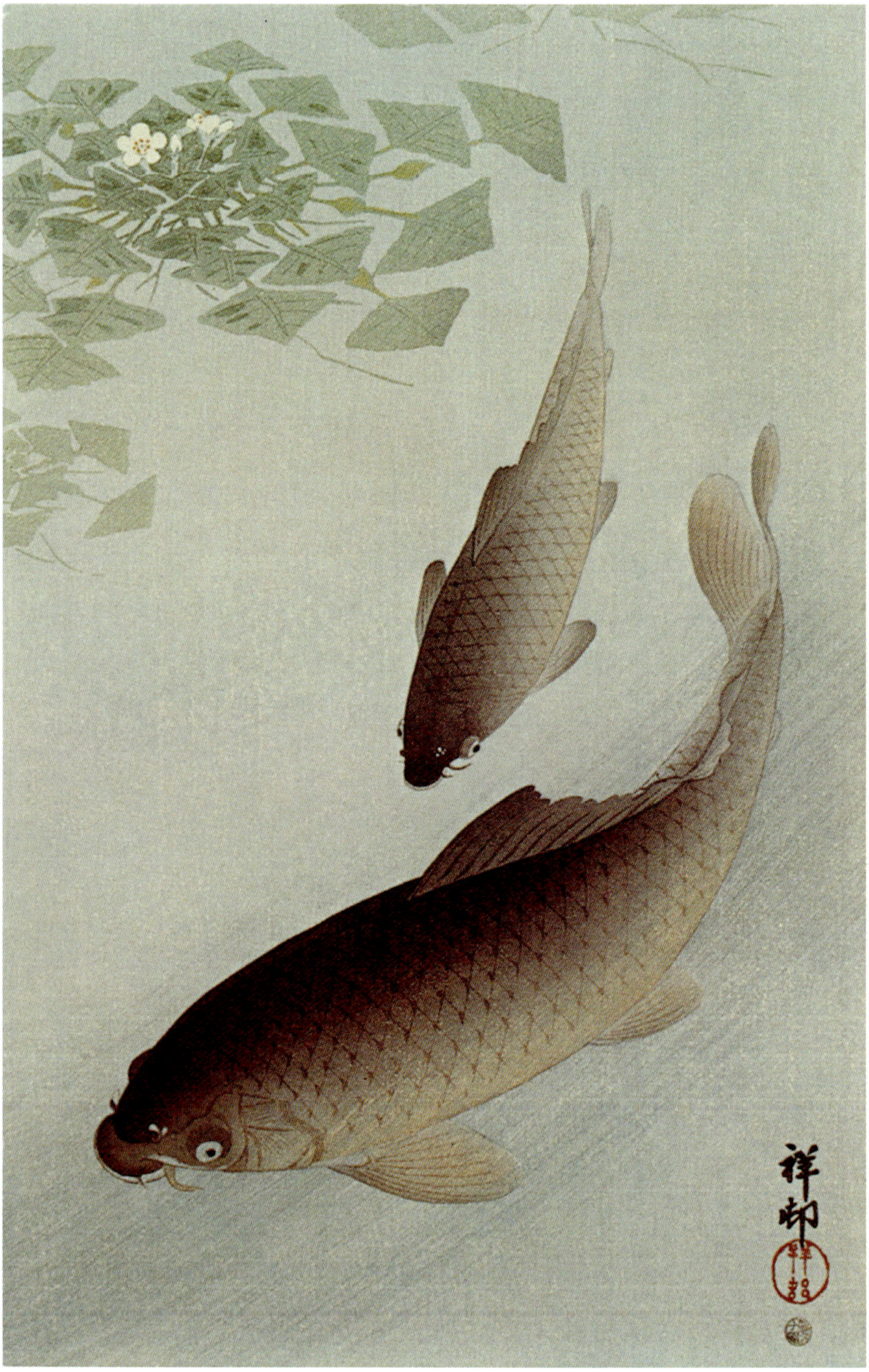

131 Ohara Shoson (1877–1945), *Carp*, woodblock print.

EELS (*Anguilla anguilla*) feed mainly at night on crustaceans, small fishes and other aquatic creatures. Adults respond to unknown stimuli, change colour from yellow-brown to silver and migrate across the Atlantic Ocean to the Sargasso Sea between the Bahamas and Bermuda to breed and die. Their elvers make their own way back to the places where their parents lived.

and Koson. He specialized in woodblocks of natural history subjects in his own realistic and restrained style. This woodblock print of a carp has been labelled as being both by Shoson and Koson. It is a simple composition on a strong diagonal with movement indicated by the irregular lines made by uneven inking of the wood block. The strong forms of the fish are delicately balanced by the water plant with a flower.

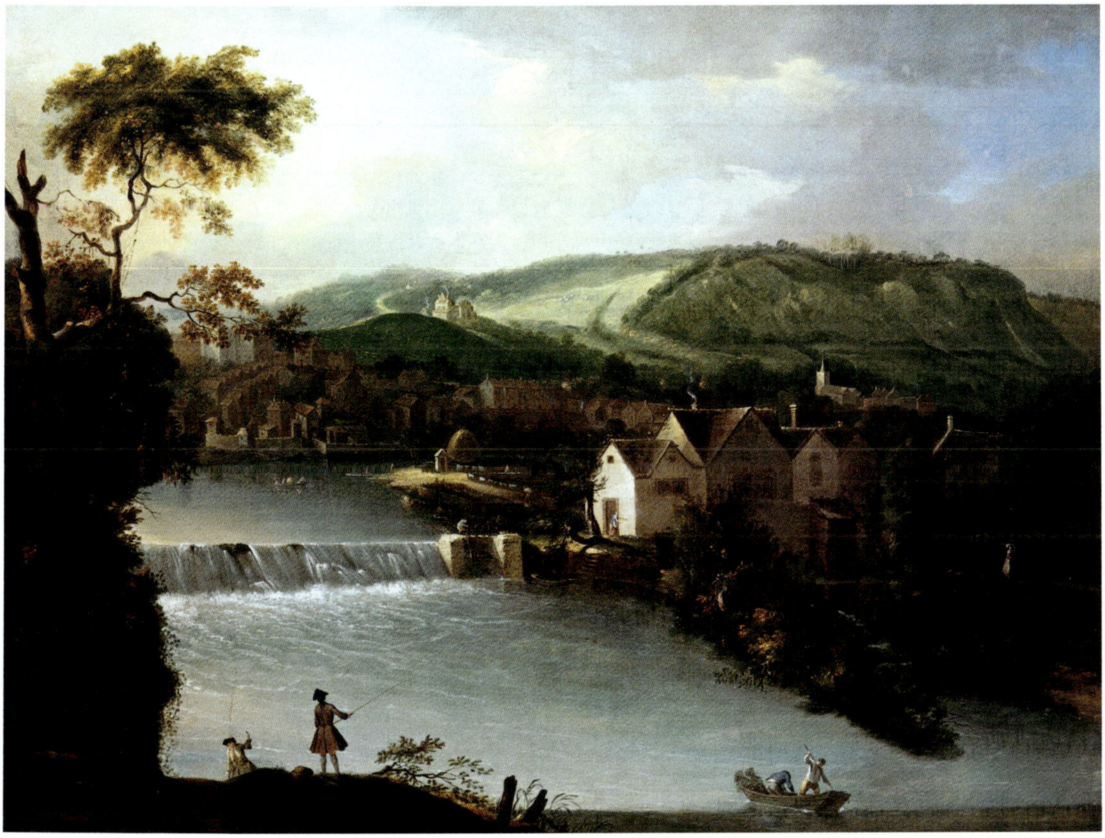

132 Thomas A. Ross, *The Weir at Bathwick and Millpond*, *c.* 1729–38, oil on canvas.

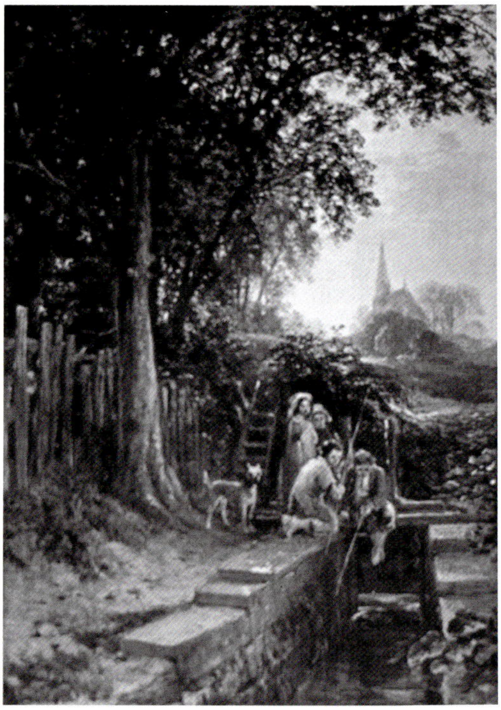

133 Samuel Bough, *Young Anglers by a Canal*, *c.* 1860, oil on panel.

At most monasteries and in many manors there were also millponds, usually well stocked with eels. Eel traps were often placed in mill cuts. More than 5,000 watermills were noted in the Domesday survey of 1086. They were used to grind the monks' and villagers' flour for bread and when the water driving the mill was too slow or shallow a small millpond was created alongside a river or stream. Old English *al-ge* and later *eleg* (eel island) is the origin of the name of the Fenland town of Ely, which the Venerable Bede maintained was derived from the vast swarms of eels caught in the surrounding meadows. Domesday entries refer to some rivers yielding 1,000 to 2,000 eels each year, occasionally recording them as 'sticks of eels', each stick bearing 25 eels.

Thomas A. Ross's painting of *The Weir at Bathwick and Millpond* also shows the millpond by the river Avon just outside Bath. Ross painted landscape scenes around the Severn Estuary and Bath between 1729 and 1738. He included two anglers in this picture, one holding aloft a fish.

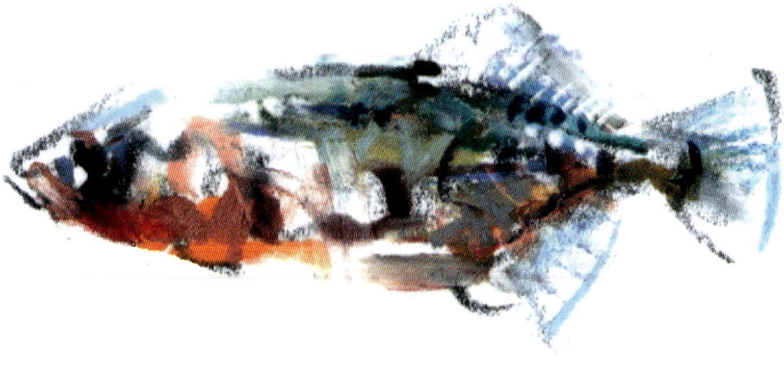

134 Carl Ellis, *Stickleback*, pastel. Contemporary artist Carl Ellis caught his first sticklebacks in a local canal and they sparked his interest in fishes and painting them.

There are many small natural canals leading off rivers, like the one where the children in Samuel Bough's painting are shown fishing. Canals were first cut in Britain by the Romans but the first wholly artificial major navigational canal in Britain was the Bridgewater Canal in Lancashire, opened in 1761. By 1830 some four thousand miles of canals had been cut, some affording new angling opportunities.

Small boys begin their careers as fishermen by catching tiny sticklebacks and carrying them home in jam jars. Carl Ellis has caught the 'jizz' or characteristic features of the stickleback. The work of this contemporary artist, who specializes in fish painting, exemplifies the late twentieth-century mode of presenting paintings of fishes. The fish are seen entering and leaving the picture area, with sketches and drawings surrounding the main finished figures showing various studies or stages of construction.

Reservoirs and gravel pits

In the second half of the twentieth century reservoirs were created, disused quarries were flooded and gravel pits allowed to fill with water when the

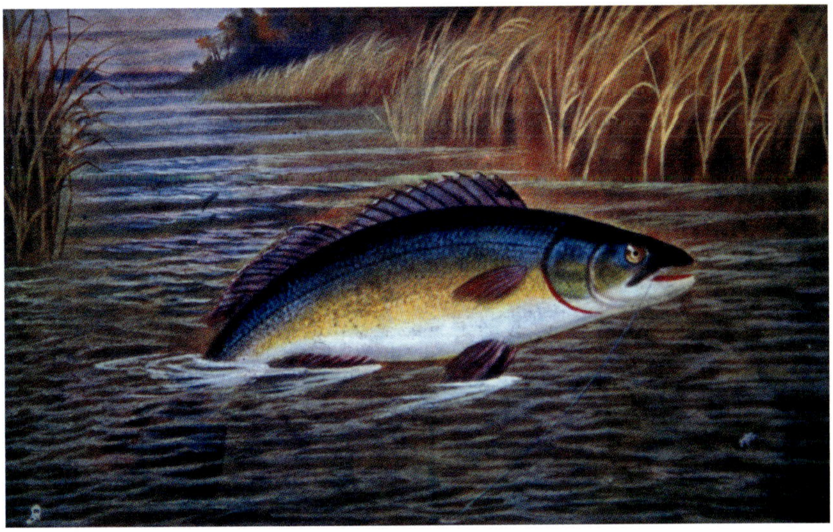

135 Arthur Roland Knight, *Black Bass*, *c.* 1920, postcard.

gravel was no longer being extracted. Former gravel pits are now good fishing spots for rudd, though it is not considered to be a prime sporting or eating fish. These still-water expanses were stocked with rainbow trout, *Oncorhynchus mykiss*, first introduced to Great Britain from its native Pacific coast basins and west-coast rivers of the United States of America in 1884 when some eggs were sent to the National Fish Culture Association in Buckinghamshire. Anglers value this species of trout because it grows very quickly in comparison with brown trout and there is no statutory close season. Fly-fishing for rainbow trout, using a longer rod to cast further into the wide expanse of water, became a new challenge for anglers. Still waters are regularly restocked with fish from fish farms. Another fish introduced for the benefit of anglers is the largemouth or black bass. It was imported from the Great Lakes of North America at the end of the nineteenth century and is established in at least two lakes in southern England.

Fish farms

So often the Romans were actively experimenting with new ideas long before the rest of the world caught up with them, and this is true of fish farming. The Chinese may have been the first to cultivate oysters but we have little knowledge of this. Pliny wrote a good deal about oyster culture, crediting Sergius Orata in the first century BC for taking the initiative in what was to become a lucrative business. The Romans appear to have hung their oysters on loosely twisted ropes. They discovered the richest natural oyster beds in Europe at the mouth of the Thames and an area centred on Colchester. Production elsewhere was facilitated later by laying down beds of young oysters to grow on.

Dutch and Flemish artists frequently included oysters in their paintings throughout the seventeenth century. Oysters were so plentiful that they were bought by the barrelful and supported many a poor household. Exhaustion of the natural oyster beds of western Europe in the mid-nineteenth century led to the development of methods of oyster

136 Wood engraving of a Surrey trout farm, from the *Illustrated London News* (1890).

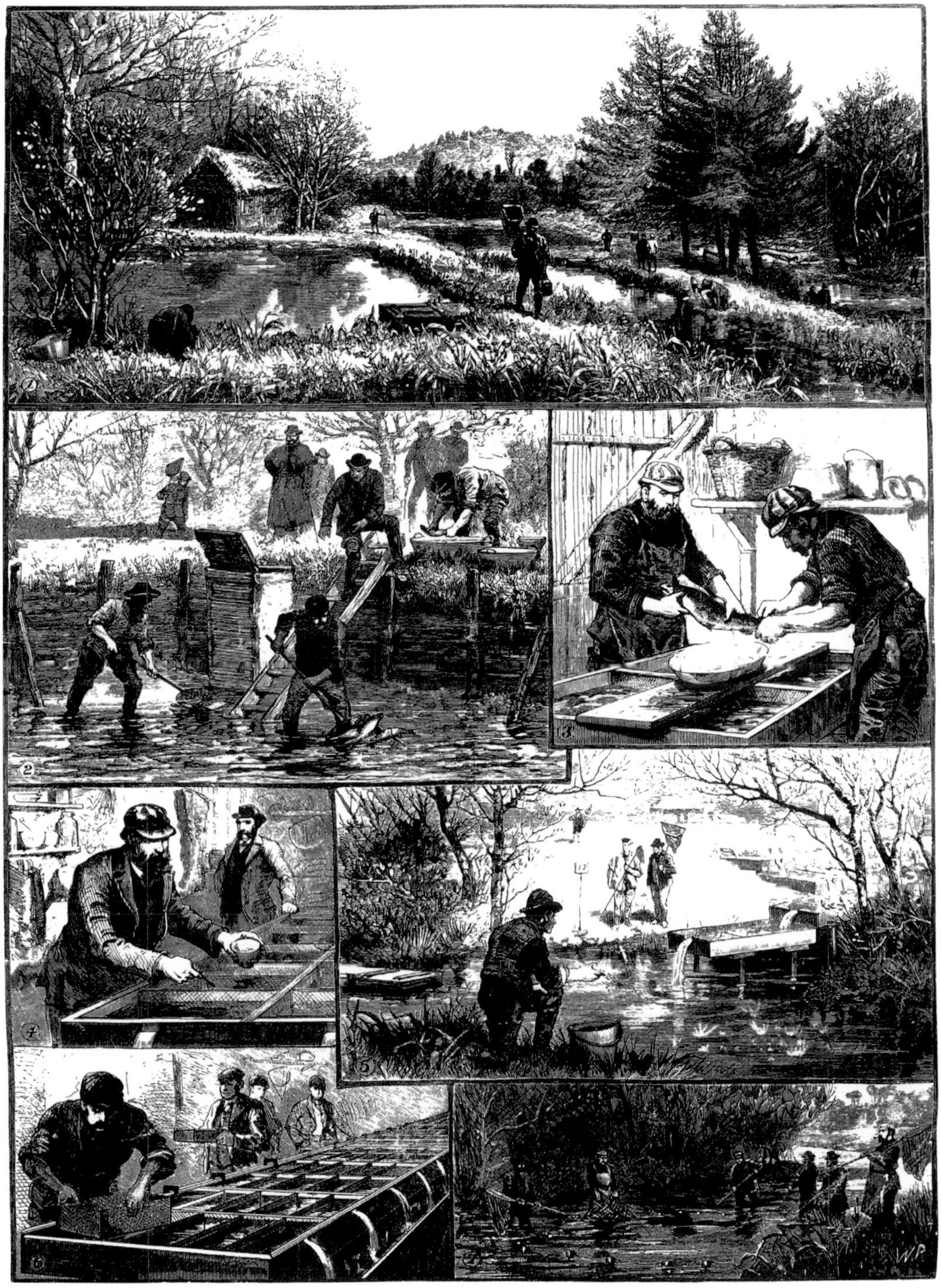

culture that in turn led to a period of intensive scientific study of oysters. The French were foremost in this study, which brought them great success. The British followed, then the Dutch, Japanese and Americans.

Small-scale fish farming of other species was carried out at the end of the nineteenth century in England. An *Illustrated London News* of 1890 has a wood engraving showing the various stages of rearing trout on a Surrey trout farm. Aquaculture, or commercial finfish farming, began in Scotland in the 1970s. Only facts and figures can convey the vast scale on which fish farming is carried out today on the thousand or more fish and shellfish farming businesses of the United Kingdom alone. They operate on 1,500 sites and employ 3,000 people, farming some 140,000 tonnes of salmon and 16,000 tonnes of rainbow trout, not to mention the production of 25,000 tonnes of carp and brown trout, turbot, halibut, cod and Arctic charr besides the molluscan shellfish (mainly mussels, oysters and clams). Some of this goes to supermarkets, including rainbow trout, while the farmed brown trout are used to stock rivers for angling.

ORFE (*Leuciscus idus*), a mainly silver fish also known as the ide (the gold-coloured variety is golden orfe) is native to the Danube basin and most parts of northern Europe except Norway. Best known in the golden form today in aquaria and ponds, it was first introduced into Britain in the 1870s to the ponds at Woburn Abbey, Bedfordshire, and is now established in a large number of lakes as well as ponds.

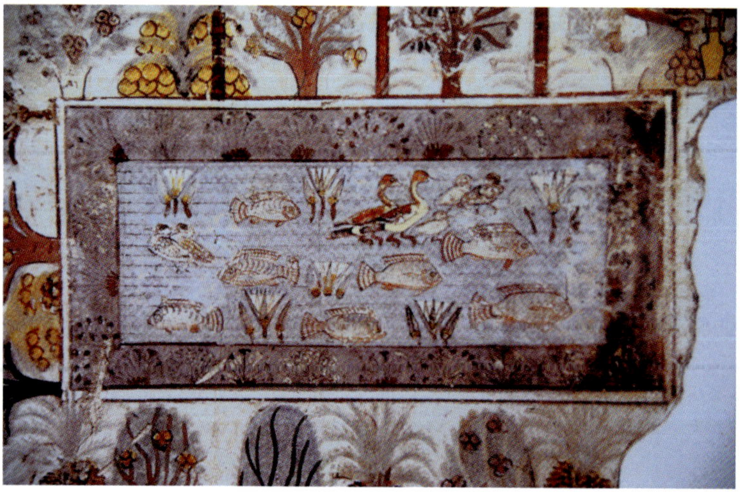

137 Egyptian pool in Nebamun's garden, dating from 1417–1379 BC.

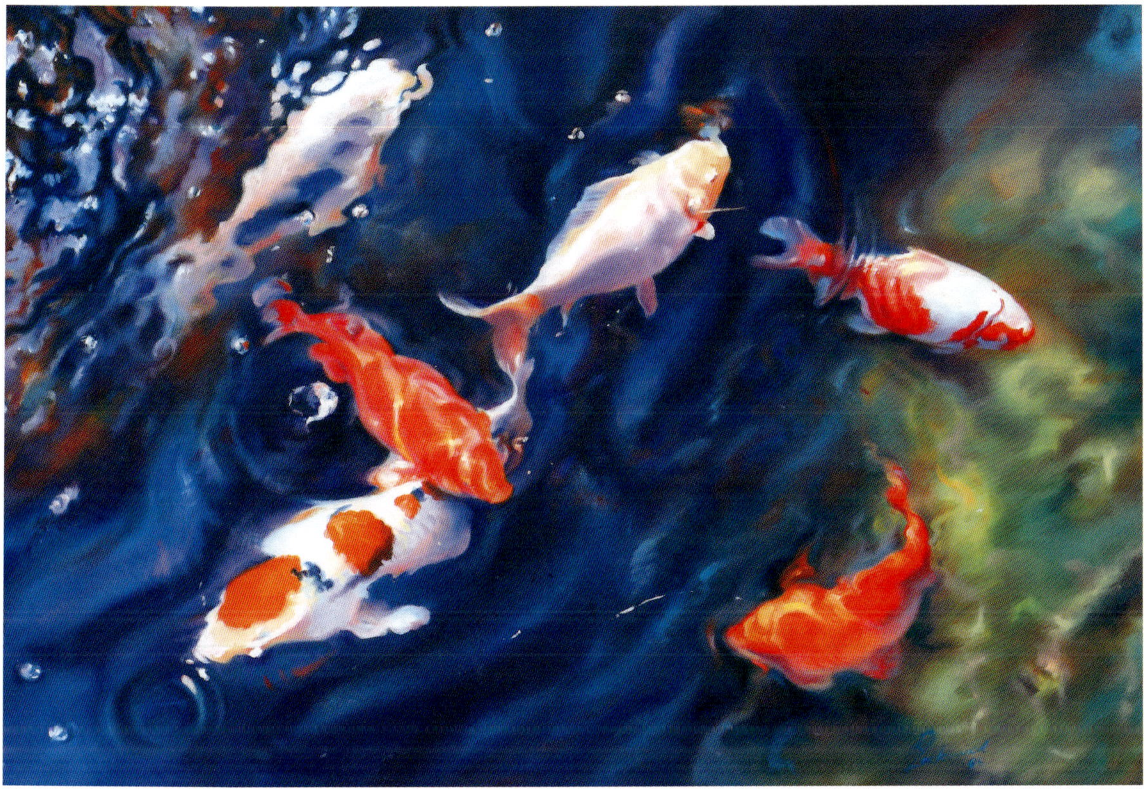

138 Rachel Lockwood, *Ogon 1*, 2004, oil on canvas.

Fish farms are not picturesque and artists are hardly likely to be inspired to paint them, but they afford close-up views of the fish with the added advantage of being able to paint freshly and easily caught specimens.

Garden ponds

Garden ponds with a few fishes swimming in them are not new phenomena, though the craze for digging garden ponds has gathered momentum over recent years. The Egyptian garden pool, with its oblong shape and straight sides, in a tomb painting of 1417–1379 BC of Nebamun's garden from the Theban Necropolis near Luxor, looks as familiar as though dug out yesterday. Nebamun had servants to maintain his small pool and many of today's owners would appreciate having them for this high-maintenance garden feature. Nebamun's pool is surrounded by date palms, sycamores and mandrakes. The pool teems with fishes provided by the goddess of the sycamore who can be seen in the top-right-hand tree, weighed down by her bounty. His fishes are swimming among sacred lotus flowers.

A touch of exoticism is seen today in garden pools that are stocked with brightly coloured golden orfe and koi carp, but most gardeners favour a few goldfishes, once exotica themselves but now common in ponds and aquaria. One of the first ornamental varieties of carp were koi carp, *Caprinus carpio*, developed in the Niigata Prefecture on the Japanese island of Honshu in the early part of the nineteenth century. he red, white and yellow fishes are traditionally kept in a bright blue bowl that is designed to show off their remarkable colours. Larger specimens are moved into garden ponds.

Goldfish bowls

Goldfish were introduced into England around 1691 during the reign of William and Mary, though the Portuguese had them many years before that. British ships collected them from Lisbon in large earthenware jars. Charles Lennox, Duke of Richmond (1701–1750), sent a jar to China for the collecting of goldfish for his ponds at Goodwood House. Goldfish are native to China, where they have been bred for different colour varieties (red, gold, white and mottled) for over 4,500 years. By the 1750s they were so common as to be kept at Vauxhall in the pleasure garden's 'purling basons'. When first kept in bowls goldfish had to be given fresh water every day or their supply of oxygen would run out and they would die. One hundred years after their introduction goldfish provided the clue to keeping freshwater fishes in aquaria successfully. Robert Warington, a chemist, introduced some

GOLDFISH (*Carassius auratus*) are now the most popular species for small ponds and aquaria, where they may survive for eight to twelve years. When young, goldfish are green-bronze above, bronze on the sides and yellowish ventrally. Mature fish are a beautiful orange-red, growing up to 30.5 cm (12 in) and a maximum weight of some 3 kg (6.5 lb). Any wild goldfish now found in European fresh water is the result of the liberation of ornamental fish that have established viable feral populations in several areas.

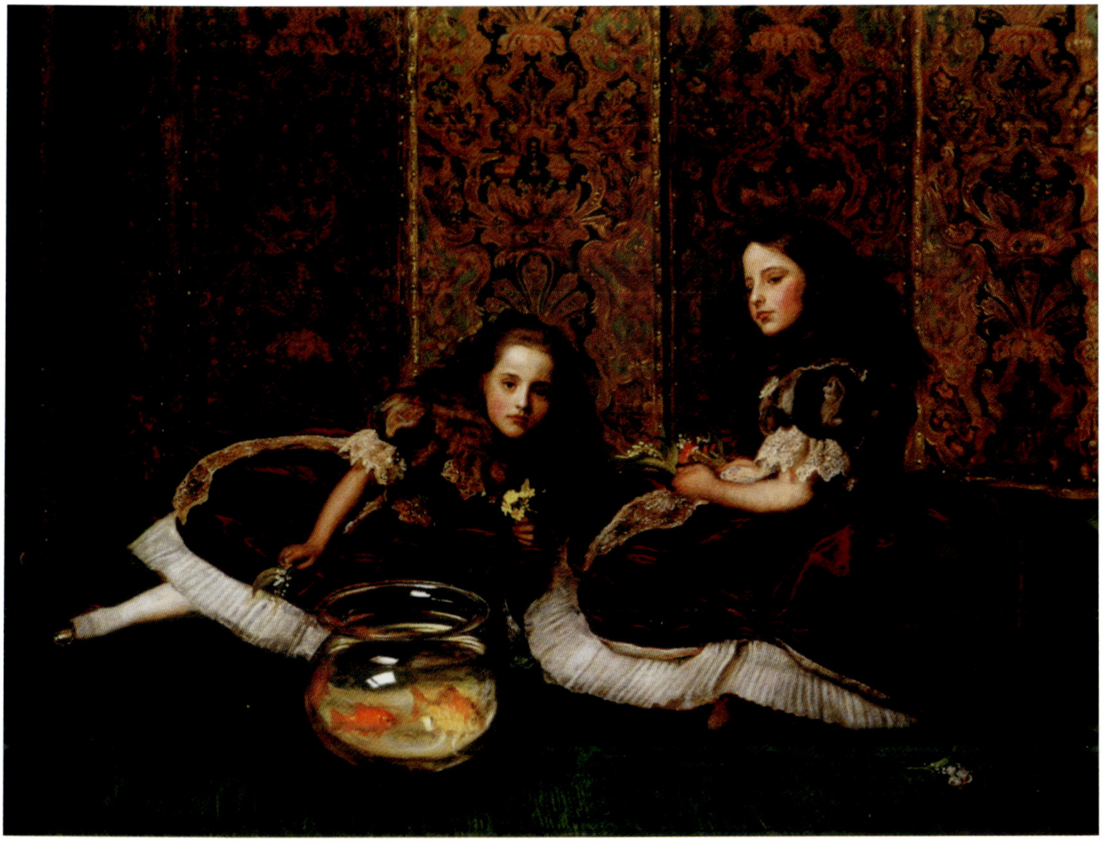

139 John Everett Millais, *Leisure Hours: Two Girls with a Goldfish Bowl*, 1864, oil on canvas.

ornamental fish into one of his tanks of aquatic plants. He found that the fishes survived better than when left without plants. He explained the principles behind this and publicized the results of his experiments. Plants absorb carbon dioxide and give out oxygen, while fishes breathe in oxygen and exhale carbon dioxide. He told the Chemical Society in 1850 how he had kept two small goldfish and a *Valisneria spiralis* plant together in a 12-gallon tank for nearly a year without changing the water. He added some pond snails and found that they kept the water clearer.

At the height of the popularity of keeping goldfish in a bowl, Sir John Everett Millais (1829–1896) painted a double portrait of two sisters with a pair of goldfish in a large glass bowl. They were Anne, on the right, and Marion, daughters of Sir John Pender of Middleton Hall, Linlithgow, a wealthy man who could afford to dress them in velvet and

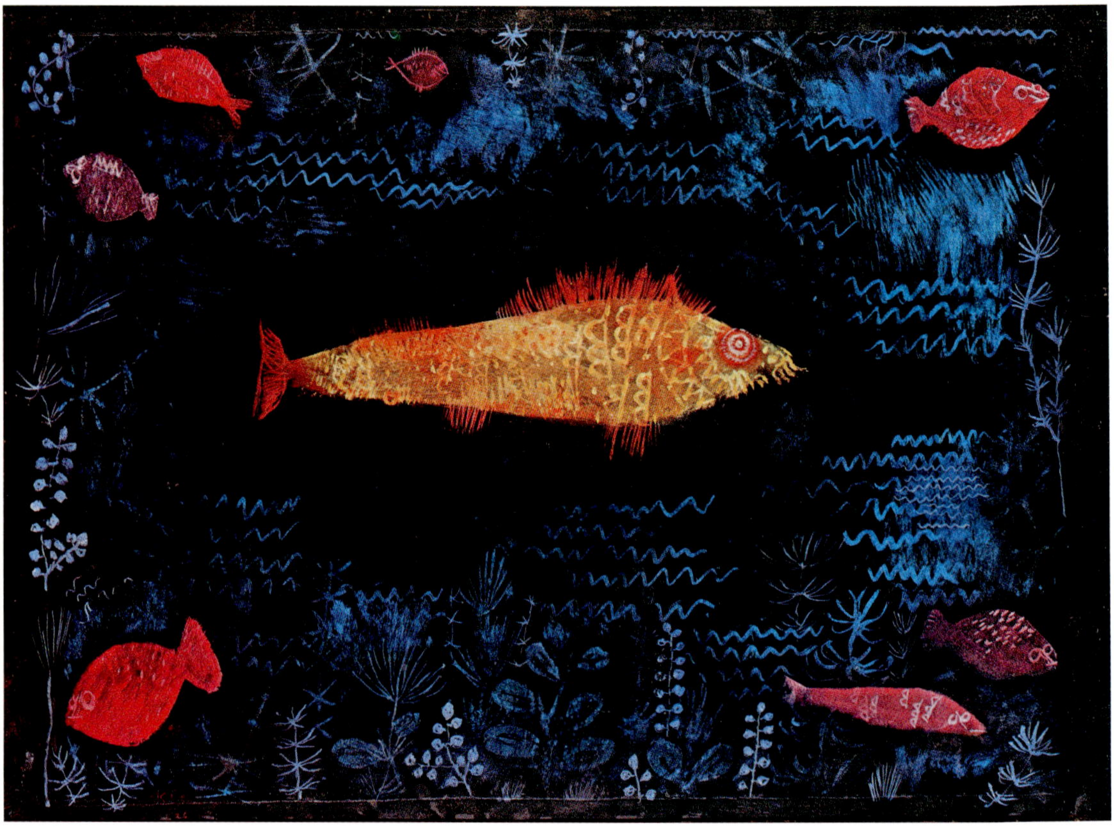

140 Paul Klee, *Golden Fish*, 1925, oil on cardboard.

provide them with the latest form of entertainment that was also deemed to be educational.

The Swiss artist Paul Klee (1879–1940) visited an aquarium in Naples and became fascinated by fishes. They inspired him to paint several pictures. Rather than paint individual species he used their shapes to introduce bright splashes of colour into his mysterious, dark underwater world. His *Golden Fish,* painted in oil on cardboard, is no particular species but a bright and cheerful centre of attention against this sombre background.

Aquaria

Aquaria, tanks or similar containers are used for the study and display of living aquatic plants and animals. We think of them as windows on

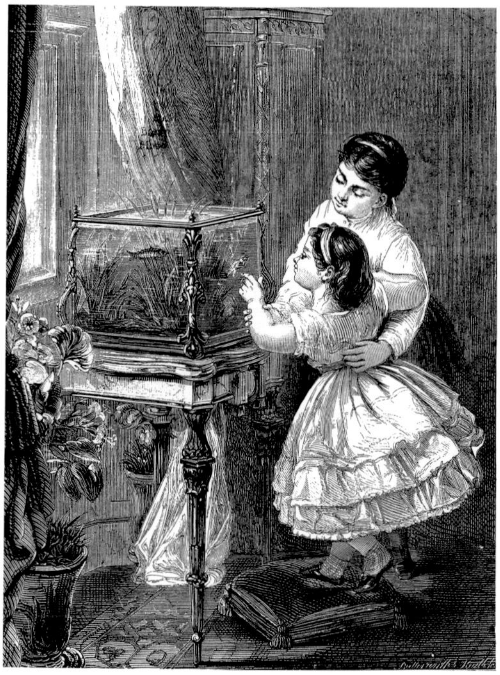

141 The aquarium, *Weekly Welcome* (1879).

a different world created for our interest and entertainment, much like the Romans who had *Vivarium piscium* recorded at various locations, probably housing bream, pike, roach and perch. Although tanks of freshwater fishes have been common ever since Roman times, they were not really popular until a way was found to keep the water oxygenated and clean without having to change it every day. Warington's paper, when read to the Chemical Society in 1850, sparked a great interest in keeping fishes in aquaria other than just goldfish, and the Victorians enthusiastically displayed small aquaria in their drawing rooms to the delight of small children and adults alike.

Philip Henry Gosse (1810–1888) was an enthusiastic amateur Victorian zoologist. He studied marine biology at his home in Devon and discovered that it was possible to keep marine species in aquaria. He introduced minute marine animals with rings of waving cilia, called rotifers, that used the oxygen from the aquatic plants which absorbed the carbon dioxide they produced. He designed a 'Marine Aquarium for the Parlour or Conservatory' that became very popular in Victorian England at a time when natural history had become a favourite pursuit. Gosse persuaded the Zoological Society of London to install a tank for marine species in the new Fish House at Regent's Park. It proved to be so popular with the public that the society opened the world's first 'marine aquivivarium' in 1853. Gosse described his experiments in aquarium-keeping in his book *A Naturalist's Rambles on the Devonshire Coast*, published in 1853, followed a year later by *The Aquarium*. Both were illustrated with chromolithographed plates from his watercolours. His work encouraged displays in showrooms across Britain and Europe. At first the tanks were small and contained sea anemones, fishes, octopuses and crabs among the water plants. A lucrative trade sprung up to supply the tanks and the live contents.

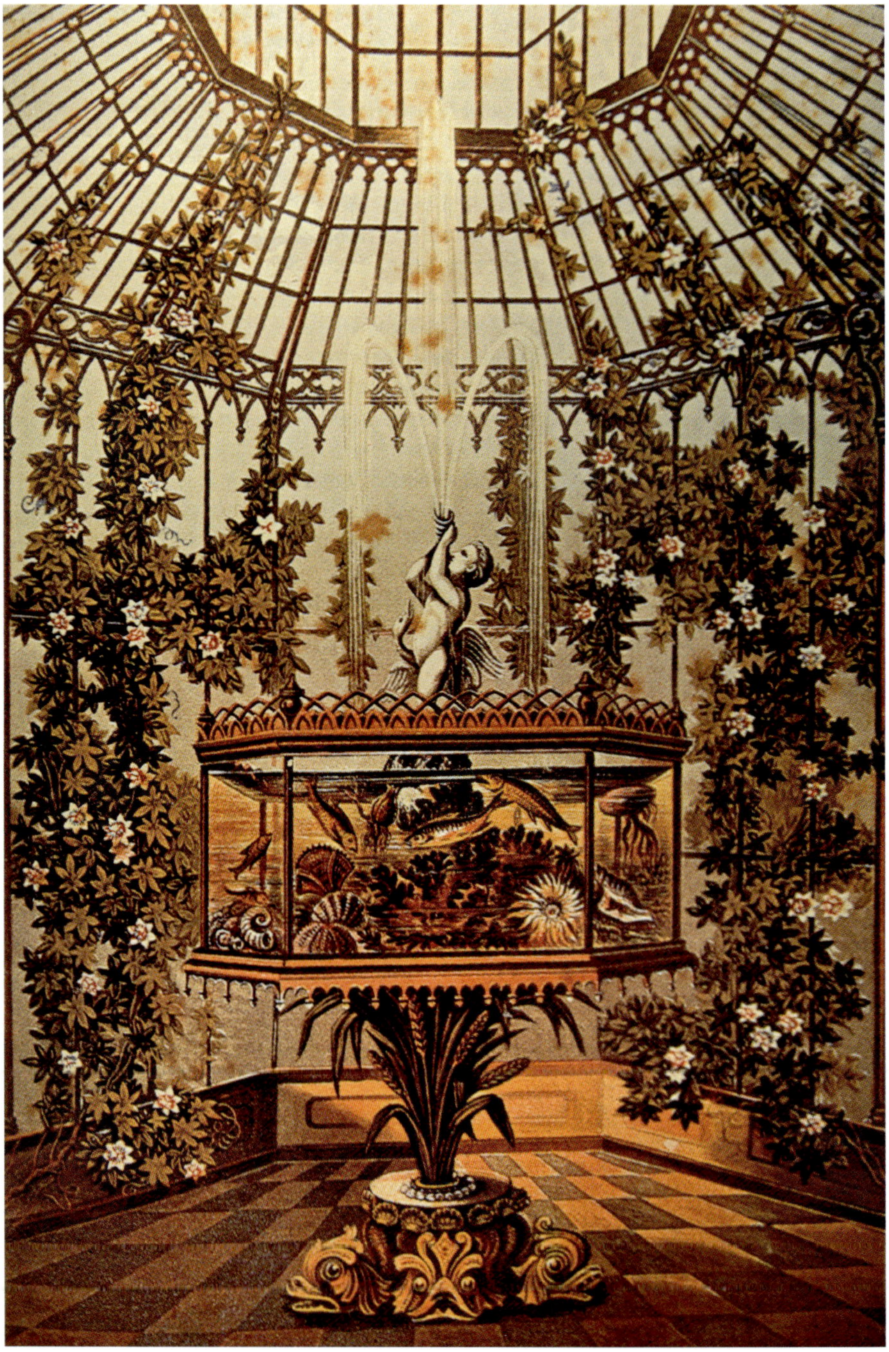

142 Aquarium and conservatory, from *Cassell's Household Guide* (*c.* 1870).

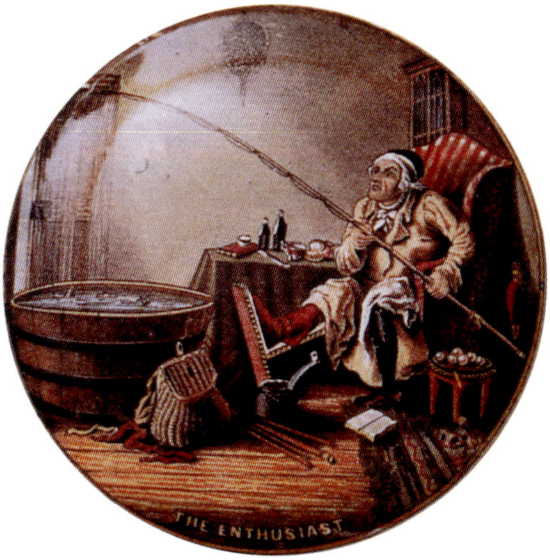

143 A ceramic pot-lid from the Pratt factory with an illustration of the watercolour *The Enthusiast (The Gouty Angler)* by Theodore Lane, *c.* 1820–28.

The craze swept through the country until superseded by newer novelties about 1868.

Technically, ways were found to increase the size of tanks so that larger fish species could be exhibited. In zoos and seaside showrooms the variety of sea creatures increased both in number and size until today we can watch large sharks as they swim in enormous tanks in an oceanarium.

Long experience in keeping cold freshwater species in aquaria means that they are now bred commercially in huge numbers. Today the occupants of fish tanks in homes may be freshwater or marine species. Temperate water marine aquaria are now gaining in popularity. The warmer water aquarium allows the fantastically shaped, intensely coloured tropical fishes with their intricate patterns to be cultivated. Having these species available for close study is of great advantage to artists painting scenes of tropical seas, especially when the aquarium also has tropical invertebrates, corals, crabs, sea anemones, shrimps, starfishes and other forms of sea-life.

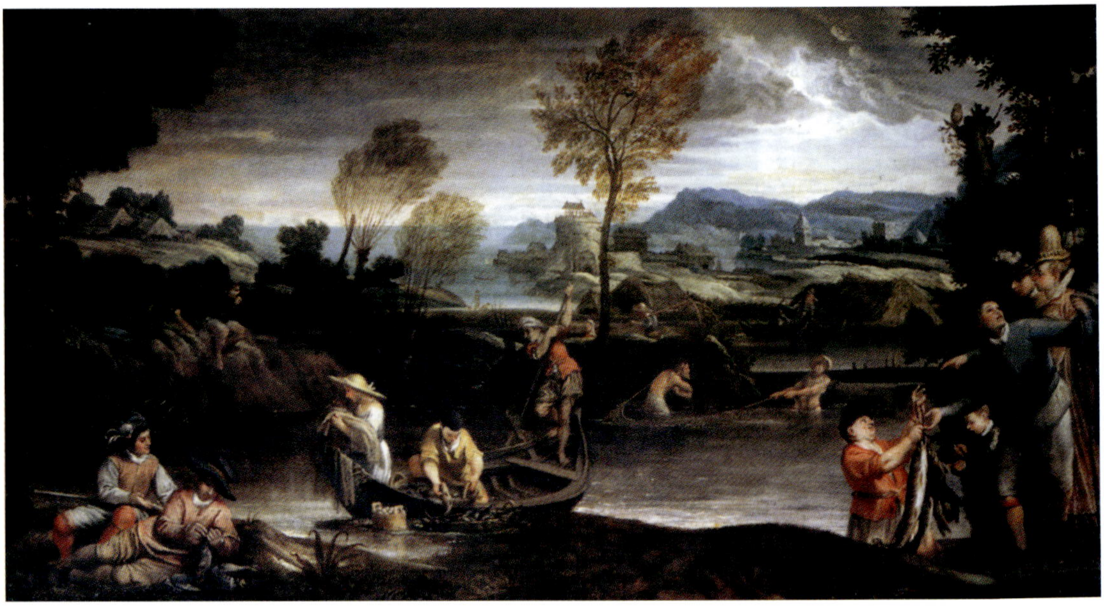

144 Annibale Carracci, *Fishing*, *c.* 1585–8, oil on canvas.

seven
Fish in the River

Four thousand years ago Egyptians were enjoying fishing in the Nile, its adjacent marshes and pools. Scenes of fishermen on the banks of the river or standing in skiffs are numerous in the tombs of ancient Egyptians. Fish was an important part of their diet. Those who were fishermen by trade used the net in preference to the line, but from the evidence of tomb paintings it is clear that fishing was a favourite pastime for Egyptian 'gentlemen'. Spearing fish with a bident (a two-pronged spear) was considered to be the most sporting way to kill fish. Where pictures show men of rank fishing with rod, line and hook, they are often using pools constructed in their own grounds. These were stocked with favourite fishes that were particularly prized for the table: several *Silurus* species (catfish), *Cyprinus* (carp), Nile perch and wrasse. Some paintings also show eels, mullet and tiger fish – all carefully delineated in the stylised wavy water. The *Oxyrhynchus* with the pointed nose was a sacred fish and it was forbidden to eat it. Several of them have been found embalmed at Thebes (illus. 146).

There are numerous ancient Greek images of Venus and her son Cupid fishing with one fish hooked – usually by Cupid, not Venus! Greek vases have images of fishermen perched on a rock by the river, fishing rod in one hand and a basket in the other. The fishes are shown swimming in the water.

The Chinese delighted to paint sinuous swimming fishes to decorate fans, scrolls and screens. During the Song Dynasty (960–1279) Liu Cai used Indian ink and colours on silk to paint a hand scroll with the title *Fish at Play among Fallen Leaves.* This very early painting is remarkable

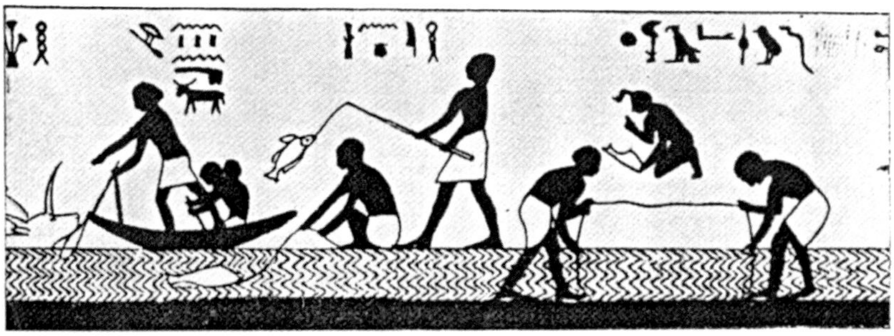

145 Egyptians fishing in the Nile, *c.* 2000 BC. This is thought to be the earliest representation of angling.

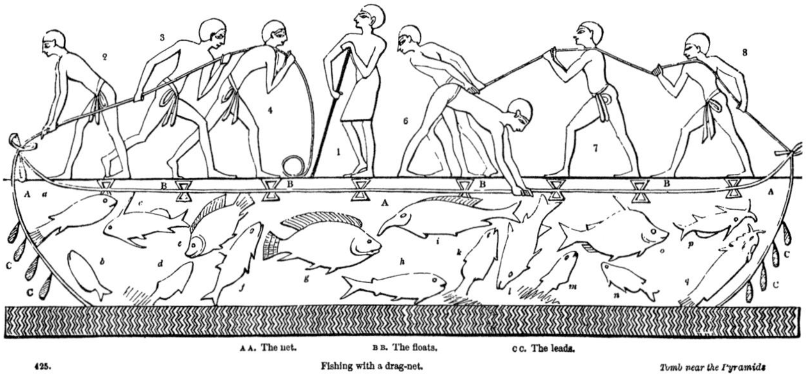

146 Woodcut of a painted fishing scene showing Egyptians in a skiff using a net, from a rock tomb at Deir el-Gebrawi. Several different species of fishes are shown: catfishes, wrasses, blennies, Nile perches and carp.

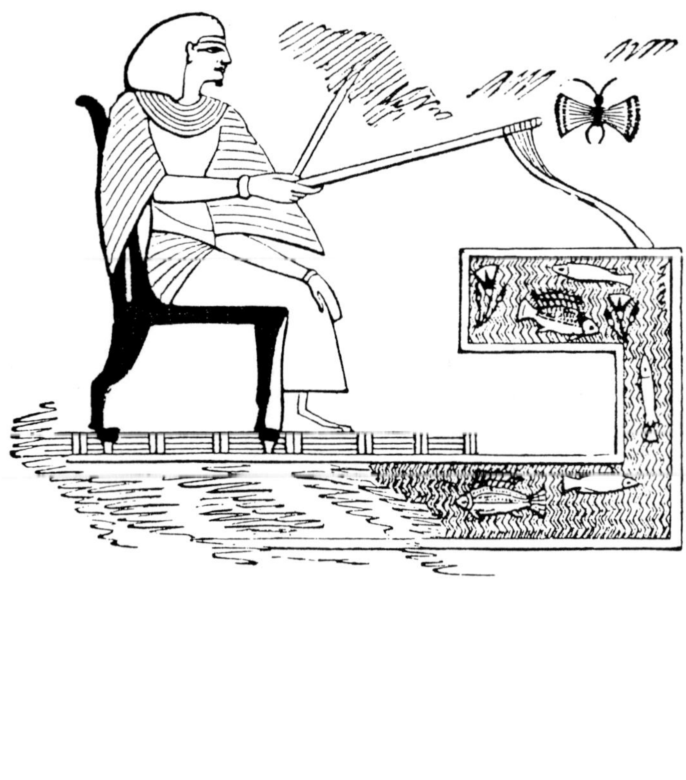

147 Seated Egyptian nobleman fishing in his pool, *c.* 1295–1069 BC, drawing on limestone.

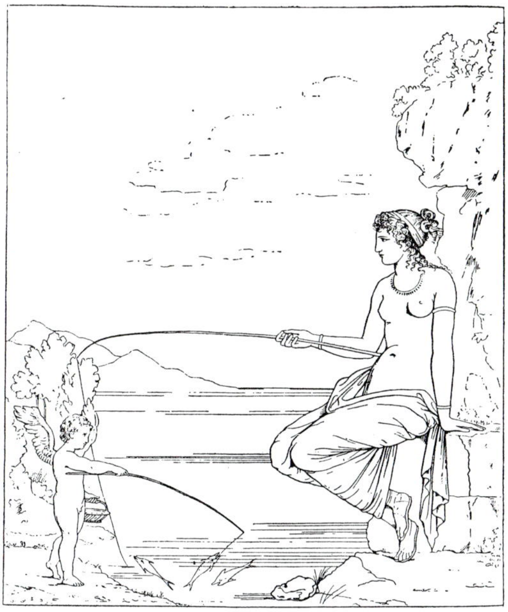

148 Venus and Cupid angling. The Greeks showed the fish in the water, with Cupid having caught one; this was a theme often repeated in Grecian art and painted on vases.

for the fluidity of the movement of the fishes as they dart through the vegetation. The idea that the fishes are at play would be entirely novel to any Western artist. Nothing either so lively or picturing the fishes in the river appeared in Western art for centuries. Another example of this versatility with the depiction of living fishes occurred in the thirteenth century, in *Fish and Water Grasses* in ink on a silk hanging scroll, painted by an unidentified artist.

An early set of European rules to control the catching and selling of freshwater fishes was drawn up by Emperor Frederick III (1415–1493). His son, Maximilian I (1459–1519), was interested in natural history and greatly encouraged both the arts and learning throughout the Holy Roman Empire. Following on from his father's edicts, Maximilian compiled a

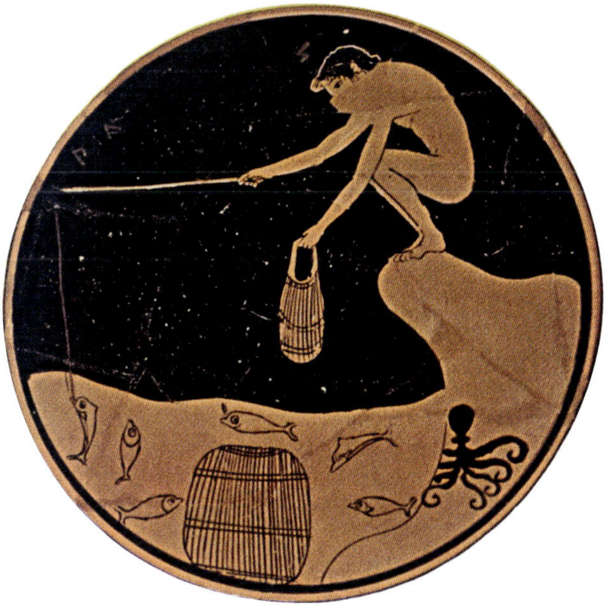

149 Greek boy fishing with rod and line and basket. From an Attic red cup by Douris, *c.* 480 BC.

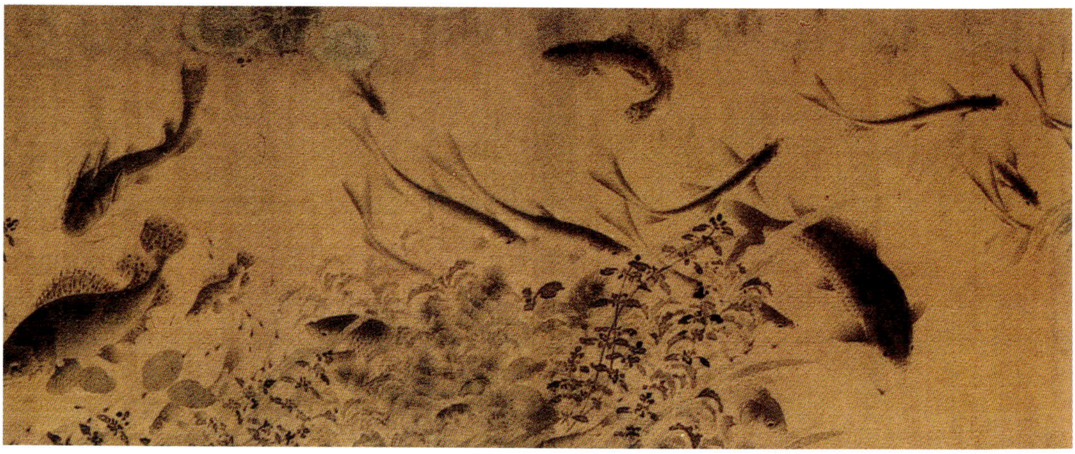

Fishing Code in 1506 that included eight well-drawn river fishes coloured with watercolour and gouache, by an unknown artist. It was essential for the fishermen obeying the code to be able to identify each species, and the illustrations are so accurate there could have been no arguments about infringement of the rules.

150 Liu Cai, *Fish at Play Among Fallen Leaves*, Song Dynasty, hand scroll, ink and colours on silk.

A bizarre portrait was painted in 1566 for Holy Roman Emperor Maximilian II, a Habsburg monarch, by one of his favourite artists, Giuseppe Arcimboldo (1527–1593). An Italian by birth, Arcimboldo moved to Prague in 1562 and became court painter to three successive emperors, Ferdinand I, Maximilian II and Rudolf II. He took the court by storm with his ingenious and original grotesques. He used flowers, fruit, vegetables or fishes to create portraits. The fish portrait was presented to Maximilian (*reg.* 1562–76) as one of a series of paintings representing *Water*, one of the *Four Elements*. He copied this many times to present at the behest of the emperor to people he wished to impress with the glory of the Habsburg court.

The author of the catalogue for an exhibition of Arcimboldo's work held in Venice in 1987 attempted to identify all the species of fishes used to create this picture, as well as the reptiles, mammals, invertebrates, crustaceans, molluscs, cephalopods and a starfish. Among the fishes were moray eel, sunfish, several catfishes, black umber, shad, pike, lung fishes, lumpfish, wrasses, gurnard, ray, dogfish and other sharks. Most of the marine animals were from the Mediterranean, while oyster pearls made up the earring and necklace.

Artists of other ancient civilizations painted men fishing in rivers and showed the species that they were attempting to net or catch by means of

151 *A Fish and Water Grasses*, 13th-century hanging scroll, ink on silk, artist unknown.

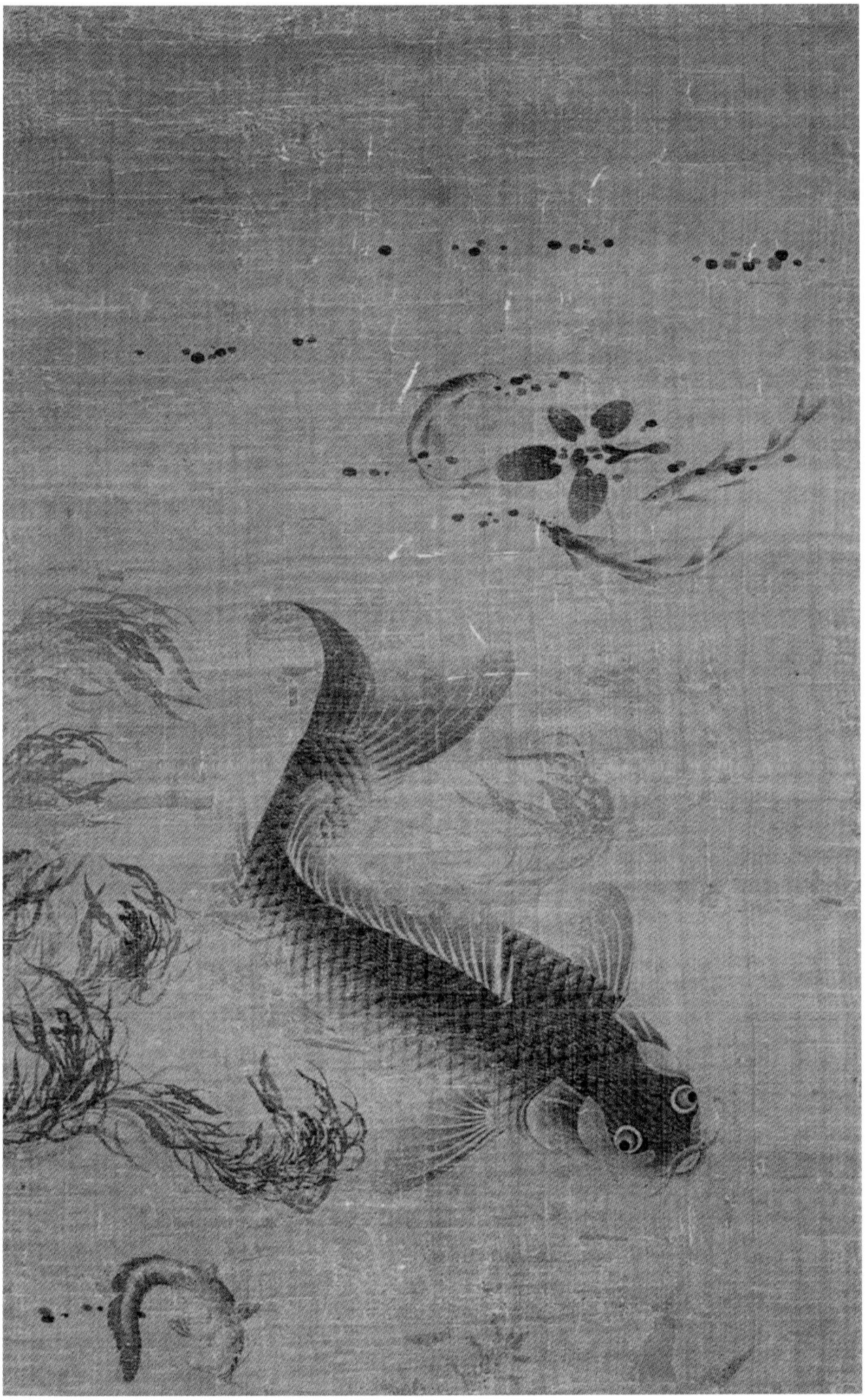

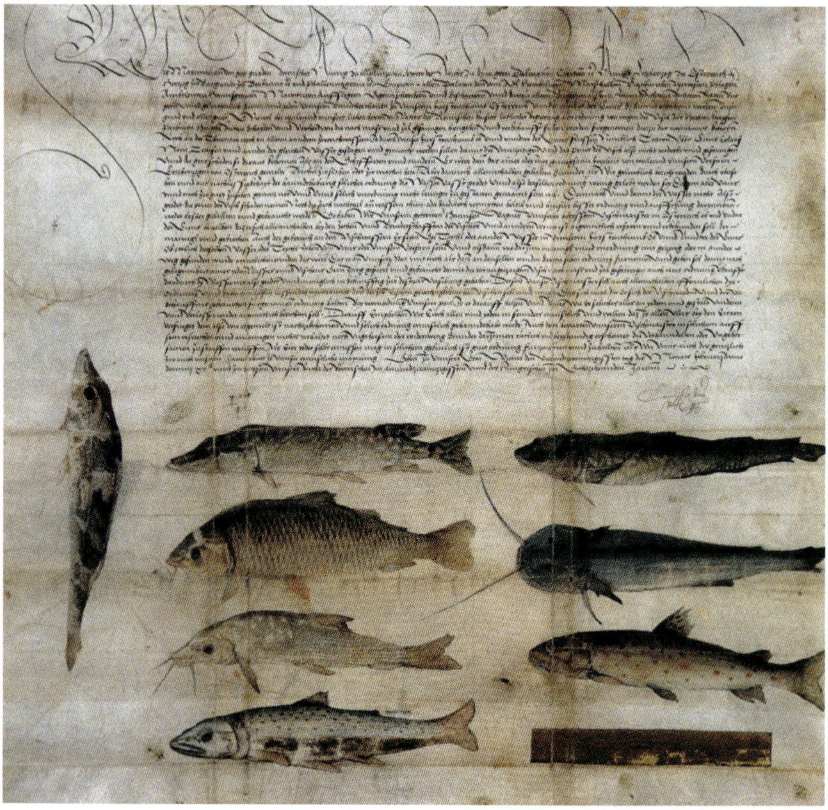

152 Fishing code commissioned by Maximilian I, 1506, artist unknown.

rod and line. This eminently sensible composition for a fishing scene was adopted by John White for his studies of natives sea-fishing in North America (illus. 11), and aborigines also show their quarry in the sea.

It is both surprising and puzzling that paintings from Continental Europe showing both the anglers and the different species of fishes in the water where they have cast their lines are very rare. The closest we come to fish in the river is when the head of a fish is seen poking out of the water after it has been hooked and is being reeled in. During the twentieth century there were studies of one or two fishes in water with plants and rocks on the riverbed, but no angler was present. Throughout our history of European freshwater fish painting, we have no hint in angling scenes of the diversity of species to be found underwater.

An early Italian painting, *Fishing*, by Annibale Carracci (1560–1609), who painted scenes around his native Bologna, including the rivers and

153 Giuseppe Arcimboldo, *Water*, 1566, oil on panel.

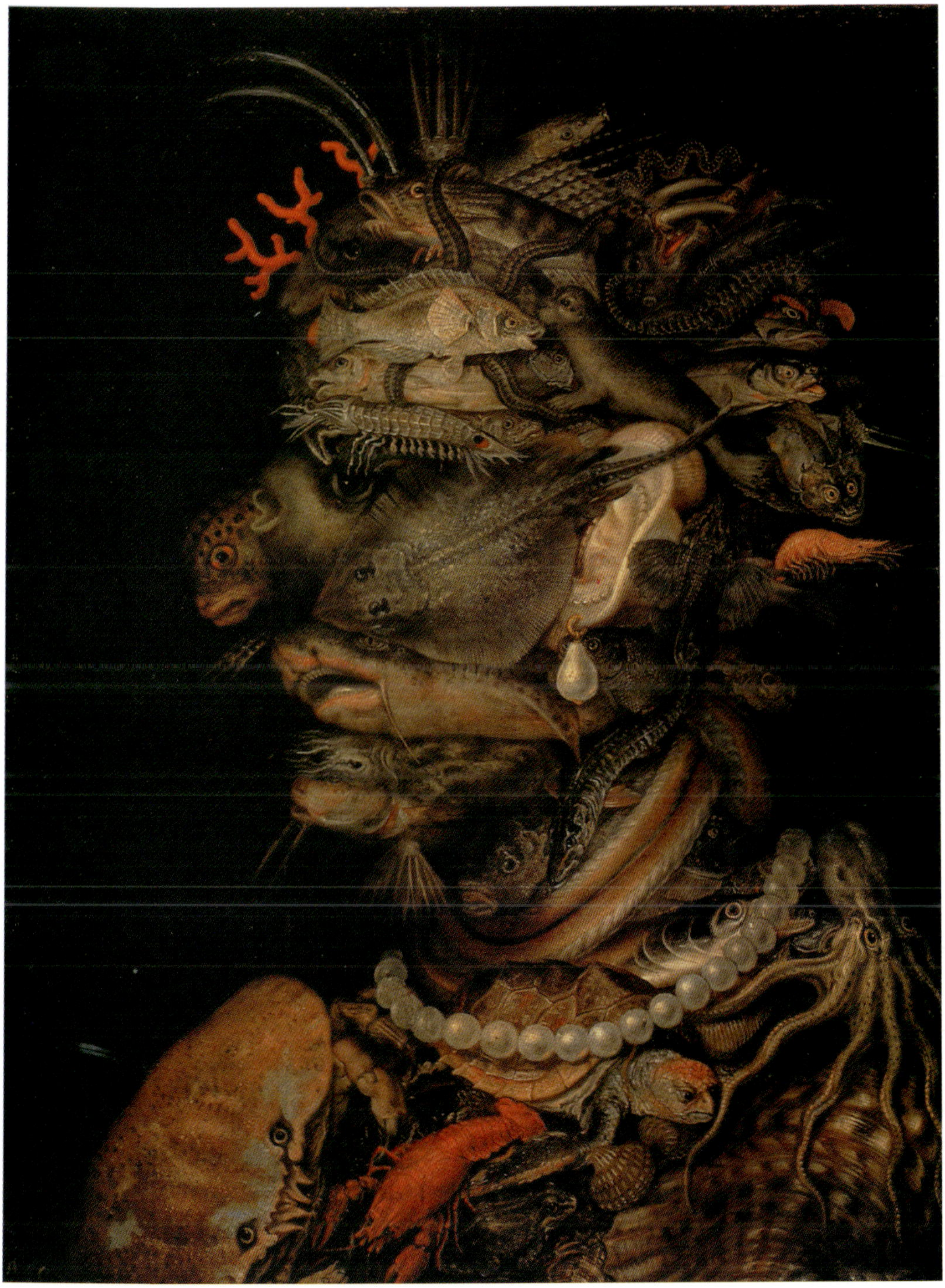

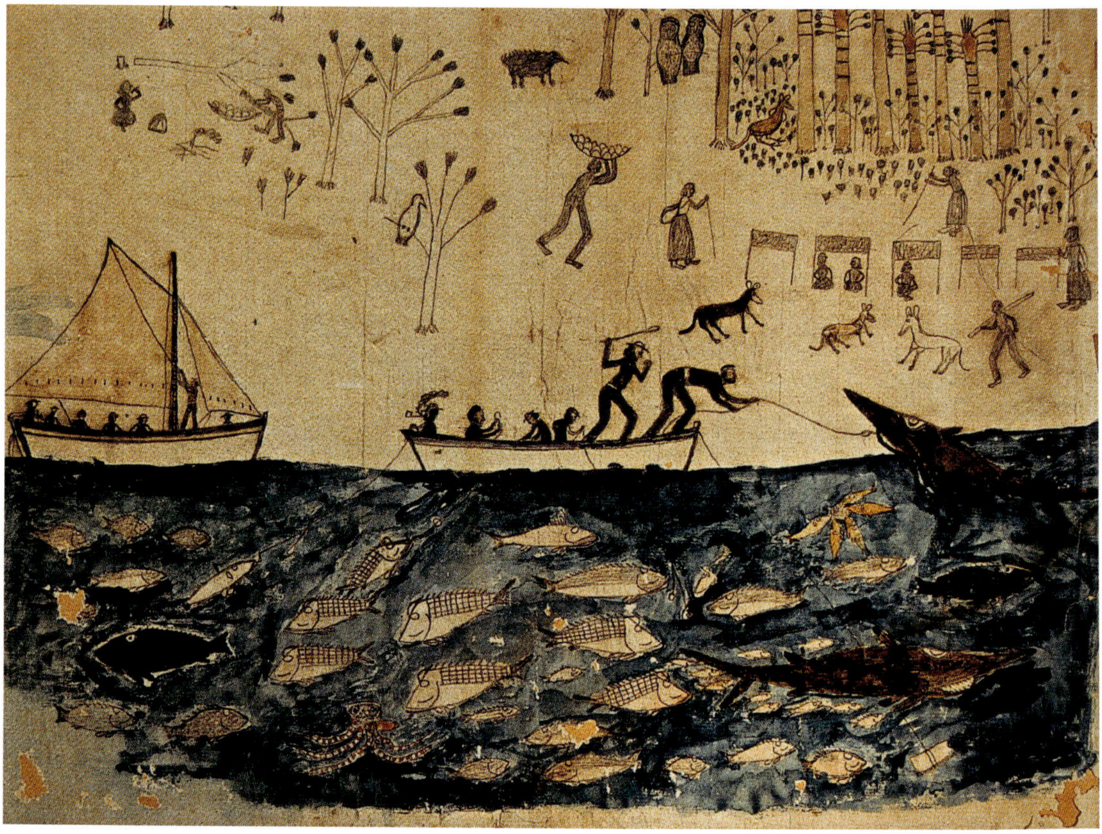

154 Mickey of Ulladulla, 'Aborigines Fishing', from his *Fishing Scenes of Daily Life: Native Flora and Fauna* (1880s).

their fishermen and boatmen, has the most unusual feature of a collection of anglers with their wives from all strata of society. The fishermen are using nets, rod and line, fishing from the bank and boats. All the fishes are shown caught and landed, not in the water.

Although more than half of the 45 or so fish species included in Dutch and Flemish fish paintings of the seventeenth century were fresh-water fishes, they were depicted after being landed, in beach and market scenes, and were mixed among the salt-water species. Paintings of fresh-water fishes have been done predominantly by British artists since the nineteenth century. Angling as a sport was developed by the British to become a favourite pastime and then taken up enthusiastically in the United States. As Tom Quinn, the author of the delightful *Angling in Art*, wrote, in other countries 'the tradition of angling as a sport simply does not exist'. As for the idea that a man will spend hours fishing, and

PERCH (*Perca fluviatilis*) is one of the most highly thought of sporting fish of slow-moving waters, readily identifiable by the broad black vertical bands. When excited, the lower fins become a vivid orange-red. It is a good fish to eat – after removing numerous bones. Mrs Beeton said it was one of the best and commonest of freshwater fishes, found in nearly all lakes and rivers in Britain. It was honoured in ancient Greece and Rome and is still eaten in Italy and France.

having caught a fish, carefully remove the hook, admire it for a few minutes and then gently ease it back into the water, that is likely to be greeted first with incredulity and then uproarious laughter by other Europeans.

The practice on the Continent is for authors of angling books to write about freshwater fishes in rivers by the zones the different species inhabit, for example, the trout zone, grayling zone, barbel zone and bream zone. The 'trout zone' refers to watercourses inhabited by brown trout and grayling. Known as trout waters, they contain the cleanest and coolest water where the fish colony is relatively sparse. Besides trout and grayling, miller's thumbs, bullheads and minnows are encountered in these areas of the river. The trout zone runs into the grayling zone as the river current gains momentum with fast-flowing stretches and deep pools, also expanses of slower-flowing water. In the grayling zone some trout are found, with miller's thumb and minnows, chub and gudgeon. These also overlap with the barbel zone of central stretches of water flowing over riverbeds of firm gravel or sand with water temperatures rising to over 25 degrees Centigrade. Unsuitable for salmonids, barbel, dace, gudgeon, pike and eels flourish here, while chub find their niches in sheltered places. Inhabitants of the lower course of the river, in the bream zone, enjoy conditions that favour roach and rudd, carp and perch.

Continental anglers fish an area and catch whatever species they can and eat their catch. Small and inedible fishes are used as bait for more desirable species. Because fishing is commercial or utilitarian, scenes of anglers at work are not particularly attractive to artists.

In Britain most fish paintings were of sportsmen angling, and most showed the angler and the river in beautiful landscapes. The greater proportion of paintings of river fishes showed them when laid on a bank, and this form of art did not occur as a popular genre until the nineteenth

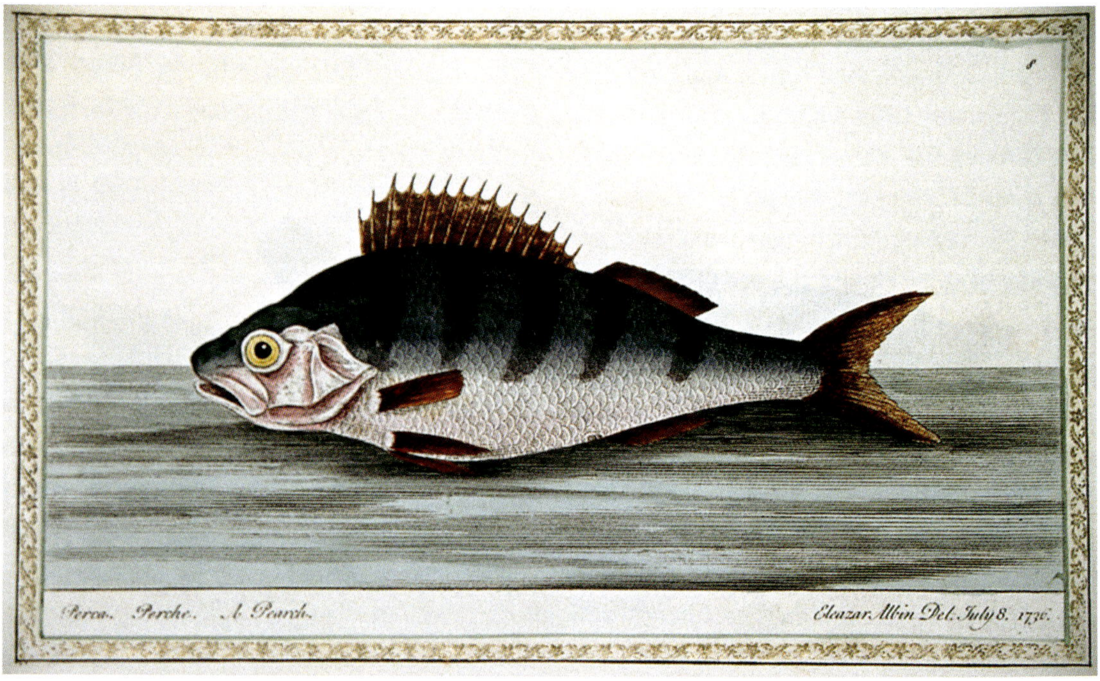

155 Eleazar Albin's illustration of a perch, 1736, from his book *Esculent Fish*, etched and then hand-painted. This was the first English book about fish to have coloured illustrations.

century. We have to search hard for fish in the river among angling paintings, hoping to catch a glimpse of the fishes every now and again.

Some of the earliest books with fish illustrations were totally unreliable because fact and fancy were mingled. The first to have hand-coloured illustrations, by Louis Renard, *Poissons, écrevisses et crabes, de diverses couleurs et figures extraordinaires,* was published in Amsterdam in around 1719. Eleazar Albin (*c.* 1680–1741/2), with the assistance of his daughter Elizabeth and son Fortinalus, published the first English colour illustrated book about fishes. The eighteen plates were first etched and then hand-painted for *Esculent [eatable] fish engraved [sic: etched] by Eleazar and Fortin Albin,* issued in London, 1735–41. It is also an early example of water being indicated, but curious in the manner in which he has painted the water and then superimposed the figure of the fish as though resting on the surface. He solved the problem of rendering waves, while using an etching needle, not by drawing parallel wavy lines, but the quicker method of using a ruler to draw a series of straight lines close together. This convention was followed for many years when water was depicted in books.

The first known English treatise on angling was printed in 1496, by Wynkyn de Worde. Called the *Boke of Seynt Albans*, there are earlier editions but this one is of particular interest because it includes, for the first time, 'A Treatise of Fysshynge with an Angle'. It named the fishes commonly caught by rod and line as trout, salmon, grayling, barbel, chub, bream, tench, perch and roach. It is frequently stated that the whole book had been written by Dame Juliana Berners or Barnes, and that she was prioress of a nunnery at Sopwell near St Albans. It has now been established that this is an eighteenth-century invention. The book is a compilation of several authors, and she may have written the section on hunting but not the ones on hawking or heraldry, or on fishing. Her association with this first treatise on angling, however, is worth noting because of the perceived involvement of a lady at this early juncture in its history.

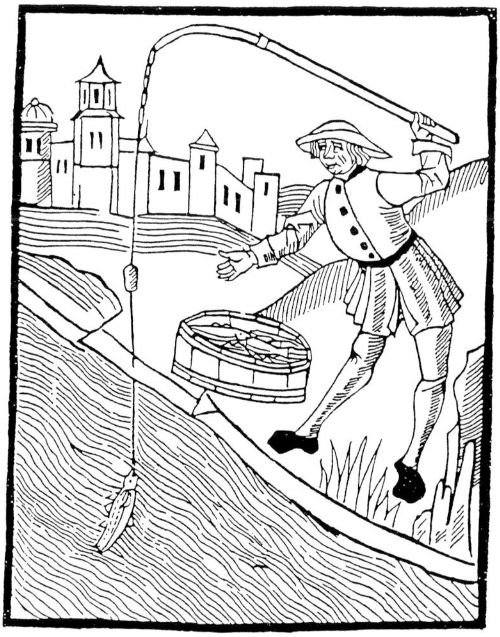

156 'A Treatyse of Fysshynge with an Angle', 1496, woodcut, from *The Boke of Saint Albans*.

The most surprising event where ladies are concerned, and much to the chagrin of male anglers, is the undeniable fact that two women hold the authenticated records for the largest salmon ever caught in British waters. On 7 October 1922 Miss Georgina W. Ballantyne spent two hours battling with a 64-lb (29-kg) salmon, having been spinning dace as the bait while sitting in her father's boat in the Boat Pool on the Glendelvine water of the river Tay in Scotland. When she finally got it on land it was the largest Scottish salmon ever caught on rod and line, and remains so to this day. Two years later another woman, 'Tiny' Morison, caught

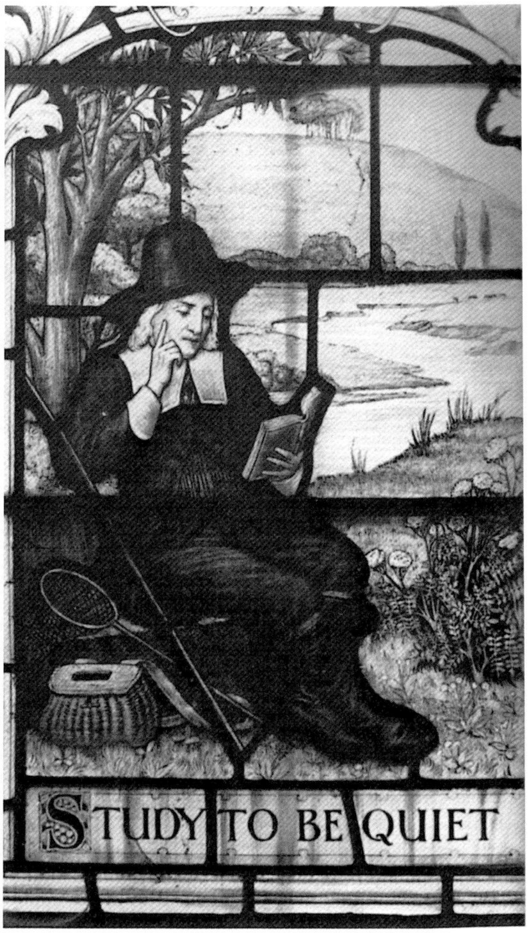

a 61-lb (28-kg) fish on a fly in the Lower Shaw Pool of the river Deveron in Aberdeenshire. A larger fish is on record as being hooked by the eighth Earl of Hume in the 1730s (a salmon of 69 lb 12 oz) from the Tweed, and the Bishop of Bristol lost a 71-pounder in 1871 that was taken in a net the next day further down the Tay. Even larger salmon have been taken in America. In Britain the ladies' records are the ones that count.

In between those remarkable events of 1496 and the 1920s there were two other milestones in the history of angling. The first was a book written by a London ironmonger, Izaak Walton, who was so successful in business that he retired early to devote his time to recreational pursuits, including his favourite, angling. In 1653 Walton's *Compleat Angler* was published and has proved to be so popular that it is still in print today. It had a profound influence on the sport of angling in Britain and led ultimately to a demand for paintings both of angling and of freshwater fishes by British artists. Walton's book gathered up what had been written previously on the art of fishing but went much further by presenting fishing not just as essential for food but as a contemplative, serene, civilized exercise. This established it as an activity that was both respectable at all levels of society and legitimately enjoyed by all. It took some time for this idea of fishing as a leisure activity to spread throughout society, but the main evidence that the gentry and new landowners had adopted it with some enthusiasm comes to us some 80 years after Walton first published the *Compleat Angler*. First, however, Walton's immediate influence is in evidence in Francis Barlow's fish paintings.

157 Part of the Izaak Walton window in Winchester Cathedral showing him by a river in Dovedale where he loved to fish.

The ATLANTIC SALMON (*Salmo salar*) is probably the most famous fish of the North Atlantic, both for its sporting quality and economic value. Salmon leave the sea to spawn upstream, in November and December. A nest or redd is scraped in gravel. The eggs hatch out in April to May into alevins or fry and progress to become parr, grilse, smolt and finally salmon. It is caught by spinning, trolling and fly-fishing and has become a major farmed species in several countries.

Francis Barlow (1626–1704) was the first English artist to record sporting scenes in prints, book illustrations and paintings. He is called the 'Father of the Sporting Print'. In 1653 he was paid £8 for a picture of fish and the diarist John Evelyn mentioned him as 'the famous painter of Fowls, Beasts & Birds' in 1656. Two years later, in *Graphice*, William Sanderson said that Barlow was among his contemporaries 'first for fowl and fish'. In 1667 he signed and dated a large painting (oil on canvas, 100 x 136 cm, now at Clandon Park, Surrey) with a title often repeated later by other artists, *After a Day's Fishing*. The foreground is strewn with recently caught pike, eels and other species. He used a landscape setting with trees and a lake and included several birds. In 1671 with Hollar as his etcher Barlow illustrated and published *Severall Wayes of Hunting, Hawking, & Fishing according*

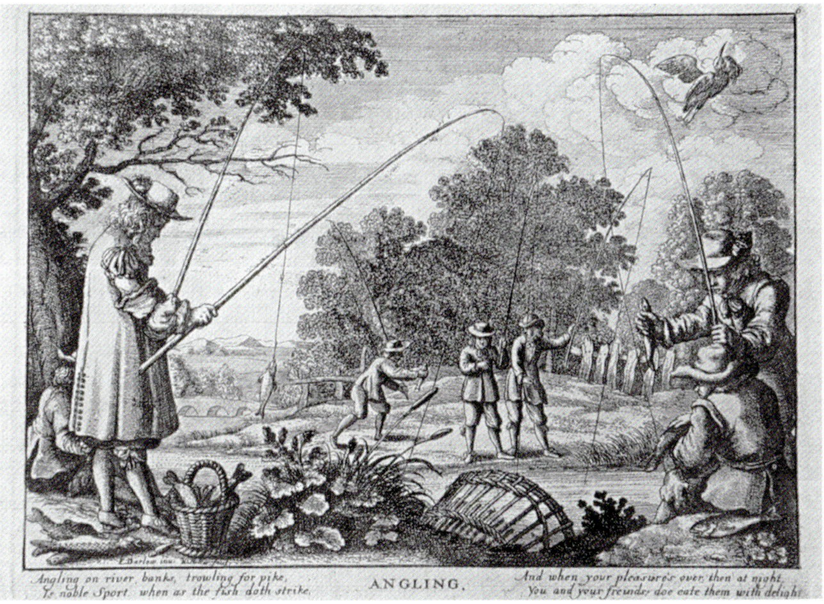

158 Francis Barlow designed this very early picture of *Angling* in England; it was engraved by Wenceslaus Hollar in 1671. The caption reads: Angling on river banks, trowling for pike / Is noble Sport when the fish doth strike / And when your pleasure's over, then at night / You and your freinds doe eate them with delight.

to the *English Manner* for the benefit of foreign sportsmen – an important publication in the history of British sports. He included three angling etchings, *Salmon Fishing*, *Angling* and *Fishing*, each with a rhyme printed underneath. The rhyme for *Fishing* describes using 'flu and codnet' in swift streams to take pike, perch and chub, poles to 'plunge' small fishes and nets to take shoals of fish. The fishes are being put into open woven baskets as though the creel had not yet been devised. In *Fishing* the consequence of this lack of a lidded basket can be seen – the eels are escaping over the sides.

In the early years of the eighteenth century Celia Fiennes made several journeys on horseback in England and wrote an account of her travels. She was impressed by the Ouse at Bedford, where, she said:

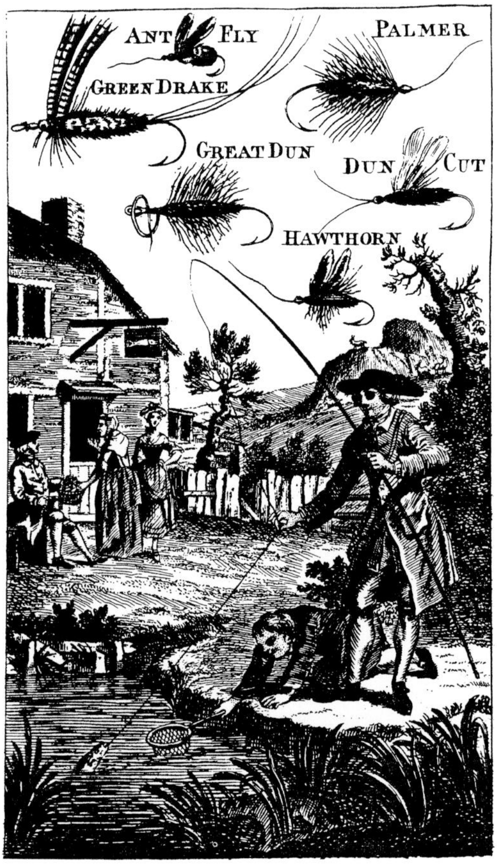

159 Richard Brookes, frontispiece from *The Art of Angling* (1790).

> The river is stored with very good fish and those which have gardens on its banks keepes sort of trunck or what they call them (it's like a receptacle of wood of a pretty size full of holes to let the water in and out) here they keep fish they catch as pike, perch, tench etc., so they have it ready for their use; this is of mighty advantage especially for the Publick houses, you see the fish taken out fresh for supper or dinner; the river runns twineing about and runns into severall notches of ground which is sett full of willows, and many little boats chained to the sides belonging to the people of the town for their diversion.

After Barlow, the next British paintings to include fishermen were the conversation pieces of the 1730s and 1740s. These portrait groups in

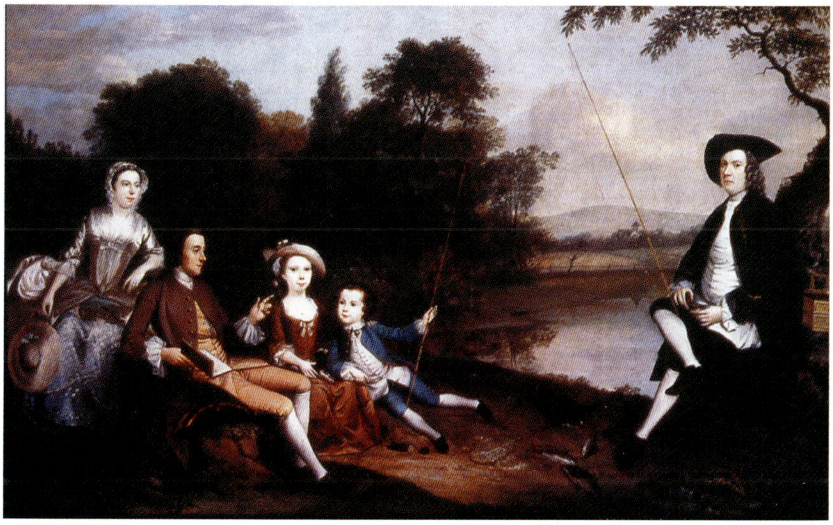

160 Arthur Devis, *The Swaine Family*, 1749, oil on canvas.

a landscape setting by a river showed a family seated on a riverbank with one or more members of the group holding a fishing rod. Conversation pieces were very popular in Britain in the mid-eighteenth century through to the early nineteenth, a time when prosperous merchants, the newly emerging middle class, were buying land and building luxury homes. The conversation piece was designed to show the owner's family relaxing by a river or lake on his property, often with his house in the background. While essentially portrait paintings they also indicated that not only was he sufficiently leisured to enjoy angling as a sport but this sport was enjoyed by all members of his family. Two artists who made a name for themselves in the 1720s for conversation pieces were Philip Mercier (1689/91–1760), a Berliner who worked mostly in England, and the better-known William Hogarth. Their conversation pieces are interesting because they show a family by the riverside with both men and women holding fishing rods. Philip Mercier's *The Wentworth Family* of 1740 includes Diana, the lady of the house, holding a rod in her right hand, and Hogarth's *A Fishing Party – The Fair Angler* is similar. They were joined in this genre by Johann Zoffany (1715–1810) and Arthur Devis

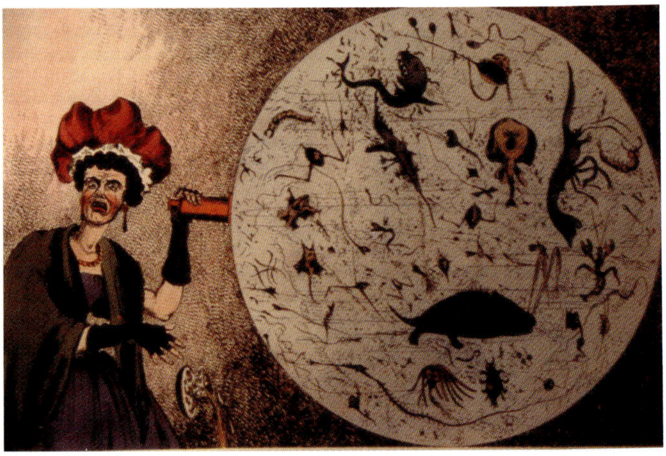

161 George Cruikshank, *Thames Water*, colour print, 1850s.

GEORGE CRUIKSHANK (1792–1878) painted this satire on the condition of the water of the Thames. The lady on the left is so astonished and mortified by what her magnifying glass revealed of the state of the source of her drinking water that she has dropped her cup of tea. The small fishes and large number of invertebrates are all gasping and grimacing as they try to survive in the polluted water. Regular outbreaks of typhus and cholera occurred in London and led, in 1855, to the Metropolitan Board of Works beginning to build sewers to carry the capital's effluent under a new embankment and downstream. In 1890 the sewage was collected at two outfalls near Tower Bridge, treated with lime and ferrous sulphate and the resulting sludge put into boats and carried out to the North Sea. This removed some of the pollutants but not all. Great efforts in recent years to clean up the river have now made the Thames the cleanest metropolitan river in Europe. More than 100 species of fishes have been found living in the river, while the estuary gives shelter to other species including bass and flounders.

(1712–1787). *The Swaine Family* by Devis is the one painting out of many conversation pieces that has identifiable fishes lying on the ground.

Of the other painters of conversation pieces, George Morland (1763–1804), Francis Wheatley (1747–1801) and Joseph Farington (1747–1821) show men and women and boys holding fishing rods. There followed several paintings of women fishing, either in groups or singly, and other pictures of children fishing, The earnest youngsters are shown catching prawns by William Collins (1788–1847) and fishing in the Thames by Edmund Bristow (1787–1876). There were many paintings of youthful fishers, some sentimental, several with village urchins, such as H. Barstowe's *Rustic Fisherboys* of 1869, with four young boys fishing. One of the boys is in the stream, possibly tickling trout. Rustic boys were acceptable subjects for Victorian angling paintings but their fathers, agricultural labourers or factory workers, were not depicted.

The aristocracy and monasteries had held much of the land in England through the Middle Ages until the dissolution of the monasteries in the 1530s. The redistribution of monastic lands (when the gentry bought the greater proportion) and the growing prosperity in England led to men investing their new wealth in land. Landownership concentrated many of the best fishing rivers and stretches into the hands of the gentry. This is the beginning of the great divide between those who had access to game fishes, salmon, trout, grayling and charr, and those who had to make do not only with less aristocratic rivers than the Helmsdale, Dee, Spey, Tweed and Tay but also other newly excluded sites. As early as the 1830s Sir William Jardine of Jardine Hall, Dumfriesshire, complained that it was becoming too expensive for him to continue to fish for salmon in the Tweed. At the same time the Industrial Revolution concentrated many former village-dwellers, who had enjoyed fishing, into crowded towns. They escaped to the countryside in their leisure time (by the spreading railway network) to fish in streams and man-made stretches of water. Unrestricted by game laws, they could fish for coarse fishes (mainly carp, perch, tench, pike, rudd, roach, eels, lampreys, burbot, shad and barbel) which were still eaten at this date, though barbel were treated with care because the roe is poisonous.

The number of fishermen increased rapidly in the second half of the nineteenth century; the bulk of them could fish only at weekends or in their holidays. Railway companies in the great industrial centres discovered a considerable source of revenue by providing cheap fares on lines running into the centres of fishing districts, such as the fens of Lincolnshire and Cambridge, the watersheds of the Trent and Nene, and the Lake District.

The PIKE (*Esox Lucius*) is a valuable food fish in Europe and well regarded as anglers' prey. Pike are voracious, aggressive and unpopular in trout rivers. In the reign of Henry VIII it was more expensive than salmon. It has attracted more legends than most fishes, and not a few lies about the size of escapees. Large eyes on the top of the head allow it to stare up malevolently at an angler. In the British Isles it can attain a weight of 24 kg (52 lb) and a length of 1.3 metres (4 feet).

The response from artists to this burgeoning interest in fishing changed to meet the demand for paintings of the anglers, then of them hooking fishes and lastly a shift in interest to the fishes themselves. The earliest nineteenth-century river fishing paintings were merely landscapes with a small figure of a fisherman added for interest. Action paintings of salmon rising, leaping, being gaffed and grassed came later. Strong, fighting trout and struggles against large pike were favourite topics. Pike are notoriously aggressive but are not usually known to take on a large mammal. In 1723 a pike suffered the fate of having its pond drained and when lifted out it was put into a wooden trough to be carried back to the village for supper. While being carried overland by two men it escaped from the trough. When its loss was discovered, three men with torches were sent back to look for it. They found the lost pike but it was not alone. A prowling fox had got too close to it and the pike had seized it by its muzzle and was not letting go. The Swiss naturalist

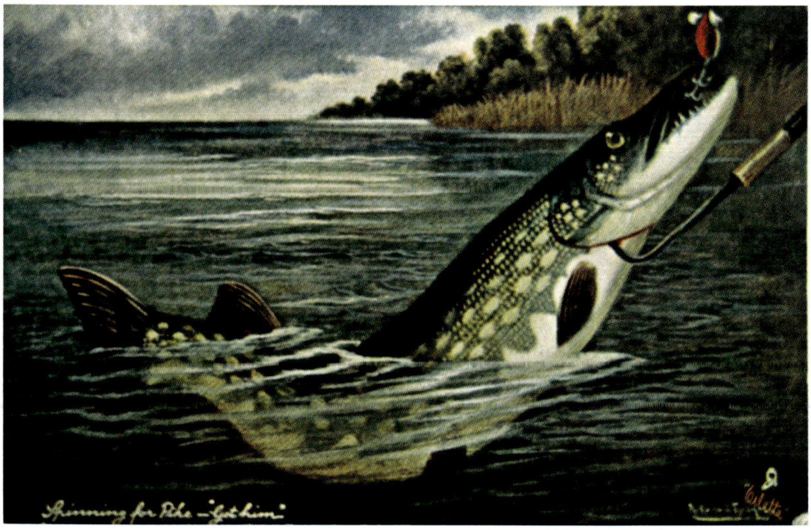

162 Arthur Roland Knight, *Spinning for Pike – Got Him*, postcard.

Conrad Gesner recounted a similar tale of a man who took his mule to a river to drink. A pike bit the mule's lower lip and would not be shaken off until, finally, the mule landed it on dry ground.

The Emperor's Pike, painted by an unknown artist in the late seventeenth or early eighteenth century (an oil, presented to the British Museum in 1881 and now in the Natural History Museum, London), has an unlikely story attached but is also a truly significant early example of fish research. Holy Roman Emperor Frederick II (1194–1250) is known to have taken a great interest in natural history and philosophy. He ruled a wide empire, stretching from Germany to Sicily, from his castle of Lautern in eastern Prussia, where he kept a menagerie. He had a lake at Lautern and marked one pike with a ring before releasing it into the lake. The Swiss naturalist Gesner wrote of this in 1558 saying that a bright copper ring had been placed under the skin of the pike, with a message engraved on it: ' I am that fish which was first of all put into this lake by the hands of the Emperor of the world, Frederick the Second, on the fifth October in the year 1230.' This might well be the earliest recorded instance of ringing or marking any wild creature.

So far the facts are believable, but the subsequent embellishments are hardly credible. The painting shows a gold ring in the lip of the pike and a large golden collar around its neck. The next record of this pike was when it was reputedly taken at Heidelberg in Germany, 267 years later, on 6 November 1497. Pike today may reach 1 metre (3 feet) in length during some fifteen years of life, but a black line placed along the edge of the picture indicates a length of 5.8 metres (19 feet). The carcase was kept in Mannheim Cathedral and when examined by naturalists in the nineteenth century was found to be a hoax. The skull had been taken from one pike while the body was made up of several others. Today we use rings and collars on wild animals to give us data on their movements and behaviour. That Emperor Frederick anticipated ringing is an amazing fact, but that the fish lived so long and grew so large is a really fishy tale.

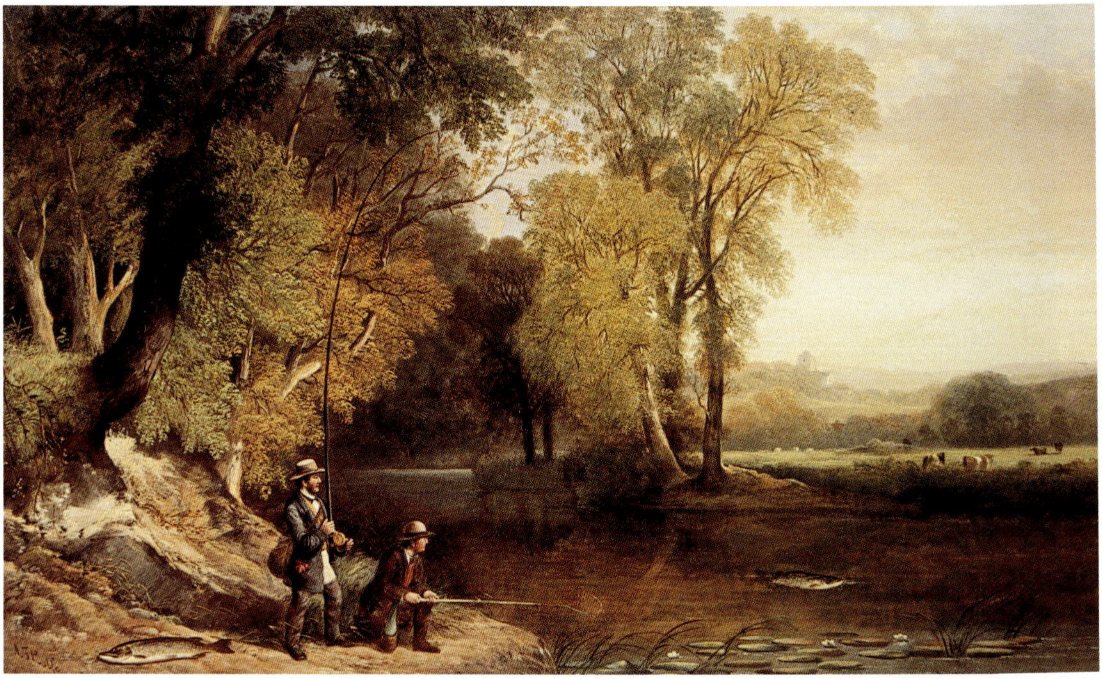

163 Alexander Frederick Rolfe, *River Landscape with Anglers Pike Fishing.*

The Rolfe family, particularly Alexander Frederick (1814–1875) and Henry Leonides (1823–1881), the most famous of the Rolfes, painted scores of fish pictures for the angling market of the second half of the nineteenth century. Paintings by Alexander Frederick Rolfe are scarce and his *River Landscape with Anglers Pike Fishing* is notable for the fish laid beside them as well as the pike in the river. Rolfe has created tension not just by the concentrated poses of the two anglers but by leaving a question mark over the pike. Will it bite and be landed?

Henry Leonides Rolfe painted a picture of a pike fishing with a kingfisher on the bank that had already had a successful strike. His *Kingfisher and a Perch Catching Fish* is a charming composition. It takes only one second for a kingfisher to dive from its perch into the water, seize a fish and return to its perch. It then stuns the fish by banging its head on the perch before turning it in its beak to face head first down its gullet. The kingfisher's enviable success rate is one strike in three attempts. Its prey includes minnow, stickleback, gudgeon and bullhead; it would find an un-netted trout hatchery or unprotected garden pool full of carp an open invitation to 'come and fish'. The Scottish Russells, John (*b.* 1851) and his father John Bucknell (1819–1893), followed a similar pattern of subjects in their work, with beautiful Scottish scenery in the background.

While the Rolfes and Russells painted river scenes with anglers dealing with pike, trout and salmon on the end of their lines, Arthur Roland Knight (*c.* 1846–1925) painted close-up pictures of the fishes that had been hooked (illus. 162). Knight was prolific with his paintings of fishes half in and half out of the river, including salmon, trout, perch, pike, roach, among other species that he knew sufficiently well to paint with accuracy and vivacity. There was too much activity sometimes, with pike making

164 Henry Leonides Rolfe, *Kingfisher and a Perch Catching Fish*, 1871, oil on canvas.

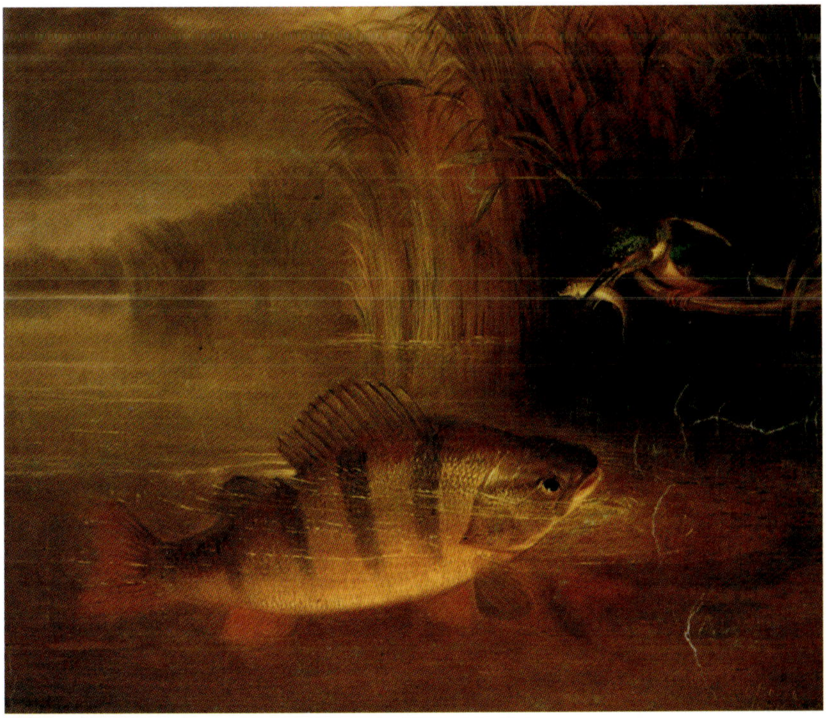

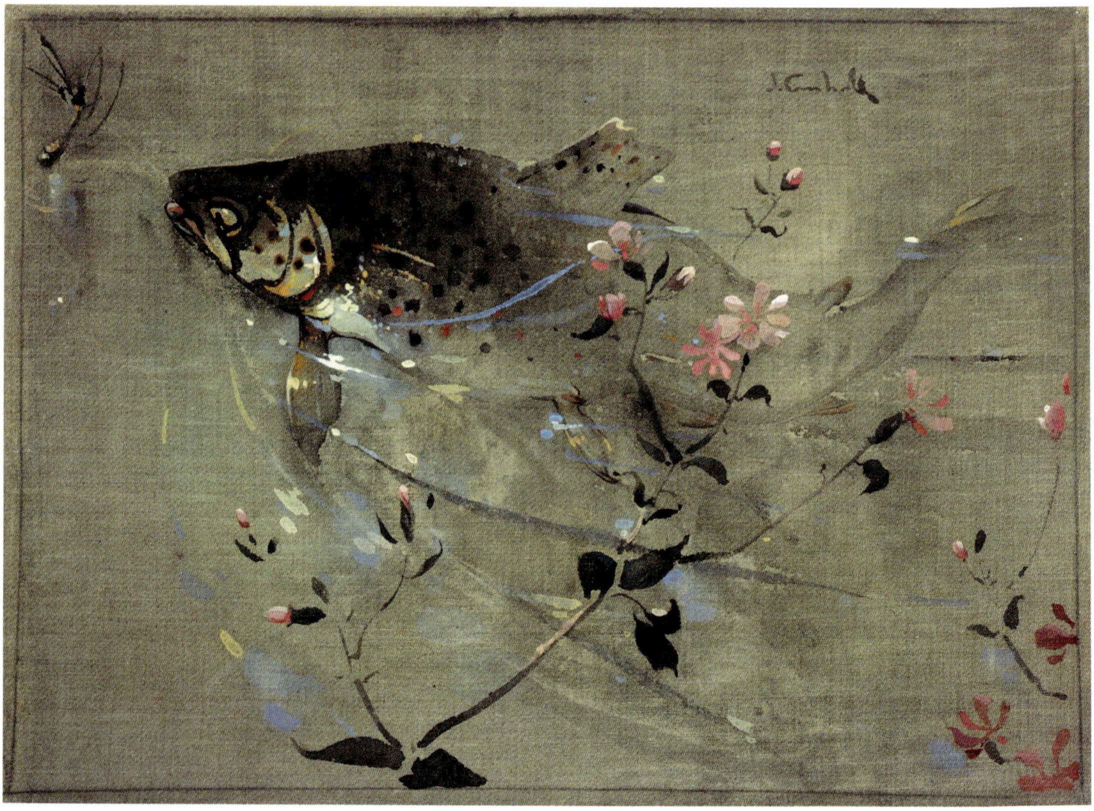

165 Joseph Crawhall, *A Trout Rising*, *c.* 1907, gouache on linen.

ridiculous leaps after fleeing roach that are flying through the air to escape, but the fishes are delightful because so well painted and animated. A large pike became a favourite subject because it can be a formidable foe. Izaak Walton valued it as 'a dish of meat too good for any but anglers, or very honest men'.

In the 1870s a different kind of sport fishing developed for anglers in poor fishing areas who could neither afford to travel to game-fish waters nor to pay the rent when they got there. Match-fishing for prize money by attempting to catch the greatest weight of fish in a given time became very popular. Up to thirty or forty anglers were ranged along the river or canal bank at regular intervals. At the end of the day the fishes were weighed and the angler with the heaviest catch won the trophy. There is a notable painting by Walter Dendy Sadler of such an event, *Pegged Down Fishing Match*, 1885, with a mixture of all levels of society fishing for coarse fishes, from a smock-frocked farmer to bowler-hatted and top-hatted traders, equipped with chairs and food for themselves, rod and baits for the fishes.

Towards the end of the nineteenth century the pattern of fish painting changed and more fishes were depicted immersed in the water with a very small section of riverbed and plants also being shown. The use of this format gathered momentum in the twentieth century when some of the finest fish artists painted them in their element. These are not only beautiful but sufficiently accurate portraits of the fishes to satisfy anglers who know these fishes intimately from having had them in the hand so frequently. One of the earliest twentieth-century paintings of this kind is Joseph Crawhall's *Brown Trout Rising*, 1907. Crawhall had a bravura style and experimented with materials and media. The trout is painted in gouache on linen.

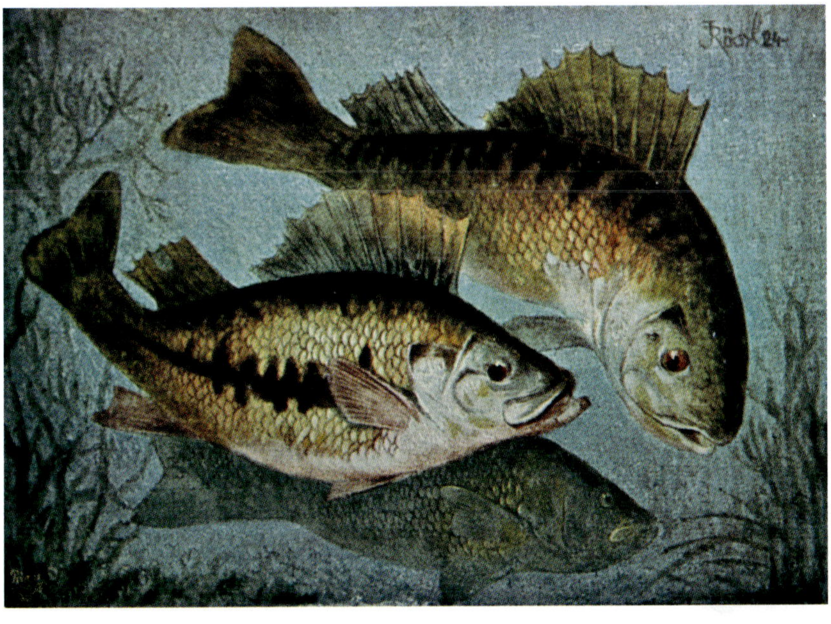

166 Joseph Rösl, *Perch in the River*, 1924, postcard.

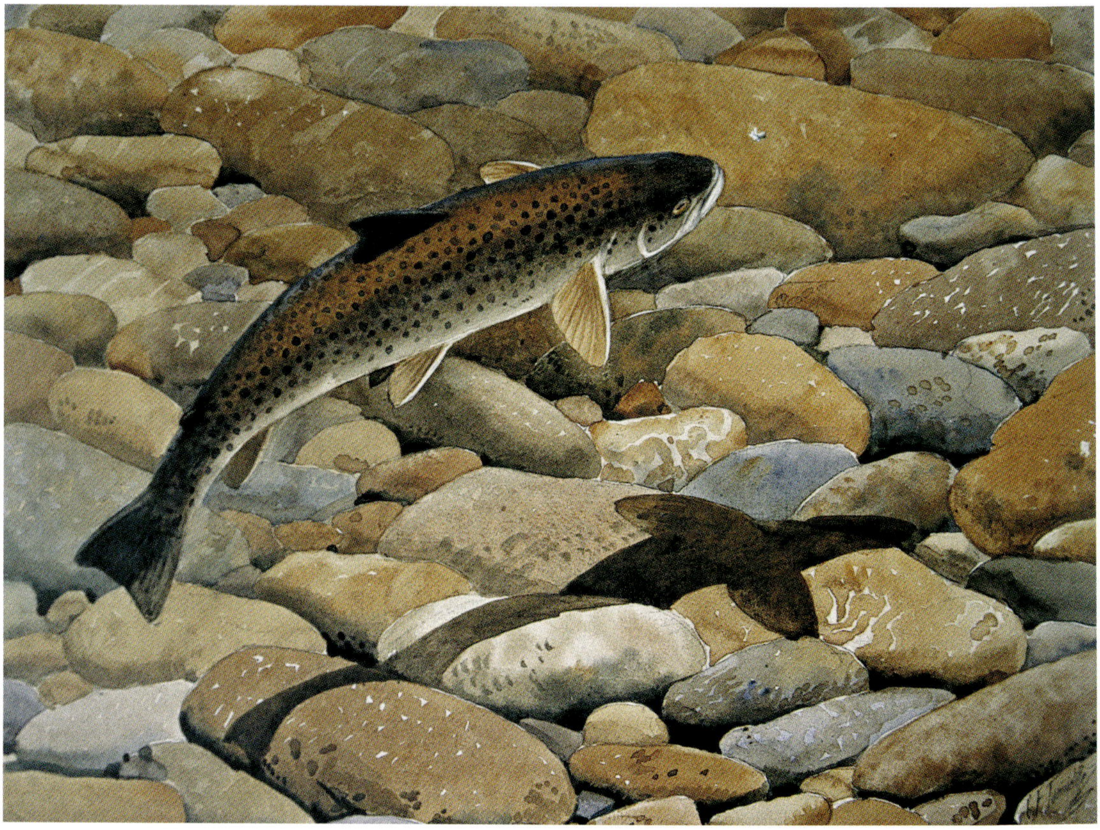

167 Charles Frederick Tunnicliffe, *Brown Trout in Shallow Waters*, watercolour.

A relatively unknown German artist working in Munich, Joseph Rösl (*b.* 1853), was mostly a painter on porcelain and stained glass for windows, but in 1924 he painted perch fully immersed in deep water. He signed and dated his picture 'J.Rösl 24'. The perch is highly thought of as a sporting fish of slow-moving or still waters, and here three perches are readily identifiable by the broad black vertical bands. When excited, the lower fins become a vivid orange-red. It may be good to eat but a lot of bones have to be removed first.

Charles Frederick Tunnicliffe (1901–1979) is well known as an outstanding painter of birds but he also painted an accurate picture of a brown trout. Strong design and clever placement are features of Tunnicliffe's work and are demonstrated clearly in this painting of *Brown Trout in Shallow Waters*. He also painted an angler playing a trout (reproduced in Negley Farson's *Going Fishing*). So many artists painted salmon, trout, pike and perch that it is refreshing to find a group of different species that are equally well regarded by some fishermen. The immaculate portrayal by Maurice J. Pledger of the barbel, roach, gudgeon and bullhead form an interesting group of coarse fishes in deep water.

Of all the river fishes, the favourite, the 'King of Fishes', is the salmon, *Salmo salar*. It is a beautiful fish, both in shape and silvery colour. Owners of parts of rivers where salmon run, guard them and their right to fish them jealously. They also create pools by building weirs to impede the fish's progress up and downstream. This is not a new practice. Our knowledge of low walls built across a river to raise the water level dates from the Middle Ages, the oldest surviving weir in England being at Chester across the river Dee, dating from around 1100. Brushwood weirs were used in rivers and on the seashore where salmon were stopped on their migration upriver. Hedges of rough brushwood were angled across the current in the shape of a shallow V with a net at

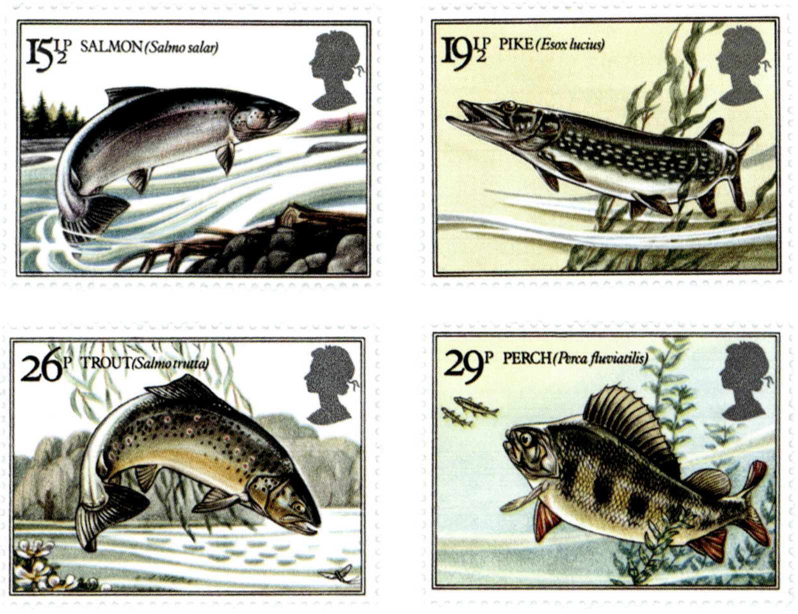

168 Alexander William Jardine designed a commemorative set of four British stamps, issued in 1983, showing salmon, pike, trout and perch.

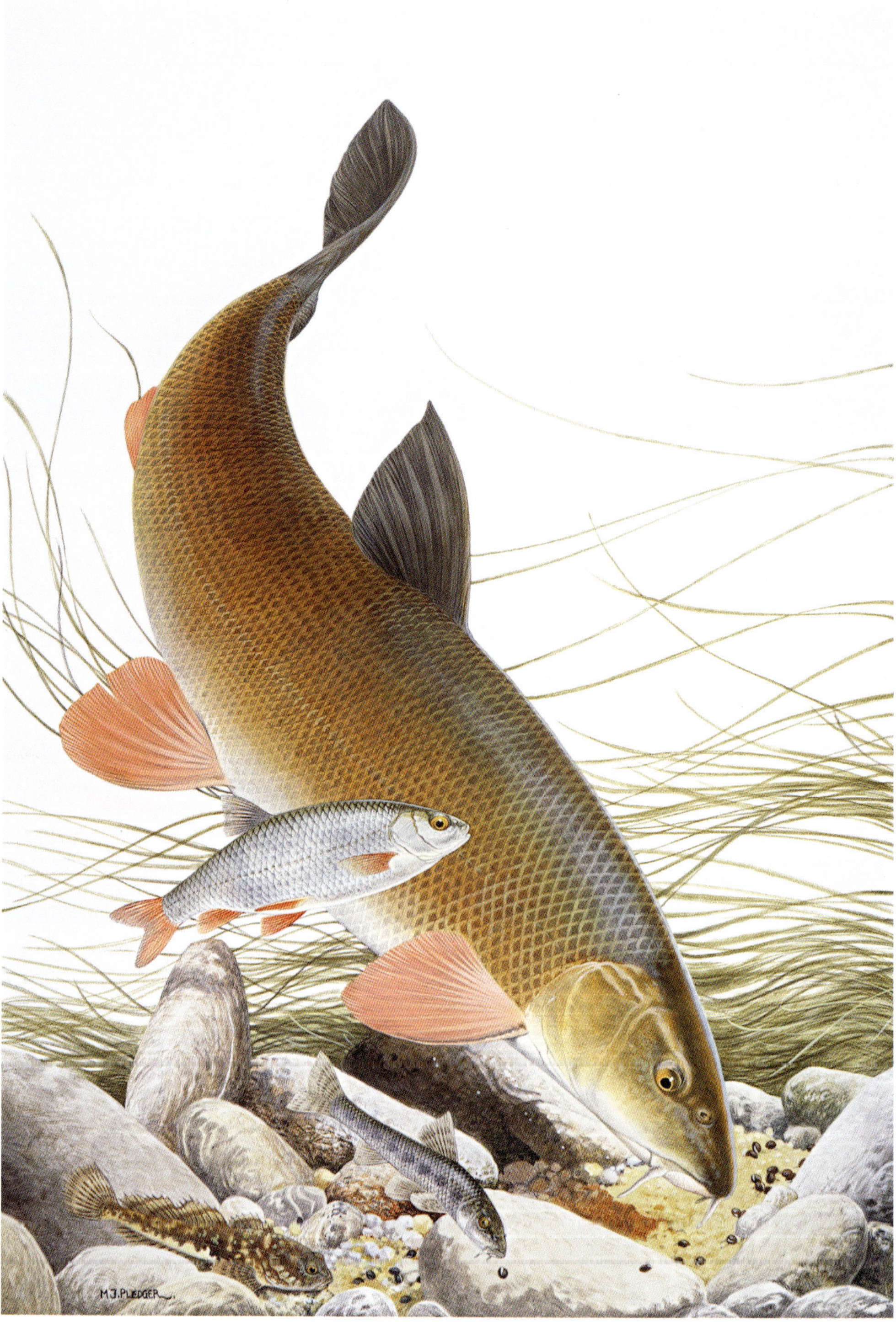

169 Maurice J. Pledger (*b.* 1955), *Barbel, Roach, Gudgeon and Bullhead*, pencil and watercolour.

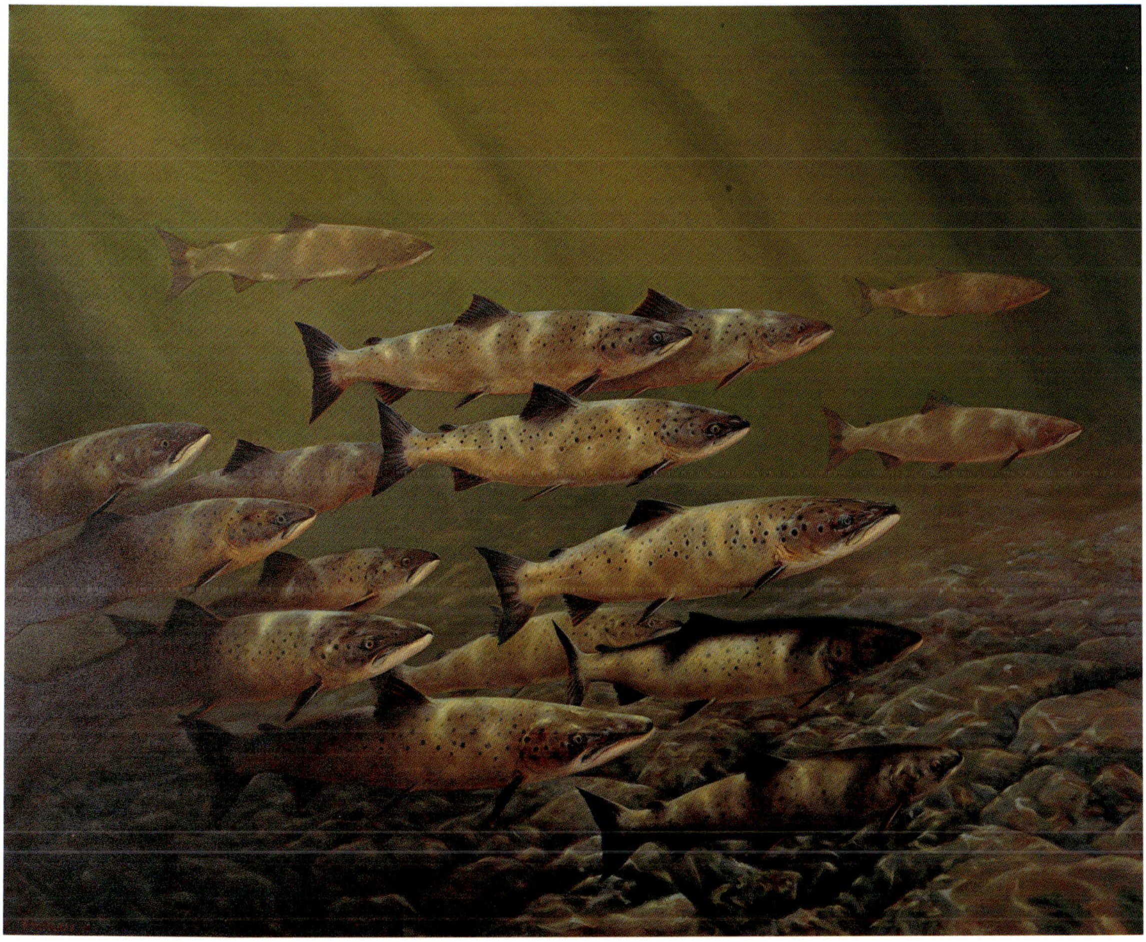

170 Roderick Sutterby, *Atlantic Salmon Waiting for the Rain*, 1996, oil on gesso canvas.

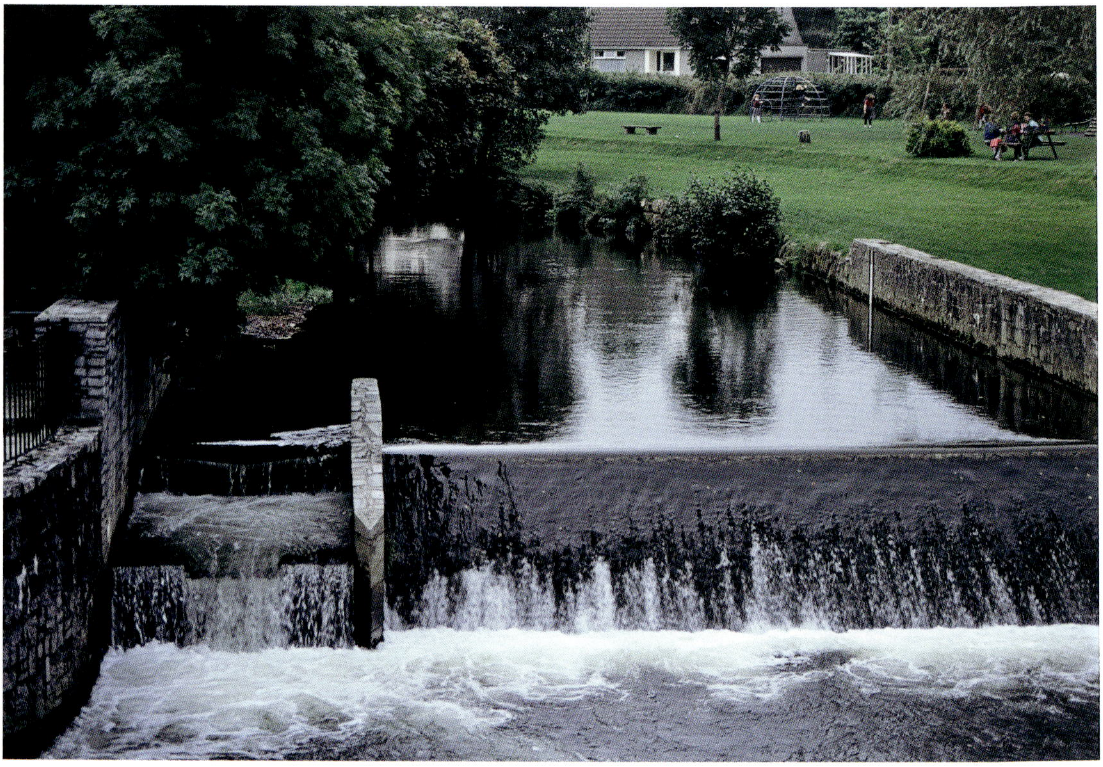

the apex. These hedges, called kiddles, gave us the phrase 'a pretty kettle [kiddle] of fish'. They caused a lot of strife between owners of the pools and other fishermen. More seriously, they could restrict the passage of salmon moving upstream to spawn.

171 Fish ladder, Horrabridge, Devon.

The collective noun for a group of salmon is a bind. Roderick Sutterby painted a bind of Atlantic salmon waiting to swim upriver. The salmon is one of the few species of fish that can transfer from salt to fresh water and back. Having left the sea to run upriver and spawn, the salmon cease to feed. From the estuary the bind moves upstream in fits and starts, on a rise in water level. Rain falling in the burns and streams feeds the river and the subsequent rise in water level stimulates the salmon to move upstream.

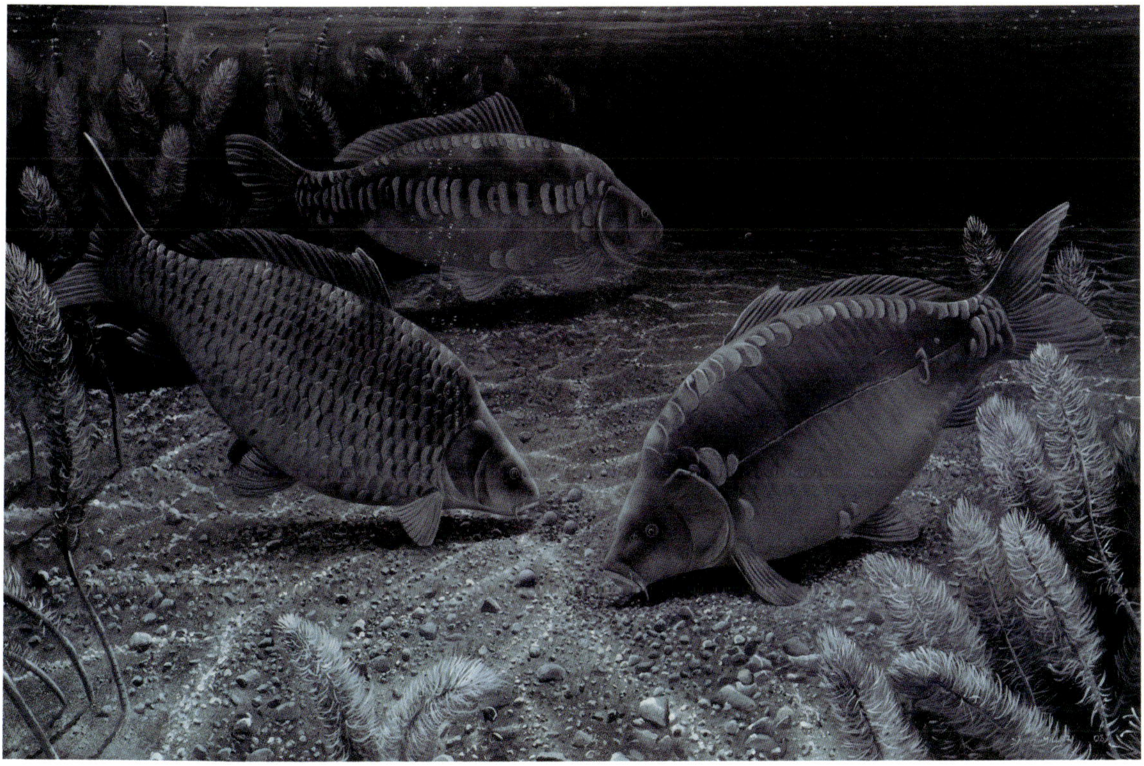

172 David Miller, *Night Fishing for Carp*, 2003, oil on board.

During the course of swimming up the river they may encounter barriers such as man-made weirs and natural waterfalls. The salmon leap falls that require prodigious feats of strength and stamina. In some places they require assistance and one solution to impediments to the salmons' progress is to provide a ladder alongside the obstruction. At Horrabridge near Tavistock is a salmon ladder built at the side of the river Tavy. An adjacent inn, the Leaping Salmon, has an appropriate inn sign. Spectacular salmon leaps while trying to mount these obstacles have been a favourite subject for artists.

Many river fishermen fish at night but it is unusual for an artist to paint a night scene in the river. David Miller's book is appropriately called *Beneath the Surface*, for he dives both by day and by night to meet his fish subjects in the river at close quarters and can convey his intimacy with them in his paintings. Carp feed at night, necessitating midnight vigils by the artist, who might also be rewarded with views of the delicate white water lily flowering underwater. An outstanding sculptor of fish, Neil Dalrymple, has made several ceramic sculptures of fine accuracy and detail that would grace any fish enthusiast's home.

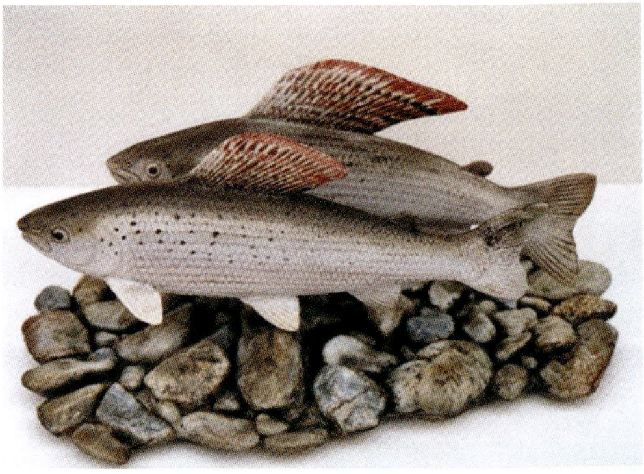

173 Neil Dalrymple (*b.* 1949), *Grayling*, ceramic.

American river paintings may be similar in concept to those of their British counterparts but are on a much grander, larger scale, with the vast wilderness portrayed in all its awesome splendour. Winslow Homer painted river scenes like his seascapes that encompass huge vistas with the fishermen reduced to small insignificant specks. Two outstanding twentieth-century American fish artists earned a living by painting angling scenes for wealthy collectors who thus financed the painters' further expeditions across America. Aiden Lassell Ripley (1896–1969) and Ogden Pleissner (1905–1983) painted imposing river

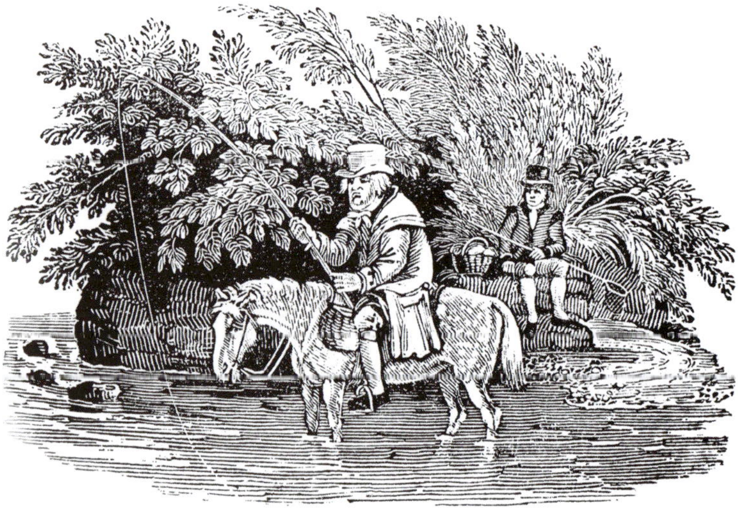

174 Thomas Bewick, tail-piece from the linnet in *The Land Birds* (1847), wood engraving.

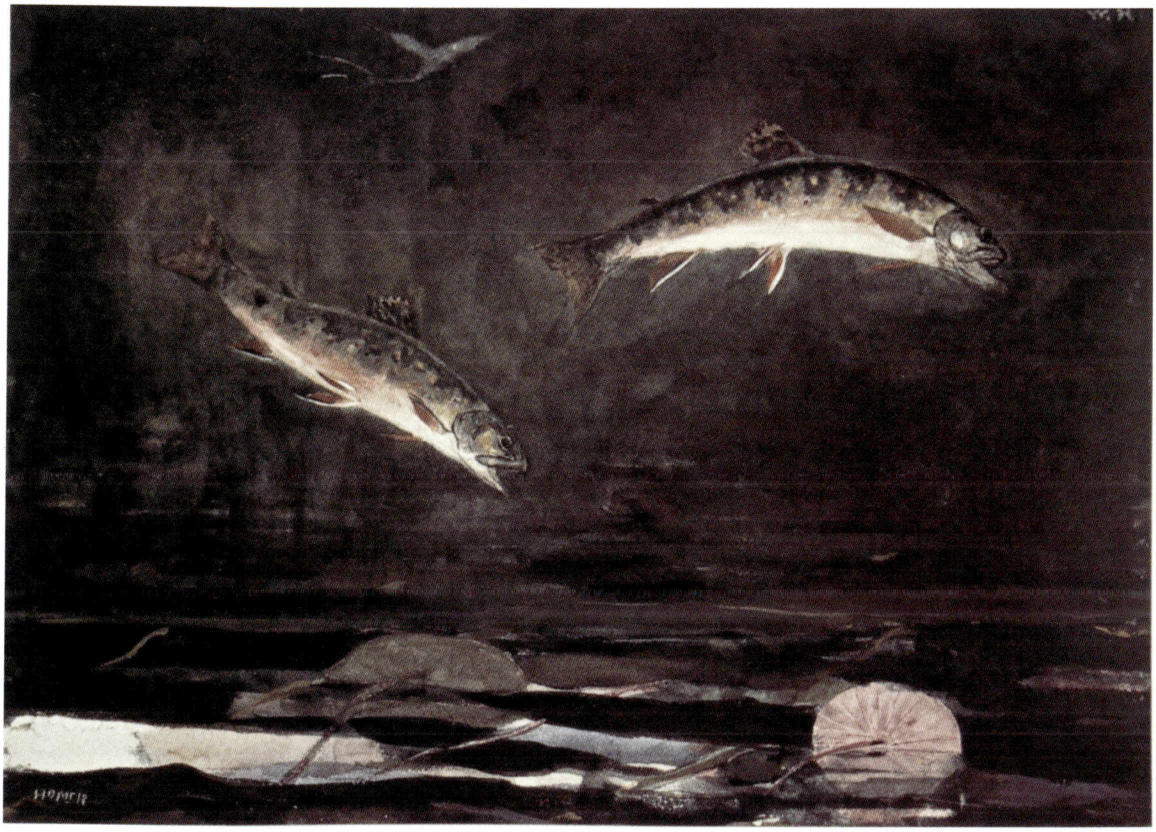

175 Winslow Homer, *Leaping Trout*, 1889, oil on canvas.

landscapes where anglers are standing in the river or sitting in boats. An innovative and interesting painting by the American artist, Fred W. Thomas, *Perfect Deception*, shows a brown trout in the river with the trout's view of an angler.

We still await paintings of an angler by the river with the fishes he is attempting to catch swimming in the river and seen as he would view them.

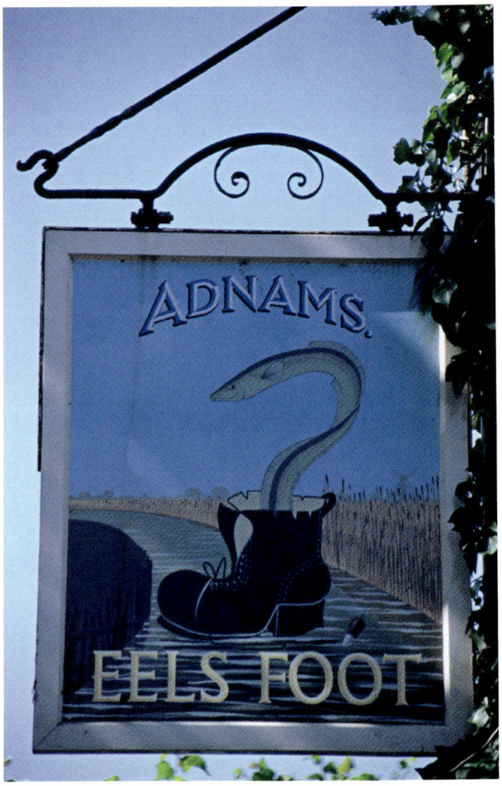

176 Eels Foot, inn sign at Eastbridge, Suffolk.

INN SIGNS Expect the unexpected when you look at inn signs. The painters of the boards can let their imagination take over and treat the subject artistically, humorously, using a pun or an allusion to local folklore, a saying or a song. They get a chance to re-do or renew the sign board every seven years or so because of weather damage. It is as well to look at both sides of inn sign boards, for there may be a different image on each side.

The Eels Foot, Eastbridge, Suffolk, illustrates a strange local event. The legend is that a thirteenth-century Eastbridge village priest, John Schorne, trapped the devil in his boot, which he then flung far out to sea. He became a local hero and was regarded as a kind of 'peasant's saint' so his shrine was made a place of pilgrimage. Eels Foot is a corruption of Devil's Boot, a name used on pub signs elsewhere and a story well known long ago. The same story is illustrated on a sign at Filby Broad, where the artist for *Eels Foot Inn* has had fun with this tale, and the little dog is certainly amused at the eels escaping over the side of the boat.

The strange practice of tickling trout as they lie near the edge of a stream is the subject of an inn sign at West Farleigh, Kent. Tickling trout was a method of catching fish described by the author of poaching tales, Richard Jeffries. He wrote in *Red Deer* in 1884: 'Groping for trout (or tickling) is tracing it to the stone it lies under, then rubbing it gently beneath, which causes the fish to gradually move backwards into the hand, till the fingers suddenly close in the gills.' The Scots have another name for it, guddling, and the Scottish artist William Geddes painted *Boys Guddling for*

Trout, exhibited at the Royal Scottish Academy in 1871. When tickling is done by a man, as on the West Farleigh inn sign, it is considered by the fishing fraternity to be thoroughly reprehensible – only a poacher would stoop to such a method. Yet it requires knowledge, patience and skill and from the trout's point of view it must surely be preferable to be gently stroked before being lifted out of the water and quickly dispatched rather than to be hooked and reeled in before being killed.

There are plenty of inns with the names of fishes and sign boards to match for the fisherman to look for and where he can celebrate – or drown his sorrows – at the end of a day spent angling. Many inns have interesting interiors, with fishing tackle, mounted specimens that were local record catches and old photographs. Just occasionally, a painting by a local artist of the nearby fishing spots brightens up the saloon.

177 Tickled Trout, inn sign at West Farleigh, Kent.

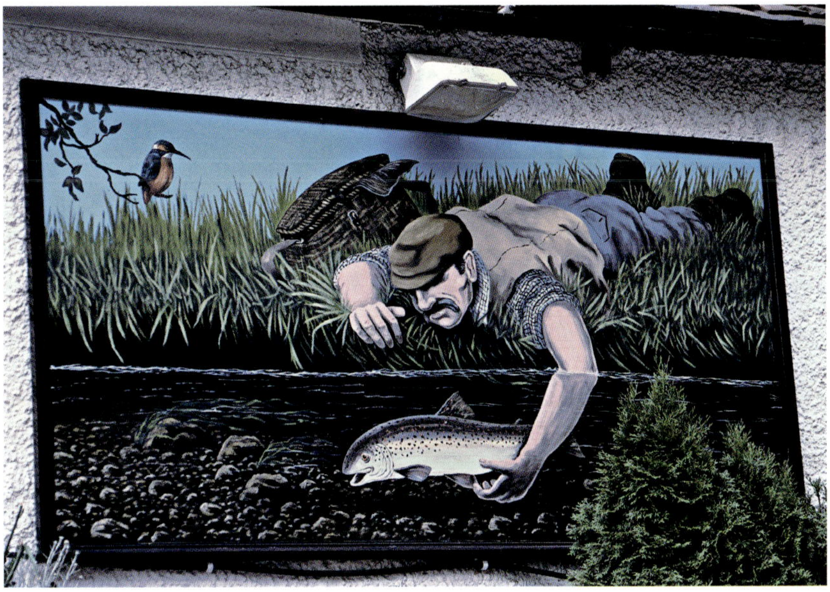

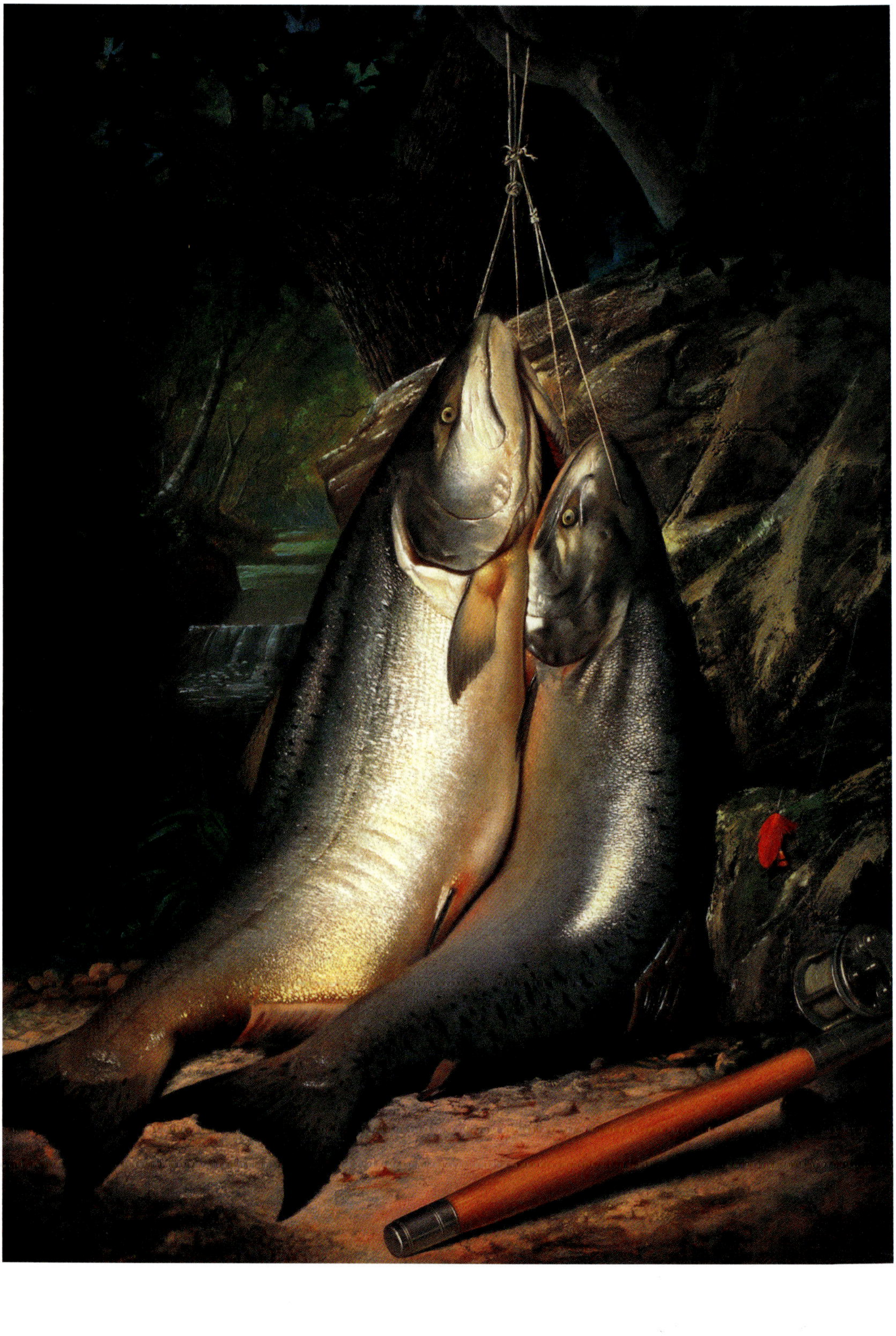

eight
Fish on the Riverbank

The best moment to see a fish in the hand is when it has just been lifted from the water. The colours are perfect, the body supple, it is gleaming and glistening; altogether a beautiful object. Quite soon, uch of the magic has disappeared. Colours fade rapidly, the scales flake, the surface dries and a limpness redolent of death takes over. No amount of dousing with water can remedy the situation. There are some wonderful paintings of fishes laid on riverbanks and the best of these were painted as soon as the fish had been caught. One or two of the artists either caught, or had another fisherman catch, a succession of fishes while they were painting to make sure of the correct unfaded colours.

In many landscape pictures the placing of a man fishing in a river merely added a point of interest to an otherwise satisfactory composition. The placement of fishes on a riverbank created a deliberate focal point of interest that was centred on the fishes. The paintings in which the fishes were so important, often entitled *Fish on a Riverbank* or *The Day's Catch*, made a statement about the artist's interest in fishes and about the fishermen who had caught them, especially when they are also present in the picture. Another important factor became the size of the catch, not in total, but each individual fish. Extra-large fish might create a record for that species, and the length and weight became important elements. A competitive spirit entered the sport and the period when paintings of newly caught fish on a bank were most popular coincided with the Victorians' enthusiasm for angling for prize specimens – the second half of the nineteenth century. The Victorians also developed a great interest in natural history, promoting many books about fishes and angling, which

178 Samuel Marsden Brookes, *Steelhead Salmon*, *c.* 1885, oil on wood.

encouraged accurate and detailed painting of the fishes. A few artists continued to paint riverbank scenes with dead fishes in the first half of the twentieth century, but they are no longer a popular format.

Several Dutch and Flemish artists painted fishes on beaches by the sea in the seventeenth century but rarely painted freshwater species laid on a riverbank. Nor did they depict scenes of the sport of freshwater fishing. However, the fish on the beach had often included freshwater species among the salt-water fishes. Few Dutch artists painted freshwater fishes almost exclusively. Pieter de Putter was one, and he used the convention for painting two pendants (one of a man facing right and another of a woman facing left, in two portraits of fisherfolk) so successfully that he repeated the format several times. However, his recently caught freshwater fishes had been taken indoors to be painted as a still-life. Similarly, Pieter van Noort's catch was taken indoors, put on a table and painted there. His *Still-life of River Fish and Fishing Tackle*, of around 1660, was a favourite subject that he repeated. There was a market for this type of fish painting that very few artists supplied.

The most famous Dutch painter of freshwater specimens with fishing tackle was a native of Utrecht, Jacob Gillig (1636–1701). His picture of pike and perch is a genuine 'on the riverbank' scene. Together with Abraham van Beyeren, Gillig is regarded as the finest of the Dutch fish painters. Gillig's *A Still-life of Freshwater Fishes, Including Perch and a Pike, Resting on a Bank with a River Beyond,* signed and dated 1693, is not typical of his work. Usually he painted the fishes grouped round an upright rod and line. This was central to the composition, with fishes arranged either side of the rod and other fishes laid on the ground. The painting of the fishes themselves is masterly.

The British instigator of portraying river fishes when caught and exhibited on the bank was Francis Barlow. He was the remarkable innovator of wildlife painting in England, painting large fish pictures, issuing prints of sporting subjects and using etching for those prints. Now he showed the way with riverbank paintings when he made the designs for

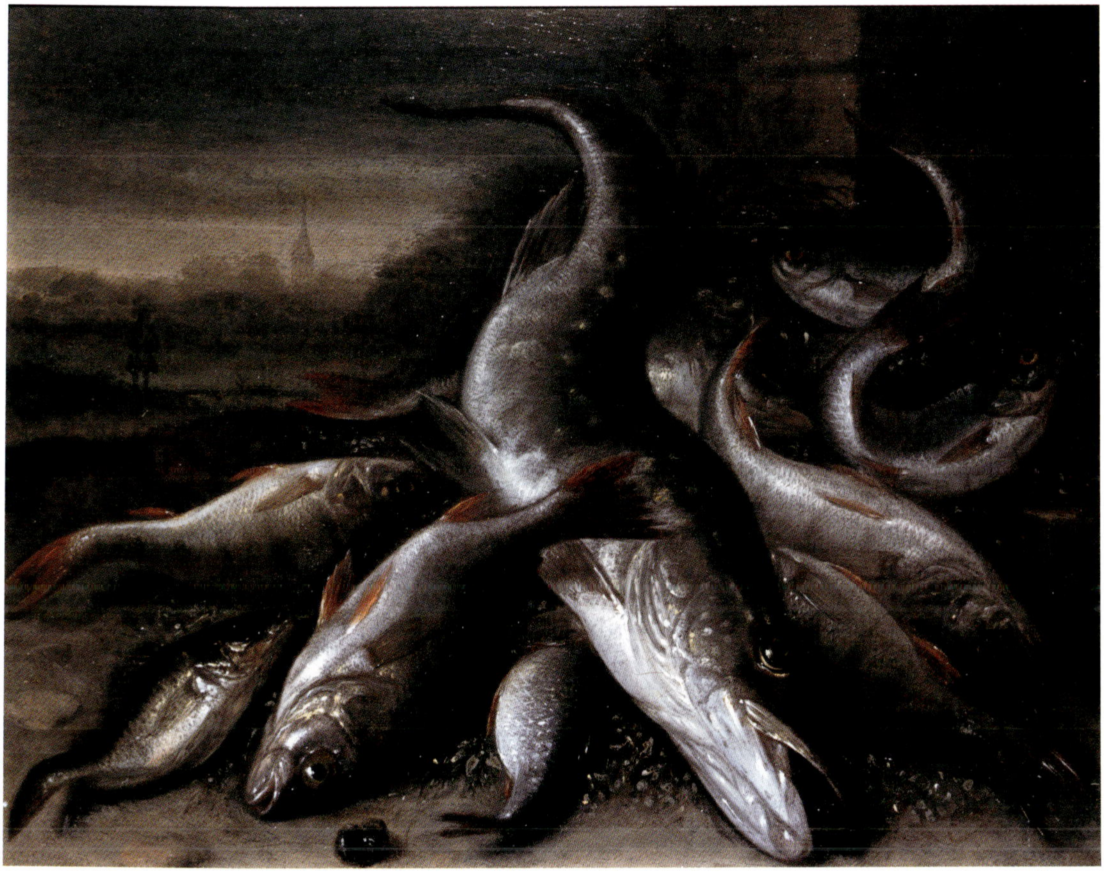

179 Jacob Gillig, *A Still-life of Freshwater Fishes, Including Perch and a Pike, Resting on a Bank with a River Beyond*, 1693, oil on canvas.

Angling (illus. 158), *River Fishing* and *Salmon Fishing*. He gave it the title *Salmon Fishing*, but the fishermen are not shown fishing. They are busy offloading their nets of salmon, eels and small fishes onto the riverbank. Wenceslaus Hollar etched the designs in 1671. A few other collections of prints had similar designs but this new idea of landed fishes was not taken up until Stephen Elmer (1717–1796) began to paint fishes in the 1760s. He established a format of a group of fishes in the foreground with a river nearby and a landscape in the background. He painted scores of pictures of a day's catch, though he did not call them that. Elmer also painted a

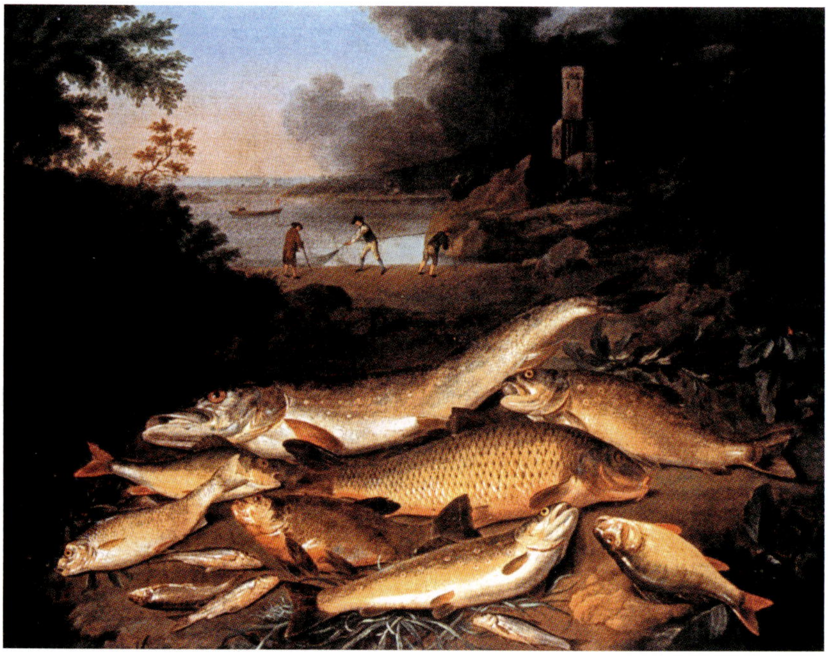

180 Stephen Elmer, *A Landscape with Freshwater Fish, Fishermen Beyond*, oil on canvas. Elmer exhibited this, or a similar painting, at the Royal Academy in 1779.

large number of similar pictures of dead birds. His paintings were very popular and because they included landscapes the Royal Academy (normally reluctant to admit a genre painter to its elite circle of artists) admitted him as a Royal Academician in 1772. He went on exhibiting fish paintings until 1795, a year before his death. This artist, considered then to be the finest British still-life painter of the time, was by trade a maltster and only painted in his spare time.

It was the British artists of the late eighteenth and nineteenth centuries who made the riverbank fish genre fashionable and this was later taken up by the Americans. At the same time Victorian paintings encapsulated clear social statements about the anglers. The social divide was made apparent between the men sufficiently wealthy to enjoy the leisure to fish and able to fish for game fishes from stretches of river they either owned or could afford to rent, and other men. Workers who had been crowded into towns by the Industrial Revolution escaped into the countryside to fish wherever they could. Even the fishes became divided by class: salmon, trout, grayling and charr were known as the game fishes, and the rest (tench, roach, rudd, pike, perch, bream, eels, dace, chub, zander), rudely defined as 'cotton wool stuffed with pins', were called 'coarse fishes'. Despite this, several coarse fishes are good eating, and were eaten.

One of the unfortunate consequences of game fishes being regarded as superior to coarse fishes is that they were favoured as subjects for 'fish on the bank' paintings. The Victorian men who could afford to commission the paintings were the ones who only wanted salmon and trout (occasionally grayling) pictured. Consequently, artists were obliged to paint an unreasonably high proportion of 'fish on the bank' pictures that portrayed salmon and trout.

During the first forty years of the nineteenth century there were a few notable painters of freshwater fishes. Frederick Richard Lee (1798–1879), a popular British painter of landscape and rustic scenes, made a name for himself with fish pictures to which he gave enticing titles: *Salmon Poachers Discovered*, *Gentleman Fishing with a Pike on his Line*, *Pike and Perch on a Bank with Fishing Tackle*, 1858, and the early *English River Fish* of about 1834. *English River Fish* includes pike, perch, trout, eels, chub, dace and gudgeon: more species than usual in riverbank paintings. He exhibited his fish paintings at the Royal Academy from 1824 to 1870, having been elected RA in 1824 after training in the Academy Schools in 1818. Painters of riverbank scenes frequently included a creel and occasionally fishing tackle. Lee's *English River Fish* differs from angling pictures where rod and line only are more often shown.

Though looking much alike, the rudd (*Scardinius erythrophthalmus*) is more a surface feeder in lakes than the roach (*Rutilus rutilus*); both occur in slow-moving water of rivers throughout Europe. The roach is common in lakes, canals and slow-flowing rivers in much of northern Europe and Asia. It was noted as 'an easy catch' in the *Boke of St Albans*. Both have large silvery scales and distinctive red fins. No longer rated as good food fish in Britain, they are used as bait for other species. The roach is a popular sporting fish for the angler and is eaten in Eastern Europe, but the rudd is less popular with anglers and not often seen in paintings.

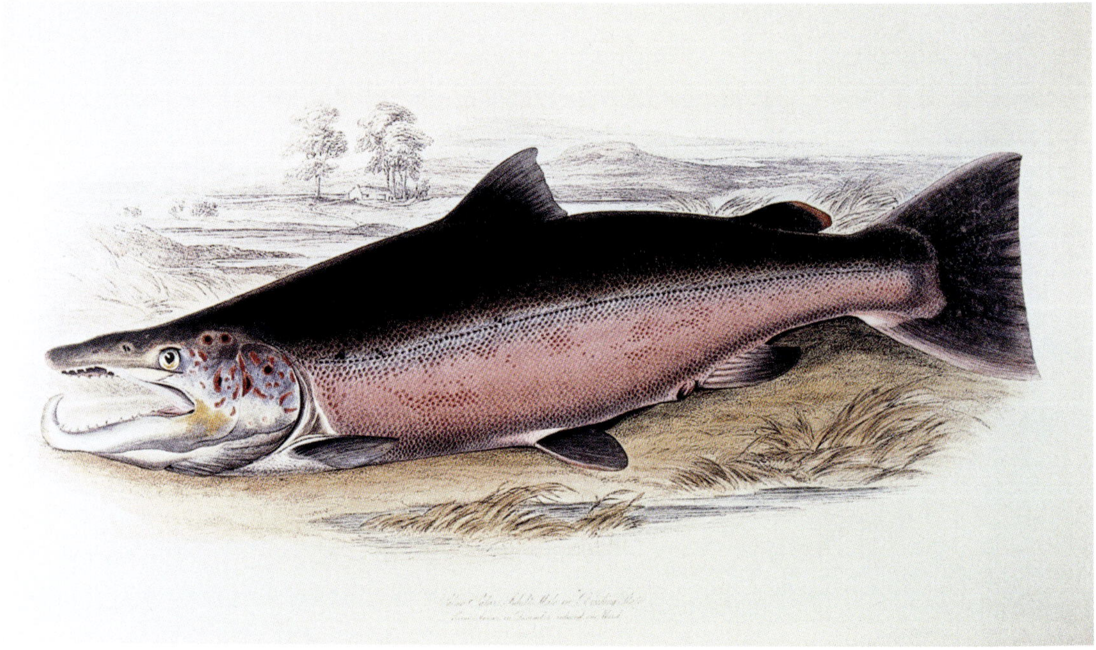

181 Sir William Jardine, 'Salmon', *c.* 1835, watercolour etching, from *British Salmonidae* (1839).

Edward Coleman (1794–1867) was a British painter of portraits, fishes, dead game, mammals and still-lifes. He clearly identified his group of fishes on the bank as being *The Day's Catch*, and signed but did not date it. He included a slight landscape background and a large creel. He was prolific in his dead fish painting output during the years 1828–48, and some are inscribed 'Birmingham', where he was baptized Edward, but later sometimes called 'John' and his pictures catalogued under that name. He lived and exhibited his pictures at Birmingham as well as at the Royal Academy, London (sixteen pictures), and the Royal Scottish Academy, Edinburgh.

Two artists, Sarah Bowdich and Sir William Jardine, made some of the finest fish studies in watercolours, intended for book illustrations. Sarah, also a naturalist and author, got an angler to catch a succession of fishes for her to paint by the riverside. Sarah Wallis (1791–1856) became Sarah Bowdich in 1813 when she married Thomas Edward Bowdich, under which name she issued *The Freshwater Fishes of Great Britain* to 50 subscribers. Each copy had a text and 48 individually hand-painted plates, issued between 1828 and 1837. These original watercolours are

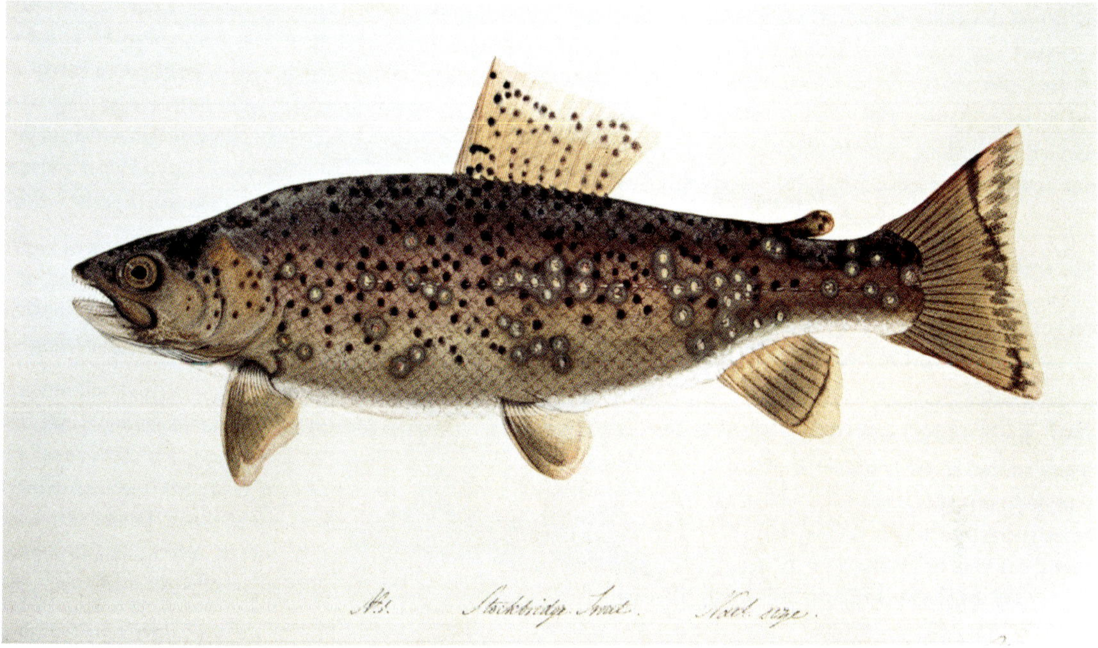

182 Sarah Wallis Bowdich, 'Stockbridge Trout', from *The Freshwater Fishes of Great Britain, Drawn and Described by Mrs T. Edward Bowdich* (1828–36).

remarkable not only for their fidelity in portrayal but also for the artist's use of silver and gold foil to catch the iridescent colours of the fishes.

Sir William Jardine (1800–1874) painted a series of 58 watercolours of salmon, twelve etched on plates with images approximately 50 × 65 cm for his *British Salmonidae*, published in Edinburgh in two volumes, 1839 and 1841. This is still the most magnificent book on the Salmonidae. A riparian owner at Jardine Hall on the river Annan, Dumfriesshire, and a keen fisherman with a naturalist's deep interest in and knowledge of salmon, he painted his newly caught specimens before their colours faded. He tagged some parr (juvenile salmon) in an attempt to trace the life history of the salmon. He also fished the Tweed while he rented a house at St Boswell's and became an acknowledged expert on both trout and salmon, researching their taxonomy, life histories and anatomy.

The most famous nineteenth-century painters of fish on the bank are the members of the Rolfe and Russell families, mentioned in the previous chapter. Alexander Frederick and Henry Leonides in particular were very good fish painters. The latter was born in France in 1823 and dated his pictures between 1840 and 1881, the year in which he died. The fish in

GRAYLING (*Thymallus thymallus*) is a European species of the salmon family, distributed from Southern France north to England and Scandinavia, east to the Ural and Volga rivers in Russia. She (a grayling is always referred to as 'she') is distinguished by the wide, high dorsal fin, silvery colour and distinctive thyme-like smell when freshly caught. Preferring cold lakes and swift-flowing rivers, this game fish is the fly-fisher's stop-gap quarry because it comes into season as trout go out of season and vice versa.

their paintings when seen today look as fresh as when taken from the river with not a sign of rigor mortis. What is more, they painted both game fishes and coarse fishes with equal loving care. In 1880 H. L. Rolfe was summoned to Scotland to paint the largest brace of salmon then caught – 50 lb and 40 lb (18 and 23 kg) – on the Tay by J. B. Haynes of Leamington. He also painted a kingfisher with a fish in its beak and an otter carrying a fish, but his huge success in commercial terms came from his paintings of fishes on a bank, sometimes with a creel, often with evocative landscapes and always superbly well-painted fishes.

Henry Leonides exhibited 36 paintings with fishes named in the title and several others with the sort of ambiguous titles attached to this type of fish painting (he was one of the few painters specializing in fish) at the Royal Academy. There is a portrait of H. L. Rolfe in front of an easel supporting a fish painting (possibly painted by his brother Alexander Frederick) in the clubhouse of the Piscatorial Club at Lower Woodford, Wiltshire, of which he was a keen member.

Alexander Frederick Rolfe exhibited only ten angling or fish paintings at the Academy, so finding one of his paintings now is a rare occurrence. Henry Leonides painted a grayling as well as trout in his *Brown Trout among Ferns*. Thought by some to be the most beautiful fish in the world, an angling society devoted to the grayling and its conservation was formed in 1978.

John Russell (son of John Bucknell Russell) exhibited at the Royal Scottish Academy and was related to a James Russell with whom he collaborated occasionally. (Another John Russell, who was born in 1849 in Cork, Ireland, also painted similar fishes.) All painted pictures of fishes on a riverbank, often with the blanket title *A Day's Catch*. The best of the Russell fish painters was John Bucknell Russell, who was initially a house

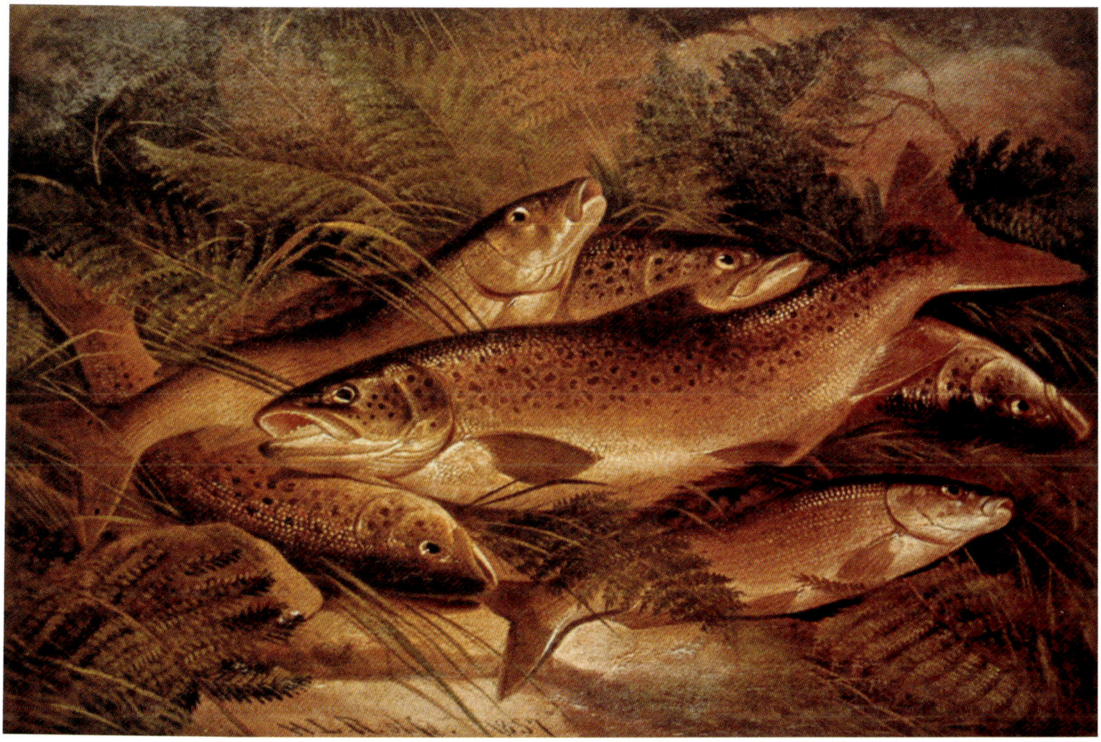

183 Henry Leonides Rolfe, *Brown Trout Among Ferns*, 1857, oil on canvas.

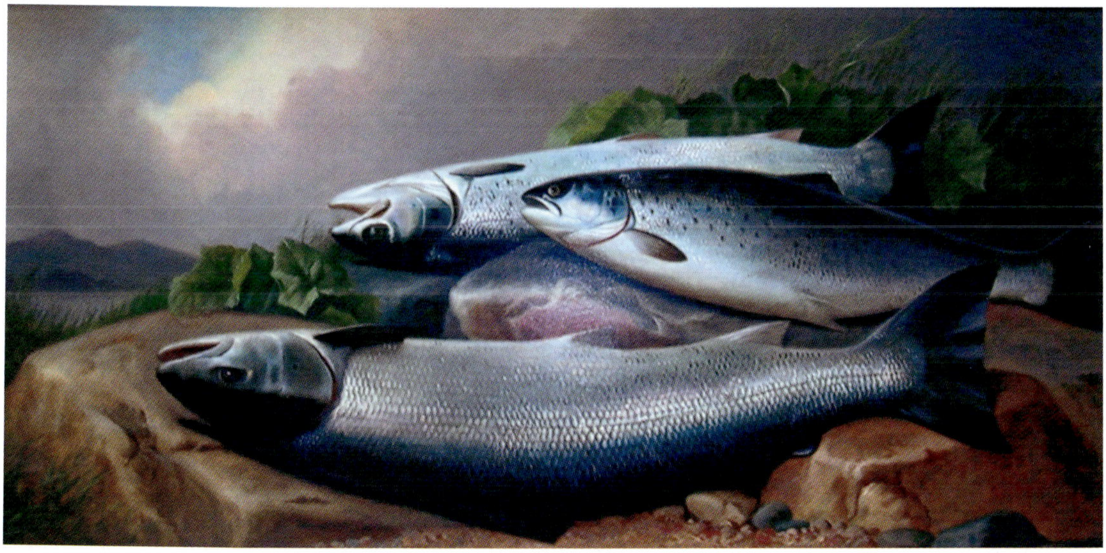

184 John Bucknell Russell, *Salmon*, oil on canvas.

painter, then a carver of fish in wood who travelled widely, astride a great white horse, in order to find subjects for his fish paintings. He finally settled at Fochabers, a village on the River Spey close to Gordon Castle near his patron, the Duke of Richmond and Gordon.

Another Victorian Scottish painter of great merit was William Geddes (1841–1884). He did some beautiful work on outstanding Scottish fishes, sometimes reflected in his titles, like *Prize Takers from the Isla*. He painted mainly sea trout, brown trout and salmon near his home in his native Blairgowrie, Perthshire.

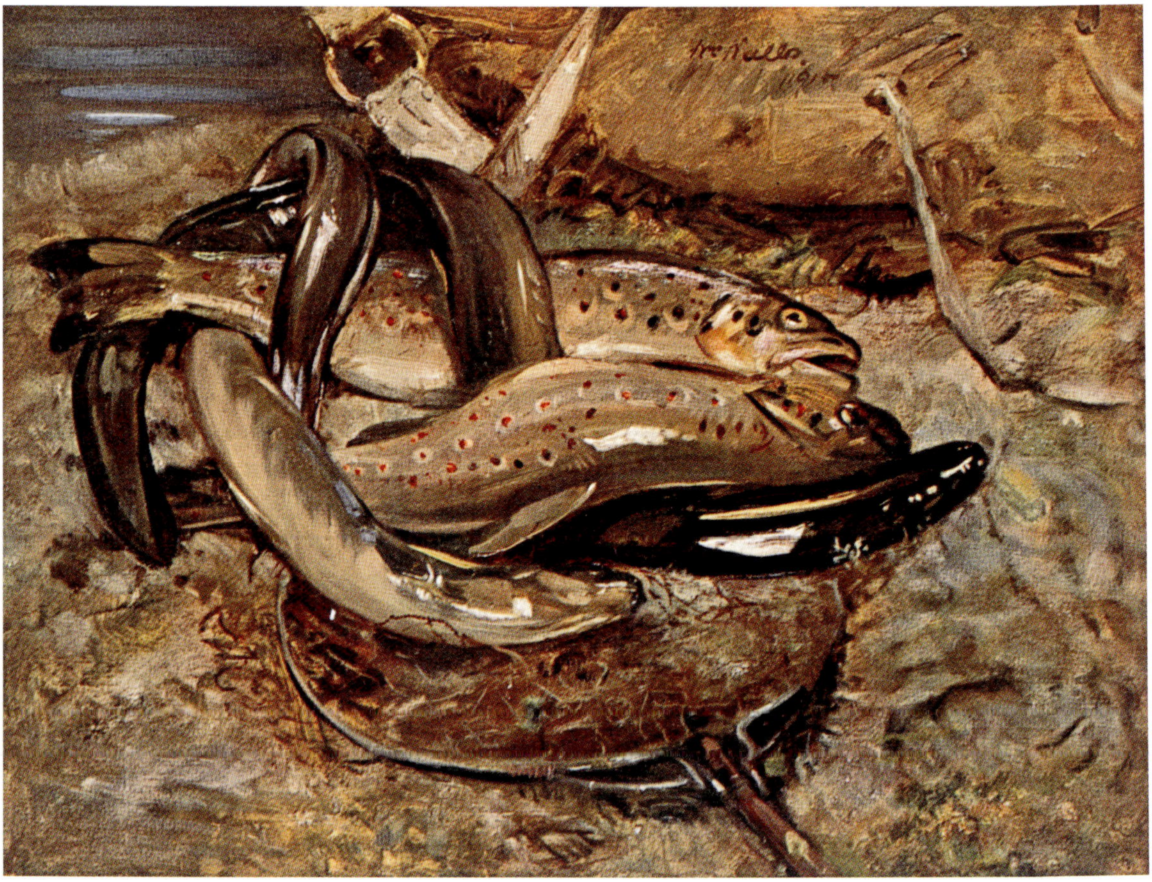

185 William Walls, *Trout and Eels on Bankside*, 1915, oil on canvas.

THERE are two basic types of trout (*Salmo trutta*), migratory (sea trout) and non-migratory (brown trout). Many young sea trout from coastal waters live in large shoals that swim into rivers in late summer when they are known as herling, whitling and finnock in different localities. A migratory species of northwestern coastal waters of Europe used to be seen in all rivers and streams within its distribution range, but it is now excluded by dams and high weirs so its numbers have dwindled.

William Walls (1860–1942) was also Scottish, born at Dunfermline and an animal painter in oils and watercolours. He was influenced by Joseph Crawhall (and like him enjoyed painting trout) and by Edwin Alexander, who became his brother-in-law. His fish paintings were done mainly before the First World War, at the end of the period when fish on the bank were in vogue. Walls said that angling pictures were difficult to paint because they need 'sure and rapid handling' and suggested this as one reason for the rarity of such paintings. Writing before 1920, he also said that he was 'aware of many Scottish painters who are anglers, but I don't know of any who have painted angling pictures except myself. The only other Scottish painter of angling pictures I can think of is William Geddes, father of Ewan Geddes R.S.W. He died a good many years ago.' A publisher, Mr Jack, sent Walls a short prayer that any angler of any generation could use:

> Lord suffer me to catch a fish
> So large that even I,
> who talking of it afterwards,
> May have no *need* to lie.'

Thomas Greenslade Target (1828–1891), resident of Salisbury, Wiltshire, exhibited pictures of animals, flowers, fruit, scenes of the chase and still-life. His fish paintings were a small part of his repertoire. *Fish on a Riverbank*, painted in 1877, has a dark background and sharply defined fishes in a clear light while *A Rainbow Trout on a Riverbank*, 1881, has a similar format but is much more loosely painted. In Target's 1877 picture several fish species are represented, among them a roach or rudd. Walton defined the rudd as a 'bastard small roach' and the two fishes are not easily distinguished by novice anglers.

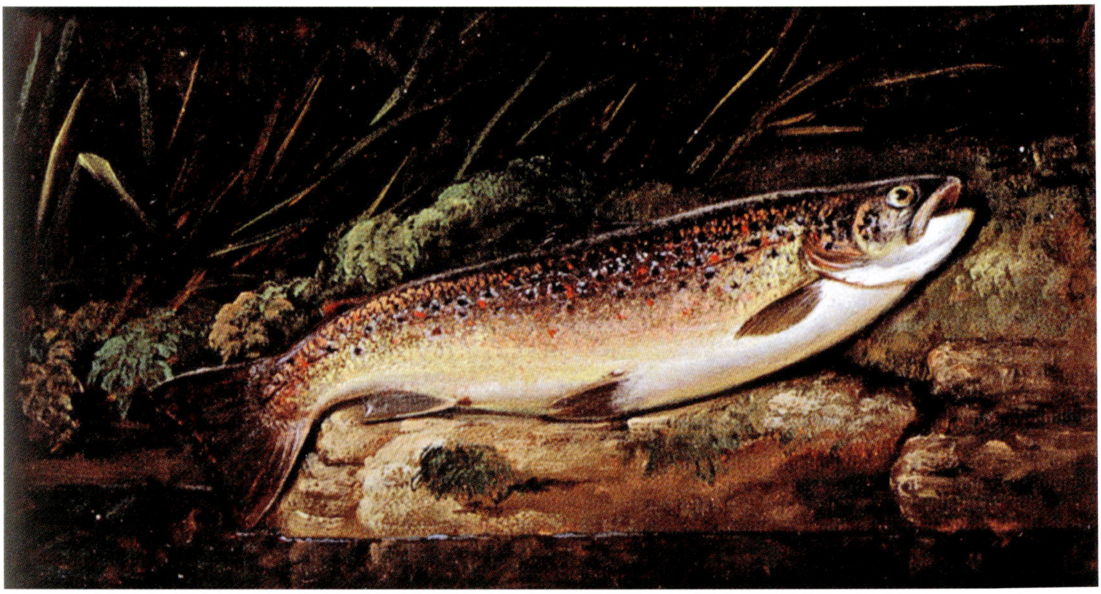

186 Thomas Greenslade Target, *A Rainbow Trout on Riverbank*, 1881, oil on board.

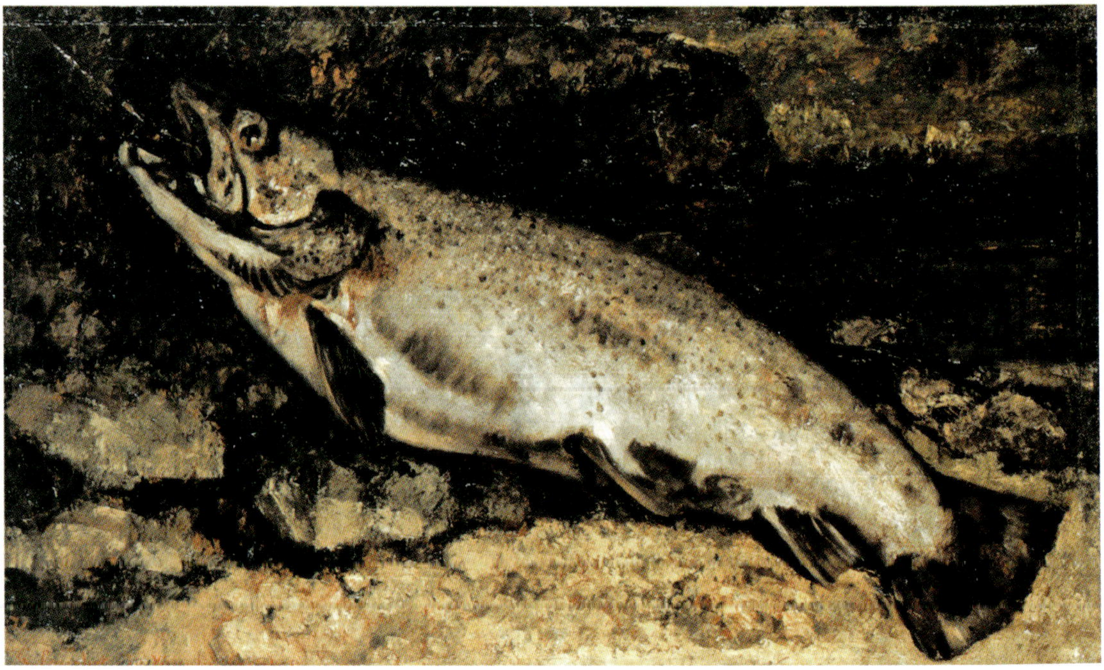

187 Gustave Courbet, *The Trout,* 1872, oil on canvas.

The French painter Gustave Courbet (1819–1877) produced a painting of a live trout caught on a hook and line in 1872 that is a lone, large fish against a bleak background. From 1857, when he abandoned Romantic influences, Courbet produced a wide range of realistic paintings based on careful drawings from nature while sketching outdoors. He was especially skilled in the use of grey and dark tones, as demonstrated by this impressive fish painting. This curious, unusual piece poses the question: is it in water or is it landed?

British fishermen of this period received welcome assistance with recognition of the fishes that they caught by the publication of a book by the Revd William Houghton. His *British Freshwater Fishes*, published in 1879, had 41 delightful and unusual plates showing fishes either in underwater scenes with plants and rocks on the riverbed among which the fish

188 A. F. Lydon, xylograph of golden and bronze carp, finished by hand-colouring, from Revd W. Houghton's *British Freshwater Fishes* (1879).

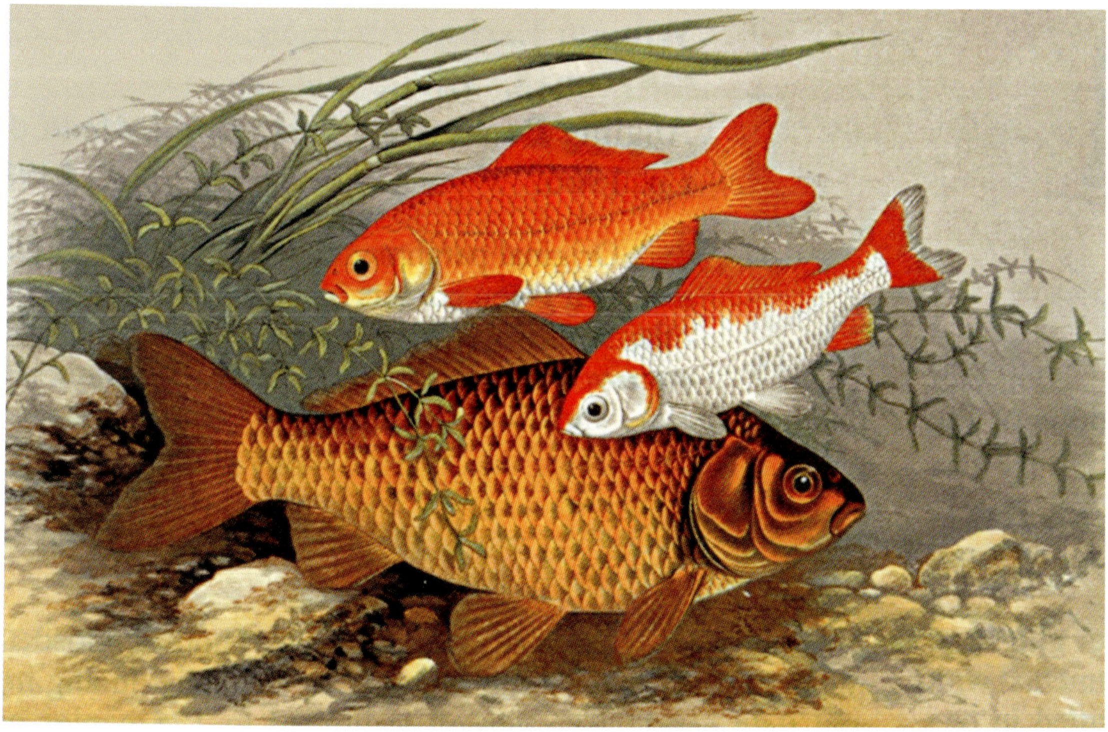

were swimming, or pretty landscapes with the fish lying on the riverbank. The xylograph illustrations were the work of A. F. Lydon, for Groombridge & Sons, and were lavishly finished by hand-colouring over the colour-printed wood engravings. All the plates had water – very fine ruled engraved lines with a blue wash – representing the river, but three had the water cunningly positioned around them to give the illusion that they were swimming in the water. The golden and bronze carp was one, the others being six sticklebacks, a bull trout and Loch Killin charr.

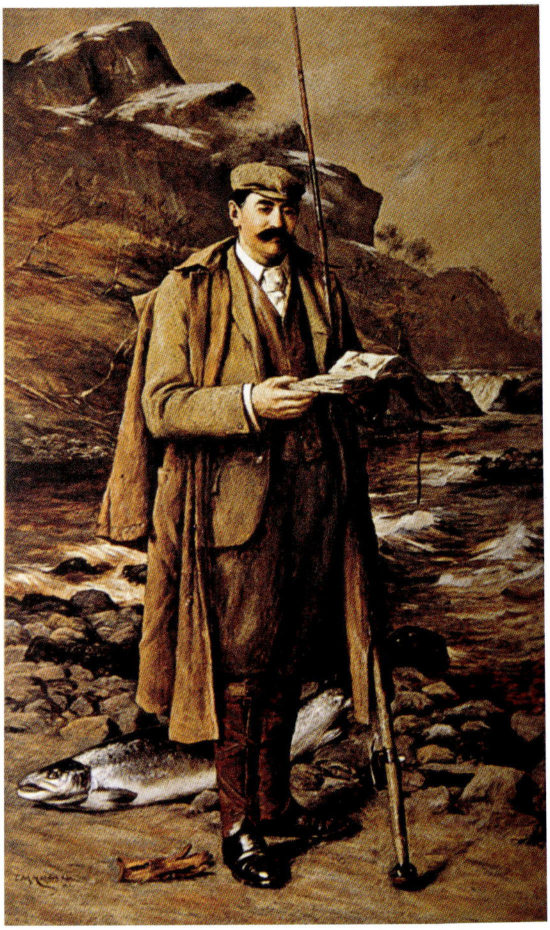

189 Charles Martin Hardie, *Julius Charles Drewe*. Drewe (1856–1931) is shown fishing at Faskally, a seat at the confluence of the Tummel and the Garry, near Pitlochry, Perthshire.

Julius Charles Drewe (1856–1931) is often cited as the archetypal self-made Victorian, who became rich from his success as a retailer from his Home and Colonial grocery stores. He retired early in life, in 1883, to live as a country gentleman and indulge his love of angling. He bought land and built a medieval-style castle (Drogo) in Devon designed by Sir Edwin Lutyens. He went fishing in the Tummel in Perthshire and had his portrait painted with a salmon he had caught lying beside him on the bank. Men like Drewe became the patrons of artists who were painting angling scenes and days' catches of fishes in Victorian times, though very few commissioned portraits of themselves alongside their catch of fish.

Some of the very wealthy British sportsmen of the late nineteenth century went to Norway to fish. The larger and faster-flowing rivers bred heavy and powerful salmon that were a delight to keen anglers. They used

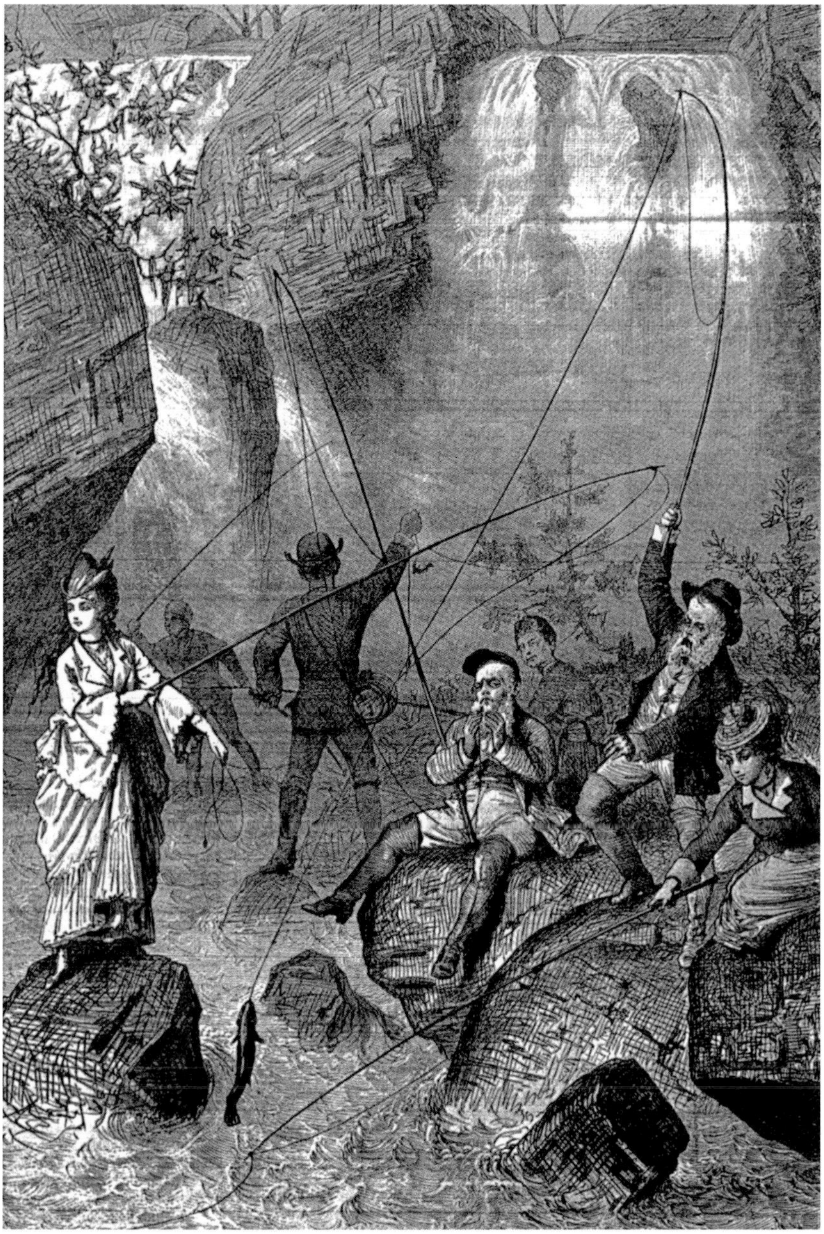

190 Knut Ekwall, 'Englishmen Fishing in Gudbrandsdal', engraving from an original drawing by Ekwall, reproduced in *Ny Illustreret Tidende* (1874).

extremely long greenheart rods fitted with huge reels that had been made especially for them by the famous manufacturers of fishing tackle, Hardy of Alnwick. John Singer Sargent (1856–1925) was of American parentage but lived much of his life in England. He painted angling pictures after visiting Norway, including *A Study of Salmon, Norway*. The Norwegians found the antics of British sports fishermen both amazing and amusing.

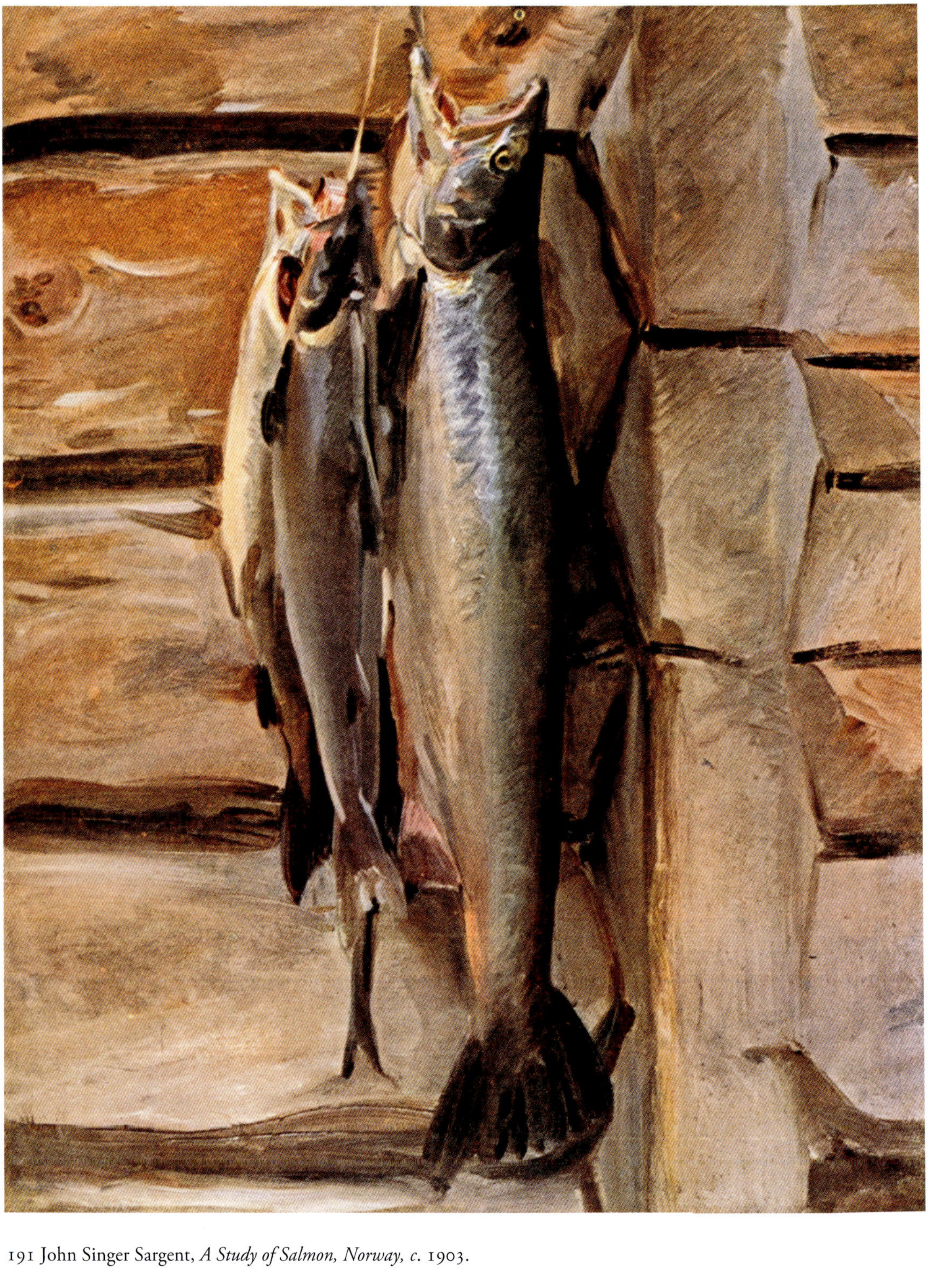

191 John Singer Sargent, *A Study of Salmon, Norway*, *c*. 1903.

A drawing by Knut Ekwall captured a group of these eccentric anglers in action as seen by a Norwegian.

There were about a score of fish painters of the late nineteenth century who painted fishes on the banks of American rivers. They incorporated some engaging gentlemen in ten-gallon hats and, like their British counterparts, other strange headgear (an unaccountable trait that endures to this day). Names to look out for are Arthur Fitzwilliam Tait (1819–1905), Walter M. Brackett (1823–1919), James F. Cafferty (1819–1869) and Gurdon Trumbull (1841–1903). One of the most sought-after was Samuel Marsden Brookes (1816–1892), an Englishman who was taken as an immigrant to America in 1833. He made his living from portraiture and then painted what he really enjoyed, fish pictures, after moving to California in 1862. His still-life pictures of fishes on the ground were painted with realistic definition. The Americans favoured hanging their fish catches (as other game, birds and mammals) on a wall or nailed to a barn door. His *Steelhead Salmon* pictures a migratory form of the rainbow trout that is more streamlined and has fewer markings below the lateral line (illus. 178). He meticulously reproduced each glistening, iridescent scale in a style greatly admired and prized. A few of his paintings were of trout while still in the water but his most unusual picture was of a live trout in a tank of murky water.

Few fish painters have been so closely studied and catalogued than Junius Brutus Stearns (1810–1885). He painted fishes with fishing tackle on a riverbank but his delightful *Elliott and his Friends,* painted in 1857, gives a new slant to this format. Stearns placed his group of anglers in the middle of a river with their catch on a rock. This is a neat way of painting portraits, river scenes, angling and a catch, all in one picture.

Very few fish paintings are *trompe l'oeil*; that is, paintings so life-like they deceive the eye and create the impression that an actual fish is present. This form of painting had a vogue in America in the mid-nineteenth century, and one or two American artists employed the technique in fish paintings. William Aiken Walker painted a picture of two of the

South's most delicious fishes hanging against pine planks. Though intended to appear as an actual dollarfish and sheepshead fish hanging there, it is not a complete success.

Probably the last man to paint the riverbank type of study of fishes was British, Leonard J. Appelbee (*b.* 1914). He made studies of *The Salmon Pool, The Catch, Pike, Salmon,* exhibiting them up to 1967. The big record catches in future were to be recorded photographically and still-life pictures were no longer acceptable. The next generation of fish painters, working after the Second World War, painted fishes in the water, singly or in very small groups. The new style was adopted early by Keith Linsell and then by a galaxy of talented fish painters, all born in the 1950s. They include Terence Lambert, Roger McPhail, Richard Smith, Charles Jardine, Don Ray, Keith Brockie, Rod Sutterby and Maurice J. Pledger. A few younger painters are now making their names, including Carl Ellis, who makes accurate studies of living fishes, while others place them in environmentally correct, often imaginative and atmospheric backgrounds, like David Miller (illus. 172). Tim Havers and Robin Armstrong are two other popular fish artists whose work is sought for the fidelity of their paintings of species in and out of the river. Their story belongs more properly to the story of 'Fish in the River'. The genre 'Fish on the Riverbank' has gone out of favour for the moment, except with collectors of Old Master and Victorian fish paintings.

Having landed a large fish, anglers wished to preserve a record of the remarkable catch to prove to the world that they had genuinely landed a notable specimen. Photography and painting did not show the exact size of a very large catch but by preserving the fish there was no shadow of doubt as to its length and girth. However, what photography and art could do was to show the colours of the fish immediately after it had been caught, which taxidermy could not achieve. Consequently, ways had to be found to colour the skin of the stuffed and mounted fish. Painting the skin was not successful, resulting in looking exactly as though a layer of paint had been applied. A few taxidermists attempted to paint the inside of the skin

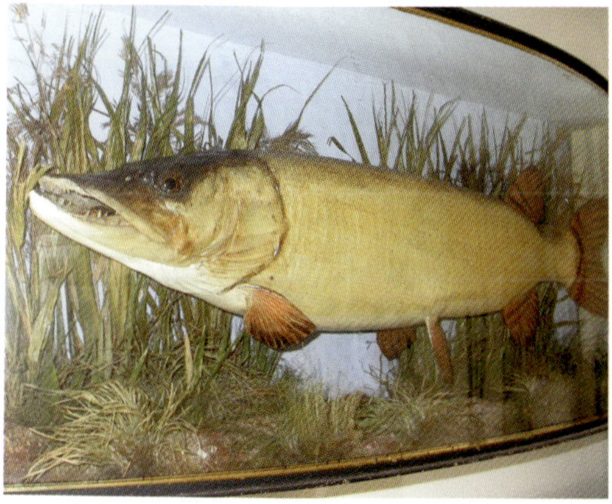

192 James Cooper, mounted pike model in bow-fronted glass case.

so that the paint shone through the translucent thin skin. Once prepared, the fish was placed inside a glass case and surrounded with reeds and other plants to create a likeness of the fish in the river. Sometimes the front glass of the cased fish was bowed (rather than the conventional flat glass) but this was an added, costly refinement.

It was preferred by some anglers to have their fish cast in plaster. Salmon was the favourite fish for preserving but among the most difficult because of the amount of oil in its skin. In mounted salmon specimens the oil could leach for some time. Plaster models recorded a special catch and were carved and then painted to represent the exact size, shape and particularities of the specimen. Preferred species were pike, perch, roach and tench. Plaster casts were very heavy, also brittle, and needed to be handled carefully. Despite these drawbacks they are highly valued today. The eccentric naturalist Frank Buckland (1826–1880) was one of the first specialists in the technique of making plaster models and the Perth firm, Malloch, was also proficient.

From the 1880s to the 1940s painted, carved wooden models of fishes were produced in two main centres and became much sought after by collectors. In London the firms C. Farlow & Company and Holbrow & Company marketed wooden models, while in Scotland the production of fish models was begun by John Bucknell Russell on Speyside. His son-in-law John Tully

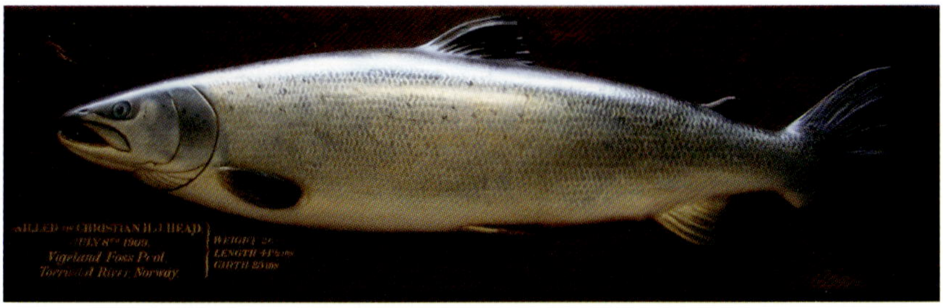

193 Painted carved wooden model.

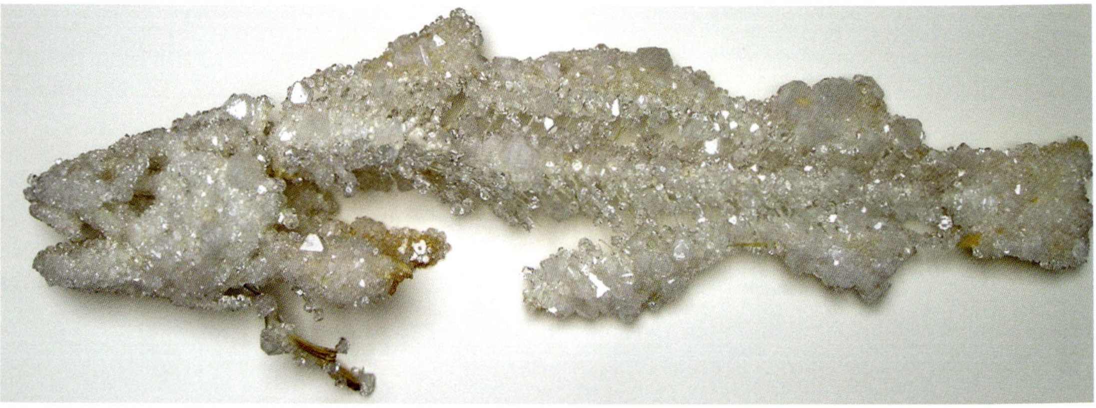

194 Heather Ackroyd and Dan Harvey, *Crystal Fish*, 2005, cod skeleton, alum crystals, Perspex display case, 86 × 30 × 19 cm.

(1862–1931) carved the models and his wife Isabella, Russell's daughter, was responsible for much of the painting. Most of the carved fishes had details of captor, weight, length, girth, the river where taken and date of capture painted onto the boards or a frame. John Tully was Clerk of Works at Gordon Castle and hundreds of these carved, painted models were bought by Scottish collectors, such as the Russells' patron, the Duke of Richmond and Gordon. Orders, usually for salmon, were received from Norway, Sweden, Japan and Canada, and for trout from New Zealand and South Africa. After Tully's death, his deputy at the castle, Bertie George, took over the carving. Some other models were produced for Malloch of Perth and the Hardy Brothers of Alnwick who, like other dealers, attached their labels to the model. Carved and painted models are hardly ever signed by the carver.

Heather Ackroyd and Dan Harvey created a *Crystal Fish* in 2005. The skeleton of a fish was cleaned before immersing it in a highly saturated alum solution that encrusted the skeleton with a chemical growth of ice-like crystals before being encased in a Perspex box. It was displayed at the Royal Society in 2011.

Nevertheless, however imposing the fishes caught and preserved for posterity, there are always fishes in the mind's eye of an angler that were larger and heavier and, unfortunately, got away. Why the biggest and the best have this annoying habit of escaping remains a mystery . . . The

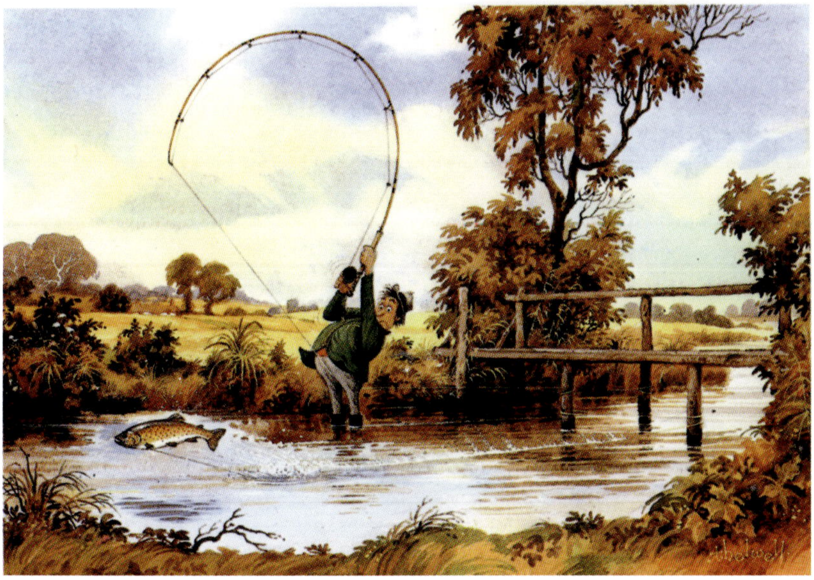

195 Norman Thelwell, 'The Compleat Tangler', from *Thelwell's Sporting Pictures* (1984).

British cartoonist Norman Thelwell graphically documented the manner in which escapees frustrate anglers in his paintings for *Thelwell's Sporting Prints* (1984). A keen fisherman, Thelwell (1923–2004) recorded them with rueful humour even though the memory of some, like the trout having woven a web of destruction for rod and line under a timber bridge, may also have been painful. Whether catching, cooking or eating them, reading about them or telling stories about them, fishes remain a constant source of fascination. We can only observe, with awe and admiration, the infinite variety of shapes, colours and behaviour of these inhabitants of a mysterious, watery world.

SELECT BIBLIOGRAPHY

Allen, Christopher, *Art in Australia from Colonization to Postmodernism* (London, 1997)

Armstrong, Robin, *The Painted Stream* (London, 1985)

Arts Council, *British Sporting Painting*, exh. cat. (London, 1976)

Art Sales Index Annual (Weybridge, 1972–2001/2), continued as *Hislop's Art Sales Index* (2002/3–)

Babinal, Natalia, *David Teniers the Younger* (London, 1989)

Banks, Fred. S., *Index of Engravings with the Names of Artists in the Sporting Magazine from the Year 1792–1870* (London, 1892)

Barlow, Francis, *Several Wayes of Hunting, Hawking and Fishing according to the English Manner* (London, 1671)

Barnes, Donna R., and Peter G. Rose, *Matters of Taste: Food and Drink in 17th Century Dutch Art* (London, 2002)

Barr, David, 'Limner of Scaly Portraits', *Country Life* (16 February 1978), pp. 404–6

Bénézit, Emmanuel *Dictionnaire critique et documentaire des peintres, sculpteurs, dessinateurs, graveurs etc.*, 10 vols (Paris, 1976)

Bergstrom, I., *Dutch Still-life Painting in the Seventeenth Century* (London, 1956)

Bernt, Walther, *The Netherlandish Painters of the Seventeenth Century*, 3 vols (London, 1970)

Bewick, Thomas, *1800 Woodcuts by Thomas Bewick and his School* (New York, 1962)

Bilbao, Museu de Bellas Artes, *El Bodegón espagnol* (Bilbao, 1999)

Billcliffe, Roger, *The Royal Glasgow Institute of Fine Art, 1861–1989: A Dictionary of the Exhibitors at the Annual Exhibition of the Royal Glasgow Institute of Fine Art*, 4 vols (Glasgow, 1990–92)

Billett, Michael, *A History of English Country Sports* (London, 1994)

Bolitho, Hector, *The Glorious Oyster* (London, 1960)

Bond, James, *Monastic Landscapes* (London, 2004)

Bradshaw, Maurice, *Royal Society of British Artists: Members Exhibiting, 1824–92; 1893–1910; 1911–1930; 1931–46; 1947–62*, 5 vols (London, 1973)
Brown, Christopher, *Scenes of Everyday Life: Genre Paintings of the Seventeenth Century* (London, 1984)
Buczacki, Stefan, *Fauna Britannica* (London, 2002)
Cherry, Peter, *Arte y naturaleza: el bodegón espanol . . .* (Madrid, 1999)
Cooke, Theodore, *Sporting Pictures at Lavington Park* (1927, privately printed)
Dance, Stanley Peter, and Geoffrey N. Swinney, *Classic Natural History Prints: Fish* (London, 1990)
David, Elizabeth, *Harvest of the Cold Months: The Social History of Ice and Ices*, ed. Jill Norman (London, 1994)
Davidson, Alan, *The Oxford Companion to Food* [1999], reissued as *The Penguin Companion to Food* (London, 2002)
Decoteau, Pamela Hibbs, *Clara Peeters, 1594–c. 1640 and the Development of Still Life Painting in Northern Europe* (Lingen, 1992)
Deuchar, Stephen, *Sporting Art in Eighteenth Century England: A Social and Political History* (London, 1988)
D'Oench, Ellen G., *The Conversation Piece: Arthur Devis and his Contemporaries*, exh. cat., Yale Center for British Art (New Haven, CT, 1980)
Ebert-Schifferer, Sybille, *Still Life: A History* (New York, 1998)
Egerton, Judy, *British Sporting and Animal Drawings, 1500–1860*, cat. of the Paul Mellon Collection (London, 1978)
Ertz, Klaus, *Jan Brueghel der Altere, 1568–1625: die Gemälde mit kritischem Oeuvrekatalog* (Cologne, 1979)
Farrington, S. K., *Atlantic Game Fishing* (New York, 1937)
Frankenstein, Albert, *After the Hunt: William Harnett and Other American Still Life Painters* (Berkeley, CA, 1969)
Friedlander, Max Julius, *Early Netherlandish Paintings* (Leiden, 1967)
Gammelbo, Poul, *Dutch Still-life Paintings from the 16th Century to the 18th Century in Danish Collections* (Leigh-on-Sea, Essex, 1960)
Garas, Klara, *Paintings in the Budapest Museum of Fine Arts* (Budapest, 1973)
Garwood, Nigel, and Rainer Voigt, *Food Mania* (London, 2001)
Gerdts, William H., and Russell Burke, *American Still Life Paintings* (New York, 1971)
Ghent Museum, *Joachim Beuckelaer: het markt en keukenstuk in de Nederlanden, 1550–1650* (Ghent, 1986)
Gilby, Sir Walter, *Animal Painters of England* (London, 1900)
Goffé, Jules, *Le Livre de cuisine* (Paris, 1869)

Graves, Algernon, *A Dictionary of Artists Who Have Exhibited Works in the Principal London Exhibitions, 1760–1893* (London, 1969)
——, *Society of Artists in Great Britain, 1760–1791; Free Society of Artists, 1761–1783; A Complete Dictionary of Contributors and Their Work, 1760–1791* (London, 1969)
——, *The British Institution, 1806–1867; A Complete Dictionary of Contributors and Their Work from the Foundation of the Institution* (London, 1969)
——, *A Dictionary of Exhibitors at the Royal Academy of Arts, 1769–1904*, 4 vols (London, 1970)
Gregori, Mina, *Paintings in the Uffizi and Pitti Galleries* (London, 1994)
Greindl, Edith, *Les Peintres Flamands de nature morte au XVII siècle* (Brussels, 1956)
Grohman, William A. Baillie, *Sport in Art from the 15th to the 18th Centuries*, 2nd edn (London, 1919)
Hackforth-Jones, Jocelyn, *Dining with the Impressionists* (London, 1991)
Halsby, Julian, and Paul Harris, *The Dictionary of Scottish Painters 1600 to the Present* (Edinburgh, 1990)
Havlice, P. P., *World Painting Index*, 2 vols (London, 1977), suppl. 1 (1973–80), suppl. 2 (1980–89, 1995)
Henisch, Bridget Ann, *Fast and Feast: Food in Medieval Society* (University Park, PA, 1976)
Hislop's Art Sales Index (London, 2002–)
Hodnett, Edward, *Francis Barlow: First Master of English Book Illustration* (London, 1978)
Hurum, Hans Jorgen, *History of the Fish Hook, and the Story of Mustad the Hook Maker, Translated from the Norwegian* (London, 1977)
Johnson, Edward Dudley Hume, *Paintings of the British Social Scene from Hogarth to Sickert* (London, 1986)
Johnson, Jane, *Royal Society of British Artists, 1824–1893* (Woodbridge, Suffolk, 1975)
Jordan, William B., and Peter Cherry, *Spanish Still Life from Velázquez to Goya* (London, 1995)
Kiers, J. Judikje, and Fieke Tissink, *The Golden Age of Dutch Art* (London, 2000)
Kurlansky, Mark, *Cod* (London, 1998)
Lambourne, Lionel, *Victorian Painting* (London, 1999)
Lank, David M., *Once-upon-a-Tyne* (Montreal, 1977)
Laperriere, Charles Baile de, ed., *The Royal Scottish Academy, 1826–1990; A Dictionary of Artists and their Work in the Annual Exhibitions of the Royal Scottish Academy* (Leigh-on-Sea, Essex, 1977)

Lucas, Edward Verrall, *The Book of Shops* [1899], illus. Francis D. Bedford (London, 1990)
Lyles, Anne, *Turner and Natural History: The Farnley Project* (London, 1988)
Maas, Jeremy, *Victorian Painters* (London, 1988)
Malcolmson, Robert W., *Popular Recreations in English Society, 1700–1850* (Cambridge, 1973)
Mayer's International Auction Record, Annual (London, 1968–94)
Meijer, Fred G., *The Collection of Dutch and Flemish Still-life in the Daisy Linde Ward Collection of the Ashmolean Museum* (Oxford, 1950)
Natural History Museum, London, *Images from Nature: Natural History Museum* (London, 1988)
Nemerov, Alexander, *Body of Raphaelle Peale: Still-life and Selfhood, 1812–24* (New York, 2001)
Norelli, Martina R., *American Wildlife Painting* (New York, 1975)
Paston-Williams, Sara, *The Art of Dining: A History of Cooking and Eating* (London, 1993)
Paviere, S. H., *A Dictionary of Flower, Fruit and Still-life Painters* (Amsterdam and Leigh-on-Sea, Essex, 1962)
Pendred, Gerald L., *An Inventory of British Sporting Art in United Kingdom Public Collections* (Woodbridge, Suffolk, 1987)
Pisano, Ronald G., *William Merritt Chase, 1849–1916; A Leading Spirit in American Art* (Seattle, 1983)
Prosek, James, *Trout of the World* (London, 2003)
Puyvelde, Leu van, *Flemish Painting: The Age of Rubens and Van Dyck* (New York, 1971)
Quinn, Tom, *Angling in Art* (London, 1991)
Robert, Paul André, *Wonders of the Sea . . . Fishes* (London, 1937)
Rogers, Millard F., 'Fishing Subjects by Junius Brutus Stearns', *Antiques*, XCVIII (August 1970), pp. 246–50
Rosenberg, Jakob, *Dutch Art and Architecture, 1660–1800* (London, 1966)
Rosenberg, Pierre, *Tout l'oeuvre peint de Chardin* (Paris, 1983)
Royal Academy, London, *Exhibitors, 1905–70* (Calne, Wiltshire, 1973)
——, *Exhibitors, 1971–89* (Calne, Wiltshire, 1989)
Rubinstein, F. W., *Gabriel Metsu* (London, 1974)
Salerno, Luigi, *Still Life Painting in Italy, 1560–1805* (Rome, 1984)
Samuel, Arthur Michael, *The Herring* (London, 1918)
Schmiechen, James, and Kenneth Carls, *The British Market Hall: A Social and Architectural History* (London, 1999)

Schneider, Norbert, *The Art of Still Life* (Cologne, 1990)
Skira, Pierre, *Still Life: A History* (Geneva and New York, 1989)
Snelgrove, Dudley, *British Sporting and Animal Prints, 1658–1874: Catalogue of Paul Mellon Collection* (London, 1981)
Society of Wildlife Art for the Nation (SWAN, then Society of Wildlife Artists), annual exhibition catalogues since 1985
Spalding, Frances, and Judith Collins, *20th Century Painters and Sculptors*, Dictionary of British Art, vol. 6 (Woodbridge, Suffolk, 1988)
Sparrow, Walter Shaw, *Angling in British Art through Five Centuries* (London, 1923)
Stechow, Wolfgang, *Dutch Landscape Painting of the 17th Century* (London, 1968)
Sterling, Charles, *Still Life Paintings from Antiquity to the Present Time* (New York, 1959)
Takács, Haraszti, *Rubens and his Age* (Budapest, 1972)
Tannahill, Reay, *Food in History* (St Albans, 1975)
Taylor, Basil, *Animal Painting in England* (London, 1955)
Walker, Stella Archer, *British Sporting Art in the 20th Century* (London, 1989)
Walton, Izaak, *The Compleat angler; or, The contemplative man's recreation. Being a discourse of rivers and fish-ponds, and fish and fishing, not unworthy of perusal of most anglers* (London, 1653)
Watson, J.N.P., *British Sporting Art in the 20th Century* (London, n.d.)
——, *Collecting Sporting Art* (London, n.d.)
Webster, Mary, *Hogarth* (London, 1978)
Weisberg, Gabriel P., and William S. Talbot, *Chardin and the Still Life Tradition in France* (Cleveland, OH, 1979)
Wheeler, Alwyne, *World Encyclopaedia of Fishes* (London, 1985)
Whiteman, Kate, *The Fish and Shellfish Kitchen Handbook* (London, 2000)
——, *The World Encyclopaedia of Fish and Shellfish* (London, 2000)
Wingfield, Mary Ann, *A Dictionary of Sporting Artists, 1650–1990* (Woodbridge, Suffolk, 1992)
Wright, Christopher, *Paintings in Dutch Museums: An Index of Oil Paintings in Public Collections in the Netherlands by Artists Born before 1870* (London, 1980)
Yood, James, *Feasting: A Celebration of Food in Art: Paintings from the Art Institute of Chicago* (Chicago, 1992)

ACKNOWLEDGEMENTS

The authors of two publications that have been invaluable for research especially deserve thanks: Tom Quinn for his *Angling in Art*, 1991, and the authors of the catalogue of the exhibition *Fish: Still Lifes by Dutch and Flemish Masters, 1550–1700,* published by the Centraal Museum, Utrecht, 2004.

The names of gallery owners who generously gave permission to use their resources: Rafael Valls, Duke Street, London; Rupert Maas Gallery, London; and Dordrechts Museum, Dordrecht, Netherlands.

We thank the trustees of the following estates for permission to reproduce paintings under their jurisdiction: Robert Gillmor, Estate of A. W. Seaby for permission to reproduce the Seaby painting.

Personal knowledge of fish paintings and suggestions for other sources were generously shared by Dr R. M. Peck, Philadelphia; Richard Prattley, for information on carved and painted wooden models; and Christopher Frost for his knowledge of postcards.

Contemporary artists who generously lent us transparencies for their paintings and whose work can be found on their websites: Patrick Chevailler of Palm Island, Caribbean; David Miller; Maurice J. Pledger, courtesy of Bernard Thornton Artists, London; Roderick Sutterby; Rachel Lockwood; Carl Ellis and Neil Dalrymple.

It is always a pleasure to find friends who take an interest and actively assist in finding paintings and advising on the subject and I thank Maureen Lambourne, Len Rogers, Professor William G. Hale and Howard Radclyffe for their comments in this capacity. I also thank Joan Watkins, Dr Laurie Jones, Joan Spalding and Keith Alison for their contribution.

Errol Fuller made useful suggestions for the text and helped with work on the illustrations. For assistance in sourcing illustrations I particularly thank Andrew B. Jackson and acknowledge a debt to him for his patience while this book was being written, for checking of the manuscript, and for his fund of knowledge of artists and their paintings. My publisher, Michael Leaman, found some additional illustrations that have improved the scope of the book, and I thank him for generously allowing so many illustrations and helping to source some.

The librarians of Cambridge University Library and Haverhill Public Library, among others, were unfailingly helpful, and I thank them for their courtesy.

PHOTO ACKNOWLEDGEMENTS

Courtesy of Heather Ackroyd and Dan Harvey: 194; Albertina, Vienna: 37; Alte Pinakothek, Munich: 51; Art Gallery of South Australia, Adelaide: 35; The Art Institute of Chicago: 98; The Ashmolean Museum, Oxford: 34; courtesy of Bernard Thornton Artists, London: 129, 169; Lynn Bogue-Hunt: 26; The British Museum, London: 11; 31; by kind permission of His Grace the Duke of Buccleuch and Queensberry, KT: 83; Cappella Brancacci, Santa Maria del Carmine, Florence; Centraal Museum, Utrecht: 2; Château-Musée, Dieppe: 53; courtesy of Patrick Chevailler: 1, 21; Christchurch Mansion, Ipswich: 101; Cleveland Museum of Art: 175; courtesy of Neil Dalrymple: 173; Detroit Institute of Arts: 68, 139; Dordrechts Museum, Dordrecht: 58, 76, 82; courtesy of Carl Ellis: 134; Fishmongers' Company, Fishmongers' Hall, London: 67; Fitzwilliam Museum, Cambridge: 6; Gallerie dell'Accademia, Venice: 10; Gemäldegalerie, Berlin: 78; Hamburger Kunsthalle, Hamburg: 140; Hermitage Museum, St Petersburg: 59; © The Hunterian, University of Glasgow, 2011: 165; Kirche St Martin, Zillis, Switzerland: 30; Kröller-Müller Museum, Otterlo: 50; Kunsthaus Zürich: 187; Kunsthistorisches Museum, Vienna: 56, 153; courtesy of Rachel Lockwood: 138; Los Angeles County Museum of Art: 115; Maas Gallery, London: 133; Masaveu Collection, Spain: 99; Mauritshuis, The Hague: 69, 77; Stanley Meltzoff: 23; courtesy of David Miller: 172; Musée d'Art et d'Histoire, Geneva: 29; Musée du Louvre, Paris: 97, 144; Musée Condé, Chantilly: 107; Museo de Artes Decorativas, Madrid: 91; Museo Mandralisca, Cefalù, Sicily: 65; Museu Nacional d'Art de Catalunya, Barcelona: 119; Museo Nacional del Prado, Madrid: 84, 100; Museum Archaeologico Nationale, Naples: 9, 94, 108, 148; Museum Boijmans Van Beuningen, Rotterdam: 62, 103; Museum of Fine Arts, Boston: 13, 149; Museum of Fine Arts, Houston: 44; Museum voor Schone Kunsten, Ghent: 57; The National Gallery, London: 70, 90; National Gallery of Art, Washington, DC: 17, 106; Naturhistorisches Museum,

Vienna: 20; The Nelson-Atkins Museum of Art, Kansas City, Missouri: 151; Oakland Museum of California: 178; Österreichische Nationalbibliothek, Vienna: 95; The Palace Museum, Beijing: 3; Palazzo Pitti, Florence: 41 (Galleria Palatina), 64; Plymouth City Museum and Art Gallery: 47; courtesy of Richard Prattley: 193; private collection: 27, 39, 40, 42, 43, 45, 46, 48, 63, 73, 75, 79, 88, 89, 92, 96, 121, 123, 130, 154, 163, 164, 167, 180, 183, 184, 186, 189, 191, 192; courtesy of Rafael Valls, London: 36, 85, 86, 87, 88, 117, 179; Rijksmuseum, Amsterdam: 60, 61, 81; Saint Louis Art Museum: 150; the estate of A. W. Seaby: 123; Keith Shackleton: 24; Staatliche Kunstsammlungen, Dresden (Gemäldegalerie Alte Meiste): 104; Staatliche Museen, Berlin: 114; Statens Museum for Kunst, Copenhagen: 93; courtesy of R. Sutterby: 170; Tate Gallery, London: 49; Norman Thelwell: 195; courtesy Tibor de Nagy Gallery, New York: 122; Victoria and Albert Museum, London: 28; Walker Art Gallery, Liverpool: 111; Wallraf-Richartz-Museum, Cologne: 54, 102.

INDEX

Numerals in *italics* are illustration numbers.